Communic Theories: Origins, Methods, And Uses In The Mass Media

THIRD EDITION

Communication Theories: Origins, Methods, And Uses In The Mass Media

Werner J. Severin

The University of Texas at Austin

James W. Tankard, Jr.

The University of Texas at Austin

Longman
New York & London

Communication Theories, Third Edition

Longman, 95 Church Street, White Plains, N.Y. 10601

Associated companies:
Longman Group Ltd., London
Longman Cheshire Pty., Melbourne
Longman Paul Pty., Auckland
Copp Clark Pitman, Toronto

Executive editor: Gordon T. R. Anderson
Development editor: Elsa van Bergen
Production editor: Kathryn Dix
Cover design: Jerry Wilke
Text art: J & R Services, Inc.
Production supervisor: Anne P. Armeny

Library of Congress Cataloging-in-Publication Data

Severin, Werner J. (Werner Joseph)
    Communication theories: origins, methods, and uses in the mass
  media / Werner J. Severin, James W. Tankard, Jr.—3rd ed.
        p.   cm.
    Includes bibliographical references and index.
    ISBN 0-8013-0463-6
    1. Mass media.   2. Communication   I. Tankard, James W.
  II. Title.
  P90.S4414   1991
  302.23—dc20
                                                                90-27477
                                                                CIP

1 2 3 4 5 6 7 8 9 10-HA-9594939291

Contents

Preface   *xi*

PART I: The Changing Media Landscape   1

---

1. Introduction to Mass Communication Theory   **3**

Concerns of the Media Practitioner   4
Concerns of the Media User   6
The New Media   7
The Impact of New Technology on Communication Theory   12
The Dynamics of User Control   13
Conclusions   14
References   14

PART II: Scientific Method and Models
of Mass Communication   17

---

2. Scientific Method   **19**

Imagination in Science   19
The Cumulative Nature of Science   20
Scientific Generalizations about Reality   21
The Process of Scientific Inquiry   23
Acquiring Empirical Data   24
Reasoning about the Data   32
Conclusions   33
References   34

3. Models in Mass Communication Research   **36**

Functions of a Model   37
Evaluation of a Model   37
Some Early Communication Models   38
Origins of Information Theory   39

The Delivery of Useful Information   41
Information Theory Applied   43
Osgood's Model   45
The Schramm Models   46
Newcomb's Symmetry Model   47
The Westley-MacLean Model   48
The Gerbner Model   50
Conclusions   52
References   53

PART III: Perception and Language Issues in the Mass Media   55

4. The Role of Perception in Communication   57

Assumptions and Perceptions   58
Cultural Expectations and Perception   58
Motivation and Perception   59
Mood and Perception   60
Attitude and Perception   61
Perception and Mass Communication   62
Other Selective Processes   64
Schema Theory   65
Subliminal Perception   66
Automatic Exposure   69
Conclusions   69
References   70

5. Problems in Encoding   72

Characteristics of Language   72
Misuses of Language   77
Three Kinds of Statements   82
Studies of Objectivity   84
Other Applications   87
Implications for Encoding   87
Conclusions   88
References   88

6. Analysis of Propaganda: First Theories of Decoding and Effects   90

What is Propaganda?   90
The Propaganda Devices   93
Effectiveness of the Propaganda Devices   104
Conclusions   106
References   106

7. The Measurement of Readability   **109**

The History of Readability Measurement   110
The Flesch Formulas   113
Using a Formula   115
Applications of Readability Formulas   117
Cloze Procedure   122
Conclusions   126
References   126

PART IV: The Social-Psychological Approach   **129**

8. Cognitive Consistency and Mass Communication   **131**

Heider's Balance Theory   133
Newcomb's Symmetry Theory   133
Osgood's Congruity Theory   135
Festinger's Theory of Cognitive Dissonance   140
Conclusions   144
References   144

9. Theories of Persuasion   **147**

The Concept of Attitude   148
Hovland's Army Research   148
One-Sided and Two-Sided Messages   150
The Yale Communication Research Program   152
Source Credibility   153
Fear Appeals   157
Resistance to Counterpropaganda   162
Inoculation Theory   162
Katz's Functional Approach   165
Attitudes and Behavior   166
Classical Conditioning of Attitudes   170
The Theory of Low Involvement   171
Techniques of Persuasion   172
New Directions in Persuasion Theory   176
Conclusions   176
References   177

10. Groups and Communication   **181**

Sherif's Research on Group Norms   181
Asch's Research on Group Pressure   183
Lewin's Food Habits Studies   184
Groups and Political Attitudes   185

Groups as Instruments of Change 188
Groups and Mass Communication 189
Conclusions 190
References 190

11. Mass Media and Interpersonal Communication 192

The Mass Media and Voting Behavior 192
The Role of the Community in Decision Making 194
Criticisms of the Two-Step Flow 197
Diffusion of Innovations 197
Conclusions 202
References 203

PART V: Mass Media Effects and Uses   205

12. Agenda Setting 207

The Chapel Hill Study 208
Precursors of the Hypothesis 209
A Change in Thinking 209
The Media Agenda and Reality 210
The Charlotte Study 211
Experimental Evidence 213
Priming 215
Agenda Setting in Television 216
Presidential Agendas 216
"The Day After" 217
The Obtrusiveness of Issues 219
Bias by Agenda 220
The Question of Time Lag 220
Agenda Building 221
The Need for Orientation 222
Who Sets the Media Agenda? 223
How Broad Is Agenda Setting? 225
How Does Agenda Setting Work? 225
Conclusions 227
References 227

13. The Knowledge-Gap Hypothesis 230

The Role of the Mass Media 231
Operational Forms of the Hypothesis 232
Possible Reasons for a Knowledge Gap 234
The Knowledge Gap in Public Affairs 234
"Sesame Street" 236
Refinement of the Hypothesis 238

The Generality of the Hypothesis   241
An Influence Gap?   242
The Knowledge Gap and the New Technology   242
Criticism of the Hypothesis   244
Conclusions   245
References   246

14. Effects of Mass Communication   **247**

The Bullet Theory   247
The Limited-Effects Model   248
Cultivation Theory   249
McLuhan's Media Determinism   250
The Effects of Synthetic Experience   252
The Spiral of Silence   252
Media Hegemony   254
Effects of Television Violence   255
The Powerful-Effects Model   258
Size of Effects   260
Toward a Synthesis   262
Conclusions   265
References   266

15. Uses of the Mass Media   **269**

Beginnings of the Uses and Gratifications Approach   269
Uses and Gratifications in an Election Campaign   270
Classifying Individual Needs and Media Uses   272
Criticisms of the Uses and Gratifications Theory   274
Empirical Tests of the Uses and Gratifications Theory   276
New Technology and the Active Audience   278
Conclusions   279
References   280

PART VI: The Media as Institutions   283

16. Mass Media in Modern Society   **285**

Four Theories of the Press   285
The News Media as Agents of Power   290
Functions of the Media   293
Values and Ideology in Support of the Society   295
Our Mental Picture of the World   298
Popular Taste and Social Action   300
Social Conformism   301
Conditions of Media Effectiveness   301
Enduring Values in the News   304

Making News: The Social Construction of Reality   306
Controlling the News Staff and Maintaining the Status Quo   307
Possibilities for Policy Deviation   310
Mass Communication and Sociocultural Integration   311
Conclusions   317
References   317

17. Media Chains and Conglomerates   **320**

Newspaper Chains   320
Broadcasting Chains   325
Media Cross Ownership   325
Media Conglomerates   328
Employee Ownership   334
Conclusions   337
References   337

PART VII: Bringing It All Together   339

18. The Overall Picture   **341**

The Model and Communication Research   341
Mass Media Research   344
In Conclusion   345
Reference   346

Index   *347*

Preface

The title of this revised third edition has been modified to more accurately reflect its contents—mass communication theories. As with the first two editions, it is aimed primarily at undergraduate students who intend to pursue careers in the mass media—journalism, advertising, public relations, radio, television, and film—and who need an introduction to the theories, foundations, and research methodology of mass communication.

This third edition revises and updates our earlier work, using recent examples from the mass media and communication research, and reflects certain organizational changes. To make the text even more useful, we have resequenced chapters and divided the book into seven parts, each prefaced by a short overview to guide readers through the body of knowledge they are building. And the chapters on models and information theory have in this edition been merged into one, as have the chapters on attitude change.

We have designed this text as a survey of the evolution of mass communication theory: to understand where we are in ongoing efforts toward a unified theoretical approach one must begin with a grounding in the origins of the field. We begin in Part I with a look at the types of problems researchers tackle and how the important changes taking place in the mass media present new challenges for researchers, media practitioners, and all of us in media audiences.

The essence of the scientific inquiry that underlies the findings we examine is provided in Part II, along with classic models and theories that have been applied to a study of mass media. Where new studies have significantly changed the course of theory and research, we include them.

Part III explores how audiences receive and use messages and how the research on these activities affects the way mass communication is generated. The methods of measurement that develop from hypotheses and scholarship are part of the science of mass communication, and a range of them are included in this book.

We proceed from views of the ways individuals process mass communication to aspects of the broader social context. Elements of general communication theory are useful in determining and interpreting reactions to media messages. The individual audience member's relation to a group, and especially to opinion leaders, influences media effects.

Media effects of course constitute a major focus of mass communication theory. In Part VI, we look at the question of the power of the media, at who is responsible for content, and how it influences us.

One result of a course in mass communication theory should be that students acquire an overview—a "big picture"—of the mass communication field, instead of focusing solely on a particular job that they might hope to hold. This is one purpose served by the chapters "Mass Media in Modern Society" and "Media Chains and Conglomerates." A complete understanding of the effects of mass communication, or even of the process of mass communication, is not possible without some consideration of ownership.

Probably no two teachers of mass communication theory see the field in exactly the same way, as indicated by surveys that show a wide variety of textbook titles used in theory courses. We have attempted to be comprehensive; instructors who feel that we have left out a topic can easily supplement the text with their own lectures or outside readings.

Communication Theories: Origins, Methods, And Uses In The Mass Media

P A R T

I

The Changing
Media Landscape

As we move into what is being called the "information age," the challenges facing the field of mass communication seem greater than ever before. A study conducted in 1990 by the Times Mirror Corporation, the publisher of the *Los Angeles Times,* showed that young adults in the United States know less and care less about public affairs than any other generation in the past 50 years. These young adults—ages 18 to 30—are less likely to read newspapers or to watch television news than their counterparts a generation ago. (On the other hand, they are more likely to read books or to use computers than Americans older than 50.) The study concluded that the information age has actually spawned an uninformed and uninvolved public.

Why are these young adults using news media less?

What do they expect or want from the news media that they are not getting?

How can these people be reached by the news media?

What are likely to be the effects on society of this decreasing attention to the news media?

What new ways of reaching people might be presented by new communication media?

It is undoubtedly possible to use several different methods to attempt to answer these questions and others. In this book, we recommend approaching questions about mass communication through the scientific method. Science—based as it is on empiricism and logic—offers powerful tools for understanding, predicting, and controlling the world around us, especially as that world becomes increasingly made up of information.

Basic to scientific method is the building and testing of theory, and Chapter 1 discusses the nature of theory as it is used in the field of mass communication. It describes some of the problems communication researchers are attempting to study in the 1990s and in so doing also gives an overview of the changing media landscape we are facing as the result of the rapid development of new communication technology. Those changes in turn affect mass communication theory itself.

1

Introduction to Mass Communication Theory

Mass communication is part skill, part art, and part science.* It is a skill in the sense that it involves certain fundamental learnable techniques such as focusing a television camera, operating a tape recorder, and taking notes during an interview. It is an art in the sense that it involves creative challenges such as writing a script for a television documentary, developing a pleasing and eye-catching layout for a magazine advertisement, and coming up with a catchy, hard-hitting lead for a news story. It is a science in the sense that certain verifiable principles involved in making communication work can be used to achieve specific goals more effectively.

Many people want to pigeonhole mass communication as involving one or two of these aspects to the exclusion of the others. This pigeonholing has sometimes reinforced unnecessary divisions in the field and obstructed the sharing of useful information. It is our position that all three aspects are valid and valuable, and that taking one approach does not mean that the others must be excluded. The *primary* focus of this book is on the aspects of communication that can be approached scientifically, but we attempt to view them from the perspective of the communication practitioner, whether this person is a newspaper reporter, a television director, an advertising copywriter, or a public relations specialist. Many important questions about mass communication that can't be dealt with in any other way can be dealt with scientifically.

Since we are taking a scientific approach, when we use the word *theory* in this book we will be referring to scientific theory. Theory can be thought of as our understanding of the way things work (MacLean, 1972). This allows us to always have *some* theory about anything we are doing. In the field of mass communication, much of our theory in the past has been *implicit*. People have relied on folklore, traditional wisdom, and "common sense" to guide much of the practice of mass communication. Sometimes these assumptions are never even stated or written down anywhere. Other times they take the forms of oversimplified *aphorisms* or *maxims*. Many of these assumptions would benefit from being tested through research. The result might be that the maxims are confirmed, disconfirmed, or confirmed only partially (within certain limits). In any of these cases, the media practitioner will have a firmer ground for taking action.

The communication scientist argues that since we have some theory operating all the

---

*We are expanding here on Mitchell Charnley's observation that reporting is a craft and an art (see Charnley, 1975).

time anyway, why not try to make it the best theory that we can? The scientist believes that the greatest faith should be placed in those statements about the way things work that have been tested and verified and that have some generality and predictive power. These are the kinds of statements that make up scientific theory. And these statements are *useful;* as social psychologist Kurt Lewin said in an often-quoted remark, "There is nothing so practical as a good theory" (1951, p. 169).

Communication theory is aimed at improving our understanding of the process of mass communication. With better understanding, we are in a better position to predict and control the outcomes of mass communication efforts. The act of communication can be observed from a number of points of view, but two of the most important are that of the source (or media practitioner), and that of the receiver (or mass communication audience). We can add to our understanding by viewing mass communication from either point of view. Some areas of mass communication theory are particularly helpful to the practitioner in trying to accomplish specific communication goals. Other areas of communication theory are more helpful in understanding the uses of mass communication by an audience member, or the effects of mass communication on an audience. Let us consider some of the important observations made during the last half of the 20th century on the roles of practitioner and audience.

Concerns of the Media Practitioner

The media practitioner—whether news reporter, public relations worker, creator of magazine advertisements, or political campaign director—usually attempts to achieve certain effects on an audience. For some, such as the reporter, the intended effect may be merely to have a news story read and understood—that is, to achieve exposure and comprehension. For other practitioners, such as the creator of an advertisement, the intended effect may be

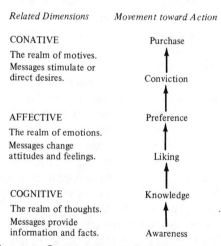

FIGURE 1.1 • STAIR-STEP MODEL OF COMMUNICATION EFFECTS

Adapted from R. Lavidge and G. A. Steiner, "A Model for Predictive Measurements of Advertising Effectiveness," *Journal of Marketing* 25 (1961): 61, published by the American Marketing Association.

to get audience members to purchase a product—that is, to achieve behavior change. The type of effect intended varies depending upon the role of the communicator and the particular communication task.

The various communication effects that can be intended have been described in several lists or typologies. In a number of these lists, the effects are presented as a hierarchy, the ones at the bottom being easier to achieve than the ones at the top. The effects are often seen as a progression, because it is necessary to accomplish a lower one before the next highest one can be achieved.

A hierarchichal model of this type, developed by Lavidge and Steiner (1961) to be applied to advertising, is presented in Figure 1.1. The model presents six steps, each of which must be accomplished before the one above it can be attempted. The six steps are grouped into three dimensions or categories: the cognitive, the affective, and the conative. The cognitive deals with our knowledge of things, the affective with our attitudes toward things, and the conative with our behavior toward things. Some media practitioners might be interested in only a portion of the effects specified by the model. The reporter, for instance, might be interested only in achieving the cognitive effects. A creator of an advertisement, in contrast, would probably be interested in achieving the full range of six steps. So, in fact, might an editorial writer attempting to get readers to vote for a certain candidate—if we replace *purchase* in the model with *vote*.

Another hierarchy of communication effects was developed by William McGuire (1973). McGuire's hierarchy of effects is presented in his "matrix of persuasion," developed particularly to clarify the process of attitude change (see Figure 1.2). The matrix lists five classes of factors within the communication process (independent variables) and six "behavioral steps" (dependent variables). McGuire's steps also specify a hierarchy. In McGuire's matrix, the steps at the top must be taken before the lower steps can be accomplished.

With either model of the hierarchy of effects, it is probably true that the lower-level effects (such as presentation) are easier to accomplish than the higher-level effects (such as behavior change).

Still another version of the hierarchy of effects model is the AIETA model, or the "awareness, interest, evaluation, trial, adoption" model (Krugman, 1977). This model

	Source	Message	Channel	Receiver	Destination
Presentation					
Attention					
Comprehension					
Yielding					
Retention					
Overt behavior					

FIGURE 1.2 • MATRIX OF COMMUNICATION FACTORS AND BEHAVORIAL STEPS

From W. J. McGuire, "Persuasion, Resistance, and Attitude Change," in I. D. S. Pool, W. Schramm, F. W. Frey, N. Maccoby, and E. B. Parker (eds.), *Handbook of Communication* (Boston: Houghton Mifflin, 1973), p. 223. Reprinted by permission.

seems to be based on the research on the adoption of innovations conducted by Everett Rogers and others (Rogers & Shoemaker, 1971).

Some later research has challenged whether the steps in these hierarchies must always take place in the same rigid sequence (Ray, 1973), but, regardless of that position, the hierarchies are useful. They remind us that mass communication can have a number of effects and they force communicators to be specific about what effect they are intending. And, as we shall see, certain variables in the communication process have more impact on some of the levels of effects than they do on others.

For most of the levels described in the hierarchies we have presented, the mass media practitioner will find that certain areas of communication theory can be helpful in achieving the intended effect. General semantics, readability, and perception, for instance, are all useful in attempting to achieve the effects of *attention and comprehension*. Attitude change, group dynamics, and interpersonal communication are all useful in attempting to achieve the effects of *yielding and retention*. Attitude change and cognitive consistency, as well as some of the others already mentioned, are useful in attempting to *change overt behavior*.

Concerns of the Media User

Mass communication can also be viewed from the point of view of the audience, and from this point of view the concerns are somewhat different. The audience member is likely to be more concerned about the *uses* of mass communication than about its *effects*. The audience member probably thinks of newspapers, radio, television, magazines, motion pictures, and other media as things to be used for specific purposes. These purposes can vary widely, from the light, such as providing leisure, relaxation, and entertainment, to the serious, such as providing warnings of dangers (tornadoes, floods, and terrorist attacks) or providing information to be used in evaluating candidates for the presidency of the United States. In between are a host of other uses, including obtaining information for daily life (weather reports, school lunch menus), shopping information (sales, announcements of new products), or news about community and neighbors.

Mass communication theory can help us understand these various uses the audience makes of the mass media and can perhaps provide valuable information about desired uses that the media are not meeting. The area of mass communication theory called "uses and gratifications" is aimed at providing just that kind of information.

The audience can also become concerned about the effects of mass communication, however, particularly when those effects might be negative or undesirable. Watching television violence might cause audience members to engage in aggressive behavior toward others. Watching pornographic films might cause men to have more callous attitudes toward women. Advertisements for beer, wine, and liquor, whether on television or in print, might lead to increased purchase and consumption of alcoholic beverages. Sexual stereotyping of men and women in advertisements and in television entertainment programs might be teaching that males and females may fulfill only certain roles, hold only certain jobs, and so forth. These are only some of the many possible undesirable effects of mass communication about which people have expressed concern—in some cases, to the point of organizing political groups boycotting certain products.

Criticisms of the mass media for producing undesirable effects has occasionally been extended to an entire medium. Television has been compared to a narcotic drug in Marie

Winn's *The Plug-In Drug* (1977) and Jerry Mander's *Four Arguments for the Elimination of Television* (1978).

Many undesirable effects are probably not intended by the producers of the messages. Nevertheless, they could be real effects with serious consequences for society. The fact that they are unintended does not mean that they are unimportant. In fact, one scholar has suggested that the main task of the social sciences is to explore the unintended social repercussions of intentional human actions (Popper, 1963).

What is crucial, however, is that these effects be investigated in the most careful and rigorous way. The answers to the questions of whether these effects exist or not should come from science—from communication theorists and researchers—and not just from arguments by people and groups who have become adversaries in a public controversy.

Another problem for audience members in the 20th century is the growing issue of information overload (Miller, 1960; Klapp, 1978). Some writers have gone so far as to say that the audience for mass communication is no longer a "receiver" but a "victim" (Hiebert, Ungarait, & Bohn, 1974). Richard Saul Wurman (1989) writes of the problem of *information anxiety*, which he says is produced by the ever-widening gap between what we understand and what we think we should understand.

Sociologist Orrin E. Klapp (1978, 1982) has described the increasing gap that is occurring between information and meaning. *Information*, as he uses it, refers to a reduction of uncertainty that can be measured in bits (see Chapter 4), while *meaning* refers to the making sense of information, to the finding of a meaningful pattern. Klapp presents the metaphor of a giant funnel with pieces of a jigsaw puzzle dropping out of the hole in the bottom. Klapp says members of the audience for mass communication are like a person sitting under the funnel trying to fit a jigsaw puzzle together. The job is difficult because not only do the pieces come faster than we can process them, but many of them do not even belong to the puzzle we are working on. Significant developments, some of them still on the horizon of the media landscape, have been altering the way media are used as well as how they are generated.

The New Media

Thirty years ago, sociologist Charles Wright defined mass communication by these three characteristics:

> 1. It is directed toward relatively large, heterogeneous, and anonymous audiences;
> 2. Messages are transmitted publicly, often timed to reach most audience members simultaneously, and are transient in character;
> 3. The communicator tends to be, or to operate within, a complex organization that may involve great expense. (Wright, 1959, p. 15)

This definition summed up a lot of what we knew about the mass media of the time—primarily newspapers, magazines, radio, television, motion pictures, phonograph records, and books.

Changes in communication technology are coming so quickly now that we frequently hear talk of a "communication revolution." Among this new technology are cable television, home computers, video cassette recorders (VCRs), satellite transmission, electronic delivery of information (videotex and teletext), hypermedia (a new medium that combines publishing, television, audio, and computers), CD–ROMs, and high definition television (HDTV). One of the consequences of the new technology is that it is no longer quite so easy to say what is mass communication and what is not. The boundary between mass communication and other forms of communication is no longer so clear.

Cable television provides alternatives to the three commercial television networks and the public broadcasting network. Available on a subscription basis, cable TV is now present in 57 percent of U.S. TV households. From cable, audiences are getting more specialized programming, with channels that are all news (Cable News Network), all sports (ESPN), all weather (The Weather Channel), all music (MTV, VH-1), all Spanish language (SIN), and all black-oriented (BET). Recent feature movies, shown without commercials, are available for an additional fee from services such as HBO and Showtime. Cable's share of the television audience at any given time has grown from essentially zero in 1980 to 18 percent in 1989 (Holloway, 1989). In addition, another 18 percent is typically watching independent stations. In the last decade, television has changed from a medium with essentially four choices for the viewer to a medium in many places with 50 or more choices. In addition, many cable systems are making public access or community access channels available as a part of their regular programming. Public access channels offer the opportunity for members of the public, usually with a minimum of training, to create their own television programs or messages and have them scheduled and transmitted (Engelman, 1990). This is a revolutionary change in television that many people have not recognized, much less taken advantage of.

Home computers have made the power and utility of the electronic computer available in a unit that the average person can afford to buy and can take home and set up on the dining room table. These home computers offer many functions, including word processing, education, financial analysis (with spreadsheet programs), and entertainment. The computer is also a creative tool that can do many of the things that traditional creative media such as the typewriter, pen and pencil, a sketch pad, and musical instruments can do—plus a lot more. The computer has been called the "first meta-medium" (Kay, 1984) because it can be used to simulate dynamically the details of any other medium. Hooked up to a modem, a home computer can also provide access to videotex services, information banks and data services, and bulletin boards dealing with all kinds of topics.

Videocassette recorders (VCRs) allow the recording and playing back of television images and programs. They can be used to tape programs or movies and play them back at another time (time shifting) or to play rented or purchased cassettes. VCRs are now present in at least 70 percent of U.S. households. A great variety of material, some of it not available through other means, can be obtained on videocassettes, including feature movies, X-rated and NC-17-rated films, exercise workout routines, and other self-help programs. In some areas of the world where commercial television broadcasting is limited, videocassettes are a major medium of communication. In Moscow, *Rambo* is said to be a popular black market videocassette movie, selling for the equivalent of $300 (Ogan, 1989).

Satellite transmission of electronic signals is being used a number of ways. Cable television networks use satellites to send their signals to the cable systems distributing their programs. Home satellite antennas purchased for $1,500 or so allow individual users to pick up these signals. Some pay cable services, such as HBO, "scramble" their satellite signals to prevent them from being picked up for free. Several newspapers that publish nationally, including the *Wall Street Journal, USA Today,* and the *New York Times,* are also using satellites to send the contents of each day's newspaper electronically to printing plants around the country. The *International Herald-Tribune* is doing the same thing to publish daily around the world.

Electronic delivery of the news is a system by which the user, at home, selects the news he or she is interested in and then sees it displayed on a television screen or home computer screen. Videotex is a form of electronic delivery of the news in which the individual uses a home computer or a special terminal to connect, usually via a telephone line, to a central computer. The user then requests news stories, advertisements, or other information that is sent over the telephone line and displayed on the computer or terminal screen. Teletext is a similar system that uses the television set and cable. In teletext, the user does not really interact with the information system, but is able to choose from a large number of "pages" that can be displayed on the home screen. Videotex and teletext might not be widely adopted as quickly as cable television and VCRs, however. High cost and difficulty of use are factors that may slow the public's acceptance of these interactive information systems (Carey, 1982; Atwater, Heeter, & Brown, 1985).

Hypermedia, combining publishing, television, audio, and computers with common access through a computer terminal, is also characterized by many links and access points, so that the user can move around easily in a multimedia information environment. A hypermedia encyclopedia, for instance, would allow the user to look up Mozart and then make choices among reading about his background, looking at some of his musical scores, and actually hearing a Mozart symphony. The user might click on "buttons" on the computer screen that would lead to additional "articles" on classical style, the sonata form, child prodigies, Salzburg, or life in 18th-century Germany. Hypercard, a program available for the Macintosh computer, illustrates some of the features of a somewhat limited form of hypermedia.

The CD–ROM (Compact Disk–Read Only Memory) is a device for storing large quantities of information on a compact disk of the same type now used for musical recordings. This new technology, which stores information optically, is so efficient that an entire encyclopedia can be stored on one disk. In addition, the CD–ROM can store many types of information, including text, audible sound, and moving visual images much like motion pictures. The CD–ROM meshes nicely with hypermedia. The CD–ROM needs some kind of interface to allow users access to its vast amounts of information. Programs like Hypercard can serve this purpose very well.

High definition television (HDTV) is a new system of television under development in which the visual screen will be capable of much greater resolution—in fact, the visual image will supposedly have the same clarity and sharpness as a 35 millimeter slide (Levy, 1989). The benefits of HDTV will go far beyond just a sharper and clearer picture, however. The nature of television programming will probably change. The low resolution television that we are used to limited the amount of detail that could be put on the screen, and this affected program content. The standard television image was effective in showing several people in the frame at one time, but not much more. This led to the development of certain kinds of programs, such as the situation comedy. HDTV will allow more panoramic and expansive scenes in television programming, and will probably change television in ways we can't imagine. HDTV will also allow multiple images, or "windowing," on the television set. This would mean a viewer could literally watch six programs at once, or monitor a football game through a small window in the upper right corner of the screen while watching a movie on the rest of the screen.

These are just some of the new technologies that are having a major effect on mass communication. There are others. In fact, the media landscape has become so complicated that a map becomes useful in understanding it. A useful map for this purpose is presented in Figure 1.3. The map defines the world of communication media with two axes or dimensions. A form-substance dimension runs from left to right across the map. The "form" end is something like the "medium" end of the continuum; the "content" end is something like the "message" end. A products-services dimension runs from bottom to top of the map. This dimension corresponds to the traditional way that companies and economists have viewed industrial activity, as providing either products or services.

Different communication media fall at different places on the map depending on their locations on the two dimensions. Books, for instance, are strong both in being a product and in providing specific content, so they fall in the extreme lower right corner. The U.S. mail, in contrast, is strong in providing a service rather than a product and in providing a channel rather than specific content, so it appears in the upper left corner. Computers, which some people suggest are *the* general, all-purpose communication device, are located in the center of the map.

One result of the new technology is that the distinctions among the media of communication are beginning to blur. As suggested by the map in Figure 1.3, the boundaries between various types of communication are not as sharp as they once were. These boundaries are likely to become even more obscure as computers, satellites, and telephone hookups become more prominent parts of communication technology.

Some blurrings are already apparent. For instance, feature movies are now available on videocassettes or through television movie services such as HBO, as well as in theaters. Newspapers and videotex, although very different in form, can contain much the same information and can be used for many of the same purposes. Satellites are further blurring some distinctions—the same satellites that are used for transmitting cable television programs such as Cable News Network or the "PTL Club" are also used to send the pages of the *Wall Street Journal* to printing plants around the country.

The newspaper *USA Today* is by itself a good illustration of the lack of a clear distinction between the media. Technologically, as we have noted, *USA Today* sends its pages to its regional printing plants by satellites—the same satellites that carry cable television programs. In content, *USA Today* is often more like other media rather than a traditional newspaper. In its use of in-depth stories and interviews and its splashy, colorful graphics, the newspaper resembles some magazines. In its short, almost bulletin-like stories on the front page, it is similar to news on television or on the radio. This style of writing the news in shorter stories is also characteristic of videotex and teletext, where stories are often limited to what can be displayed on the screen in one "page" or viewing. *USA Today* makes no secret of the fact that it is attempting to appeal to the audience of television viewers—the distribution boxes from which *USA Today* is sold on the streets are even designed to look like television sets (Seelye, 1983).

One of the implications of the map in Figure 1.3 is that it might be a mistake for a student of mass communication to focus too narrowly on any one medium. The media are becoming more interchangeable and indistinguishable. The map gives new impetus to a

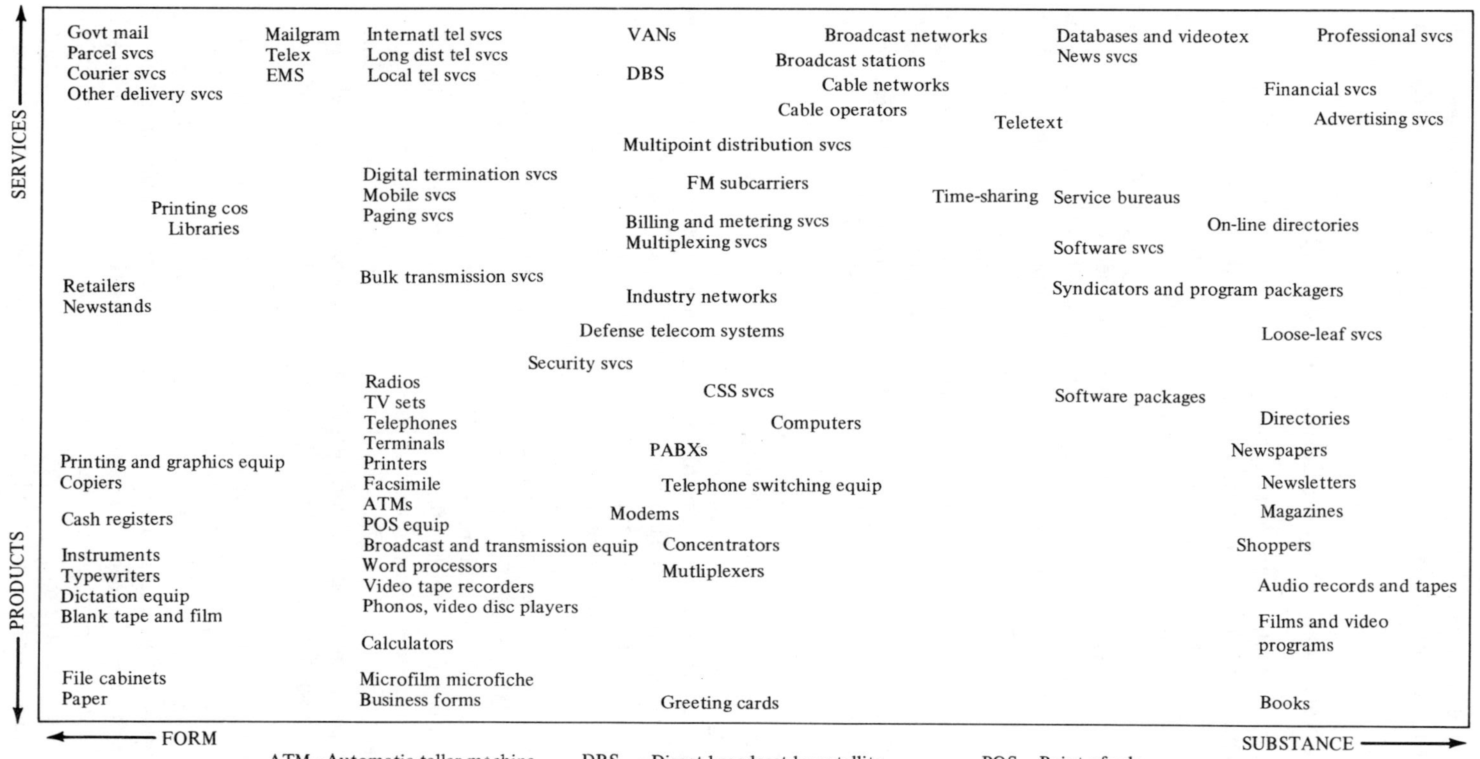

SERVICES

Govt mail · Parcel svcs · Courier svcs · Other delivery svcs
Mailgram · Telex · EMS
Internatl tel svcs · Long dist tel svcs · Local tel svcs
VANs · DBS
Broadcast networks · Broadcast stations · Cable networks · Cable operators
Databases and videotex · News svcs
Professional svcs · Financial svcs · Advertising svcs
Printing cos · Libraries
Multipoint distribution svcs
Digital termination svcs · Mobile svcs · Paging svcs
FM subcarriers
Teletext
Time-sharing · Service bureaus
On-line directories
Billing and metering svcs · Multiplexing svcs
Software svcs
Retailers · Newstands
Bulk transmission svcs
Industry networks
Syndicators and program packagers
Loose-leaf svcs
Defense telecom systems
Security svcs
CSS svcs

PRODUCTS

Printing and graphics equip · Copiers
Cash registers
Instruments · Typewriters · Dictation equip · Blank tape and film
File cabinets · Paper
Software packages
Computers
PABXs · Telephone switching equip
Modems · Concentrators · Multiplexers
Radios · TV sets · Telephones · Terminals · Printers · Facsimile · ATMs · POS equip
Broadcast and transmission equip · Word processors · Video tape recorders · Phonos, video disc players
Calculators
Microfilm microfiche · Business forms
Greeting cards
Directories · Newspapers · Newsletters · Magazines · Shoppers
Audio records and tapes · Films and video programs · Books

Axes: ← FORM → · ← SUBSTANCE → · SERVICES · PRODUCTS

Legend:

ATM – Automatic teller machine
cos – companies
CSS – Carrier "smart" switch
DBS – Direct broadcast by satellite
EMS – Electronic message service
PABX – Private automatic branch exchange
POS – Point-of-sale
svcs – services
VAN – Value-added network

FIGURE 1.3 • THE INFORMATION BUSINESS

From John F. McLaughlin with Anne Louise Antonoff, *Mapping the Information Business* (Cambridge, Mass.: Program on Information Resources Policy, Harvard University, 1986). Reprinted by permission.

more general approach to the study of mass communication—one to which communication theory, with its emphasis on general processes and general effects, is particularly appropriate.

The Impact of New Technology on Communication Theory

The new technologies are introducing many changes to mass communication, and communication theories must be developed or revised to keep up with the changes.

One of the ways the new technology is affecting mass communication in general is by giving the user more control over the communication process. Cable television channels and videotapes give the audience member access to specialized programs and material, far beyond what is available on the three commercial television networks and public television. Videotex and teletext offer the user a wide selection of news stories or other information. CompuServe, a computer information service that can be accessed through home computers, has 550,000 subscribers (Couzens, 1989). One CompuServe service called "IQuest" gives users access to more than 700 data bases, each of them filled with information on a particular subject (Gerber, 1986). CompuServe also offers a large number of "special interest groups" (SIGs) or forums dealing with specialized topics. These special interest groups allow people who are interested in the same topic—science fiction, poetry writing, an arcane computer programming language such as FORTH—to communicate with one another. This is a big change from the way communication through media has largely taken place in the past. In a SIG on CompuServe, messages are not being chosen for the audience by someone else and imposed on them, but are being shared by people who are more or less equal but have a common interest in a topic.

VCRs are also giving the user more control over mass communication. Once a program has been videotaped from a commercial network broadcast, it becomes possible to skip the commercials by pushing the fast-forward button on the remote control of the VCR. This procedure, called "zapping," has become a major concern in the advertising industry.

One of the effects of the new technology, then, is a shift away from the "ideal type" of a centralized broadcasting or publishing organization sending out the same content to large and stable audiences (McQuail & Windahl, 1981, p. 8). In a sense, this heightened selectivity due to the new technology could create a kind of balance that has been lacking in mass communication, with the audience and the message producers being more *equal* in power. The decentralization of communication due to the new technology can be seen taking place in the U.S. Government Printing Office, which plans over the next 10 years to shift to much heavier dissemination of information by individual agencies and through electronic mail, on-line data bases, floppy disks, magnetic tapes, and CD–ROMs (U.S. Congress, 1988).

The trend toward greater control and activity on the part of the user means communication theorists are going to have to shift to models and theories that recognize the interactivity of the new media (Rogers & Chaffee, 1983). One consequence is that we probably should have theories that give less emphasis to the effects of mass communication and more emphasis to the ways audience members are *using* mass communication. This shift might give increased importance to the uses and gratifications approach to the study of mass communication (see Chapter 15).

The coming of cable television and, to a lesser extent, VCRs also means mass communication theorists should change the way they think about the audience, particularly the audience of television. It is no longer possible to think of television as a uniform or monolithic system, transmitting essentially the same message to everyone. This realization has consequences for a number of theories of mass communication that assume to some extent a uniform television message, or a uniform media message (Webster, 1989). These theories include Gerbner's cultivation theory and Noelle-Neumann's spiral of silence (Chapter 14), as well as, to a lesser extent, the agenda-setting function (Chapter 12). Essentially, it appears that the fragmented or segmented audience that is characteristic of the new media probably leads to a lessening of the impact of the mass media suggested by cultivation theory, the spiral of silence, and the agenda-setting function.

The Dynamics of User Control

The increase in user control that is coming with the new technology may have a beneficial effect of giving users more control over the information explosion. It could help them cope with information overload or "meaning lag." By being more selective, users can get more control over the flow. Each could select the information that he or she wants and eliminate the rest. Rather than become inundated by pieces of puzzles, many of them for the wrong puzzle, one could request the particular piece that one needs.

The new technology may also require the creation of new kinds of jobs—"guides" to help us through the electronic wilderness. These people would help users sort out information and prevent information overload. Some of these new professionals might be a kind of extension of the traditional librarian—experts who help people find information, but do so through the new electronic information systems. Others might be a new kind of information integrator and synthesizer—someone who puts the little bits of information together in a meaningful way.

We can also expect that some of this help in processing information will come from the computer itself. Some day in the future when we are using the computer to obtain information, we might interact with an "agent" who will do our bidding (Kay, 1984). The agent could work for us while we are asleep. For instance, it could scan the hundreds of data banks for us during the night and present us the next day with a personal newspaper created just for us. The agent is likely to be presented to us in some kind of quasi-intelligent form, so we can "converse" with it. The agent might "say" to us at some point, "Mary (or John), I notice you haven't been reading the stories I have selected for you dealing with 'ancient Egyptian hieroglyphics.' Would you like me to take that category off your list?" A major purpose of the agent would be to make computer information retrieval more "user friendly." The form of the agent should not be something we think of as too intelligent, however, because the agent will make mistakes. One possibility is that the agent will take the form of a cartoon animal.

Of course, it is not certain that these new technologies of communication will be made available to everyone or that everyone will use them equally. One concern is that the new technology, because it is expensive and is more likely to be used by people of higher education, could end up contributing to a kind of widening gap between the information "haves" and "have-nots." The result could be a kind of "knowledge gap" (Chapter 13).

Another undesirable side effect of the selectivity being introduced by the new technology could be that it will lead audience members to isolate themselves from information that they might find unpleasant or disturbing. Perhaps processes of selective exposure and selective perception will be heightened by the new communication technology. This could cut down severely on the kind of open debate that a free society needs to function.

In general, the rapid changes in communication technology suggest that researchers should try to formulate communication theory in terms that go beyond the details of a specific medium or technology. For example, we probably should avoid phrasing our theories in terms of *newspaper reading* or *television exposure* and instead phrase it in terms of variables like *public affairs information seeking, the need for companionship, degree of user control,* and so forth. In doing so, we would be making the shift from what sociologist Jerald Hage has called *specific nonvariables* to *general variables* (Hage, 1972).

Conclusions

This book deals with the scientific study of mass communication. The end product of scientific research is theory. Mass communication theory is aimed at improving our understanding of how mass communication works. Mass communication theory can be used to help the media practitioner communicate better. It can also be used to inform consumers, and other interested parties, about the effects of mass communication.

Much is said and written these days about the "information explosion" and the "communication revolution." Undoubtedly, a tremendous amount of information is available today through a variety of media, leaving the audience feeling "bombarded." In addition, a rapid influx of new technological innovations has caused the media to begin to overlap in their functions and their forms. The distinctions between mass communication and interpersonal communication and between interpersonal communication and intrapersonal communication are not as sharp as they used to be. Much of this communication technology is bringing more control to the user, or, to put it another way, making communication more "two-way" or more interactive.

The information explosion and the communication revolution are quite possibly giving communication theory an even more important role than it has ever had before. As the distinctions between the various communication media begin to blur, the study of the communication process in general becomes more useful. All communication deals with symbols, messages, and receivers, whether those messages are in a newspaper, on a television screen, in a radio broadcast, or on a videotex page displayed on a home computer. The media practitioner of the future needs to feel at home with mass communication messages, no matter what the medium or format, and communication theory can help achieve that goal.

References

Atwater, T., C. Heeter, and N. Brown (1985). Foreshadowing the electronic publishing age: First exposures to Viewtron. *Journalism Quarterly* 62: 807–815.

Carey, J. (1982). Videotex: The past as prologue. *Journal of Communication* 32, no. 2: 80–87.

Charnley, M. V. (1975). *Reporting*. 3rd ed. New York: Holt, Rinehart, and Winston.

Couzens, M. (1989). Closing up shop. *Channels*, Dec., pp. 80–81.

Engelman, R. (1990). The origins of public access cable television, 1966–1970. *Journalism Monographs* no. 123, October.

Gerber, C. H. (1986). The search is over: IQuest makes information accessible. *Online Today* 5, no. 5: 30–31.

Hage, J. (1972). *Techniques and Problems of Theory Construction in Sociology.* New York: John Wiley.

Hiebert, R. E., D. F. Ungarait, and T. W. Bohn (1974). *Mass Media: An Introduction to Modern Communication.* New York: David McKay.

Holloway, D. (1989). Cable in the '80s nibbles away at audience. *Austin American-Statesman.* Dec. 24, p. 7.

Kay, A. (1984). Computer software. *Scientific American* 251, no. 3: 53–59.

Klapp, O. E. (1978). *Opening and Closing: Strategies of Information Adaptation in Society.* Cambridge: Cambridge University Press.

——— (1982). Meaning lag in the information society. *Journal of Communication* 32, no. 2: 56–66.

Krugman, H. E. (1977). Memory without recall, exposure without perception. *Journal of Advertising Research* 17, no. 4: 7–12.

Lavidge, R., and G. Steiner (1961). A model for predictive measurements of advertising effectiveness. *Journal of Marketing* 25, no. 6: 59–62.

Levy, S. (1989). Next picture show. *Rolling Stone*, June 15, pp. 91–103.

Lewin, K. (1951). *Field Theory in Social Science: Selected Theoretical Papers*, p. 169. New York: Harper & Row.

MacLean, M. (1972). *Journalism education: Whence and where to.* Paper presented at a conference honoring Prof. Henry Ladd Smith on his retirement, University of Washington, Seattle.

Mander, J. (1978). *Four Arguments for the Elimination of Television.* New York: Morrow.

McGuire, W. J. (1973). Persuasion, resistance, and attitude change. In I.D.S. Pool, W. Schramm, F. W. Frey, N. Maccoby, and E. B. Parker (eds.), *Handbook of Communication,* pp. 216–252. Chicago: Rand McNally.

McQuail, D., and S. Windahl (1981). *Communication Models for the Study of Mass Communication.* London: Longman.

Miller, J. G. (1960). Information input overload and psychopathology. *American Journal of Psychiatry* 116, no. 8: 695–704.

Ogan, C. L. (1989). The effects of new technologies on communication policy. In J. L. Salvaggio and J. Bryant (eds.), *Media Use in the Information Age: Emerging Patterns of Adoption and Consumer Use,* pp. 43–58. Hillsdale, N.J.: Lawrence Erlbaum.

Popper, K. R. (1963). *Conjectures and Refutations: The Growth of Scientific Knowledge.* New York: Harper & Row.

Ray, M. (1973). Marketing communication and the hierarchy of effects. In P. Clarke (ed.), *New Models for Communication Research,* pp. 147–176. Beverly Hills, Cal.: Sage.

Rogers, E. M., and S. H. Chaffee (1983). Communication as an academic discipline: A dialogue. *Journal of Communication* 33, no. 3: 18–30.

Rogers, E. M., and F. F. Shoemaker (1971). *Communication of Innovations: A Cross-Cultural Approach.* New York: Free Press.

Seelye, K. (1983). *USA Today:* Gannett's technicolor baby. *Columbia Journalism Review* 21, no. 6: 27–35.

USA Today (1989). The '80s: Plugged in to TV. Dec. 1, p. 1A.

U.S. Congress, Office of Technology Assessment (1988). *Informing the Nation: Federal Information Dissemination in an Electronic Era.* Washington, D.C.: U.S. Government Printing Office.

Webster, J. G. (1989). Television audience behavior: Patterns of exposure in the new media environment. In J. L. Salvaggio and J. Bryant (eds.), *Media Use in the Information Age: Emerging Patterns of Adoption and Consumer Use,* pp. 197–216. Hillsdale, N.J.: Lawrence Erlbaum.

Winn, M. (1977). *The Plug-In Drug.* New York: Viking.

Wright, C. R. (1959). *Mass Communication: A Sociological Perspective.* New York: Random House.

Wurman, R. S. (1989). *Information Anxiety.* New York: Doubleday.

PART II

Scientific Method and Models of Mass Communication

Scientific theory has the great advantage of being solidly grounded in observations. It is easy to spin out many different theories of mass communication effects, some quite grandiose (and some quite menacing). But stating at the beginning that our theories should be scientifically testable means that they ultimately have to be verifiable through observations. This not only cuts out a lot of lengthy debate over matters that can never be resolved, but also means that our theories are more likely to be related to the real world and thus are more likely to have some practical applications.

Communication scientists also develop models of communication. A scientific model is not quite the same as a scientific theory. A model is more limited, and is usually an attempt to identify the crucial parts of a process or phenomenon. Theories are ordinarily constructed to *explain* communication phenomena, while models usually do little more than *describe*. Nevertheless, the process of communication is so complicated that models can do a great deal to help us understand it.

Chapter 2 describes the scientific method as it is used to develop and test communication theories, and Chapter 3 presents a number of models that have been found useful for detailing the communication process.

2
Scientific Method

Science serves as a guard against untested assumptions about the world we live in. The scientific method differs from other methods of obtaining knowledge in that it is based on observation and the testing of our assumptions (hypotheses) against the evidence of the "real" world (empiricism).

Methods of establishing truth that were commonly employed before development of the scientific method include *intuition, authority,* and *tenacity* (Cohen & Nagel, 1934).

- Many times intuition is based on personal values or early socialization. Frequently it argues for what is "self-evident." For example, it was "self-evident" to many people that the sun revolves around the earth.
- A reliance on authority often results in seeking truth from sources in religion, morals, and politics. Authorities in religion once held that the earth was the center of the universe. Such a view fit their theology.
- Tenacity accounts for many of the beliefs that we have always held to be true. Reinforcement from others and frequent repetition support these beliefs, even when we have no verifiable evidence and when the beliefs may be false.

Unfortunately, these methods are often used today, although they are more subject to error and bias than the scientific method.

This book deals instead with the findings of *research* from a number of disciplines or fields. Nearly all of the findings are derived, however, from the application of scientific method, in this case in what have come to be known as the social or behavioral sciences. There are two qualities characteristic of science that we should consider before exploring its basic nature and usefulness for communication theory.

Imagination in Science

Thomas H. Huxley, a great 19th-century scientist, once defined science as "trained and organized common sense" and added that theory building is something you engage in "every day and every hour of your lives."

The father of the relativity theory, Albert Einstein, said, "The whole of science is nothing more than a refinement of everyday thinking."

This is not to imply that first-rate science does not require large quantities of imagination—in identifying significant areas of inquiry, in the ability to perceive unrecognized

19

relationships and causes, in the ability to translate abstract hypotheses into real world variables (operational definitions) that can be measured, in the ability to devise measuring instruments to "get a handle" on elusive data, and in many other aspects of science.

Certainly it took imagination for Nicolaus Copernicus to visualize the sun at the center of our solar system and to break with the astronomy of Ptolemy, which for 15 centuries had held that the sun revolved around the earth. It also took imagination for Galileo to see the possibilities of applying a new instrument, the spyglass, to the heavens and to demonstrate that Copernicus's guess, or hypothesis, was right. In doing so, Galileo created the modern scientific method: he built the apparatus, did the experiment, and published the result. As is so often the case with new ideas, many people felt their authority threatened by Galileo's findings, and they did everything within their power to suppress his new notions of the universe. (Bronowski, 1973, gives an excellent brief account.)

Every scientist *assumes* an approach or a particular orientation when dealing with a subject or issue. This approach determines the concepts, questions, perspectives, and procedures the scientist applies. It also shapes the hypotheses tested and eventually the theory generated. The approach, then, is the framework within which a theory is tested.

As has often been observed, the business of science is theory. Put another way, theory is what science is all about; it is the product of scientific research. The scientist seeks to make generalizations about the nature of reality. In our field we wish to be able to make generalizations about the way people communicate. Verified theory then enables us to make predictions about the outcome of certain events. In this case the goal is to make predictions concerning the process and effects of communication.

The Cumulative Nature of Science

Science, as all scholarship, is also cumulative; that is, it builds on the work that has preceded it. Sir Isaac Newton summed this up three centuries ago when, in one of the most important aphorisms in the history of science, he said, "If I have seen further, it is by standing on the shoulders of giants."

Robert K. Merton, a pioneer in the sociology of science, has pointed out that Newton's aphorism "does not only apply to science. In its figurative meaning it explains the growth of knowledge and culture in virtually every area of learning you can mention." Merton adds, "Newton's aphorism means that no investigator starts out with a tabula rasa, or clean slate. It denies the great man notion" (Whitman, 1976).

The cumulative nature of scholarship and science is made possible by its transmissibility, its ability to overcome barriers of geography, language, and social, economic, and political systems. Transmissibility is possible in part because science, like all knowledge, deals with abstractions about reality. The special language of any discipline is composed of these abstractions.

For cumulation to take place, scholars must share an approach or orientation, or at least a system of scholarly values. Some people believe that if scholarship is to be transmissible across social classes and political systems, it must, to a great extent, be "detached, objective, unemotional and nonethical" (Westley, 1958, p. 162). This point has been the cause of much concern in recent years. Well known is the debate, which continues among atomic scientists, concerning the development of the atomic and hydrogen bombs. At the height of the Vietnam War a Harvard University scientist defended the development of napalm, the jellied gasoline used in warfare, often with devastating effects on civilian populations. He said that he would do it again and added that the moral issues were outside his realm (*New York Times,* Dec. 27, 1967, p. 8).

There are, on the other hand, scholars who feel that "value-free research is a delusion." In its theme, an October 1989 Nobel Conference stated, "We have begun to think of science as a more subjective and relativistic project, operating out of and under the influence of social ideologies and attitudes—Marxism and feminism, for example" (*New York Times,* Oct. 22, 1989).

"Legally your researchers are free, but they are controlled by the passions of the day," observed Alexander Solzhenitsyn in a 1974 speech at Harvard University.

The history of science is filled with attempts to impose philosophical and political positions on scientific findings and to make scientific findings conform with untested preconceived notions (often held on the basis of intuition, authority, or tenacity), or to fit current political policies. Well known and already mentioned was the reaction of established authority to Galileo's verification of Copernicus's hypothesis, which placed the sun and not the earth at the center of our solar system. In our own century Soviet agriculture and genetics had Marxist dogma imposed on it by Trofim Lysenko. He rejected conventional theories of heredity and asserted that the basic nature of plants and even animals could be radically affected by changes in environment. Discussion and experimentation related to opposing views was forbidden, and it is claimed that Soviet agriculture was set back by 25 years (Salisbury, 1976). More recently a top U.S. government scientist charged that the White House's Office of Management and Budget had changed the text of testimony scheduled to be delivered to Congress. He said the changes made "his conclusions about the effects of global warming seem less serious and certain than he intended" (Shabecoff, 1989).

Scientific Generalizations about Reality

Scientists seek to make generalizations about the nature of reality. They accomplish this by repeatedly testing (replication) generalizations (hypotheses) about reality until sufficient confirmations are obtained to warrant calling these generalizations tentative laws. In science the tests of generalizations are accomplished through controlled observations. A scientist must be able to demonstrate that any variables that could provide an alternative explanation for the findings of an experiment have been controlled. This must be accomplished in such a way that it can be repeated by another investigator. The replicability and verifiability of science serve as its guard against fraud and bias.

Scientific Hypotheses

As has been pointed out, the end product of science is theory to enable the making of predictions. A hypothesis (or scientific proposition) is usually framed in what is known as a conditional form ("if . . . , then. . . . "). Although usually unstated, it is assumed that this statement is preceded by *ceteris paribus,* Latin for "all other things being equal." A scientist who establishes a conditional relationship is dealing with *cause and effect.* It is these causal relations that science ultimately seeks. Scientists assume that the subjects they deal with are natural phenomena or a part of nature, ordered in a natural way, and not a result of supernatural ordering. This implies that the objects of investigations are determined and that causal connections can be found to account for them.

As a scientific discipline develops, it works toward the explanations that are the most parsimonious. As one writer aptly put it, "The parsimonious explanation is the one that accounts for the most variance with the fewest propositions" (Westley, 1958, p. 167). In other words, science tries to explain as much as possible with the fewest generalizations. A twin goal of science, along with parsimony, is a striving for closure. If the scientist works with lawful, ordered, or natural data, it is assumed that eventually the universe is knowable. The sciences work toward understanding the areas that remain unknown—in pursuit of the goal of closure.

Whereas every scientist assumes an approach or orientation when dealing with an issue, science concerns itself with what is, what exists, or what happens when, not with questions of what is right or what should be. This is not to say that social sciences do not deal with ideologies, attitudes, and value systems, but that social scientists, in selecting or framing their methods of inquiry, must take into account the observers' or investigators' biases in these areas. Questions of values, or what should be, are dealt with by the fields of religion, ethics, and philosophy rather than science.

Safeguards against Bias and Fraud

As two famous authors in the area of logic and scientific methods have said, "By not claiming more certainty than the evidence warrants, scientific method succeeds in obtaining more logical certainty than any other method yet devised" (Cohen & Nagel, 1934, p. 396).

The safeguard of science against bias or fraud lies in the publication of findings and the replication of results. Researchers bear in mind a number of questions:

Can colleagues in the discipline agree that the hypotheses have been put to a valid test?

Are the conclusions drawn from the data reasonable?

Are the generalizations made from the data within the bounds of the phenomena examined, or do the conclusions go beyond the data?

Can the findings be replicated?

In March 1989 two scientists at the University of Utah startled the scientific community by announcing the discovery of a simple method of obtaining unlimited, cheap, and safe power with "cold fusion." The claims were announced in a press conference, rather than the usual published scientific paper, and the two scientists were widely criticized for not having submitted their findings to prior peer review and for refusing to provide details needed for replication. After hundreds of scientists failed to duplicate the process the Utah scientists were called "deluded, incompetent and outright frauds." A University of Utah physicist, who was invited to monitor the experiments in the Utah labs in May and June, published a paper in the British journal *Nature* in early 1990 saying he was unable to measure any nuclear reaction (Associated Press, 1990). There remains, however, a residue of provocative findings of strange heats and erratic results, as yet unexplained. Teams of university and corporate scientists in the United States, India, and Japan have continued to search for scientific bases for the unexplained results (Browne, 1989; Broad, 1989a). Many say that the findings go beyond the bounds of classical physics. A respected physicist at the Brookhaven National Laboratory says, "People I trust are finding things they can't explain" (Broad, 1990). In the history of science many experiments have produced unintended findings, resulting in entirely new directions of inquiry.

In contrast to the Utah announcements, two Japanese scientists reported in the December 1989 *Physical Review Letters* that small gyroscopes lose weight when spun under certain conditions. Commenting on their report, one writer (Broad, 1989c) said:

> Experts who have seen the report said it seemed to be based on sound research and appeared to have no obvious sources of experimental error . . . the current results are presented with scientific understatement. The authors do not claim to have defied gravity, but simply say their results "cannot be explained by the usual theories." . . . More important, the experiment is outlined in rich detail, insuring that other scientists can try to duplicate and assess it . . . the next step is for independent researchers to see if the results of the Japanese scientists can be duplicated . . . their apparatus is accurately and well described. It should be easy to replicate. Most of the equipment is available in any lab. We'll have the answer shortly.

An example of a check on bias in mass communication research is an article by the noted Columbia University professor of sociology Herbert J. Gans. He examined the findings of three other researchers, reported in two widely published surveys, that contended that U.S. journalists impose a liberal or left bias on the news and mislead the American people (Gans, 1985). Gans questioned the way the researchers analyzed their data and reported their findings. He said that their approach often diverges sharply from scientific methodology and that the researchers have not published or released detailed information about their methods, despite repeated requests (p. 30). Gans argued that, based on what the researchers have published, both studies

1. hide a political argument behind a seemingly objective study, highlighting the data which support that argument;

2. report findings about journalists which do not accurately reflect the answers they gave to the survey questions they were asked;

3. violate basic survey methodology by first inferring people's opinions from answers to single questions, and then treating their answers as strongly felt opinions in a way that makes the journalist appear militant and radical;

4. violate scientific norms by forgetting an explicit promise to their respondents;

5. present a mass of data on the personal backgrounds and alleged political opinions and values of the journalists without any evidence that these are relevant to how the journalists report the news. (Gans, 1985, pp. 29–33)

Several critics have recently charged laxity in the peer review process and the publication of erroneous and fraudulent scientific papers. They have made several proposals to make scientific journals more accountable (Altman, 1989; Broad, 1989b; Goleman, 1988; Maddox, 1988; Stagner, 1989; Wade, 1988).

The Process of Scientific Inquiry

Scientific inquiry employs both *induction* and *deduction*. Induction uses particular or specific instances as observed by the scientist to arrive at general conclusions or axioms. This is the use of data or evidence to arrive at generalities, often called empiricism. The mathematical expression of induction is found in statistical inference: the scientist examines many cases and arrives at a conclusion. Deduction, in contrast, begins with what is general and applies it to particular cases; this is often called logic or rationalism. Deduction is employed by the scientist in making the leap from a hypothesis (a generalization) to an operational definition so that the hypothesis can be tested with specific real-world phenomena or cases.

Several definitions will assist us in summarizing what we have learned thus far. Two authors of a well-known text in comparative politics provide these reasoned and, for our purposes, highly useful definitions (Bill & Hardgrave, 1973, p. 24):

> Generalization: A statement of uniformities in the relations between two or more variables of well-defined classes.
> Hypothesis: A generalization presented in tentative and conjectural terms.
> Theory: A set of systematically related generalizations suggesting new observations for empirical testing.
> Law: A hypothesis of universal form that has withstood intensive experimentation.
> Model: A theoretical and simplified representation of the real world.

It is important to remember that a model is neither a generalizing nor an explanatory device. (Chapter 3 deals with models, especially communication models, in greater detail.)

> A model is a theoretical and simplified representation of the real world. It is an isomorphic construction of reality or anticipated reality. A model, by itself, is not an explanatory device, but it does play an important and directly suggestive role in the formulation of theory. By its very nature it suggests relationships. . . . The jump from a model to a theory is often made so quickly that the model is in fact believed to be a theory. A model is disguised as a theory more often than any other concept. (Bill & Hardgrave, 1973, p. 28)

Acquiring Empirical Data

In mass communication research several methods are frequently employed to acquire empirical data in a systematic fashion. The most common are survey research, content analysis, experimental design, and case studies.

Survey Research

The sample survey is used to answer questions about how a large number of subjects feel, behave, or are, especially with regard to variables that change over time.

Survey research is the study of a portion or sample of a specific "population" (magazine subscribers, newspaper readers, television viewers, the population of a community or state). If done according to statistical principles, generalizations can then be made from the sample to the population with a certain degree of assurance or confidence. A sample is less costly than a census, which is an enumeration of all the members of a population. A census allows statements to be made about actual population parameters. However, the sample, which is less costly than a census, forces the researcher to make generalizations about the population within a degree or range of probability (called the "confidence interval"), which can be calculated statistically for any given sample.

Sample surveys can also compare relationships between variables by correlation (moving toward answers to questions of cause and effect). Often variables of interest to the researcher cannot be manipulated in an experiment (e.g., age, race, occupation). The survey allows for comparisons between people who differ on a given characteristic and also for differences in their behaviors (e.g., how individuals of various ages, occupations, or educational levels differ in their perceptions of media credibility or in their media use).

A Survey to Check News Accuracy   An example of the survey technique is the use of mail questionnaires to check on news accuracy. Tankard and Ryan (1974) clipped articles dealing with science news over a three-month period from a random sample of 20 newspapers taken from 167 newspapers in the 26 states east of the Mississippi that have a circulation exceeding 50,000. Cover letters, questionnaires, clippings, and return envelopes were mailed to 242 scientists involved in the news articles. The scientists were asked to indicate possible types of errors in the articles on the checklist of 42 kinds of errors, to express their attitudes toward science news coverage in general, and to provide information regarding their recent activities with representatives of the press.

The survey resulted in 193 usable returns (only 2 scientists refused to cooperate, and 13 mailings were returned as undeliverable).

The investigators were able to specify the types of errors the scientists perceived as made most often, the scientists' agreement or disagreement with nine short statements regarding science writing in general, and the relationship between nine "predictor" variables and perceived error rate (such things as content category [medicine, biology, social sciences, etc.], origin of the report [staff, wire service, etc.], circulation of the newspaper, whether or not a story was bylined).

Tankard and Ryan reported that the mean number of kinds of errors was 3.50 when the scientist read the story before publication and 6.69 when the scientist did not read the story before publication. The attitude items indicated strong criticism by scientists of the accuracy of science news reporting in general. Large majorities of the sample indicated that headlines on science stories are misleading and that information crucial to the understanding of research results is often omitted from news stories (Tankard & Ryan, 1974, p. 334).

A Survey of Media Credibility   An example of the sample survey using personal interviews in communication research is a study done by Westley and Severin (1964b) concerning perceived media credibility. A sample of 1,200 households was drawn from the population of an entire state, and one randomly selected adult in each household was interviewed by a professional interviewer. The sample resulted in 1,087 usable completed interviews.

In the course of the interviews the interviewees were asked to indicate which medium (television, radio, or newspaper) they would be most likely to place their trust in should they receive conflicting reports concerning several types of news and also to indicate the time they spend on a typical day with each of the media. Questions were also asked concerning the interviewees' behavior in several other areas (voting, group memberships, offices held, visiting patterns, etc.) and were gathered on demographic variables (age, sex, educational level, occupation, income, place of residence, etc.).

It was then possible to "cross-tabulate" responses to identify the types of persons who claim to place the greatest trust in one of the media and the types of persons who report the greatest and least amount of time spent with each of the media.

The investigators concluded, among other things, that the "ideal type" of media user who was especially likely to assign relatively high credibility to the newspaper was a man who had at least some college, resided in an urban area, and had a high-status occupation. He regarded himself as middle-class, and his father also had a high social status. He was most likely to be an independent in politics and, if he acknowledged any party, to have had only a weak party identification. He belonged to a moderate number of organized groups and tended to hold office in them but was not especially gregarious (Westley & Severin, 1964b, p. 334).

In another analysis of the data the investigators profiled the daily newspaper nonreader. They found the nonreader to be most often a rural or small-town resident with few memberships in formal organizations, including churches, and infrequent in attending church and in visiting with friends and relatives. The nonreader tended to have no political identification or even political leaning and to be a nonvoter (Westley & Severin, 1964a, p. 51).

Ten years later the survey was replicated in another state by another group of researchers. They concluded that by and large the newspaper nonreader was approximately the same type of person found earlier. A discouraging factor these researchers found was that significantly larger numbers of people had decided not to read the newspaper, especially the poorer and the less educated (Penrose, Weaver, Cole, & Shaw, 1974).

These samples were drawn according to sampling theory, and an error term for these specific samples was calculated. The researchers were able to make generalizations about the media use and assigned credibility patterns for the population of a state as a whole within stated parameters with a high degree of assurance. In the Westley and Severin study, survey research allowed making generalizations to a population of more than 4 million from a sample of little more than 1,000.

Content Analysis

Content analysis is a systematic method of analyzing message content. It is a tool for analyzing the messages of certain communicators. Instead of interviewing people or asking them to respond to questionnaires, as in survey research, or observing behavior, as in the human experiment, the investigator using content analysis examines the communications that have been produced at times and places of his or her own choosing. It has been described as the "objective, systematic, and quantitative description" of communication content (Bernard Berelson, cited in Budd, Thorp, & Donohew, 1967, p. 3).

A sophisticated use of content analysis couples it with additional information about source, channel, receiver, feedback, or other conditions of the communication situation, such as attitude, personality, or demographic characteristics. This enables predictions to be made about the communication process. In such cases content analysis is a tool used with other methods of inquiry to link message content with other parts of the communication setting. It allows the investigator to deal with larger questions of the process and effects of communications.

After selecting a question to be investigated or a hypothesis to be tested, the content analyst must define the population he or she will work with (publications, newscasts, time span, etc.). If the population is large, a sample is drawn, as in survey research. Categories must then be defined for classifying message content (a crucial step) and the content of the sample is coded according to objective rules. The coded content may be scaled or differentiated in some way to arrive at scores. If the content is to be related to other variables, these scores can then be compared with them.

As with all quantitative research, these scores must then be analyzed (usually using the data reduction techniques of statistical analysis) and the findings interpreted according to the concepts or theories that have been tested.

Magazine Coverage of Vietnam War Objectors   A good example of the use of content analysis to test hypotheses based on theory and prior research is a study done to measure positions taken by 21 magazines toward objectors to the Vietnam War (Showalter, 1976).

The investigator began by citing prior theory and research concerning wartime restrictions on freedom of expression, value-consensus theory, the mass media's major function of enforcement of social norms, and studies of press performance in treatment of dissenters to previous American wars. He concluded that wartime minorities received little press backing.

As a result of the literature review, the researcher's primary hypothesis was, "Conscientious objectors, a legally recognized ideological minority in wartime, receive negative treatment in magazine editorial content since objectors counter the dominant norm of duty to country."

Twenty-one popular magazines indexed in the *Reader's Guide to Periodical Literature* were selected for the study. All entries under "Conscientious Objectors"—a total of 110 articles and 28 letters to the editor—were analyzed. The 138 items yielded 999 assertions about conscientious objectors. Five coders classified these assertions in accordance with evaluative assertion analysis procedure.

The primary hypothesis was not confirmed. The researcher found that only 2 of 21 magazines viewed conscientious objectors negatively.

Showalter's second hypothesis, "Opponents to the Vietnam War who perform services more nearly commensurate with military duty receive less negative editorial treatment than those who express their opposition in less acceptable channels," was generally supported.

His third hypothesis, "Magazine editorial positions toward objectors vary inversely with size as measured by circulation," was substantiated.

His fourth hypothesis was "Public opposition to the Vietnam War and magazine editorial treatment of objectors are positively correlated." The data indicate positive correlations; however, they were generally not statistically significant.

Showalter concludes: "American magazine journalists exercised more freedom in covering an ideological minority during the Vietnam War than the theoretical and historical literature had suggested."

The larger question raised by this study concerns trends in press positions toward all minority groups. Additional research is needed to determine whether journalists—in all media—are fulfilling their responsibilities in coverage of ethnic, religious, economic, and other minorities.

Such studies have implications for the well-being of the press itself. Tolerance and understanding of diverse points of view in the society can help the press preserve its own claims to freedom.

Reagan's China Policy in Three Elite Newspapers   Another content analysis dealt with Reagan's China policy as covered by three elite American newspapers (Chang, 1984).

Citing prior theory and research indicating the important role the press plays in the process of policymaking, the investigator raised these research questions:

1. How did coverage of Reagan's China policy in some elite newspapers differ before and after he took office?
2. What is the newspaper's treatment of Reagan's China policy?

Chang chose the *Los Angeles Times,* the *New York Times,* and the *Washington Post* because of their prestige status and their importance in national politics. He defined the press agenda as "emphasis on specific problems or issues in the newspaper's coverage of Reagan's China policy" and measured the number of paragraphs published on a certain subject.

News, editorials, columns, and features dealing with China, international relations, and Taiwan were analyzed.

The study period was divided into two nine-month periods, one before and one after Reagan's first inauguration, January 20, 1981.

The data indicated that the three newspapers ran roughly the same number of items about and devoted the same number of paragraphs to Reagan's China policy. However, coverage of Reagan's China policy differed significantly before and after his inauguration. In the former period the emphasis was on Reagan's views concerning U.S.–Taiwan relations, whereas after inauguration it shifted to U.S.–China policy.

The evidence indicates that coverage of Reagan's China policy was more negative before than after his inauguration. Still to be answered is the question of whether the president sets the agenda for the newspapers or vice versa.

Both the Showalter and Chang investigations are good examples of how content analysis can be applied to the media to measure objectively how they deal with the news. The effect of media content on the society is, of course, a matter for further investigation. Content analysis is also used to measure media positions taken on various other issues, alleged bias in the media in politics, and changes in media positions, often, as we have seen, in correlation with events.

The Portrayal of Education in Prime-time Television Mayerle and Rarick (1989) used content analysis to examine 40 prime-time television series that featured education or educators as central concerns during the period 1948 to 1988. They found that such series were rare and transient. The researchers analyzed

> longevity and frequency of scheduling of education series, program formats, locale and educational level portrayed, role portrayals (job title, gender and race of lead and major supporting cast), and dramatic theme of the series. Two coders independently coded each program according to these variables. (pp. 141–142)

They concluded:

> The world of television education, while presented positively, is less diverse in settings, activities and role depictions than the world of actual education. Television's teachers are dedicated, work with interested students in urban high schools or colleges, and often have conflicts with cranky or inept administrators. White males far outnumber females and minorities in most occupational roles. Themes about nontraditional educators, family life of students and teachers, and educational problems are common. (p. 139)

Experimental Design

Experimental designs are the classic method of dealing with questions of causality. An experiment involves the control or manipulation of a variable by the experimenter and an observation or measurement of the result in an objective and systematic way. When it is possible to use the experimental method, it is the research method most apt to provide answers of cause and effect. The classic experiment will answer questions of whether and to what degree a variable (the experimental or independent variable) affects another variable (the dependent variable).

In the simplest form of the classic experiment, two matched groups are randomly selected from a population (defined by and of interest to the experimenter), and one is given the experimental variable (in communication research it may be a news story, documentary film, piece of propaganda, etc.). After the experimental group has been exposed to the variable in question, both groups are observed or measured and any differences between them are construed as effects of the experimental treatment.

Many experiments modify the classic design, for reasons such as practical difficulties or costs. Some experiments are made far more complex in order to provide answers to additional questions (e.g., how long the effects of a message will last, the effects of various types or combinations of messages, the effect of a number of different independent variables that may interact).

An Experiment of Communicator Credibility   A classic experiment in communication research, conducted by Hovland and Weiss (1951), dealt with the effects of communicator credibility on acceptance of the content of a message. Identical messages were presented to two groups, one from a source with high credibility and the other from a source with low credibility. Opinions were measured before and after the messages were presented and also one month later. Four different topics were used (each in affirmative and negative versions) and presented to some subjects by trusted sources and to other subjects by sources held in much lower esteem.

Each subject received one article on each of the four topics, with the source given at the end of each article. Before reading the articles the subjects indicated their trust in each of a long list of sources, including those used in the experiment. The four high-credibility sources used in the experiment were judged so by 81 to 95 percent of the subjects; with the low-credibility sources the scores were only 1 to 21 percent.

The initial attitudes held toward the sources clearly affected how the subjects evaluated the presentations. Those from low-credibility sources were judged "less fair" and conclusions "less justified" than those by high-credibility sources, even though the articles were identical. The researchers concluded that "judgments of content characteristics, such as how well the facts in a given communication justify the conclusion, are significantly affected by variations in the source" (Hovland, Janis, & Kelley, 1953, p. 29).

The researchers found greater opinion change in the direction advocated by the message when the source was of high credibility than when it was of low credibility.

However, when opinion data were obtained four weeks later, the differential effectiveness of the sources had disappeared. There was less acceptance of the viewpoints of high-credibility sources and greater acceptance of the positions advocated by low-credibility sources. At that time measures were also obtained of the subject's memory of the sources for each communication.

After ruling out other explanations, the researchers concluded that there exists a "sleeper effect" for subjects who showed increased belief in messages attributed to sources of low credibility; in the investigators' words, "There is decreased tendency over time to reject the material presented by an untrustworthy source" (Hovland, Janis, & Kelley, 1953, p. 256).

The main advantages of the experimental method are the control it allows the investigator and the inherent logical rigor it offers. However, many experiments are "artificial" or oversimplified in their settings and the findings must be translated to the "real" world. For this and a number of other reasons, often seemingly conflicting results are obtained from experimental designs and survey research. Carl Hovland, a pioneer in communication research, addressed this problem as it applies to studies of attitude change and suggested methods for its resolution. He concluded by noting the virtues of each method and the need for both methods in communication research (Hovland, 1959).

"Natural" Experiments Often "natural" experiments can be set up outside the laboratory. An example of a planned natural experiment in communication is the "split-run" technique, whereby two versions of an advertisement or other message are run and the relative effectiveness of each is assessed. This may be done through follow-up questions asked over the telephone or in personal interviews, through tabulation of responses from coupons coded to identify which version has resulted in the response, or through other means.

Sometimes the experimenter may be interested in a theoretical question or in the test of a hypothesis and can design a study for an appropriate natural event. The experimenter then "follows up" the event with fieldwork. Such is the case involving the question of the effects of price advertising on the sales of beer and ale. This is a question of considerable controversy in many parts of the United States and an issue of concern for brewers, for the advertising industry, and for consumer groups concerned over alcohol consumption, its negative health aspects, and drunk driving.

In the state of Michigan price advertising of beer and wine was prohibited, allowed, and again prohibited between May 1981 and April 1984. The researcher (Wilcox, 1985) examined total sales of brewed beverages (beer and ale) as reported by a sample of 65 retail outlets in lower Michigan in A. C. Nielsen in-store audits every two months over the three-year period. The researcher also examined data showing the number of surveyed retail outlets engaging in local advertising during the period of no restrictions on price advertising (March 1982 to May 1983).

Examination of the data indicated that a significantly higher percentage of retail stores engaged in local advertising during the nonrestrictive period. However, the presence of price advertising appeared to have no significant effect on sales of brewed beverages (Wilcox, 1985, p. 37).

Case Studies

While a survey examines one or a few characteristics of many subjects or units, a case study is used to examine many characteristics of a *single* subject (e.g., a communicator, newsroom, newspaper, news syndicate, television station, ad agency). The case study usually tries to learn "all" about the area the investigator is interested in for the specific case over a period of time.

The Wire Editor as Gatekeeper "Gatekeeper" studies are classic media case studies. With the cooperation of the wire editor of a morning newspaper with a 30,000 circulation in a midwestern city of 100,000, White (1950), in what is *the* classic gatekeeper study, was able to compare wire copy used with that actually received during one week from three major wire services.

The wire editor saved all unpublished wire copy, about nine times as much as that which was published, and at the end of each day spent one and one-half to two hours noting his reasons for rejecting each item not used.

With the data available, the investigator was able to compare the amount of wire copy actually received for each of a number of categories, both in column inches and in percentages of the total received, as compared with that used. He was also able to tabulate the number of times stories were rejected for various reasons.

The "gatekeeper" was then asked to consider at length four broad questions about the basis on which he selected news, his own prejudices, his concept of the audience he was making selections for, and any specific tests of subject matter or style that may enter into the selection of stories.

The researcher carefully qualified his conclusions with the parenthetical remark, "If Mr. Gates is a fair representative of his class," recognizing that a case study deals with one example and is not a sample that can be logically or scientifically generalized. The study has, of course, provided considerable insight and information that has served as the basis for further investigation.

A Case Study of Television News Gatekeeping Using Content Analysis   More recently, Berkowitz (1990) did a gatekeeper case study combining observational research with content analysis to examine the selection of local news items for a network-affiliated television station in Indianapolis. He refined the metaphor of the news "gate" and reshaped the notion of gatekeeping to fit the local television situation. Working in the newsroom, he coded a total of 391 potential stories during a four-week period.

Berkowitz found that news selection decisions were based on several considerations besides news values, including information that was easy to explain, that would draw audience, and that could be assembled with efficiency of effort. As a result of 220 hours of newsroom observation and later interviews, Berkowitz concluded that rather than use textbook news values, newsworkers used their instincts, citing interest, importance, and visual impact, although the latter was rarely mentioned during story conferences.

The structure of the newscast format, which called for an approximate quota of stories from various categories, had almost as much to do with story selection as did the news merits of potential stories. Berkowitz says that "this helps explain why gatekeepers do not always agree on specific stories, but they do tend to agree on the kinds of stories that constitute a balanced news mix" (p. 66).

Berkowitz concludes:

> . . . this study found that decision-making didn't fit the traditional mold of a lone wire editor sitting next to a pile of stories and making decisions based on either newsworthiness or personal preferences. . . . First, decision-making seemed to be a group process; content, therefore, was shaped by group dynamics. . . . Second, the keys to the lock—interest, importance, visual quality—were different than the keys searched for by past studies of newspaper wire editors or those taught in journalism classes. Whether these keys could even be used was partly dictated by organizational demands such as resource constraints and newscast formats. . . . Stories that passed through one gate faced still other gates on their way toward being broadcast. Spot news closed the gate on planned event stories. Resource constraints and logistical problems sometimes closed the gate on spot news stories. (p. 66)

Histories as Case Studies   Most histories of media institutions can also be classified as case studies. An exception in communication research is an investigation of three centuries of the British press and its regulation by Siebert (1952). In this nonquantitative study hypotheses are formulated and tested and conclusions drawn, giving it some of the properties of scientific research. A later example is a test of one of Siebert's propositions in North Carolina by Shaw and Brauer (1969), using the historical method in focusing on one editor and the Newcomb ABX model of symmetry from the field of social psychology to make predictions. Case studies usually cannot be generalized to other similar situations. Most often the results are based on a single example and rarely are hypotheses formulated and tested, making it difficult, if not impossible, to generalize to other situations. The method does provide a great many observations, ideas, and insights that can be followed up with other types of investigations to yield results that can be generalized.

Reasoning about the Data

Statistics

Scientific investigators rely on statistics to aid them in making inferences from the object of their studies to the populations they seek to generalize about. Statistics are a tool used in the process of reasoning about the data gathered.

Statistics can be used in a number of ways. One of the most common uses is in data reduction, in bringing large quantities of data to manageable form by providing summaries. These are known as descriptive statistics, which provide information such as the mean, median, variance, and percentiles for a body of data.

Perhaps even more important for our purposes is the use of sampling or probability statistics to enable scientists to make estimates of population characteristics. This use of statistics enables scientists to draw inferences from data at specific levels of confidence. A scientist using the sample survey method can make inferences from the sample data to the population from which the sample was drawn. This is done within parameters that can be calculated after specifying the confidence level (the "odds" of being in error) that the scientist is willing to accept. For example, the range of the mean daily television viewing of a population can be predicted from a random sample from that population once the chances of error are stated (a 5 percent level of confidence would indicate 1 chance in 20). As scientists increase the degree of confidence they expect in the prediction, the interval within which they can make the prediction (confidence interval) also increases.

The investigator who employs the experimental method randomly assigns subjects to various groups. Random assignment assures that there will be no systematic bias in subject assignment. After the experimental group or groups have been exposed to the variable under investigation, observations and measurements are made about the effects of the variable. The resulting data are analyzed with statistical methods to determine if any differences between groups in the effects of the experimental variable could have been by chance and at what level of probability. For example, what is the probability that the group that received a specific message and scored higher on an attitude measure following the message did so only by chance? If the probability is very low, and if other basic requirements of the experimental method were observed, the scientists can then infer that the difference between the groups is due to the different treatment (in this case the message).

Validity, External and Internal

When evaluating scientific findings and the generalizations made from them, scientists ask questions regarding validity and reliability. Did the experiment, survey, or content analysis measure what the investigator claims it measures?

More specifically, external validity deals with the question of whether the phenomena observed and measured by an investigator are representative of the real world phenomena the scientist wishes to generalize about.

The work of Shere Hite, author of three books dealing with male and female sexuality, has been challenged for the representativeness of the samples upon which her conclusions are based. Her third book, *Women in Love,* is based on 4,500 responses to 100,000 questionnaires she mailed out, largely to women's groups. Critics have argued that sampling members of women's groups, and a return of only 4.5 percent, does not provide a valid sample of the population of women in general, to which she projects her findings. An earlier book, *The Hite Report on Male Sexuality,* was described as "social science fiction" by the then editor of the *New York Times Book Review* (McDowell, 1987).

Internal validity is required in experimental research if conclusions are to be drawn from the data. It raises the question of whether differences obtained resulted from the experimental treatment or whether they can be explained by other factors. Internal validity deals with extraneous or alternate variables that must be controlled in the research design to rule out their being a cause of any effects that may be observed. Put another way, the experimenter wishes to rule out any explanation for the results or findings other than the experimental or independent variable.

Operationally Defining the Hypothesis

The act of translating abstract hypotheses to real-world phenomena is called "operationally defining" the hypotheses. For example, the hypothesis "If an individual is a social isolate, then that individual is less apt to use the mass media than one who is socially integrated into his or her community" needs to be defined in terms that can be measured.

The investigator can define *social isolate* and *socially integrated* in terms of frequency of visits with neighbors, relatives, coworkers, and others and *media use* in terms of reported time spent with the mass media. A comparison can then be made between individuals who report little social interaction with others and those who report considerable social interaction with others, and subgroup reports of time spent with various mass media can be analyzed. The question of validity then becomes whether the measures of social integration actually measure what social integration is, as defined for that study.

Reliability

Reliability deals with the consistency of measurement. External reliability is the ability of a measure to provide the same results time after time, within acceptable margins of error, if applied to the phenomena under the same conditions. Internal reliability refers to the question of whether various subparts of a test provide comparable data.

Conclusions

As a scientist in any field of investigation develops and tests hypotheses about the nature of the world in a particular area of interest, the process of observation, testing, replication, cumulation, and closure continues. All of this contributes to the building of a theory that will provide explanations and make possible predictions.

In communication research there has been a gradual and long-term shift from applied research to basic research (sometimes, with unfortunate connotations, called "pure" science). The field of mass communication research, like so many other fields, is moving from answers to specific questions dealing with immediate problems toward theory building to provide the general explanations of how humans communicate.

References

Associated Press (1990). Utah monitor of "cold fusion" casts doubt on its validity. *New York Times,* Mar. 29, p. A8.

Altman, L. K., M.D. (1989). Errors prompt proposals to improve 'peer review' at science journals. *New York Times,* June 6, p. 20.

Berkowitz, D. (1990). Refining the gatekeeping metaphor for local television news. *Journal of Broadcasting & Electronic Media* 34: 55–68.

Bill, J. A., and R. L. Hardgrave, Jr. (1973). *Comparative Politics: The Quest for Theory.* Columbus, Ohio: Charles E. Merrill. Especially pp. 21–40 dealing with the scientific method.

Broad, W. J. (1989a). Despite scorn, some scientists still seek cold-fusion clues. *New York Times,* Oct. 31, p. 17.

———— (1989b). Question of scientific fakery is raised in inquiry. *New York Times,* July 12, p. 7.

———— (1989c). Two men and a gyroscope may rewrite Newton's Law. *New York Times,* Dec. 28, p. 10.

———— (1990). "Cold fusion" claimants review puzzling results. *New York Times,* April 3, p. B5.

Bronowski, J. (1973). *The Ascent of Man.* Boston: Little, Brown. Especially Chapter 6, "The Starry Messenger," dealing with Copernicus, Galileo, and the birth of the scientific method.

Browne, M. W. (1989). Fusion claim is greeted with scorn by physicists. *New York Times,* May 3, p. 1.

Budd, R., R. Thorp, and L. Donohew (1967). *Content Analysis of Communications.* New York: Macmillan.

Chang, T. K. (1984). How three elite papers covered Reagan's China policy. *Journalism Quarterly* 61: 429–432.

Cohen, M. R., and E. Nagel (1934). *An Introduction to Logic and the Scientific Method.* New York: Harcourt Brace and World.

Gans, H. J. (1985). Are U.S. journalists dangerously liberal? *Columbia Journalism Review,* Nov.-Dec., pp. 29–33.

Goleman, D. (1988). Test of journals is criticized as unethical. *New York Times,* Sept. 27, p. 21.

Hovland, C. (1959). Reconciling conflicting results derived from experimental and survey studies of attitude change. *The American Psychologist* 14: 8–17. Reprinted in W. Schramm and D. Roberts (eds.) (1971), *The Process and Effects of Mass Communication,* rev. ed., pp. 495–515. Urbana: University of Illinois Press.

Hovland, C., I. L. Janis, and H. H. Kelley (1953). *Communication and Persuasion.* New Haven: Yale University Press.

————, and W. Weiss (1951). The influence of source credibility on communication effectiveness. *Public Opinion Quarterly* 15: 635–650.

Maddox, J. (1988). A too-polite silence about shoddy science. *New York Times,* Sept. 26, p. 27.

Mayerle, J., and D. Rarick (1989). The image of education in primetime network television series 1948–1988. *Journal of Broadcasting and Electronic Media* 33: 139–157.

McDowell, E. (1987). Agent for Hite resigns amid a controversy. *New York Times,* Nov. 13, p. 45.

New York Times (1989). Does ideology stop at the laboratory door? A debate on science and the real world. Oct. 22, Sect. E, p. 22.

Penrose, J., D. Weaver, R. Cole, and D. Shaw (1974). The newspaper nonreader 10 years later: A partial replication of Westley-Severin. *Journalism Quarterly* 51: 631–638.

Salisbury, H. (1976). Trofim L. Lysenko is dead at 78; Was science overlord under Stalin. *New York Times,* Nov. 24, p. 36.

Shabecoff, P. (1989). Scientist says U.S. agency altered his testimony on global warming. *New York Times,* May 8, p. 1.

Shaw, D., and S. Brauer (1969). Press freedom and war constraints: Case-testing Siebert's Proposition II. *Journalism Quarterly* 46: 243–254.

Showalter, S. W. (1976). American magazine coverage of objectors to the Vietnam War. *Journalism Quarterly* 53: 648–652; 688.

Siebert, F. S. (1952). *Freedom of the Press in England 1476–1776.* Urbana: University of Illinois Press.

Stagner, R. (1989). Bogus research shows experts to be embarrassingly human. *New York Times,* Apr. 23, Sect. 4, p. 22.

Tankard, J., and M. Ryan (1974). News source perceptions of accuracy of science coverage. *Journalism Quarterly* 51: 219–225.

Wade, N. (1988). Looking hard at science's self-scrutiny. *New York Times,* Aug. 21, Sect. 4, p. 9.

Westley, B. (1958). Journalism research and scientific method. *Journalism Quarterly* 35: 161–169; 307–316. Reprinted in R. O. Nafziger and D. M. White (1963), *Introduction to Mass Communication Research* as "Scientific Method and Communication Research" (Chapter 9). Baton Rouge: Louisiana State University Press.

Westley, B., and W. Severin (1964a). A profile of the daily newspaper nonreader. *Journalism Quarterly* 41: 45–51.

——— (1964b). Some correlates of media credibility. *Journalism Quarterly* 41: 325–335.

White, D. (1950). The "Gate Keeper": A case study in the selection of news. *Journalism Quarterly* 27: 383–390.

Whitman, A. (1976). Newton's other law is hailed on its tercentenary. *New York Times,* Feb. 6, p. 21.

Wilcox, G. (1985). The effect of price advertising on alcoholic beverage sales. *Journal of Advertising Research* 25 (Oct.-Nov.): 33–38.

3
Models in
Mass Communication Research

Whether we realize it or not, we are using models every time we try systematically to think about, visualize, or discuss any structure or process, be it past, present, or future. The effectiveness of such activity depends in large measure on how well our model fits the thing we are supposedly modeling.

In Chapter 2 we discussed the nature of the scientific method, the role of theory, and the advantage of being able to make predictions. We gave a definition of a model as a "theoretical and simplified representation of the real world" and quoted two authors who observed that models are often confused with theories.

If a model is not a theory, what then *are* models, why use them, how does one evaluate them, and what are some of the important models in communication research? The answers to these questions make up this chapter.

A model is not an explanatory device by itself, but it helps to formulate theory. It *suggests relationships,* and it is often confused with theory because the relationship between a model and a theory is so close.

Deutsch (1952) points out that a model is "a structure of symbols and operating rules which is supposed to match a set of relevant points in an existing structure or process." Models "are indispensable for understanding the more complex processes." This is a form of selection and abstraction, which as we shall see later is used far more often than most of us realize. Because we select the points we include in a model, a model implies judgments of relevance, and this, in turn, implies a theory about the thing modeled. Of course, abstraction carries with it the danger of oversimplification.

A model provides a frame within which we can consider a problem, even if in its early versions it does not lead to successful prediction. A model may also point out important gaps in our knowledge that are not apparent, and it may suggest areas where research is needed (the goal of closure). Failure of a model when it is tested may lead to an improved model.

The use of theoretical models unites the natural and social sciences, as does the scientific method itself. In nearly all areas of scientific endeavor, symbols are used to describe the essential aspects of reality a particular scientist wishes to focus on.

The structures and processes we are interested in modeling have to do with how humans communicate, especially with the mass media. This can be the way one individual deals with reality within his or her own mind; how a newspaper, television network, advertising agency, or information office is structured and functions; how information flows in a society; or how innovations are adopted or rejected in a social system.

Functions of a Model

Deutsch (1952, pp. 360–361) has discussed the uses of communication models in the social sciences. He cites four distinct functions of models: organizing, heuristic, predictive, and measuring.

The *organizing* function of a model is seen in its ability to order and relate data and to show between data similarities and connections that had not previously been perceived. If a new model explains something that was not understood, it almost always implies *predictions* that can be made. If it is operational, a model implies predictions that can be verified by physical tests.

Predictions, even if they cannot be verified at the time for lack of measuring techniques, can be *heuristic* devices that may lead to new unknown facts and methods. Models also allow a range of predictions, from the simple yes-or-no type to completely quantitative predictions dealing with when or how much.

When a model allows us to make completely quantitative predictions with a degree of precision about when or how much, it becomes related to *measurement* of the phenomena we are interested in. If the processes that link the model to the thing modeled are clearly understood, the data obtained with the help of a model constitute a measure, whether it be a simple ranking or a full ratio scale.

Evaluation of a Model

Each of these functions, in turn, forms a basis for evaluating models.

1. How *general* is a model? How much material does it organize, and how effectively?
2. How *fruitful* or *heuristic* is the model? How helpful is it in discovering new relationships, facts, or methods?
3. How *important* to the field of inquiry are the predictions that can be made from it? How *strategic* are they at the stage of development a field is in?
4. How *accurate* are the *measurements* that can be developed with the model?

Deutsch (1952, pp. 362–363) also adds the following criteria for the evaluation of models:

1. How original is the model? Or how improbable is it? How much new insight does it provide?
2. What is the model's simplicity, economy of means, parsimony? (This is linked to the model's efficiency or its attainment of an intended goal with the greatest economy. An unsurpassed example is Einstein's theory that energy and matter are interchangeable, expressed as $E = mc^2$.)
3. How real is the model? To what degree may we rely on it as a representation of physical reality?

Some Early Communication Models

Lasswell's Model

An early verbal model in communication is that of Lasswell (1948):

> Who
> Says What
> In Which Channel
> To Whom
> With What Effect?

Lasswell's model allows for many general applications in mass communication. He implies that more than one channel can carry a message. The "who" raises the question of the control of the messages (e.g., the "gatekeeper" study cited in Chapter 2). The "says what" is the subject of content analysis (e.g., the studies of the portrayals of conscientious objectors in the media). Communication channels are studies in media analysis. "To whom" deals with the receiver and audience analysis (e.g., the newspaper nonreaders in Chapter 2). The diffusion study and the communicator credibility studies cited in Chapter 2 can be viewed as effect studies.

Lasswell's model has been criticized because it seems to imply the presence of a communicator and a purposive message. It has also been called oversimplified, but, as with any good model, it focused attention on important aspects of communication.

Norbert Wiener published *Cybernetics* in the same year (1948). This book emphasized two important concepts, the statistical foundation of communication and *feedback*, one of the most frequently borrowed concepts in communication.

The Mathematical Theory of Communication

Shannon and Weaver's *Mathematical Theory of Communication* (1949) has been the most important and influential stimulus for the development of other models and theories in communication. The Shannon model is based on the statistical concept of signal transmission, which was first emphasized by Wiener. In the second part of *The Mathematical Theory of Communication*, Warren Weaver presented a schematic diagram of communication that resulted in many other models of the communication process. In this model (Figure 3.1) the information source produces a *message* to be communicated out of a set of possible messages. The message may consist of spoken or written words, music, pictures, and so on. The *transmitter* converts the message to a signal suitable for the channel to be used. The *channel* is the medium that transmits the *signal* from the transmitter to the receiver. In conversation the information source is the brain, the transmitter is the voice mechanism producing the signal (spoken words), transmitted through the air (the channel).

The *receiver* performs the inverse operation of the transmitter by reconstructing the message from the signal. The *destination* is the person or thing for whom the message is intended.

Other major contributions are Shannon and Weaver's concepts of a message composed of *entropy* and *redundancy* and the necessary balance between them for efficient communication while offsetting noise in a channel. Briefly, the more noise in a channel, the greater the need for redundancy, which reduces the relative entropy of the message (e.g., the wireless telegrapher transmitting in a noisy channel repeats key portions of the message to

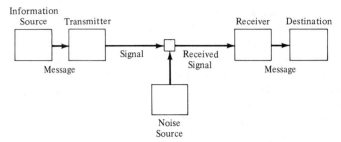

ensure their reception). By using redundancy to overcome the noise in the channel, the amount of information that can be transmitted in a given time is reduced.

Origins of Information Theory

Claude Shannon developed the mathematical theory of signal transmission while he was a research mathematician at Bell Telephone Laboratories and a professor of science at the Massachusetts Institute of Technology.

A direct result of Shannon's information theory is digital communication technology, which became commonplace in the 1980s. We now have digital audio recording on compact disk and tape (Pollack, 1990), and the technology is rapidly spreading over the entire field of telecommunications, including the telephone, radio, and television.

One writer (Fantel, 1989) says:

> What we have witnessed is more than a shift in technology. It is a shift in mentality. We have developed new ways of seeing and representing certain natural phenomena. . . .
>
> But by the middle of the 20th century—in 1948, to be precise—a new General Theory of Information had been formulated by Dr. Claude Shannon of Bell Laboratories. This theory, expressed in elegant mathematics, enabled us to break down the analog entities of our normal perceptions (such as sight and sound) into separate digital bits. The advantage was that the bit language would be intelligible to machines and, through computers, could be manipulated very quickly and with virtually no distortion or loss in the process.

The theory also has important and far-ranging applications outside the engineering field for which it was developed, including the social sciences and communications theory. Warren Weaver, then a consultant on scientific projects at the Sloan Foundation, summarized the main concepts of Shannon's mathematical theory and suggested important applications of the theory to the whole problem of communications in society. The *Philosophical Review* called it "a beautiful example of a theory that unifies hitherto separate branches of physical science, and Dr. Weaver makes important suggestions as to how this unity may be extended" (60:399).

Information theory, as the mathematical theory of communication has become known, is described as "exceedingly general in its scope, fundamental in the problems it treats, and of classic simplicity and power in the results it reaches" (Shannon & Weaver, 1949, p. 114). Weaver suggested that the theory is general enough that it can be applied to written language, musical notes, spoken words, music, pictures, and many other communication signals. The term *communication* is used in a "very broad sense to include all of the procedures by which one mind may affect another" (Weaver, 1949, p. 95). The purpose of communication is defined as an attempt to influence the conduct of the destination with a broad definition of conduct (p. 97).

The concepts of information theory provide insight, and they have been applied to mass communication situations. As has already been noted, the theory has provided the impetus for many other models of the communication process. The theory gives insights into relationships within many forms of communication. Weaver says it is so imaginative that it deals with the core of communication—relationships that exist no matter what form communication may take.

Information theory is essentially a theory of signal transmission. At first it may seem disappointing to the student of the mass media because it has nothing to do with meaning and it may even seem a bit bizarre because information theory equates information with uncertainty. As we shall see, these are two of the theory's greatest assets in that they provide a new and fruitful way of viewing the communication process.

The communication process (see Figure 3.1) begins with the source selecting a message out of all possible messages. This message can be in the form of spoken or written words, musical notations, the music itself, pictures, mathematical notations, symbolic logic, body movements, facial expressions, or a host of other forms we have available. The transmitter operates on the message to produce a signal suitable for transmission over a channel. The message exists only between the source and the transmitter and between the receiver and the destination. Only a signal travels between the transmitter and the receiver.

When we use the telephone, the channel is the wire, the signal is the electrical current passing through the wire, and the transmitter (mouthpiece) transforms the sound pressure of the spoken word into varying electrical current. In oral speech the source is the brain, the transmitter is the human voice mechanism or vocal system, the channel is the air, and the signal is the varying pressure passing from the vocal system of one person to the ear of another. The transmitter functions to encode the message; and when it is received, the receiver (in this case the ear) must decode the message (convert the varying sound waves coming through the air into neural impulses for the destination, the brain.).

The *signal*, of course, takes different forms, depending on the communication system we are examining. We have seen that in speech the signal is varying sound pressure traveling through the air (the channel). In radio and television the signal is an electromagnetic wave, while newspapers, magazines, and books use the printed word and illustrations as the signal on a page (the channel). The channel is, as implied, the medium used to transmit the signal from the transmitter to the receiver.

Channel capacity, in information theory terms, is not the number of symbols a channel can transmit but rather the information a channel can transmit or a channel's ability to transmit what is produced out of a source of information (Weaver, 1949, p. 106). Of course, all channels, be they electronic, mechanical, or human, have an upper limit of capacity. For example, the human eye can resolve and transmit far more information in a period of time than the brain can process and store. As we shall see, all communications are composed of chains of systems, and as with any chain, they are no stronger than their weakest link. Channel capacity is also limited by the space or time available to the editor or newscaster and by the time available to the destination to spend with the media.

Once a transmitter has encoded a message for transmission over a channel, a receiver must reconstruct the message from the signal transmitted. Ordinarily the receiver's operation is the inverse of the transmitter's; that is, the receiver changes the transmitted signal back into a message and passes this message on to a destination. In broadcasting the receiver is, as the term implies, the radio or television set. In speech the receiver is the ear and its part of the nervous system. With print material it is the eye and its associated nervous system.

The *destination* is the person or thing for whom the message is intended. With the mass media the destination is, of course, a member of the audience—the reader, listener, or viewer. The destination can also be a thing. A thermostat communicates with a heating or cooling system; a governor communicates with a motor or the fuel supply to an engine. Computers can be programmed to communicate with one another.

The thermostat or governor provides feedback to allow a system to make corrections in its own operation. The concept of *feedback* was first introduced by Norbert Wiener of MIT in his book *Cybernetics* (1948). In the mass media we have many forms of feedback from the destination to the source to help the communicator correct subsequent output. Letters and telephone calls from readers and listeners are a form of feedback, as are responses to advertising campaigns, audience ratings in broadcasting, and increases or decreases in newsstand sales or subscriptions. Feedback in the classroom can take many forms including puzzled looks or signs of boredom, which inform the instructor that a point needs to be clarified or that it is time to move on to another topic.

The Delivery of Useful Information

So far you have probably had little difficulty with information theory. But its most unique feature and most valuable contribution to our understanding of the communication process may be harder to grasp: its approach to what constitutes *information*. As defined by Weaver, the term *information* is used in a very special way. It is most important that you not confuse information with meaning, as is commonly the case (1949, pp. 99–100). Each one of us adds our own meaning to the information we receive, as we shall see in subsequent chapters. Information, in terms of the mathematical theory of communication, or information theory, according to Weaver, "relates, not so much to what you do say, as to what you could say" (1949, p. 100). Information becomes a measure of our freedom of choice in selecting a message to transmit. In information theory terms, information is very similar to *entropy* in the physical sciences—it is a measure of the degree of randomness. Entropy is the uncertainty or disorganization of a situation. In information theory it is associated with the amount of freedom of choice one has in constructing a message.

A highly organized message does not have a high degree of randomness, uncertainty, or choice. In such a case the entropy or information is low because any parts of the message that are missing when it is received have a high probability of being supplied by the receiver. For example, because of the organization (entropy) of the English language, a receiver who is familiar with it can correct most misspellings. Individuals familiar with a given subject can provide missing elements in a passage. We shall see how this has been applied to measure the "readability" of a passage.

The part of the message that is not entropy or information is called, as we might expect, redundancy. *Redundancy* is defined as the portion of the message that is determined by the rules governing the use of the symbols in question or that is not determined by the free choice of the sender. Redundancy is unnecessary in that if it were missing the message would be essentially complete or could be completed (1949, p. 104). When we use the English language about half of our choices are controlled by the nature of the language and the rules for its usage.

Redundancy can be used to offset noise in a communication channel. The fact that English is about 50 percent redundant makes it possible to correct errors in a message that has been received over a noisy channel. However, key or important items are often repeated in transmission (a form of redundancy) to ensure their reception when transmitting through a noisy channel ("will arrive Tuesday, repeat Tuesday").

Redundancy is a measure of certainty or predictability. The more redundant a message is, the less information it is carrying. Sometimes, however, increased redundancy will increase the efficiency of a communication system.

Noise is defined as anything added to the signal that is not intended by the information source. Noise can take many forms. The example that comes most readily to mind is that of static on the radio. In information theory terms, noise can also be distortions of sound in telephony, radio, television, or film, distortions of shape or shading in a television image, a smudged reproduction of a printed photo, or errors of transmission in telegraphy. Noise can also take the form of a speaker's distracting mannerism—added to the signal, but not intended by the information source.

Noise increases uncertainty and, both paradoxically and technically, in an information theory sense, noise increases information. According to Weaver (1949, p. 109), information as used in information theory can have good or bad connotations. Noise is spurious information. For the sender or source, a high degree of uncertainty or freedom of choice (entropy) is desirable, but from the destination's point of view, uncertainty because of errors or noise is undesirable. To get useful information, the destination must subtract the spurious information (noise) from the received message.

From the standpoint of the destination, noise can also be competing stimuli from outside the channel. Obvious examples are a low-flying airplane that blocks out the sound of a newscast, a crying baby, a barking dog, or quarreling children. Noise can also take the form of whisperers at the cinema or the woman who habitually arrives late for class wearing revealing attire. The woman is obviously communicating information, but from the standpoint of the lecturer it is information not intended by the communicator. The communicator must then increase the level of redundancy in the lecture (usually by repeating a point) to offset the noise introduced by a competing source.

The mass communicator usually tries to reduce noise as much as possible in his or her own transmission and expects noise to be present when the message is received. As has been pointed out, this noise can be offset through increased redundancy. The art of the right balance between entropy and redundancy is much of what makes a good editor— striking a balance between predictability and uncertainty. This, in turn, becomes a function of how an editor defines what an audience wants, what it can absorb, and what the editor feels it should have, all, of course, within the limits or constraints of the medium used to communicate.

When *rates of transmission* are at less than channel capacity, noise can be reduced to any desired level through improved coding of the message. However, if the rate of transmission of information exceeds channel capacity, noise cannot be reduced below the amount by which the rate of transmission exceeds channel capacity. In most communication situations, the capacity of the individual to process information is the limiting factor. If the channel is overloaded, error increases dramatically. A major decision for any communicator when encoding a message becomes that of finding the optimum level of redundancy.

Information Theory Applied

Any human communication consists of a series of systems coupled into chains. A *system* is defined as any part of an information chain that is capable of existing in one or more states or in which one or more events can occur (Schramm, 1955, p. 132). A communication system can be the telephone wire, the air, or a human optic nerve. Systems include the channels of information but also include sources, transmitters, receivers, and destinations. Systems must be coupled with one another in order to transfer information, and the state of any system depends on the state of the system adjoining it. If the coupling is broken, information is not transferred (e.g., when a student's attention wanders while reading an assignment).

Human communication contains many coupled systems. This coupling or "interface" between two systems is a *gatekeeper* point. A gatekeeper determines what information is passed along the chain and how faithfully it is reproduced. This principle applies to reporters, photographers, editors, commentators, and all others who decide what information to use in the media from the vast array of information available. How much do they filter out? How much emphasis is changed? How much distortion is there, both systematic distortion through bias and random distortion through ignorance or carelessness? A newspaper or a broadcasting station is a gatekeeper, deciding what to present to its audience. It must select from all of the local, state, national, and international news available. The human destination (reader, viewer, or listener) also acts as a gatekeeper by selecting and interpreting material according to his or her own individual needs.

Human communication systems, however, are *functional systems,* as opposed to Shannon's structural system—that is, they can learn. When we say that the human central nervous system is a functional system because it is capable of learning we mean that its present state depends on its own past operation. As Schramm (1955) pointed out very early, the mathematical formulas of information theory are based on probabilities, and learning alters those probabilities (p. 132). This prevents the direct application of Shannon's mathematical theory to human communication.

Communication systems may be corresponding or noncorresponding. *Corresponding systems* can exist in identical states. The telegraph transmitter or key and the telegraph receiver or magneto coil accept and repeat the same series of dots and dashes (minus any noise introduced in transmission). *Noncorresponding systems* cannot exist in identical states. For example, the information given the telegraph operator does not correspond to the message transmitted, nor is the message transmitted identical to the current on the wire or the radiation transmitted through the air in the case of radiotelegraphy.

In information theory terms, communication takes place "when two corresponding systems, coupled together through one or more noncorresponding systems, assume identical states as a result of signal transfer along a chain" (Schramm, 1955, p. 132). In human communication we have very long chains (e.g., foreign reporting). The material of a reporter or photographer on the scene in the Middle East or Asia passes through a great many gatekeepers before it is offered to a potential audience member in the United States. At each step it can be edited, discarded, distorted, reorganized, or changed.

The mass media are usually characterized by a relatively high output compared with a low input; or to state it differently, the mass media are *high amplifiers*—relatively few people produce the news, entertainment, advertising, and public relations that are seen, heard, or read by millions. This is simply another aspect of the industrial revolution whereby, through the application of modern technology, a relatively small number of workers in an industry produce commodities for a much larger number of consumers. This reflects the application of corporate and industrial economic efficiency in creating and distributing the commodity called "information."

The mass media themselves are made up of groups of people, and as with any group, *communication networks* must be established and maintained if a group is to function. Communication networks are equally important in all groups in society as well as in electronic and mechanical communications. Schramm (1955) cites a number of measures derived from information theory that suggest new ways of studying communication activity in small groups (p. 143). Some of them are *traffic,* or who does most of the talking and how much talking is done; *closure,* or how open is the group to outsiders and ideas from the outside; and *congruence,* the question of whether members are equal participants in group communication or whether some are primarily originators of communications while others are primarily recipients.

Information Theory Applied to Readability

A direct and practical application of information theory's concepts of entropy and redundancy to message content is the *"Cloze Procedure,"* developed by Wilson Taylor in 1953. This procedure (examined in greater detail in Chapter 7) provides us with a useful way of estimating the entropy or redundancy of a passage of writing for a given audience. Taylor's procedure deletes every nth word in a passage and then asks readers to supply the missing word. The frequency with which words are provided for the various deletions and the number of different words provided for a particular deletion indicate the predictability of the passage for a given audience or for one individual. Here the concepts of entropy and redundancy in messages are put to work to measure a specific audience's familiarity with a specific content and also the difficulty of the level of writing for a specific audience.

Paisley (1966) demonstrated how the measurement of entropy can be used to determine the authorship of various samples of English prose and verse. He used letter redundancy to identify numerous biblical and classical passages that varied in topic, time of composition, structure, and authorship.

In a series of studies (Krull, Watt, & Lichty, 1977; Watt & Welch, 1982), information theory has been applied to measure television program complexity as related to viewer preferences. One finding was that static complexity has a negative impact on visual attention but dynamic complexity is positively related to attention.

Finn and Roberts (1984) have argued that few researchers have used Shannon's concepts in their research because of a failure to distinguish between two fundamental orientations in Shannon's theory: the relationship between source and destination and the technical characteristics of transmission channels.

These researchers say that communication researchers have had success applying information theory to their problems when they

> have been sensitive to Shannon's entropy formula as a probabilistic measure of information and his realization that communication requires that source and destination be intimately linked by a shared set of messages . . . the assumed linear flow of the diagram obscures what we believe is Shannon's most fundamental notion—that the communication process presumes the existence of a set of messages shared by both information source and destination prior to signal transmission. (Finn & Roberts, 1984, pp. 454–455)

Finn and Roberts argue that

> Shannon's conceptualization suggests a reorientation of our approach to such perennial concerns of communication research as selective perception and message comprehension. The focus of such research may need to shift from such topics as channel characteristics and noise in the system to more basic questions regarding the initial degree of correspondence between message sets held by the source and the destination. (p. 460)

Shannon's entropy measure can be applied beyond the technical problems of signal transmission. It makes possible the analysis of categorical (nominal) data as continuous data, which allows the use of more sophisticated and powerful quantitative statistical methods (McMillan, 1953, p. 17; as cited in Finn & Roberts, 1984, p. 459).

A recent article (Ritchie, 1986) raises serious questions about Weaver's interpretation of Shannon's mathematical theory and the way the model has been applied in three decades of communication research. Ritchie concludes that

> Shannon's . . . theorems may serve as the basis for theorizing in our own field in three different ways. First, where our problems can be broken down into subproblems, and where any of these subproblems satisfy the assumptions of Shannon's theorems, the theorems can be applied straightforwardly. Second, where our problems resemble Shannon's transmission problems, but do not seem to satisfy his assumptions, we might strive to develop a theory somewhat parallel to Shannon's theorems, but based on a set of assumptions that we can justify with our own data. Third, we can consider how Shannon's assumptions might apply to our field, taking the assumptions themselves as problematic, and develop a line of inquiry based on exploring the hypotheses suggested by Shannon's assumptions. (p. 295)

Osgood's Model

Osgood (1954) contended that the technical communication model of Shannon and Weaver, developed for application to engineering problems, was never intended for human communication. His own model is developed from his theory of meaning and from psycholinguistic processes in general.

Osgood provides for both the sending and receiving functions within one individual, and he takes into account the "meaning" of symbols. (We have seen that the Shannon and Weaver model specifically excludes meaning from the definition of information.) The Shannon and Weaver model implies separate sources, destinations, transmitters, and receivers. While this is usually true of mechanical systems, it is not true of human communication systems. An individual functions as both a source and a destination, as both a transmitter and a receiver by decoding the messages he or she encodes through a number of feedback mechanisms.

In this model the "input" is some form of physical energy or a "stimulus" coded in a form that is converted (decoded) to sensory impulses.

In Osgood's view, each person in a "speech community" is viewed as a complete communicating system corresponding to the Shannon and Weaver model. Osgood has rearranged the Shannon model into what he calls a "communications unit" to send and receive messages.

Osgood stresses the social nature of communication and says:

> Any adequate model must therefore include at least two communicating units, a source unit (speaker) and a destination unit (hearer). Between any two such units, connecting them into a single system, is what we may call the message. For purposes of this report, we will define the message as that part of the total output (responses) of a source unit which simultaneously may be a part of the total input (stimuli) to a destination unit. When individual A talks to individual B, for example, his postures, gestures, facial expressions and even manipulations with objects (e.g., laying down a playing card, pushing a bowl of food within reach) may all be part of the message, as of course are events in the sound wave channel. But other parts of A's total behavior (e.g., sensations from B's own posture, cues from the remainder of the environment) do not derive from A's behavior—these events are not part of the message as we use the term. These R-S message events (reaction of one individual that produces stimuli for another) may be either immediate or mediate—ordinary face-to-face conversation illustrates the former and written communication (along with musical recordings, art objects, and so forth) illustrates the latter. (1954, pp. 2–3)

The Schramm Models

Schramm does not make the sharp distinction that Shannon and Osgood make between technical and nontechnical communication, but he does acknowledge that many of his ideas are inspired by Osgood.

In an early series of models, Schramm (1954) proceeded from a simple human communication model to a more complicated model that accounted for the accumulated experiences of two individuals trying to communicate and then to a model that considered human communication with interaction between two individuals (Figure 3.2). The first model bears a striking similarity to that of Shannon. In the second model Schramm introduces the notion that only what is shared in the fields of experience of both the source and the destination is actually communicated, because only that portion of the signal is held in common by both source and destination.

The third model deals with communication as an interaction with both parties encoding, interpreting, decoding, transmitting, and receiving signals. Here we see feedback and the continuous "loop" of shared information.

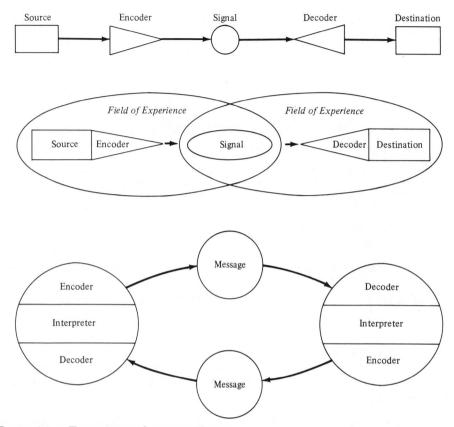

FIGURE 3.2 • THREE OF THE SCHRAMM MODELS

From W. Schramm, "How Communication Works," in W. Schramm (ed.), *The Process and Effects of Mass Communication* (Urbana: University of Illinois Press, 1954). Copyright © 1954 by the University of Illinois. Reprinted by permission.

Newcomb's Symmetry Model

Theodore Newcomb's (1953) approach to communication is that of a social psychologist concerned with interaction between human beings. His model (Figure 3.3) is reminiscent of the diagrams of group networks made by social psychologists and is one of the early formulations of cognitive consistency. In its simplest form of the communication act, a person, A, transmits information to another person, B, about something, X. The model assumes that A's orientation (attitude) toward B and toward X are interdependent, and the three constitute a system comprising four orientations (pp. 393–394):

> 1. A's orientation toward X, including both attitude toward X as an object to be approached or avoided (characterized by sign and intensity) and cognitive attributes (beliefs and cognitive structuring)
> 2. A's orientation toward B, in exactly the same sense (For purposes of avoiding confusing terms, Newcomb speaks of positive and negative attraction toward A or B as persons and of favorable and unfavorable attitudes toward X.)

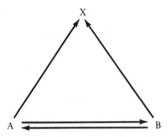

FIGURE 3.3 • THE BASIC NEWCOMB ABX MODEL

From T.M. Newcomb, "An Approach to the Study of Communicative Acts," *Psychological Review* 60 (1953): 394. Copyright © 1953 by the American Psychological Association. Reprinted by permission.

3. B's orientation toward X
4. B's orientation toward A

In the Newcomb model, communication is the common and effective way in which individuals orient themselves to their environment. This is a model for intentional, two-person communicative acts. Newcomb derives the following postulates from his model:

> 1. The stronger the forces toward A's coorientation with respect to B and X, (a) the greater A's strain toward symmetry with B with respect to X and (b) the greater the likelihood of increased symmetry as a consequence of one or more communicative acts. (p. 395)
> 2. The less the attraction between A and B, the more nearly strain toward symmetry is limited to the particular Xs toward which coorientation is required by conditions of association. (p. 399)

Newcomb's model implies that any given system may be characterized by a balance of forces and that any change in any part of the system will lead to a strain toward balance or symmetry, because imbalance or lack of symmetry is psychologically uncomfortable and generates internal pressure to restore balance.

Symmetry has the advantage of a person (A) being readily able to calculate the behavior of another person (B). Symmetry also validates one's own orientation toward X. This is another way of saying we have social and psychological support for the orientations we hold. When Bs we hold in esteem share our evaluations of Xs, we tend to be more confident of our orientations. It follows that we communicate with individuals we hold in esteem about objects, events, people, and ideas (Xs) that are important to us to try to reach consensus or coorientation or, in Newcomb's term, symmetry. Asymmetry is also included in Newcomb's model when people "agree to disagree."

The Westley-MacLean Model

Westley and MacLean, in the process of reviewing and classifying research in journalism and mass communications, felt the need for a different model (Westley, 1976). Because of their interest in news they realized that the communication process can be started by an event as well as by an individual. The linear and noninteractive nature of both Shannon's and Lasswell's models were also sources of concern. Although neither of these models was satisfactory for their purposes, they do acknowledge the influence both had on their own model.

Westley had been influenced by the Newcomb model while a student of Newcomb at Michigan. Newcomb's model provided a starting point for the Westley-MacLean (1957) model of the mass communication process. Westley and MacLean took the Newcomb model, added an infinite number of events, ideas, objects, and people (Xs from X_1 through X_∞), which are "objects of orientation," placed a C role between A and B, and provided for feedback (Figure 3.4).

The Westley-MacLean model provides for As and Xs outside the immediate sensory field of B. The new role, C, allows these additional As and Xs to contribute to B's orientation of the environment. The C role has three functions:

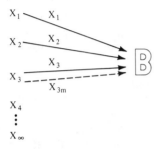

(a) Objects of orientation ($X_1 \ldots X_\infty$) in the sensory field of the receiver (B) are transmitted directly to him in abstracted from ($X_1 \ldots X_3$) after a process of selection from among all Xs, such selection being based at least in part on the needs and problems of B. Some or all are transmitted in more than one sense (X_{3m}, for example).

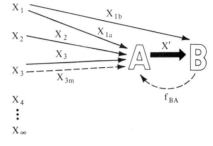

(b) The same Xs are selected and abstracted by communicator (A) and transmitted as a message (X') to B, who may or may not have part or all of the Xs in his own sensory field (X_{1b}). Either purposively or nonpurposively, B transmits feedback (f_{BA} to A).

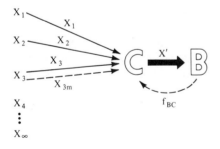

(c) What Xs B receives may be owing to selected abstractions transmitted by a nonpurposive encoder (C), acting for B and thus extending B's environment. C's selections are necessarily based in part on feedback (f_{BC}) from B.

(d) The messages C transmits to B (X'') represent his selections from both messages to him from As (X') and C's selections and abstractions from Xs in his own sensory field (X_{3c}, X_4), which may or may not be Xs in A's field. Feedback not only moves from B to A (f_{BA}) and from B to C (f_{BC}) but also from C to A (f_{CA}). Clearly, in the mass communication situation, a large number of Cs receive from a very large number of As and transmit to a vastly larger number of Bs, who simultaneously receive from other Cs.

FIGURE 3.4 • STEPS IN THE PROGRESSION OF THE WESTLEY-MACLEAN MODEL

From B. H. Westley and M. MacLean, "A Conceptual Model for Communication Research," *Journalism Quarterly* 34 (1957): 32–35. Reprinted by permission.

1. To select the abstractions of object X appropriate to B's need satisfactions or problem solutions
2. To transform them into some form of symbol containing meanings shared with B
3. To transmit such symbols by means of some channel or medium to B.

Westley and MacLean acknowledge their indebtedness to Newcomb for his emphasis on the shared symbol system.

In effect, C observes, selects, encodes, and transmits a limited portion of Xs to fulfill B's information needs. This is the "gatekeeper" role played by the media. In this model B can be a person, a group, or an entire social system.

Unlike the Newcomb model, in the Westley-MacLean model messages can be purposive (with the intent of modifying B's perception of X) or nonpurposive (without any intent on the part of the communicator to influence B). Feedback can also be purposive (e.g., a letter or call to the editor) or nonpurposive (e.g., a purchase or a subscription that becomes a part of a statistic that indicates the effect of a commercial or liking for a publication).

In the Westley-MacLean model As become advocacy roles ("the communicator"). As can be a personality or a social system that selects and transmits messages purposively.

Bs (behavioral system roles, to use the authors' term) are what is usually meant by the "destination" or the "public." These are individuals, groups, or social systems that need and use information about their environment to help satisfy needs and help solve problems.

Cs (channel roles) serve as agents of Bs by selecting and transmitting nonpurposively the information Bs need, especially information that is not readily available to Bs.

Xs are the objects and events "out there," in message form (abstractions of X in a form that can be transmitted).

Channels are the means by which Xs (messages) are transmitted through As to Bs. Channels include C who may alter messages (acting as "gatekeepers").

Encoding is the process by which As and Cs abstract from Xs the messages (X') transmitted in channels. Decoding takes place when Bs receive the message and interiorize it.

Feedback provides As and Cs with information about the effect of their messages on Bs.

Westley and MacLean took the Newcomb model and extended it to include mass communication. For this reason, we shall return to this model in our summary chapter as a means of organizing the contents of this book.

The Gerbner Model

Gerbner (1956) elaborated on Lasswell's model and provided a verbal model that implies 10 basic areas of communication research:

Verbal Model	*Areas of Study*
1. Someone	Communicator and audience research
2. perceives an event	Perception research and theory
3. and reacts	Effectiveness measurement
4. in a situation	Study of physical and social setting
5. through some means	Investigation of channels, media, controls over facilities

6. to make available materials	Administration; distribution; freedom of access to materials
7. in some form	Structure, organization, style, pattern
8. and context	Study of communicative setting, sequence
9. conveying content	Context analysis, study of meaning
10. of some consequence	Study of overall changes

These 10 aspects represent shifts in emphasis only, rather than tight compartments for the study of communication.

Gerbner also provides a pictorial model (Figure 3.5), which he discussed in detail.

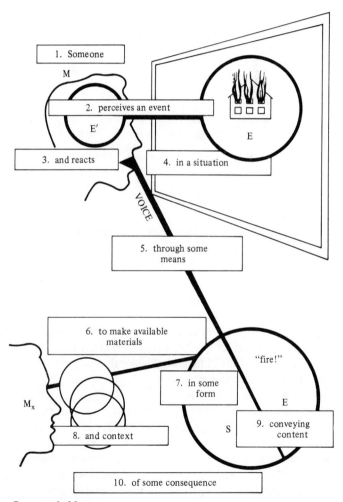

FIGURE 3.5 • GERBNER'S MODEL

From G. Gerbner, "Toward a General Model of Communication," *AV Communication Review* 4 (1956): 175. Reprinted with permission of the Association for Educational Communications and Technology, 1126 16th Street N.W., Washington, DC 20036.

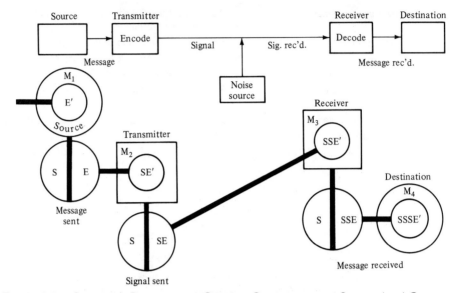

FIGURE 3.6 • SHANNON'S DIAGRAM OF A GENERAL COMMUNICATION SYSTEM (TOP) COMPARED WITH THE PROGRESS OF A SIGNAL IN THE SAME SYSTEM AS ILLUSTRATED IN FIGURE 3.5.

From G. Gerbner, "Toward a General Model of Communication," *AV Communication Review* 4 (1956): 191. Reprinted by permission of the Association for Educational Communications and Technology, 1126 16th Street NW, Washington, DC 20036.

Gerbner's model appears to be an extension of the Lasswell model, but Gerbner includes a comparison with the Shannon model (Figure 3.6). Once again we see the influence of Shannon.

Conclusions

Shannon's mathematical theory of communication, or, perhaps more accurately, signal transmission, is the most important single contribution to the communication models in use today. It not only has stimulated much of the later thinking in this area, but his schematic diagram of the communication process has also been the impetus for many subsequent diagrams of communication models.

Shannon provides a concept of information as entropy or uncertainty. Messages are composed of entropy and redundancy, the latter of which can be used to offset noise that may enter the channel during transmission. The theory is very general in its scope, treats fundamental problems, and attains results with a classic simplicity and power.

As we have seen, this concept of information, which has nothing to do with meaning, is not only not disappointing but is highly fruitful in the paths it leads to. Upon close inspection, a concept of information that is identified with uncertainty is hardly bizarre.

If we evaluate information theory according to the criteria given we find that it does allow one to organize, order, and relate data and shows similarities and connections that had previously not been perceived. It implies predictions that can be verified with physical tests. It has been heuristic in that it has led to new, unknown facts and methods. It provides formulas for the measurement of phenomena of central interest to communication researchers.

Information theory is general enough to organize a great deal of material, much of which is strategic or central to the concerns of communication researchers. It is a model of simplicity or parsimony, yet it is highly original and provides many new insights.

The student who wishes to examine the theory more fully, especially the mathematical bases, is directed to the following references.

In addition to the models discussed in this chapter, there are a number of other models used in communication research and theory building. Several of them will be introduced in other chapters of this book.

As we said earlier, each model emphasizes certain points its creator feels are relevant in the communication process or structure. By selecting certain aspects of communication to be included in a model, the originator of a model implies judgments of relevance, and a theory about the process or structure that is modeled.

No one model can "do it all." Even if it could, it would defeat the purpose of a model—a simplified representation of the real world. Therefore, we select the model that best fits our purposes for the immediate problem at hand. If none is available to do the job required, the researcher might well be forced to modify an existing model, as we have seen in this chapter, or even invent a new one, as we have also seen.

References

Deutsch, K. (1952). On communication models in the social sciences. *Public Opinion Quarterly* 16: 356–380.

Fantel, H. (1989). The advance was digital, and it's just a beginning. *New York Times,* Dec. 31, Section 2, p. 28.

Finn, S., and D. Roberts (1984). Source, destination, and entropy: Reassessing the role of information theory in communication research. *Communication Research* 11: 453–476.

Gerbner, G. (1956). Toward a general model of communication. *Audio Visual Communication Review* 4: 171–199.

Krull, R., J. H. Watt, and L. W. Lichty (1977). Entropy and structure: Two measures of complexity in television programs. *Communication Research* 4: 61–86.

Lasswell, H. D. (1948). The structure and function of communication in society. In L. Bryson (ed.), *The Communication of Ideas.* New York: Harper & Bros. Also reprinted in W. Schramm (1960), *Mass Communications,* pp. 117–130. Urbana: University of Illinois Press.

McMillan, B. (1953). Mathematical aspects of information theory. In B. McMillan et al. (eds.), *Current Trends in Information Theory,* pp. 1–18. Pittsburgh: University of Pittsburgh Press.

Newcomb, T. M. (1953). An approach to the study of communicative acts. *Psychological Review* 60: 393–404.

Osgood, C. E. (ed.) (1954). Psycholinguistics: A survey of theory and research problems. *Journal of Abnormal and Social Psychology* 49 (Oct.). Morton Prince Memorial Supplement.

Paisley, W. J. (1966). The effects of authorship, topic, structure, and time of composition on letter redundancy in English texts. *Journal of Verbal Learning and Verbal Behavior* 5: 28–34.

Pollack, A. (1990). 2 stereo makers promise digital tape in 1990. *New York Times,* Jan. 8, pp. 1, 25.

Ritchie, D. (1986). Shannon and Weaver: Unravelling the paradox of information. *Communication Research* 13: 278–298.

Schramm, W. (ed.) (1954). How communication works. In *The Process and Effects of Mass Communication,* Ch. 1. Urbana: University of Illinois Press. Also in revised edition, 1971, W. Schramm and D. Roberts (eds.).

Schramm, W. (1955). Information theory and mass communication. *Journalism Quarterly* 32: 131–

146. Also in B. Berelson and M. Janowitz (eds.) (1953) *Reader in Public Opinion and Communication.* 2nd ed. New York: Free Press. Also in A. Smith (ed.) (1966) *Communication and Culture.* New York: Holt, Rinehart, and Winston.

Shannon, C., and W. Weaver (1949). *The Mathematical Theory of Communication.* Urbana: University of Illinois Press.

Taylor, W. (1953). Cloze procedure: A new tool for measuring readability. *Journalism Quarterly* 30: 415–433.

Watt, J. H., and A. Welch (1982). Visual complexity and young children's learning from television. *Human Communication Research* 8: 133–145.

Weaver, W. (1949). Recent contributions to the mathematical theory of communication. In C. E. Shannon and W. Weaver, *The Mathematical Theory of Communication,* pp. 95–117. Urbana: University of Illinois Press.

Westley, B. H. (1976). MacLean and I and "The Model." In L. Manca (ed.), *Journal of Communication Inquiry* (Spring), pp. 26–34. Essays in Honor of Malcolm S. MacLean, Jr.

Westley, B. H., and M. MacLean (1957). A conceptual model for communication research. *Journalism Quarterly* 34: 31–38.

Wiener, N. (1948). *Cybernetics.* New York: John Wiley.

P A R T
III

Perception and Language
Issues in the Mass Media

Viewing communication from the point of view of the receiver—the individual person who is exposed to (or "bombarded" by) countless messages—involves some important questions regarding how individuals receive and process messages, how they assign meaning to those messages, and what kinds of factors can increase or decrease understanding.

The starting point for the processing of messages is the individual act of perception. Chapter 4 discusses scientific research on the process of perception and relates it to the act of communication.

Messages are often, although not always, encoded in language. Chapter 5 focuses on what perspective the area of general semantics provides for a study of encoding and includes some important information on the ways language can be used and misused in the process of communication.

Messages can be put together with different strategies, and some of these are basic and well known. Among the strategies for message creation are the propaganda devices identified by the Institute for Propaganda Analysis in the 1930s. These devices, which are still relevant to communication in the 1990s, are discussed in Chapter 6. Analysis of propaganda led to early theories of how we are affected by mass communication.

Clarity and ease of communication are goals that are shared by both sources and receivers of communication. We know that some pieces of writing are easy to understand and others are difficult. Some of the factors most related to the difficulty of understanding of writing for various media have been identified by research, and these are discussed in Chapter 7.

4
The Role of Perception
in Communication

During a presidential campaign, a television spot showed one candidate chatting with a group of disabled veterans. One viewer of the commercial expressed this reaction: "He really cares what's happening to disabled vets. They told him how badly they've been treated and he listened. He will help them." Another viewer of the same commercial expressed this reaction: "[He] was talking with these disabled vets. He doesn't really care about them. He's just using them to get sympathy" (Patterson & McClure, 1976, p. 89).

These viewers were demonstrating *selective perception,* or the tendency for people's perception to be influenced by wants, needs, attitudes, and other psychological factors. The first viewer was a 37-year-old supporter of the candidate shown in the television spot; the second was a 33-year-old supporter of the candidate's opponent.

Selective perception plays an important role in communication of any sort. Selective perception means that different people can react to the same message in very different ways. No communicator can assume that a message will have the intended meaning for all receivers or even that it will have the same meaning for all receivers. This complicates our models of mass communication. Perhaps mass communication is not just a matter of hitting a target with an arrow, as some models suggest. The message can reach the receiver (hit the target) and still fail to accomplish its purpose because it is subject to the interpretation of the receiver.

The process of receiving and interpreting a message is referred to in many communication models as *decoding.* The process involves perception, or the taking in of information through the senses, an area that psychologists have studied in considerable detail. Before we consider the operation of perception in the decoding of a mass communication message, we will discuss some of the research findings about perception in general.

Modern psychology has shown perception to be a complex process, rather different from the naive view that many people held a century ago. The old view—which we might refer to as the commonsense view—saw human perception as largely a physical or mechanical process. The human eye and the other sense organs were thought to work much like a camera or a tape recorder. This view of perception held that there was a quite direct correspondence between an "external reality" and a person's perception, or what was in the mind. This view would hold that everybody perceives the world in essentially the same way.

Psychologists have found perception to be a more elaborate process than that. One definition (Berelson & Steiner, 1964) states that perception is the "complex process by which people select, organize, and interpret sensory stimulation into a meaningful and coherent picture of the world" (p. 88). This definition brings out the active role that a person plays in perception. The person doing the perceiving brings something to the act of perception, just as does the object being perceived. Putting it another way, perception is influenced by a number of psychological factors, including assumptions based on past experiences (that often operate at an almost unconscious level), cultural expectations, motivation (needs), moods, and attitudes. A number of experiments have demonstrated the effects of these factors on perception.

Assumptions and Perception

Much of the research showing that perception is influenced by assumptions has come from a group of researchers working at one time or another at Princeton University. These researchers, who have included Adelbert Ames, Jr., Hadley Cantril, Edward Engels, Albert Hastorf, William H. Ittelson, Franklin P. Kilpatrick, and Hans Toch, have presented what has been called the "transactional view" of perception. The concept is abstract and somewhat philosophical, but essentially it means that *both* the perceiver and the world are active participants in an act of perception (Toch & MacLean, 1962).

The transactional thinkers have developed a number of convincing demonstrations that perception is based on assumptions. One of the most striking, invented by Adelbert Ames, Jr., is called the "monocular distorted room." This room is constructed so that the rear wall is a trapezoid, with the vertical distance up and down the left edge of the wall longer than the vertical distance up and down the right edge of the wall. The rear wall is positioned at an angle so that the left edge is further back than the right edge. This angle is carefully selected so that the room will appear to be an ordinary rectangular room to an observer looking through a small hole at the front of the room. If two people walk into the room and stand in the rear corners, something interesting happens. The one on the right appears to a viewer looking through the hole to be very large because he or she is closer to the viewer and fills most of the distance from the floor to the ceiling. The one on the left appears to be very small because he or she is farther away and fills less of the distance from the floor to the ceiling. This illusion occurs because the mind of the viewer is assuming that the rear wall is parallel to the front wall of the room. This assumption is based on prior experience with other rooms that looked similar. The illusion is so strong that if the two people in the corners switch places, one will appear to grow larger and the other will appear to get smaller, right before the viewer's eye.

Cultural Expectations and Perception

Some of the most striking evidence for the influence of cultural expectations on perception comes from research on binocular rivalry (Bagby, 1957). It is possible to construct a device that has two eyepieces like a pair of binoculars, but can be used to present a different picture to each eye. When this is done, people seldom see both pictures. They more often see one picture and not the other or one picture and then the other. Sometimes they see a mixture of some elements of each picture, but this usually occurs after seeing one picture alone first. Bagby used this instrument to investigate the effect of cultural background on perception.

Subjects were 12 Americans (6 males and 6 females) and 12 Mexicans (6 males and 6

Table 4.1

PERCEPTUAL PREDOMINANCE IN 10 PAIRS OF PICTURES
FOR MEXICAN AND AMERICAN SUBJECTS

	Trials Where Mexicans Dominated	*Trials Where Americans Dominated*	*Total Number of Trials*
Mexican males (6)	44	16	60
Mexican females (6)	45	15	60
American males (6)	7	53	60
American females (6)	12	48	60

From J. W. Bagby, "A Cross-cultural Study of Perceptual Predominance in Binocular Rivalry," *Journal of Abnormal and Social Psychology* 54 (1957): 333. Copyright © 1957 by the American Psychological Association. Reprinted by permission.

females). Except for one matched pair made up of a person from each country, the subjects had not traveled outside their own country. Bagby prepared ten pairs of photographic slides, each pair containing a picture from the American culture and a picture from the Mexican culture. One pair, for instance, showed a baseball scene and a bullfight scene. Subjects were exposed to each slide for 60 seconds and asked to describe what they saw. The assignment of the Mexican or the American picture to the left or right eye was randomized to eliminate the effect of eye dominance. The first 15 seconds of viewing for each slide were scored for which scene was dominant—the Mexican or the American. Dominance was determined by the scene that was reported first or was reported as showing up for the longest period of time. The results (Table 4.1) indicate a strong tendency for subjects to see the scenes from their own culture rather than the scenes from an unfamiliar culture.

Toch and Schulte (1961) used the binocular rivalry procedure to investigate whether training in police work led a person to perceive violent scenes more readily. Subjects who received training were advanced students in a three-year law enforcement course. Control groups were beginning students in the same course and introductory psychology students. Subjects were given half-second exposures through a binocular instrument presenting a picture of a violent scene (such as a man with a gun standing over a body) to one eye and a picture of a neutral scene to the other eye. There were nine pairs of pictures. Subjects were asked to describe the objects they saw. The violent pictures were alternately presented to the left and right eyes, to control for eye dominance. In a second run of the experiment each violent scene was presented to the eye it was not presented to the first time. The results (Table 4.2) showed that the advanced police students saw the violent scenes about twice as frequently as people in either control group. Police training apparently increased the expectation of seeing violent scenes.

Motivation and Perception

One of a number of experiments that show the effect of motivation on perception was done by McClelland and Atkinson (1948). The type of motivation being investigated was hunger. Subjects were Navy men waiting for admission to a submarine training school. One

Table 4.2
PERCEPTION OF VIOLENT PICTURES BY DIFFERENT GROUPS

	Average Number of "Violent" Pictures Perceived (out of 18 presentations)
Control group 1 (27 psychology students)	4.03
Control group 2 (16 beginning trainees)	4.69
Experimental group (16 advanced trainees)	9.37

From H. H. Toch and R. Schulte, "Readiness to Perceive Violence as a Result of Police Training," *British Journal of Psychology* 52 (1961): 391. Reprinted by permission of Cambridge University Press.

group had gone 16 hours without food, a second 4 hours without food, and the third 1 hour without food. All subjects were told they were participating in a test of their ability to respond to visual stimulation at very low levels. The men went through 12 trials in which a picture was supposedly projected, but actually nothing was projected at all. To make this realistic, during the instructions they were shown a picture of a car and then the illumination was turned down until the car was only faintly visible. In some of the trials subjects were given clues such as: "Three objects on a table. What are they?"

The results (Table 4.3) showed that the frequency of food-related responses increased reliably as the hours of food deprivation increased. Furthermore, in another phase of the experiment food-related objects were judged larger than neutral objects by hungry subjects but not by subjects who had recently eaten.

Mood and Perception

An experiment using hypnosis demonstrated that mood has an effect on perception. Leuba and Lucas (1945) hypnotized subjects, suggested to them that they were experiencing a certain mood, and then asked them to tell what they saw in a picture. Each subject was put

Table 4.3
FOOD-RELATED RESPONSES

Hours of Food Deprivation	*Mean Number of Food-Related Responses (maximum: 14)*
1	2.14
4	2.88
16	3.22

Adapted from D. C. McClelland and J. W. Atkinson, "The Projective Expression of Needs: I. The Effect of Different Intensities of the Hunger Drive on Perception," *Journal of Psychology* 25 (1948): 212. Reprinted with permission of the Helen Dwight Reid Educational Foundation. Published by Heldref Publications, 4000 Albemarle St. N. W., Washington, D.C. 20016. Copyright © 1975.

in a happy mood and then shown six pictures. Then the subject was told to forget the pictures and what had been said about them and was put in a critical mood and again shown the same six pictures. Finally the subject was given the same treatment once more except that the suggested mood was anxious.

The descriptions of the pictures were drastically different depending on the mood the person was in. They differed not only in the train of thought the pictures suggested but also in the details noticed.

One picture showed some young people digging in a swampy area. Here is one subject's description of that picture while in a happy mood:

> It looks like fun; reminds me of summer. That's what life is for; working out in the open, really living—digging in the dirt, planting, watching things grow.

Here is the same subject describing the same picture while in a critical mood:

> Pretty horrible land. There ought to be something more useful for kids of that age to do instead of digging in that stuff. It's filthy and dirty and good for nothing.

Here is the same subject describing the same picture while in an anxious mood:

> They're going to get hurt or cut. There should be someone older there who knows what to do in case of an accident. I wonder how deep the water is.

Another study provides some evidence that even exposure to different types of communication is influenced by mood. Meadowcraft and Zillmann (1987) investigated the relationship between menstrual cycle and choice of television programming. Previous studies had established a relationship between menstrual cycle and mood, with women experiencing more unpleasant moods during the premenstrual and menstrual phases of the cycle. Meadowcraft and Zillmann surveyed a sample of women on three separate dates. Women were asked to imagine how they would spend an evening free for watching television, and they were given a choice of 10 television comedies, 7 game shows, and 10 drama programs. Women were also asked to report where they were in the menstrual cycle.

The findings were that women in the premenstrual and menstrual phases were more likely to choose the comedy programs, apparently in an effort to relieve their unpleasant mood states.

Attitude and Perception

The effects of attitude on perception were documented in a study of perception of a football game by Hastorf and Cantril (1954). The 1951 football clash between Dartmouth and Princeton was an exciting and controversial one. Princeton's star player Dick Kazmaier was taken out of the game in the second quarter with a broken nose. In the third quarter, a Dartmouth player received a broken leg. Discussion of the game continued for weeks, with editorials in the two campus newspapers charging the other school with rough play. Hastorf and Cantril took advantage of this situation to conduct a study in perception. They showed a film of the game to two groups: two fraternities at Dartmouth and two undergraduate clubs at Princeton. Students from both schools saw about the same number of infractions by the Princeton team. But Princeton students saw an average of 9.8 infractions by the Dartmouth team, while Dartmouth students saw an average of 4.3 infractions by the

Dartmouth team. That is, the Princeton students saw more than twice as many violations by the Dartmouth team as did the Dartmouth students. Hastorf and Cantril state, "It seems clear that the 'game' actually was many different games and that each version of the events that transpired was just as 'real' to a particular person as other versions were to other people" (p. 132).

Perception and Mass Communication

So far this discussion of research has shown that perception in general is influenced by assumptions (often unconscious), cultural expectations, needs, moods, and attitudes. The same kinds of forces are at work when people respond to mass communication messages, as the following examples show.

A Time *Magazine Cover*

The cover of an issue of *Time* magazine showed a hand with an American flag pattern on it shaking hands with a red hand with a Soviet hammer and sickle on it. The cover story, "Space Spectacular," dealt with the Apollo-Soyuz orbital linkup and cooperation in space.

Not everyone perceived this theme of cooperation, however. A few weeks later, the following letter to the editor from D. Vincent O'Connor of North Adams, Massachusetts, appeared in *Time:* "The cover illustrates very well that the Russians have got us."

The Carter-Ford Debate

The *New York Times* and CBS News conducted a poll of 1,167 respondents after the first televised debate between presidential candidates Jimmy Carter and President Jerry Ford (Apple, 1976). Overall, 37 percent of the respondents thought Ford had won, 24 percent thought Carter had won, 35 percent called it a draw, and 4 percent were unwilling to express an opinion. If the results are examined separately for Carter supporters and Ford supporters, however, some striking differences in reaction show up. Table 4.4 shows that Ford supporters were more likely to see the debate as a victory for Ford, while Carter supporters were more likely to see the debate as a tie. All viewers were exposed to the same televised debate, and yet people came away with very different views, depending on their own initial attitudes. Similar evidence of selective perception was found in studies of the earlier Kennedy-Nixon debates (Kraus, 1962).

Table 4.4

HOW SUPPORTERS OF FORD AND CARTER PERCEIVED THE FIRST DEBATE

	Ford Supporters (%)	Carter Supporters (%)
Who won the first debate?		
Ford	66	14
Carter	6	40
Tie	24	42
Don't know	4	4

Based on R. W. Apple, "Voter Poll Finds Debate Aided Ford and Cut Carter Lead," *New York Times*, Sept. 27, 1976, p. 1.

Antiprejudice Cartoons

Satire is a familiar journalistic device. It has been used in works ranging from Jonathan Swift's *Gulliver's Travels* to Garry Trudeau's "Doonesbury" comic strip. But how is satire perceived?

The American Jewish Committee was interested in studying the effects of satire in reducing prejudice. It sponsored a study by Eunice Cooper and Marie Jahoda (1947) that investigated the effects of antiprejudice cartoons. The cartoons featured an exaggerated figure named "Mr. Biggott," who appeared in situations designed to make prejudice appear ridiculous. For instance, one cartoon showed Mr. Biggott lying in a hospital bed and dying. He is saying to the doctor, "In case I should need a transfusion, doctor, I want to make certain I don't get anything but blue, sixth-generation American blood!" The intention was that people looking at the cartoon would see how ridiculous prejudice is and would lessen their own feelings of prejudice.

Cooper and Jahoda tested the cartoons on 160 white, non-Jewish working-class men. About two-thirds of the sample misunderstood the cartoons. Some said the purpose of the cartoons was to legitimize prejudice. These people explained that the cartoons showed that other people had attitudes of prejudice, so the viewer should feel free to have those attitudes also. The cartoons were most likely to be understood by respondents low in prejudice and most likely to be misunderstood by respondents high in prejudice. Cooper and Jahoda suggested that fear of disapproval by a social group was one of the factors leading to this evasion of propaganda. They argued that accepting the antiprejudice message threatened the individual's security in groups the individual valued.

This study suggests that making fun of prejudice is not an effective way of reducing it. People tend to view satiric cartoons differently, depending on their own attitudes. Both prejudiced and unprejudiced people tended to see elements in the cartoons that confirmed their existing attitudes.

"All in the Family"

When the television program "All in the Family" appeared in 1971, some television critics began immediately to suggest that the program might have a harmful effect of reinforcing bigotry. They pointed out that the main character, Archie Bunker, was portrayed as a "lovable bigot," and that this condoned and perhaps even encouraged bigotry. They also pointed out that the program was teaching racial slurs such as "coon," "chink," and "wop," some of which might have been fading from the American scene at the time.

Producer Norman Lear replied that the program actually reduced prejudice by bringing bigotry out into the open and showing it to be illogical. He said the program showed Archie to be a fool, and that the program was a satire on bigotry. He claimed that the program showed Archie losing at the end to Mike, who made more sense. Carroll O'Connor, the actor who played Archie, also defended the program. He stated in a *Playboy* interview that the effect of the program was to help reduce prejudice. The Los Angeles chapter of the NAACP agreed with this favorable evaluation and gave the program an award in 1972 for its contribution to racial relations.

Neil Vidmar and Milton Rokeach (1974) conducted a study to determine how the program was being perceived by viewers. They conducted surveys of a sample of U.S. adolescents and a sample of Canadian adults. Contrary to the opinion of Lear, neither sample indicated that Archie was the one seen as being made fun of. U.S. adolescents were most likely to pick Mike as the one most often being made fun of, and Canadian adults were most likely to pick Edith as the one most often being made fun of. In another question, respondents were asked whether Archie typically wins or loses at the end of the program. People low in prejudice were most likely to say Archie loses, but people high in prejudice were most likely to say Archie wins. The Vidmar and Rokeach study shows the operation of selective perception in viewing "All in the Family." Viewers high in prejudice and viewers low in prejudice were likely to perceive the program in line with their existing attitudes.

The findings that viewers tend to exercise selective perception in viewing "All in the Family" were supported in other studies. For instance, Brigham and Giesbrecht (1976) found that whites who were high in prejudice showed a strong tendency to like and agree with Archie and to see Archie's racial views as valid.

Producer Norman Lear has changed his tune about the effects of "All in the Family." "To think about what the show might accomplish is to defeat the creative process," Lear has said. "I seriously question what a half-hour situation comedy can accomplish when the entire Judeo-Christian ethic has accomplished so little in the same area" (Gross, 1975).

Other Selective Processes

Three other processes that are similar to selective perception sometimes come into play in mass communication. These are selective exposure, selective attention, and selective retention.

Selective exposure is the tendency for a person to expose himself or herself to those communications that are in agreement with the person's existing attitudes and to avoid those communications that are not. The notion of selective exposure follows nicely from Festinger's theory of cognitive dissonance (Chapter 8), which suggests that one way to reduce dissonance after making a decision is to seek out information that is consonant with the decision. Nevertheless, the research findings show that under several conditions people will expose themselves to dissonance-producing materials (see Chapter 8).

However, individuals often cannot judge beforehand the message content. Selective attention is the tendency for a person to pay attention to those parts of a message that are consonant with strongly held attitudes, beliefs, or behaviors and to avoid those parts of a message that go against strongly held attitudes, beliefs, or behaviors (see Chapter 8).

Selective retention is the tendency for the recall of information to be influenced by wants, needs, attitudes, and other psychological factors. Some evidence for selective retention comes from studies of rumor transmission by Allport and Postman (1947), in which they found that details were frequently left out when people passed on stories or descriptions of pictures. In another study supporting selective retention, Jones and Kohler (1958) found that people in favor of segregation learned plausible prosegregation and implausible antisegregation statements more easily than they learned plausible antisegregation and implausible prosegregation statements. The reverse was true for antisegregationists. Both groups learned most easily the information that would be useful in protecting their own attitudinal positions. In a third study supporting selective retention, Levine and Murphy (1958) found that subjects confronted with pro- or anti-Soviet material learned it more slowly and forgot it more quickly when it conflicted with their own attitudes.

The selective processes can be thought of as four rings of defenses, with selective exposure as the outermost ring, followed by selective attention, then selective perception, and finally selective retention. Undesirable information can sometimes be headed off at the outermost ring. A person can avoid those publications or programs that might contain contrary information. If one expects a mix of information in a message, a person can pay selective attention to only the parts of the message that are agreeable. If this fails, the person can then exercise selective perception in decoding the message. If this fails, the person can then exercise selective retention by simply failing to retain the contrary information.

Sometimes one of these selective mechanisms will be more appropriate or more possible to use than the others. For instance, in watching a televised debate between two presidential candidates, you might not want to practice selective exposure, avoiding the message entirely. If you want to see and hear the candidate you agree with, you may watch only that candidate, practicing selective attention. If you do see and hear the opposition candidate and are exposed to contrary material, you can always fall back on selective perception and hear only what is agreeable or on selective retention and forget all but the points that reinforce your original point of view.

In another study of "All in the Family," this one conducted in Holland, selective exposure seemed to be the mechanism preferred over selective perception. Wilhoit and de Bock (1976) found a tendency for selective exposure among persons who might not like to see a bigoted, rigid person being made fun of. That is, persons high in parental authoritarianism or life-style intolerance tended to avoid watching "All in the Family." There was less of a tendency for people to practice selective perception. Contrary to the selective perception hypothesis, persons high in parental authoritarianism or life-style intolerance who did watch the program often perceived the satiric intent.

Earlier reviews of the research relating to selective exposure tended to cast doubt on the validity of the phenomenon (Sears & Freedman, 1967), but later research has found more support for selective exposure. Cotton and Hieser (1980) required subjects opposed to nuclear power plants to write essays favoring locating such plants near populated areas. They manipulated the amount of dissonance by putting some people in a low-choice (low-dissonance) condition and others in a high-choice (high-dissonance) condition. After writing the essays, subjects were given the opportunity to indicate on rating scales how much they would like informational pamphlets dealing with four issues, one of which was nuclear power. The high-choice (high-dissonance) subjects expressed a greater desire for consistent information than did the low-choice (low-dissonance) subjects. They also expressed less desire for inconsistent information than did low-choice subjects. This latter finding of an active avoidance of dissonant information provides stronger support for selective exposure than many early studies were able to do.

Cotton reviewed a number of studies from 1967 to 1983 and concluded that "the later research on selective exposure, generally more carefully controlled, has produced more positive results. Almost every study found significant selective-exposure effects" (1985, p. 25).

Schema Theory

One concept that might add to our understanding of how people process information from mass communication is the idea of *schema*. Although scholars do not agree about exactly what a schema is, the following definition is useful: "In a nutshell, a schema is a cognitive structure consisting of organized knowledge about situations and individuals that has been abstracted from prior experiences. It is used for processing new information and retrieving stored information" (Graber, 1988, p. 28). The concept of schema has become widely used by psychologists, cognitive scientists, political scientists, and communication researchers because of its apparent usefulness in understanding how people process information.

Fiske and Kinder describe schemas as "serviceable although imperfect devices for coping with complexity" (1981, p. 173). They suggest that people are "cognitive misers" whose limited complexity for dealing with information forces them to practice "cognitive economy" by forming simplified mental models (p. 172).

Doris Graber (1988) has done research that indicates that people use schemas to process news stories from newspapers or news broadcasts. She found that people processing news stories choose from a number of strategies, including straight matching of a news story to a schema (interpreting a political candidate as "another Nixon"), processing through inferences (deducing that a cease-fire in Lebanon would not work well because cease-fires had not worked well in Northern Ireland), and multiple integration of a story with several schemas or schema dimensions (a story on national defense can be related to parity in defense capabilities with the Soviet Union or to the effect of defense spending on the U.S. budget). Graber found that in processing news stories, people tend to store the conclusions drawn from the evidence, rather than the evidence itself. She argued that processing news through schemas is an effective means of dealing with information overload, a problem we have discussed in Chapter 1.

Finally, Graber points out that the matching of news stories with schemas is influenced by *cueing*, and notes that the mass media are a major source of cueing information. Thus, in the example of a story concerning national defense mentioned above, the news media themselves can, by means of headlines, pictures, captions, and so forth, help determine whether the story is seen as dealing with keeping up with the Russians or spending too much of the taxpayer's money on nuclear missiles. This kind of cueing can also influence schema development, so that when the next story on national defense comes along it is more likely to be related to either the "keeping up with the Russians" schema or the "wasting taxpayers' money" schema.

In summary, the notion of schema can help us to understand how people may process many news stories. It appears that they attempt to match the information in a news story to some existing schema through a number of different matching strategies. If a match can be found, some part of the information or inferences from the information is likely to be stored in the form of a modified schema. If a match cannot be found, the information is likely to pass by without being assimilated.

Subliminal Perception

One other topic involving perception and mass communication is the controversial and rather dubious technique known as *subliminal perception.* This is the notion that people can be influenced by stimuli of which they are not aware.

Subliminal perception first came to public attention in 1957 when James M. Vicary of the Subliminal Projection Company began attempting to sell a special projector. The machine was reported to flash a message on a motion picture screen every five seconds at the same time that a regular motion picture projector was showing a film on the same screen. The message flashes were very brief in duration—1/3,000 of a second.

Vicary reported that he had conducted an experiment in a New Jersey movie house in which subliminal messages stating "Eat popcorn" and "Drink Coca-Cola" were flashed on the screen. He said he achieved a 57.5 percent increase in popcorn sales and an 18.1 percent increase in Coca-Cola sales. Vicary said subliminal advertising would be a boon to the consumer because it would eliminate bothersome commercials and allow more entertainment time (*Advertising Age*, Sept. 16, 1957, p. 127).

Vicary's claims provoked quite a negative reaction. Norman Cousins (1957), the editor of *Saturday Review*, wrote an editorial that began with the sentence "Welcome to 1984." Some people were worried that subliminal ads would be used to force people to drink alcohol against their will. Subliminal advertising was banned in Australia and Great Britain, and in the United States it was prohibited by the National Association of Broadcasters.

Vicary's movie theater study was never described fully enough that researchers could evaluate it. Other researchers began to look into the phenomenon, however. Much of the research on subliminal perception was undertaken by the advertising industry. It was concerned because the controversy about subliminal perception was giving the advertising industry a bad name.

Researchers attempting to study subliminal perception immediately ran into some problems. Subliminal perception is supposed to be perception that takes place below the threshold of awareness. One of the first problems is that there is no sharp threshold of awareness (Wiener & Schiller, 1960). At one moment a person might need 1/25 of a second to be able to identify a stimulus, but a short time later the same person might be able to identify a stimulus shown for only 1/100 of a second. Psychologists have typically solved this problem by defining the threshold as the point where the subject identifies the stimulus 50 percent of the time. But this is essentially an arbitrary definition. Also, thresholds differ from person to person and for the same person depending on fatigue and other factors. It is not clear which of the various thresholds should be used.

A number of studies of subliminal perception have shown that people can respond to a stimulus below the threshold of awareness. For instance, a person who has been given a shock when exposed to certain nonsense words will sometimes show a galvanic skin response reaction indicating fear when these nonsense words are flashed so briefly that the person still cannot recognize them (Lazarus & McCleary, 1951).

The results of research on subliminal persuasion have been mixed, but the preponderance of the evidence has been against the effect. For instance, in a recent experiment Beatty and Hawkins (1989) investigated the possible effect on thirst of presenting the word *Coke* subliminally. Subjects were randomly divided into three groups. All three groups were given the cover story that the purpose of the experiment was to establish recognition thresholds for names of brands of automobiles. The automobile names were presented 15 times, with the exposure time starting below the threshold of awareness and becoming slightly longer each time. In between these exposures, the subjects in two groups were exposed to two different subliminal stimuli. One group received the word *Coke* at an exposure time below the threshold of awareness. A second group received the nonsense syllable *NYTP* at an exposure time below the threshold of awareness. A third group was shown the word *Coke* along with the automobile brand names, so that it became increasingly visible as the presentations continued. Subject thirst was measured with a Perceptual Health Inventory, which also contained other measures aimed at disguising the purpose of the experiment. Statistical analysis showed no difference in thirst ratings for the three groups.

In fact, there is some evidence that no magic change in perception occurs just because the "threshold" of awareness has been crossed. The main effect may be that the message will not be perceived at all because it is of lower impact (Klass, 1958). Interestingly enough, it appears that selective perception may operate even in subliminal perception. That is, instead of the subliminal message stimulating a need or want, the message is interpreted in terms of existing needs or wants. Some indication of this comes from a study in which the word *beef* was flashed subliminally in an attempt to make people hungrier for beef sandwiches (Byrne, 1959). The test audience was made up of college students, and two of them reported later they thought they had seen the word *beer*.

Berelson and Steiner (1964), in their summary of scientific findings about human beings, drew this conclusion about subliminal perception:

> There is no scientific evidence that subliminal stimulation can initiate subsequent action, to say nothing of commercially or politically significant action. And there is nothing to suggest that such action can be produced "against the subject's will," or more effectively than through normal, recognized messages. (p. 95)

Claims for the effectiveness of subliminal perception continue to be made, despite the absence of scientific research to support the phenomenon. Wilson Bryan Key has presented a variation of the old idea in his books *Subliminal Seduction* (1972) and *Media Sexploitation* (1976). Key claims that many advertisements contain within them subtle printings of the word *sex* as well as disguised representations of male and female sex organs. These hidden words and symbols are called *embeds.* According to Key's theory, which is loosely based on Freudian theory, the viewer perceives these embeds unconsciously and is influenced by them to desire the advertised product, whether it is a bottle of perfume or an automobile tire. Key's books contain little in the way of scientific documentation. His proof rests more on the reproduction of advertisements supposedly containing embeds. Most of these are ambiguous at best. In keeping with perception theory, one begins to wonder if the fact that Key sees these pictures as filled with sexual references does not tell us something about Key rather than something about the advertisements!

Subliminal perception popped up in still another form in 1978. Newspapers reported that Hal Becker of Metairie, Louisiana, had developed a system for preventing theft in department stores by putting hidden messages deep in the background of a music system similar to Muzak (Garvin, 1978). Two of the messages were "I am honest" and "I will not steal." Becker claimed that he had conducted an experiment in a store in an Eastern city for six months and had cut the annual theft rate from $1.6 million to less than $900,000.

Hope springs eternal, however. In 1984 a newspaper consumer affairs columnist, under the headline "Subliminal Phrases Flash on TV Screen," responded to a question about where to buy a new machine for weight reduction that had been advertised on television. After providing the name of a physician and a San Antonio address, the columnist cited a machine called "Subliminal" for $130. The advice columnist added:

> It attaches to your TV or computer.
> It works like this: A message is flashed on the screen every two minutes for 1/30 of a second. Messages could be: "I see me as thinner," "Exercise is fun," "I am attractive," "I am okay," "I see me as disciplined," "I see me as healthy," "I am relaxed."

Each program costs $39.95 and you can choose from programs on weight or smoking control, stress management, success motivation, increased memory power and improved self-image. (Rucker, 1984)

The great American circus pitchman P. T. Barnum said, "There's a sucker born every minute." Unfortunately, our media often aid and abet this gullibility, usually unwittingly, not only in advertising but sometimes even in their advice columns. It's true that Barnum's press agents gave blocks of free tickets to the local newspapers when the circus came to town for favorable free publicity. But at least the "big top" provided clean, wholesome, low-cost entertainment.

Automatic Exposure

Exposure to mass communication may not always be highly deliberate or purposeful. Many times people seem to be making their way through the mass communication environment while on a kind of "automatic pilot" (Donohew, Nair, & Finn, 1984). Common, everyday examples of this phenomenon include people working at their desks with the radio on in the background, or washing dishes while also giving some attention to the television news.

The following description of the process of automatic exposure is drawn from Donohew, Nair, and Finn (1984). In general, the cognitive system may be ready at any given time to devote whatever amount of attention is appropriate to a given task. If there is attention that is left over, the system may use the leftover attention to daydream or solve problems. But if a change in the stimulus—movement, color, loudness—suggests that more attention may be appropriate, the system can switch very quickly to a more alert state in which it may use its full processing capacities. This view suggests that much use of mass communication might involve a low level of attention, and, in fact, might be appropriately labeled *ritualistic* or *habitual*. With this low level of attention operating, much of our selection of particular mass communication messages (the decision to read a particular news story, for instance) might be guided by very minor cues suggesting the pleasantness or unpleasantness of being exposed to a particular message.

The notion of automatic exposure reminds us that much selection of mass communication might not be for the purposes of reducing uncertainty, protecting our attitudes, or carrying out a type of *surveillance* function. A great deal of exposure to mass communication is apparently carried out in a nearly *mindless* state, where the intention is to seek mildly pleasant stimuli, and past experience with the same or similar content becomes a strong determinant.

Conclusions

There is a great deal of scientific evidence for selective perception, or the tendency for people's perception to be influenced by their wants, needs, attitudes, and other psychological factors. Selective perception occurs in the receiving of the messages of mass communication just as it does in other areas. This complicates our models of mass communication. The communicator cannot be sure that the meaning intended in a message will be seen there by members of the audience. The receiver of the message has a very active role in assigning meaning to that message. As communication scholar Dean C. Barnlund (1970) has put it, "It should be stressed that meaning is something 'invented,' 'assigned,' 'given,' rather than something 'received' " (p. 88).

Communication scholar Franklin Fearing (1970) has put the same idea another way: *"All communications contents are in some degree ambiguous.* This may be termed the Principle of Necessary Ambiguity, and is basic to the understanding of all communications effects" (p. 50).

The ambiguity that Fearing was talking about is perhaps most obvious in a rich and complicated television program like "All in the Family," where some viewers can identify with one character while other viewers identify with another. But the ambiguity is also present in a presidential State of the Union address, a newspaper editorial, or the six o'clock television news.

We should also remember that not all exposure to mass communication is the result of an active process of reducing uncertainty, protecting our attitudes, or carrying out a type of *surveillance* function. Much exposure to mass communication is ritualistic or habitual, is aimed primarily at mood enhancement or entertainment, and involves a low level of attention.

References

Allport, G. W., and L. Postman (1947). *The Psychology of Rumor.* New York: Henry Holt.

Apple, R. W. (1976). Voter poll finds debate aided Ford and cut Carter lead. *New York Times,* Sept. 27, p. 1.

Bagby, J. W. (1957). A cross-cultural study of perceptual predominance in binocular rivalry. *Journal of Abnormal and Social Psychology* 54: 331–334.

Barnlund, D. C. (1970). A transactional model of communication. In K. K. Sereno and C. D. Mortensen (eds.), *Foundations of Communication Theory,* pp. 83–102. New York: Harper & Row.

Beatty, S. E., and D. I. Hawkins (1989). Subliminal stimulation: Some new data and interpretation. *Journal of Advertising* 18: 4–8.

Berelson, B., and G. A. Steiner (1964). *Human Behavior: An Inventory of Scientific Findings.* New York: Harcourt, Brace, & World.

Brigham, J. C., and L. W. Giesbrecht (1976). *All in the Family:* Racial attitudes. *Journal of Communication* 26, no. 4: 69–74.

Byrne, D. (1959). The effect of a subliminal food stimulus on verbal responses. *Journal of Applied Psychology* 43: 249–252.

Cooper, E., and M. Jahoda (1947). The evasion of propaganda: How prejudiced people respond to anti-prejudice propaganda. *Journal of Psychology* 23: 15–25.

Cotton, J. L. (1985). Cognitive dissonance in selective exposure. In D. Zillmann and J. Bryant (eds.), *Selective Exposure to Communication,* pp. 11–33. Hillsdale, N.J.: Lawrence Erlbaum.

Cotton, J. L., and R. A. Hieser (1980). Selective exposure to information and cognitive dissonance. *Journal of Research in Personality* 14: 518–527.

Cousins, N. (1957). Smudging the subconscious. *Saturday Review,* Oct. 5, p. 20.

Donohew, R. L., M. Nair, and S. Finn (1984). Automacity, arousal, and information exposure. In R. N. Bostrom (ed.), *Communication Yearbook 8,* pp. 267–284. Beverly Hills, Cal.: Sage.

Fearing, F. (1970). Toward a psychological theory of human communication. In K. K. Sereno and C. D. Mortensen (eds.), *Foundations of Communication Theory,* pp. 40–54. New York: Harper & Row.

Fiske, S. T., and D. R. Kinder (1981). Involvement, expertise, and schema use: Evidence from political cognition. In N. Cantor and J. F. Kihlstrom (eds.), *Personality, Cognition, and Social Interaction,* pp. 171–190. Hillsdale, N.J.: Lawrence Erlbaum.

Garvin, G. (1978). Mind over Muzak? *Austin American-Statesman,* April 14, pp. B1–B2.

Graber, D. A. (1988). *Processing the News: How People Tame the Information Tide.* 2nd. ed. New York: Longman.

Gross, L. (1975). Do the bigots miss the message? *TV Guide,* Nov. 8, pp. 14–18.

Hastorf, A. H., and H. Cantril (1954). They saw a game: A case study. *Journal of Abnormal and Social Psychology* 49: 129–134.

Jones, E. E., and R. Kohler (1958). The effects of plausibility on the learning of controversial statements. *Journal of Abnormal and Social Psychology* 57: 315–320.

Key, W. B. (1972). *Subliminal Seduction: Ad Media's Manipulation of a Not So Innocent America.* Englewood Cliffs, N.J.: Prentice-Hall.

Key, W. B. (1976). *Media Sexploitation.* Englewood Cliffs: N.J.: Prentice-Hall.

Klass, B. (1958). The ghost of subliminal advertising. *Journal of Marketing* 23: 146–150.

Kraus, S. (1962). *The Great Debates: Background, Perspective, Effects.* Bloomington: Indiana University Press.

Lazarus, R. S., and R. A. McCleary (1951). Autonomic discrimination without awareness: A study of subception. *Psychological Review* 58: 113–122.

Leuba, C., and C. Lucas (1945). The effects of attitudes on descriptions of pictures. *Journal of Experimental Psychology* 35: 517–524.

Levine, J. M., and G. Murphy (1958). The learning and forgetting of controversial material. In E. E. Maccoby, T. M. Newcomb, and E. L. Hartley (eds.), *Readings in Social Psychology,* 3rd ed., pp. 94–101. New York: Holt, Rinehart, and Winston.

McClelland, D. C., and J. W. Atkinson (1948). The projective expression of needs: I. The effect of different intensities of the hunger drive on perception. *Journal of Psychology* 25: 205–222.

Meadowcraft, J. M., and D. Zillmann (1987). Women's comedy preferences during the menstrual cycle. *Communication Research* 14, no. 2: 204–218.

Patterson, T. E., and R. D. McClure (1976). Political campaigns: TV power is a myth. *Psychology Today,* July, pp. 61ff.

"Persuaders" get deeply "hidden" tool: Subliminal projection. (1957). *Advertising Age* 28, no. 37: 127.

Rucker, E. (1984). Subliminal phrases flash on TV screen. *Austin American-Statesman,* Feb. 25, p. B1.

Sears, D. O., and J. L. Freedman (1967). Selective exposure to information: A critical review. *Public Opinion Quarterly* 31: 194–213.

Toch, H., and M. S. MacLean, Jr. (1962). Perception, communication, and educational research: A transactional view. *Audio Visual Communication Review* 10, no. 5: 55–77.

Toch, H. H., and R. Schulte (1961). Readiness to perceive violence as a result of police training. *British Journal of Psychology* 52: 389–393.

Vidmar, N., and M. Rokeach (1974). Archie Bunker's bigotry: A study in selective perception and exposure. *Journal of Communication* 24, no. 1: 36–47.

Wiener, M., and P. H. Schiller (1960). Subliminal perception or perception of partial cues. *Journal of Abnormal and Social Psychology* 61: 124–137.

Wilhoit, G. C., and H. de Bock (1976). *All in the Family* in Holland. *Journal of Communication* 26, no. 4: 75–84.

5
Problems in Encoding

Encoding is the translation of purpose, intention, or meaning into symbols or codes. Often these symbols are the letters, numbers, and words that make up a language such as English. But of course encoding can also take place through photographs, musical notes, or images on motion picture film.

Encoding is in many ways a mysterious process. How do the "preverbal tensions" (or whatever you want to call the feelings that precede words) become converted into words? It is not an easy process even to describe.

Some help in understanding encoding is provided by the work of a group of students of language called general semanticists. These thinkers have not explained all the mysteries of encoding, but they have identified some characteristics of language that make encoding (at least in language) difficult.

Characteristics of Language

The general semanticists were first led by Alfred Korzybski, a Polish count who emigrated to the United States. His seminal work, *Science and Sanity,* was popularized by Wendell Johnson. These scholars have been concerned with language and how it relates to our success in everyday living and our mental health. They argue that we run into many of our problems because we misuse language. They say we would misuse language less if we used it more the way scientists use it—so that it constantly refers to the realities it represents.

The general semanticists point out several characteristics of language that make it difficult to use it carefully. These characteristics cause difficulty in *encoding* and make communication difficult.

Language Is Static; Reality Is Dynamic

Words themselves do not change over a period of time, yet the world around us is full of change. Modern science has shown that *matter* is ultimately made up of small particles moving very rapidly. A wooden table that appears to be solid is actually decaying and oxidizing. Twenty years from now it might not be a table at all, but a pile of firewood. Einstein's formula $E = mc^2$ brought out that even matter and energy are not distinct but can be converted one into the other.

Modern biology shows the same pattern of constant change. The caterpillar becomes a butterfly. The hard shell crab loses its shell and temporarily becomes a soft shell crab so that it may grow bigger. The theory of evolution brought out that even the species are not permanent and distinctive but are changing and developing through time.

Reality is a process, yet the language we must use to describe it is fixed and static. Another example of the process nature of reality is the cycle of the day. The sun is constantly moving, and its position in the sky changes throughout the day. The words we have to describe that ever-changing process are primarily two: *night* and *day*. Anyone who has watched a sunset and tried to say exactly when it has become night recognizes the difficulty of fitting those two words to reality in an exact way. People have invented a few other words to help deal with that problem: *twilight, dusk, dawn.* But we still have only a handful of words to refer to an ever-changing process.

The Greek philosopher Heraclitus said, "One cannot step in the same river twice." The Way of Practical Attainment in the teachings of Buddha puts it this way: "Everything is changeable, everything appears and disappears." George Bernard Shaw is supposed to have said, "The only man who behaves sensibly is my tailor: he takes my measure anew each time he sees me, whilst all the rest go on with their old measurements and expect them to fit me." T. S. Eliot in *The Cocktail Party* wrote, "What we know of other people is only our memory of the moments during which we knew them. And they have changed since then . . . at every meeting we are meeting a stranger."

The Chinese 13th-century classic *Romance of the Three Kingdoms* in the opening, "All Under Heaven," begins, "Such is the grand scheme of all under heaven, things that are separated will eventually come together, things that are together will eventually break apart."

Towns and people change, yet the words (names) we have to refer to them usually remain the same. The fact that the word does not change over time can blind us to the fact that the reality is changing. A man might spend twenty years dreaming of retiring in Pleasant Valley, a town he visited as a young man, only to go there and find that it has become a busy city. Eldridge Cleaver in 1968 was a militant, critical of almost everything American. Eldridge Cleaver today is a converted Christian who says things are better in the United States than they are in most countries. The name stayed the same; the behavior of the person being referred to changed drastically. The general semanticists recommend a technique of *dating* to help remind ourselves of this kind of change. Putting a date after the name would help remind us which Eldridge Cleaver we are referring to: Eldridge Cleaver$_{1968}$ or Eldridge Cleaver$_{1990}$.

Alvin Toffler, author of *Future Shock* and *The Third Wave*, said, among other things:

> We felt the metaphor of waves offers a powerful way to characterize periods of fundamental change in society. . . . The emphasis on process that Korzybski stressed is present in all the intellectual work my wife and I have done over the years. (Toffler, 1989)

The world changes much faster than words do. We are always using verbal models that are somewhat out of date and no longer describe the world we live in. The survival of civilizations and individuals depends on their ability to adapt to change. Failure to recognize change with time leads to generalizations like "If Tom said it, it's a lie. He's lied to me before" or "Once a failure, always a failure."

True?.

Language Is Limited; Reality Is Virtually Unlimited

Wendell Johnson (1972) points out that there are 500,000 to 600,000 words in the English language and that they must represent millions of individual facts, experiences, and relationships. The vocabularies that people ordinarily use are much smaller. In telephone conversations, people typically use a vocabulary of about 5,000 words, and the average novel uses a vocabulary of about 10,000 (Miller, 1963, p. 121). This might suggest that our vocabularies are normally sufficient for everyday communication, but it is not difficult to think of cases in which our vocabularies begin to appear limited.

Suppose someone were to place a dozen oranges on a table before you and randomly pick one of them and ask you to describe it in words. Could you describe it in such a way that someone else who had not been present could later pick that orange out of the dozen? Unless by luck the orange had some obvious deformity, the task would probably be difficult. The point is that we can make more distinctions in reality than we have words to describe easily.

The same kind of problem shows up on a more practical level in giving physical descriptions of people. Sometimes it seems as if people are only a little easier to describe than the oranges in the example just given. The problem shows up frequently in law enforcement work, where people have to describe another person so exactly that the person can be recognized by other people. Many people often aren't very good at this, partly because they don't observe carefully but also because only a limited number of words exist for describing people.

Or think of the problem of describing in words some continuous process, such as playing a violin, riding a bicycle, or tying a shoe. Most people would find these acts difficult to convey in words, and they are the kinds of things that are typically taught by one person showing another. Something as simple as the correct way to hold a guitar might be almost impossible to express in words, and a guitar book for beginners will usually contain a picture to get the message across. The writer of a beginner's guitar manual has a similar problem in communicating what certain guitar effects are supposed to sound like when they are done correctly. Such a writer might be forced to describe a certain rhythm pattern by inventing words such as "*boom*-chicka, *boom*-chicka." Even these invented words would only approximate the desired sound.

Because of the limited nature of our knowledge and our language, general semanticists stress you can never say *all* about anything. Thomas Edison said, "We don't know one millionth of one percent about anything." General semanticists recommend a technique of putting *etc.* at the end of any statement to remind yourself that more could be said about anything. (If you don't actually say or write the *etc.*, you can at least *think* it.) The general semanticists named their journal *ETC.* to stress the importance of this idea.

Language Is Abstract

Yes

Abstraction is a process of selecting some details and leaving out other details. Any use of language involves some abstraction. And indeed, abstraction is one of the most useful features of language. It allows us to think in categories, and this gives us the ability to generalize.

In classifying a number of fruits into categories—apple, pear, orange, and peach, for instance—we are selecting some details, such as their color, shape, and texture, and ignoring others, such as their weight. We could classify them another way, into categories such as six-ounce fruits, seven-ounce fruits, eight-ounce fruits, and so forth; in this case we would be selecting a different detail, their weight, and ignoring the details we paid attention to at first.

Much human knowledge is intimately bound up in the process of categorizing or classifying; we learn that certain red, round objects are good to eat, and giving those objects a name makes it easier to remember that knowledge and pass it on to others.

Abstraction is a useful characteristic of words, but it is also one that can lead to problems, particularly when people are not aware of abstraction.

All words involve some abstraction, or leaving out of details, but some words are more abstract than others. And as words become more and more abstract, their correspondence to reality becomes less and less direct. S. I. Hayakawa (1964, p. 179) has developed a useful diagram to show the way words can have differing degrees of abstraction. His diagram, called an "abstraction ladder," is based on a concept developed by Korzybski (1958, p. 397) called the "structural differential." An example of an abstraction ladder appears in Figure 5.1.

The abstraction ladder in Figure 5.1 takes a particular object, an automobile belonging to one of the authors of this text, and shows how it can be referred to at different levels of abstraction. The lowest level of abstraction, at which no details are left out, is the process level, the level at which scientists using instruments can observe the car. The second level is the car as the object that we can experience with our senses. Notice that even at this level, the level of everyday observation, some details are being left out. This is partly because the eye can process more information than the brain. But it is also because we can observe from only one point at a time. When we observe the car from the front, we do not see the details at the back. And we see only the surface, not the internal structure of the car. Even in *observation*, some abstraction or leaving out of details takes place. The third level is the first verbal level, the first level involving the use of words. At this level there is one word or phrase that refers uniquely to the one car being described. This could be the phrase *Werner Severin's Accord*. At this level, the word being used refers to the one particular object. At the fourth level, we can use the word *Honda* to refer to the same object. We have then assigned the object to a category, the category of all Hondas. We have left out the detail that would distinguish that particular Honda from all other Hondas. At the next level, that of the word *car*, we would be including not only Hondas but also Volkswagens, Fords,

Verbal Levels

8	transportation
7	land transportation
6	motor vehicle
5	car
4	Honda
3	Severin's Honda Accord

Nonverbal Levels

2 (object level)	the maroon Honda Accord in the parking lot that we can see and touch
1 (process level)	the car as atomic process

FIGURE 5.1 • THE ABSTRACTION LADDER

Cadillacs, and all other makes, so still more distinguishing detail would be left out. At the sixth level, we could refer to the car as a *motor vehicle,* putting it into a category that also includes trucks and jeeps and leaving out still more detail. At the seventh level, we could use the term *land transportation,* categorizing the car with railroad trains and snowmobiles. And at the eighth level, we could refer to the car with the word *transportation,* putting it in a class that would also include airplanes and ships. Notice that at each level more detail is left out until at the eighth level we come to a very abstract word, *transportation.* This word does not suggest a particular picture to the mind the way the word *Honda* does. Some people might hear the word *transportation* and visualize a boat, while others might visualize a truck, and many others would have no clear picture of anything. That is one of the characteristics of abstract words: they do not suggest a clear picture of something in reality, and people often have very different meanings in mind for them.

Because our language is limited and because we abstract and categorize, language compels us to emphasize similarities but *permits* us to ignore differences. We see similarities by ignoring differences. There are similarities among different things, just as there are differences among similar things.

A well-known historian and philosopher of science, J. Bronowski, said, "The action of putting things which are not identical into a group or class is so familiar that we forget how sweeping it is. The action depends on recognizing a set of things to be alike when they are not identical. . . . Habit makes us think the likeness obvious" (Bronowski, 1951, p. 21).

With the exception of proper nouns, our language has no words for unique events, feelings, and relationships. We speak, perceive, and think of the world in categories. These categories are in our language and in our heads; they are not in nature.

We can use language to group together any two things (categorization). We can use language to place anything in more than one category. We can use language to treat things as identical (through categorization) when, indeed, they are unique. Language is sometimes used in this way to imply "guilt by association." What we call a person depends on our purpose, our projections, and our evaluations, yet the person does not change when we change the label.

One political campaign handbill depicts a red scorpion, the body labeled "DEMO PARTY" and the segments of the long tail, which ends in a poisonous stinger, labeled "queens; communist party programs; funny farm refugees; dope fiends; etc." The bottom of the handbill contains a mail-in coupon that includes the statement, "I certify that I am of good character with Anglo Saxon blood foaming and churning through my veins." This handbill supposedly originates with an organization called Americans to Restore Freedom.

Another leaflet listed 52 "reasons" why a candidate for the presidency should be defeated, including:

> Favorite candidate of the national homosexual-lesbian society.
>
> Favorite candidate of the marijuana cult.
>
> Has the support of all left wing organizations everywhere.
>
> Favorite candidate of the left wing *New York Times.*
>
> Supported enthusiastically by the widow of Martin Luther King.
>
> He is the enthusiastic choice of the treason machine, sometimes referred to as the national networks.

Supports Cesar Chavez, who is considered as a spearhead of the Marxist revolution among farm workers.

Supports the World Council of Churches which donates to international revolutionary activities.

Assumptions Built into Languages

The structure and vocabulary of every language contains many assumptions about the nature of reality. Many are so ingrained that we are no longer aware of them. Wendell Johnson observed that the language we use not only puts words in our mouths, but it also puts notions in our heads. Benjamin Lee Whorf put it this way:

> And every language is a vast pattern-system, different from others in which is culturally ordained the forms and categories by which the personality not only communicates, but analyzes nature, notices or neglects types of relationships and phenomena, channels his reasoning, and builds the house of his consciousness. Each language performs this artificial chopping up of the continuous spread and flow of existence in a different way. (Whorf, 1952, p. 173)

One example of hidden assumptions in the English language is the many instances of sexism, often unperceived. The women's movement has made us aware of many of them. Other languages face the same problems. For example, the Chinese language is built of ideograms (characters, symbols, or figures that suggest the idea of an object without expressing its name). The ideogram representing *woman* is often combined with other ideograms for other meanings. The combination of woman and child means *good;* woman and eyebrow means *flattery;* and woman repeated three times means *treachery.* The ideogram *woman* is also used in other combinations, including *adultery* and *lustful.*

As Wendell Johnson observed, the language we use not only puts words in our mouths, but it also puts notions in our heads—a major point mass communicators need to be aware of.

Misuses of Language

Because of the static, limited, and abstract nature of language, certain misuses of language are likely to occur. One of the great contributions of the general semanticists has been to identify some of these for us. Four common misuses are dead-level abstracting, undue identification, two-valued evaluation, and unconscious projection.

Dead-Level Abstracting

This concept, described by Wendell Johnson (1946, p. 270), refers to getting stuck at one level of abstraction. The level could be high or low.

High-level abstractions are words like *justice, democracy, freedom, mankind, Communism, peace with honor,* and *law and order.* When words like these are used in a message that does not also contain words at lower levels of abstraction, it is difficult to know what the message is saying. Words at a high level of abstraction that are not accompanied by more concrete words have been referred to as "words cut loose from their moorings" (Hayakawa, 1964, p. 189). They are not anchored to lower levels of abstraction.

Much political rhetoric gets stuck at a high level of abstraction. When the expression *law and order* was used in a presidential campaign, what it referred to at a less abstract level was not clear. Did it mean that a police officer would be assigned to every street corner? Did it mean that a 6 P.M. curfew would be enforced in major cities? Did it mean that demonstrators in the streets would be arrested and placed in jail without being charged (as actually happened in Washington, D.C., in May 1971)? It was hard to know, because we were given the high-level abstraction but no translation at a concrete level.

The motion picture *Cabaret* contained an example of the way high-level abstractions can be baffling. In one scene some Germans are sitting around a living room at the time the Nazis were rising to power, and one of them says, "If all the Jews are bankers, how can they be Communists too?"

Language can also get stuck at a low level of abstraction in one message, and this is another type of dead-level abstracting. An example of this might be someone recounting every detail of his or her day. A message that stays at a low level of abstraction usually does not come to a general conclusion, and it is often difficult to see the point of what is being said. Receiving a message stuck at a low level of abstraction can be something like reading a mail-order catalog.

The general semanticists say that the most effective communication *ranges up and down* the ladder of abstraction. An effective message contains generalizations at a high level of abstraction, but there are also specific details at a low level of abstraction. One effective technique for doing this that many skilled teachers use is to give lots of *examples.*

Undue Identification

This is the failure to see distinctions between members of a category or class. The term points out that they are seen as identical, or *identified.* Another term for this is *categorical thinking.* In everyday discourse, it is sometimes referred to as *overgeneralization.* One common kind of undue identification is *stereotyping.*

The following statements all show a failure to see distinctions between members of a class:

"If you've seen one tree, you've seen them all."

"I'll never trust another woman."

"You can't believe a thing you read in the newspapers."

"Statistics don't prove anything."

The stereotyping of mothers-in-law as interfering and critical or of Italians as great lovers are other examples of undue identification.

Feminist writer Germain Greer once said on the William Buckley program "Firing Line" that "advertising is universally depraving." Buckley asked her about a message telling people to get a chest X ray, pointing out that her statement was probably an overgeneralization.

Often such categorization with language and failure to recognize differences between individuals leads to *stereotyping,* which makes some subgroup out to be greedy, stupid, lazy, cowardly, or the like. Sometimes this is reflected in cultural jokes. For example, so-called Polish jokes ignore the fact that Poles like Frederic Chopin, Marie Curie, Joseph Conrad, and Nicolaus Copernicus are recognized for major contributions to civilization. Such jokes ignore heroism like that of the 5,000 men of the First Parachute Brigade of the Polish Army in Exile (based in England) who in September 1944 jumped at Arnhem in

Holland. They did so to relieve pressure on the British First Airborne Division, then surrounded by the enemy, and with the knowledge that they were jumping to almost certain death.

The French film *Classified People* illustrates an effect of classification because of South African apartheid. The children of a mixed marriage are unable to live with their black father after their white mother dies.

Journalistic overgeneralization was the topic of an op-ed article by the Jordanian ambassador to the United States. He said, in part,

> I am perturbed by the continuing tendency of the American media to utilize the simplistic equation "Moslem-terrorist-Arab."
>
> There are almost 200 million Arabs and close to a billion Moslems in the world. Is it honest or fair that they be blanketed with the "terrorist" label through the indiscriminate use of an identifying "Moslem" or "Arab" adjective in media coverage of terrorist actions emanating from the Middle East?
>
> Journalists, even those who pride themselves on objective reporting, are curiously selective in their descriptions. They never refer to the Baader-Meinhof Gang as "Christian terrorist." The Japanese Red Army Faction is never called "Shinto terrorist." The obliteration of camps and towns in Lebanon is not called "Jewish terrorism."
>
> . . . The press would not think of writing "black thief" or "Christian murderer." Why then does a qualifying racial or religious adjective become acceptable when it is "Arab" or "Moslem"?
>
> Moreover, the American media apparently found it convenient to ignore a resolution at the Islamic summit that unanimously condemned terrorism in any form as contrary to the teachings of Islam. Such a failure is but another form of the discrimination I have defined here. (Kamal, 1987).

A person who goes around saying "I can't spell" is showing a similar kind of overgeneralization (Stoen, 1976, p. 324). Indeed, the person can spell some words but not others; the remark is an overstatement. It may be a remark with important consequences, too, if it makes people think they are worse spellers than they are and leads to a defeatist attitude.

General semanticists sometimes recommend the use of *index numbers* to prevent undue identification. If we were to attach an index number to a word like student each time we use it, we might be less likely to think of all students as alike. This would remind us that student$_1$ is not student$_2$, or to take another example, that Arab$_1$ is not Arab$_2$. Of course, the important thing is not so much actually to use index numbers in our writing and talking but to *think* them—to be aware that members of a class share some characteristics but are different in terms of many others. Each classification tells us something about the way an object is considered similar to other objects, but it also tells us about the way it is considered different from certain other objects. No two things are identical.

Two-valued Evaluation

This misuse is also known as *either-or thinking* or *thinking with the excluded middle*. It involves thinking that there are only two possibilities when there are actually a range of possibilities. Language contributes to this tendency because often only two words that are opposites are available to describe a situation. Familiar examples are words like *night* and *day, black* and *white, right* and *wrong*. As we discussed earlier, *night* and *day* are two words that do not begin to reflect the many different states that occur during the cycle of the day. Many people would say that the same is true of the other pairs of opposites. This is reflected in the commonplace statement when referring to moral questions: "It's not a matter of black and white; there are shades of gray."

Some examples of two-valued evaluation can be found in the rhetoric of student demonstrators and their critics during the late 1960s. The demonstrators who were critical of society sometimes said, "You're either part of the problem or part of the solution." The statement leaves no room for a middle ground. But there must have been some people—children, perhaps, or people in iron lungs in hospitals—who even the protesters would say were neither part of the problem nor part of the solution.

Critics of the demonstrators would sometimes reply with two-valued evaluation of their own. Consider the bumper sticker reading "America—Love it or leave it." This excludes the existence of other possibilities, such as "staying and changing it." In times of confrontation it is also common to hear people speaking of "them" and "us," another example of either-or thinking.

A support group dedicated to assisting former members of fundamentalist religions describes its activities this way:

> We try to help people who have problems with religious addiction or a problem with the fundamentalist view of God, which is characteristically either/or, black/white thinking— no neutral ground. Either you think the *right* way or you are condemned. There are a lot of guilt feelings and self-esteem problems. (*Austin American-Statesman,* 1988)

Shortly before he resigned as CIA director, William Colby appeared on a television news program and said, "Are we going to acknowledge our place in the world or go on an isolationist binge as we did in the twenties?" In this case we not only see two-valued evaluation, but we also see one of the choices being given a negative label in an effort to make the other choice more attractive—a common rhetorical device.

The same technique can be seen in this statement from a document of the Symbionese Liberation Army, the group that kidnapped Patty Hearst: "The choice is yours alone, to be and show yourselves as lovers of the people and our children and true to your word revolutionaries or as egotistic opportunists and lovers of the group and organization and enemies of the people."

Wendell Johnson (1946, pp. 9–10) points out that applying two-valued evaluation to ourselves can lead to mental health problems. If a person begins to think "I am either a failure or a success" and takes the statement too seriously, some major problems can develop. The next line of thinking is liable to be, "Boy, I sure don't feel like a success, so I must be a failure!" This kind of thinking could in some cases lead to suicide, even though it is to a large extent a delusion of language. Treffert (1976) told of a 15-year-old girl who had received straight A's who hanged herself when she got her first B. She wrote in her suicide note, "If I fail in what I do, I fail in what I am."

In reality, most of us have some small successes and some small failures every day. Summing it all up with a general conclusion about whether one is a success or a failure is not necessary and can never reflect reality accurately.

The cure the general semanticists suggest for two-valued evaluation is *multivalued evaluation,* thinking in terms of a range of possibilities instead of two.

Alvin Toffler, speaking of the influences of Korzybski on his own thinking and writing, said:

> Reality did not come packaged with "either-ors"—at least to me—and I think it is still part of the way I like to analyze things. I think in terms of multiple models, rather than a single model. I think of things overlapping, blending into each other, and so on; and change, which is my preoccupation, is really a complex process. (Toffler, 1989, p. 197)

Unconscious Projection

Unconscious projection is a lack of awareness that one's statements are to a degree statements about oneself. Wendell Johnson (1972, p. 304) went so far as to claim that "basically we always talk about ourselves." An example is the statement "The room is hot." It is a statement about the room, but it is also a statement about the condition of the nervous system of the person making the statement. The same is true of the statement "The orange is sweet." It might be sweet to one person but sour to another. Many people might be aware of their own projection when they say something is "hot" or "sweet." But people seem less aware that their statement is about themselves when they say something like "The art exhibit is ugly." That sounds like a factual statement about the art exhibit, when actually it is a statement that involves a great deal of personal reaction. It is not difficult to see how unconscious projection can lead to problems when we recall that people sometimes get into fights over whether or not an art exhibit is ugly.

The statement "Who cares?" is usually high in projection; it implies that nobody cares but really translates as "I don't care."

We are all familiar with the "Pollyanna" optimist who always sees the world through rose-colored glasses and the chronic pessimist who has a sour view of the world. These people are involved in projection: their own moods and opinions influence the way they see and describe the world.

Novelist Erica Jong once said on the "Today" show on television that "marriage is an invention for making lawyers rich." Since she had recently been through a divorce, we can assume that the statement was high in projection (although it may not have been *unconscious* projection, since Jong appears to be a careful user of language).

Unconscious projection can become dangerous when it occurs in government leaders or other persons with great responsibility. President Nixon once complained during a televised news conference that television coverage of his administration was "outrageous," "vicious," and "distorted." When the National News Council asked the White House to supply the specific details that supported the charge, they were never provided. President Nixon was apparently not aware that his statement was to a large degree an expression of his own personal reaction. When such statements became the basis of official and unofficial actions—and there is evidence that the Nixon administration was taking steps against the television networks (Whiteside, 1975)—we begin to see the seriousness of the consequences of unconscious projection by government leaders.

Psychologist Earl C. Kelley (1947) has said, "When we take in our surroundings, we select from them, not at random, but in accordance with our past experience and our purposes" (p. 48). William Shakespeare said, "Nothing is good or bad, but thinking makes it so" (as cited by Brown, 1988, p. 16). A contemporary writer, H. Jackson Brown, Jr., in a compilation *A Father's Book of Wisdom,* writes, "We do not see things as they are. We see things as we are" (p. 106). It is the I behind the eye that does the seeing. Seeing goes on inside of our heads and inside of our nervous systems. What we see is our response to what we look at.

The general semanticists suggest that a cure for unconscious projection is to add "to me" at the end of any statement you make. Again, it might not be necessary to write or say the words but it would help at least to think them.

Three Kinds of Statements

A major debate in journalism has concerned objectivity—whether it is good or bad and whether it is even possible to achieve it. Some well-known journalists, including Hunter Thompson, Bill Moyers, and David Brinkley, have described objectivity as a myth, while other well-known journalists, such as Clifton Daniel and Herbert Brucker, have defended objectivity as essential to reporting.

Some concepts introduced by S. I. Hayakawa can help the journalist to make some sense out of the controversy over objectivity. Hayakawa (1964) discusses three kinds of statements people can make—reports, inferences, and judgments—and the related issue of slanting.

A *report* is a statement that is capable of verification and excludes inferences and judgments. An example is the statement "The low temperature last night in Durham, North Carolina, was 47 degrees." This statement is capable of verification, of being checked out. You could go to the weather station in Durham and examine the records or interview the meteorologist there. Other examples of reports would be these statements:

> "The City Council approved a budget of $237 million for the fiscal year 1991." (Either they did or they didn't, and the action can be verified by checking with council members, eyewitnesses attending the meeting, and the official minutes of the meeting.)

> "Robbery suspect Larry Joe Smith was seen at Municipal Airport Saturday afternoon." (This would be more difficult to verify, and it might not be verified until Smith is apprehended and identified in court by an eyewitness or in a lineup, but the statement is still capable of verification.)

An *inference* is a statement about the unknown made on the basis of the known. Any statement about another person's thoughts or feelings is an example of an inference. You might observe a person pounding a fist on the table, raising her or his voice, and becoming red in the face. These would be the known aspects. If you then made the statement "Chris is angry," you would be making a statement about the unknown, the person's emotions. You would be making an inference. In many cases, the safest course is to stick to what is known and report it—the pounding of the fist, the raising of the voice, and the reddening of the face. Statements about these observable characteristics are verifiable and are reports.

Any statement about the future is an inference, since the future is unknown. The statement "The president will enter the hospital Thursday for a checkup" is an inference, since it deals with the future. The safer statement in this case would be "The press secretary said that the President will enter the hospital Thursday for a checkup." That is capable of verification—a report.

A man who was mugged said of his assailant: "He must have been six-feet-two and probably high on something." The conclusion that the mugger was "high on something" was an inference, although it might be most accurate to refer to it as a *labeled inference* since the word probably was used.

Inferences sometimes appear in news articles. A wire service story contained this sentence: "The hearing room was crowded and, judging from the number of yellow legal pads seen, many in the audience were lawyers." A statement about the unknown—the number of lawyers in the room—was being made on the basis of the known—the number of legal pads. This was also a labeled inference, since the word judging was included to let the reader know an inference was being made.

In another example of a labeled inference, a television correspondent describing Congress's failure to override a presidential veto of an emergency job bill said: "The Democrats seemed bewildered by what happened."

A *judgment* is an expression of approval or disapproval for an occurrence, person, or object. For example, students sometimes use words like great (approval) or terrible (disapproval) to describe a teacher.

Letters to the editor of a newspaper sometimes contain judgments. Consider the letter describing the television series "Roots" as an "ethnic hate-mongering diatribe" and "overdone fiction."

In an unusual departure from wire service objectivity, United Press International filed a news story with the following lead sentence: "Elizabeth Ray, the secretary whose intimate services led to the resignation of former Rep. Wayne Hays, has launched an acting career with a shoddy performance that nearly ruined the show." The last phrase—"with a shoddy performance that nearly ruined the show"—is clearly a judgment. In defense of UPI, however, some specific detail supporting the evaluation appeared later in the story.

Sometimes the source of a news story will state a judgment, and it might be necessary for an alert journalist to challenge it. During some textbook hearings in Texas, a feminist critic of sexism in books told a television interviewer: "This year there are some books we almost like, and there are a lot of bad books." The interviewer asked, "What's a bad book?" The critic was ready with an answer, however: "A bad book is one that shows 75 percent or more of males in the working roles." This shifted the interview out of the realm of judgments into the realm of reports.

A journalist can do a great deal toward being objective by eliminating inferences and judgments and sticking as much as possible to reports. But this alone will not guarantee objectivity. Another factor must be considered, as Hayakawa points out. That factor is slanting. *Slanting* is selecting details that are favorable or unfavorable to the subject being described.

In describing large outdoor demonstrations, for example, a newspaper often has several estimates of crowd size from which to choose. Leon Mann (1974) studied coverage of an antiwar rally in Washington, D.C., in October 1967 and found that antiwar newspapers were more likely to choose a large estimate of the crowd size and prowar newspapers were more likely to choose a small estimate.

Time magazine showed some slanting in its description of Dr. Lorene Rogers when she was appointed acting president of the University of Texas. Dr. Rogers had served previously as vice president of the university and as associate dean of the graduate school and had been a member of the national Graduate Record Examination Board. *Time* referred to her only as "Lorene Rogers, 60, a professor of home economics."

Absolute objectivity might not be possible, but in fact a journalist (or any other communicator) can go a long way toward being objective by sticking as much as possible to reports (and excluding inferences and judgments) and by making a conscious effort to avoid slanting. Furthermore, these concepts provide some specific terms for discussing the ways in which reporting might or might not be objective.

Studies of Objectivity

Journalism professor John Merrill (1965) used general semantics concepts as well as concepts of his own in his study "How *Time* Stereotyped Three U.S. Presidents." He set up the following six categories of bias: attribution bias (for example, "Truman snapped"), adjective bias (Eisenhower's "warm manner of speaking"), adverbial bias ("Truman said curtly"), outright opinion (equivalent to Hayakawa's judgments; for example, "Seldom has a more unpopular man fired a more popular one"), contextual bias (bias in whole sentences, whole paragraphs, or the entire story; six judges had to agree), and photographic bias ("What overall impression does the photograph give? How is the President presented in the picture—dignified, undignified; angry, happy; calm, nervous; etc.? What does the caption say/imply?").

Merrill examined a sample of 10 issues of *Time* for each president—Truman, Eisenhower, and Kennedy—and counted the occurrences of bias in each of the six categories. The results, summarized in Table 5.1, showed a strong negative bias toward Truman, a strong positive bias toward Eisenhower, and a rather balanced portrayal of Kennedy. The portrayals of Truman and Eisenhower are good examples of *slanting*—over a period of time the details selected almost overwhelmingly added up to either a favorable or an unfavorable impression of these presidents.

Fourteen years after the publication of Merrill's study, three other researchers replicated it to find out if things had changed (Fedler, Meeske, & Hall, 1979). They said:

> Since Merrill's study was published in 1965, the editors of *Time* have insisted that their magazine has become fairer, and the *Wall Street Journal* has reported that "even critics concede that *Time*'s political coverage now is more balanced than in its anti-Truman and pro-Eisenhower days." (p. 353)

The authors added that observations about the magazine's growing impartiality are contradicted by its coverage of the war in Vietnam and other developments. They also ob-

Table 5.1

INSTANCES OF BIAS SHOWN BY *TIME* MAGAZINE
IN 10-ISSUE SAMPLES FOR EACH OF THREE PRESIDENTS

	Truman	*Eisenhower*	*Kennedy*
Total Bias	93	82	45
Total Positive Bias	1	81	31
Total Negative Bias	92	1	14

Adapted from J. C. Merrill, "How *Time* Stereotyped Three U.S. Presidents," *Journalism Quarterly* 42 (1965): 565. Reprinted by permission.

served that since the Merrill study the magazine's circulation had grown by nearly 40 percent and that a survey showed that even the nation's journalists rely heavily on *Time*.

The replication (done as similarly as possible to the Merrill study for consistency) examined *Time*'s treatment of presidents Johnson, Nixon (both before and after Watergate), Ford, and Carter. The three investigators, all experienced journalists, working separately, read copies of all the articles about the presidents that *Time* published during randomly selected 10-week periods and independently recorded instances of apparent bias.

After a detailed analysis of the data they concluded:

> *Time* continues to use most of the bias techniques reported by Merrill, although the manner in which some are used seems to have changed. *Time* continues to use a series of devices that guide readers' opinions of the news and that enable *Time* to editorialize in its regular news columns. (Fedler et al., 1979, p. 335)

The 1979 data indicated that *Time*'s news columns were neutral toward Johnson, favored Nixon before Watergate and were critical after Watergate, supported Ford, and opposed Carter. Note that the data were drawn from news columns of *Time*, not from editorials. The researchers said:

> This study indicates that *Time* continues to weave facts into semi-fictionalized language patterns that are designed to lead the reader's thinking. While this produces a style of writing that is interesting to read, it obscures the preferential positions taken by the magazine. . . . The reader who enjoys a clever and racy style will undoubtedly enjoy *Time* because the style is entertaining. However, the careful and thoughtful reader who does not expect to find the opinions of the magazine in its unsigned articles may not find *Time* very satisfying. *Time* has never claimed to be objective. It is still not. (Fedler et al., 1979, p. 359)

More recently, in what is essentially a case study of news bias, Herman (1985) used content analysis to examine the treatment of similar new stories. The researcher hypothesized that the mass media often treat similar events differently, depending on their political implications for U.S. interests. He contends that the effectiveness of the mass media as normally cooperative dispensers of official or establishment views is enhanced by the credibility the media acquire in their occasional tiffs with established institutions, like corporations or government. Mass media credibility also derives from the fact that their frequently homogeneous behavior arises "naturally" out of industry structure, common sources, ideology, patriotism, and the power of the government and top media sources to define newsworthiness and frameworks of discourse. Self-censorship, market forces, and the norms of news practices may produce and maintain a particular viewpoint as effectively as formal state censorship.

In one of two case studies, Herman compares the *New York Times*'s coverage of the 1984 elections in El Salvador and Nicaragua, the former openly sponsored and supported by the U.S. government, the latter openly opposed by the U.S. government.

He argues that the mass media would be expected to "disregard unfavorable human rights conditions as irrelevant to elections in the client state but would feature them prominently in covering an election in a disfavored state."

He content-analyzed 28 articles about the Salvadoran election and 21 articles about the Nicaraguan election that were published in the *New York Times* during 1984.

Herman says that from a propaganda framework one would predict that where the United States supports the government in power, the apparent "democratic aspects" of the election would be stressed over any aspects that might detract from the election's legitimacy, which would be downplayed or ignored. One would also expect the media to downplay the foreign sponsor's role in organizing and funding the election, the public relations purpose of the election from the sponsor's viewpoint, and a number of other major factors.

In the case where the United States opposes the government in power, Herman says the same framework would lead to the prediction that coverage would reveal a total reversal of topical emphasis.

Herman argues that the human rights violations were, in many cases, far more extreme in the election the United States supported than in the election the United States opposed, yet the data from the content analysis indicated that the news coverage ignored most of the former while emphasizing most of the latter.

He concluded, "In sum, although basic electoral conditions were far more compatible with a free election in Nicaragua in 1984 than they were in El Salvador in either 1982 or 1984, U.S. news coverage gave El Salvador a triumphant vindication of democracy and Nicaragua an electoral experiment discredited by Sandinista intransigence and totalitarian controls" (Herman, 1985, p. 145). The researcher's generalization from a case study of the *New York Times* to "U.S. news coverage" would be considered unwarranted by most, lacking further data about U.S. news coverage on these topics. Nevertheless, the researcher has provided data on how one of the most prestigious newspapers in the United States covered these two elections and has provided a framework for further investigations of similar events.

The author adds:

> The media campaigns . . . embody sharply dichotomous manipulations of symbols and political agendas. These media campaigns were quite successful in scoring political points and making important ideological statements to the general public and the world at large. In these cases dissident voices in the United States were not available in any of the major media, even when those voices might have suggested relevant information that had been "overlooked" or "selected out." These two case studies are offered as illustrations that a propaganda framework is frequently applicable to the performance of the U.S. mass media and that in such cases meaningful diversity of opinion may be absent from media coverage of important news issues. (p. 145)

The Merrill and the Fedler, Meeske, and Hall studies are good examples of the application of principles from general semantics and content analysis applied to an examination of one of the major media in the United States. The follow-up is also a good example of the cumulative nature of science discussed in Chapter 2.

Another journalism professor, Dennis Lowry (1971), used the Hayakawa categories of reports, inferences, and judgments as the basis for a study of whether Vice President Spiro Agnew's famous Des Moines speech had an intimidating effect on television newscasters. Lowry notes the following major criticisms of the media made by Agnew:

> 1. The fact that "a little group of men . . . wield a free hand in selecting, presenting and interpreting the great issues of our Nation"; these men are the "anchor men, commentators and executive producers" of the TV newscasts

2. The "slander" and attacks which emanate from "the privileged sanctuary of a network studio"

3. "Whether a form of censorship already exists when the news that 40 million Americans receive each night is determined by a handful of men responsible only to their corporate employers and filtered through a handful of commentators who admit to their own set of biases." (*New York Times*, Nov. 14, 1969, p. 24, cited in Lowry, 1971, p. 205)

Lowry studied a random sample of network newscasts before and after the Agnew address. He looked only at statements dealing with the presidential administration, and he sorted them into these nine categories: attributed reports, unattributed reports, labeled inferences, unlabeled inferences, attributed favorable judgments, attributed unfavorable judgments, unattributed favorable judgments, unattributed unfavorable judgments, and others. Lowry found an increase in the percentage of attributed reports, the safest kind of statement, after the Agnew speech. There were hardly any judgments in the newscasts before or after the Agnew speech, indicating that critics who accused the networks of being biased against the Nixon administration were apparently not noticing judgments. The critics may have been objecting to unlabeled inferences, the category with the highest percentage before and after the Agnew speech (49 percent each time). The critics might also have objected to slanting, but that would be difficult to study since it involves omission of material.

Other Applications

Occasionally the mass media have called directly on a general semanticist to help analyze language. Four days after Patricia Hearst was kidnapped, a radio station received a letter from the Symbionese Liberation Army stating that they had taken her. Journalists became interested in analyzing that message and some others received previously from the SLA to get information about her captors. The *New York Times* quoted Dr. S. I. Hayakawa as saying that the writings showed a "high grade of intellect devoted to revolutionary ideology" (Turner, 1974). A few weeks later, CBS News brought in a similar kind of language expert. A tape-recorded message was received from "Cinque," the leader of the SLA. "CBS Morning News" on February 26, 1974, featured a psycholinguist as a guest. He analyzed the message and pointed out the categorical thinking in phrases such as "the Hearst empire" and "I am the nigger that you fear in the night."

Implications for Encoding

Now we can return to our original question of what general semantics can tell us about *encoding*, the translating of purpose, intention, or meaning into symbols or codes. The lesson from general semantics is that encoding is a difficult task often fraught with pitfalls. There are only a limited number of words available in the English language, and often these words correspond to the real world in only a rough way. Any writer facing the common problem of trying to find the "right word" to express an idea is aware of the difficulty of encoding.

Alvin Toffler recalls an experience he had while working as a journalist covering a Senate disarmament hearing in Washington and trying to condense several hours of testimony into 500 words. He says:

> I knew that I couldn't capture the full reality . . . since then I have regarded page one of the newspaper as a kind of fiction, a distorted map of a territory, too complex and too fast-changing to map. Nevertheless it is a fiction that we live by. (Toffler, 1989, p. 198)

Furthermore, it is possible to encode in such a way that one is actually saying very little about the real world. This is true when language stays at a high level of abstraction.

Finally, the concept of projection makes us aware of the difficulty of being objective. Any statement is to some degree a statement about the speaker and is thus subjective. The best way to overcome the problem of subjectivity is to stick to verifiable statements, or reports.

Conclusions

General semantics deals with the relationship between language and reality and with the ways in which language influences our thinking.

General semantics has a number of implications for the practitioner of mass communication. First, it points out the difficulty of encoding, of expressing meaning in symbols or codes. Second, it provides a basis for analyzing and talking about objectivity—a major communications concept. Third, it can help the mass communicator—or anyone else—in sorting out information and misinformation. The general semanticists have identified some misuses of language—dead-level abstracting, undue identification, two-valued evaluation, and unconscious projection—that are widespread. Knowledge of these misuses could be very beneficial to the reporter interviewing a news source. Such knowledge could also help the consumer of mass communication—the ordinary citizen trying to cope with the daily barrage of information and misinformation from the mass media.

References

Austin American-Statesman (1988). Ellie Rucker column, Nov. 6, Sect. E., p. 1.

Brown, H. (1988). *A Father's Book of Wisdom.* Nashville, Tenn.: Rutledge Hill Press.

Bronowski, J. (1951). *The Common Sense of Science.* London: William Heinemann.

Fedler, F., M. Meeske, and J. Hall (1979). *Time* magazine revisited: Presidential stereotypes persist. *Journalism Quarterly* 56: 353–359.

Hayakawa, S. I. (1964). *Language in Thought and Action.* 2nd ed. New York: Harcourt, Brace, and World.

Herman, E. S. (1985). Diversity of news: "Marginalizing" the opposition. *Journal of Communication* 35: 135–146.

Johnson, W. (1946). *People in Quandaries: The Semantics of Personal Adjustment.* New York: Harper & Row.

——— (1972). The communication process and general semantic principles. In W. Schramm (ed.), *Mass Communications,* 2nd ed., pp. 301–315. Urbana: University of Illinois Press.

Kamal, Mohamed (1987). Why tar Arabs and Islam? *New York Times,* Feb. 16, p. 17.

Kelley, E. (1947). *Education for What Is Real.* New York: Harper.

Korzybski, A. (1958). *Science and Sanity: An Introduction to Non-Aristotelian Systems and General Semantics.* 4th ed. Lakeville, Conn.: The International Non-Aristotelian Library Publishing Co.

Lowry, D. T. (1971). Agnew and the network TV news: A before-after content analysis. *Journalism Quarterly* 48: 205–210.

Mann, L. (1974). Counting the crowd: Effects of editorial policy on estimates. *Journalism Quarterly* 51: 278–285.

Merrill, J. C. (1965). How *Time* stereotyped three U.S. presidents. *Journalism Quarterly* 42: 563–570.

Miller, G. A. (1963). *Language and Communication.* New York: McGraw-Hill.

Stoen, D. (1976). Stuttering pencils. *ETC.* 33: 323–325.

Toffler, A. (1989). The relevance of general semantics. *ETC. et cetera* 46: 197–199. Remarks when invited to speak after dropping in at the 1988 International Conference on General Semantics at Yale University.

Treffert, D. A. (1976). Five dangerous ideas our children have about life. *Family Weekly,* Sept. 19, pp. 26–27.

Turner, W. (1974). Release of 2 may be kidnapping "price." *New York Times,* Feb. 9, p. 27.

Whiteside, T. (1975). Annals of television: The Nixon administration and television. *New Yorker,* Mar. 17, pp. 41–91.

Whorf, B. (1952). Language, mind, and reality. *ETC.* 9: 167–188.

6

Analysis of Propaganda:
First Theories of Decoding
and Effects

Propaganda was the topic of a number of books between the world wars. When Harold Lasswell's doctoral dissertation on the use of propaganda in World War I was published as a book in 1927, one reviewer called it "a Machiavellian textbook which should promptly be destroyed" (Dulles, 1928, p. 107). The reviewer's reaction indicates the kind of fear with which the techniques of propaganda were viewed following World War I. One book on American propaganda in World War I even had the title *Words that Won the War* (Mock & Larson, 1939). In this climate, it is no wonder that people were concerned about the effects of propaganda as World War II began to draw near.

Propaganda was thought to have great power. For our purposes its significance was that some of our first theoretical thinking about the effects of mass communication came out of the various analyses of propaganda. As we look back on it now, much of it appears to be rather primitive theory. Nevertheless, two important areas of communication theory have their roots in this early thinking about propaganda. One of these is *attitude change*, traditionally one of the major areas of communication research. What are the most effective methods for changing people's attitudes? The study of propaganda provided some tentative answers to this question. The second area is theoretical thinking about the *general effects* of mass communication. What effects does mass communication have on individuals and society? How do these effects take place?

What Is Propaganda?

The term *propaganda* comes from the *Congregatio de propaganda fide,* or Congregation for the Propagation of Faith, established by the Catholic Church in 1622. This was the time of the Reformation, in which various groups were breaking away from the Catholic Church, and the Congregation was part of the Church's Counter-Reformation. One of the great issues of this period was the struggle between science and religion as the source of knowledge about the world. One of the principal figures in this struggle was Galileo, who argued on the basis of observations through a telescope that the earth revolved around the sun. This idea ran directly against the teachings of the Catholic Church and was in fact one of the Church's forbidden propositions. Galileo was tried and convicted by the Inquisition in 1633 and was made to renounce his statements that the earth revolved around the sun. The Church was left in the position of defending an indefensible idea. Perhaps the term *propaganda* picked up some of its negative associations or its connotations of untruth from this major incident in which the Church was left arguing for a position that was scientifically demonstrable as false. In 1980 the Church undertook a new study of Galileo to determine if he had indeed been guilty of heresy. It was reported that the move was part of a new effort to give the Church a central and credible role in culture and science (Fleming, 1980).

Lasswell's classic work, *Propaganda Technique in the World War* (1927), presented one of the first careful attempts to define propaganda: "It refers solely to the control of opinion by significant symbols, or, to speak more concretely and less accurately, by stories, rumors, reports, pictures and other forms of social communication" (p. 9).

Lasswell (1937) presented a slightly different definition a few years later: "Propaganda in the broadest sense is the technique of influencing human action by the manipulation of representations. These representations may take spoken, written, pictorial or musical form" (1937, pp. 521–522).

Both of Lasswell's definitions would include most of advertising, and in fact, would appear to include all of what is often referred to as *persuasion*. In fact, Lasswell has stated that "both advertising and publicity fall within the field of propaganda" (1937, p. 522).

Lasswell's definitions would include a teacher influencing a class to study, an act many people would not want to call propaganda. Thus Lasswell's definitions may be too broad for some purposes.

Psychologist Roger Brown (1958) attempted to deal with this problem by making a distinction between propaganda and persuasion. Brown defined *persuasion* as "symbol-manipulation designed to produce action in others" (p. 299). He then pointed out that persuasive efforts are labeled propaganda "when someone judges that the action which is the goal of the persuasive effort will be advantageous to the persuader but not in the best interests of the persuadee" (p. 300). In other words, there are no absolute criteria to determine whether an act of persuasion is propaganda—that is a judgment someone makes. And as far as the techniques used are concerned, persuasion and propaganda are identical. Only when someone perceives that the source is benefiting but not the receiver can an act or message be called propaganda.

As defined by both Lasswell and Brown, propaganda would include much of advertising (where the aim is not the good of the receiver but greater sales for the advertiser), much of political campaigning (where the aim is not the good of the receiver but the candidate's election), and much of public relations (where the aim is often not the good of the receiver but the most favorable image of a corporation).

Lasswell also discussed four major objectives of propaganda:

1. To mobilize hatred against the enemy
2. To preserve the friendship of allies
3. To preserve the friendship and, if possible, to procure the cooperation of neutrals
4. To demoralize the enemy (1927, p. 195)

These are obviously wartime objectives that would not apply to advertising or other peacetime types of persuasion.

Wartime Propaganda

Wartime propaganda can be traced back to *The Art of War,* a book written by Sun Tsu before the birth of Christ (Read, 1941). But it came into its own in World War I, when it was used on a scale and with an effectiveness that had never been seen before. This was in large part because people were naive about propaganda. One expert has pointed out that the 1913 edition of the *Encyclopaedia Britannica* did not even have an article on "propaganda" (Read, 1941). One of the most effective techniques, particularly in achieving Lasswell's first objective of mobilizing hatred against the enemy, was the use of atrocity stories, which were spread by both sides. The Allies were very successful in whipping up hatred for the Germans with a widely reported story that German soldiers in Belgium were cutting the hands off Belgian children. Atrocity stories were often part of speeches given in movie theaters in the United States by "four-minute men," speakers with talks carefully timed to four minutes (Mock & Larsen, 1939). Most of these atrocity stories were false, but they did a great deal to make World War I propaganda effective because people believed them.

Propaganda Education

Propaganda education became a major concern in the United States in the period prior to World War II. Perhaps some Americans were worried that the techniques the United States had used so effectively in World War I were about to be used against them.

Social psychologist Hadley Cantril (1965) described how sometime during the 1930s he gave a radio talk over a Boston radio station on the subject of propaganda. The next day he received a telephone call from Edward A. Filene, the successful merchant who organized the credit union movement in the United States and founded the Twentieth Century Fund. Filene wanted to finance an undertaking to teach people how to think, and he asked Cantril to spend an evening with him talking over the idea. They finally decided that they might not be able to teach people how to think but that they might have some success in teaching people how *not* to think. The result was the establishment in 1937 of the Institute for Propaganda Analysis, with Cantril as its first president. The advisory board of the institute included names of several other people who later made various contributions to communication theory, including Edgar Dale and Leonard Doob.

The institute was concerned about the rise of the Nazis to power in Germany and the effects that Nazi propaganda might have in the United States. Hitler and his propaganda minister, Joseph Goebbels, seemed to be having great success with propaganda in Germany. The institute was concerned about the possibility of a Hitler figure rising to power in the United States. This may seem unlikely now, but we should remember that Nazi rallies were being held in Madison Square Garden and across America in the 1930s. Furthermore, there was even a fairly likely candidate to become the American Hitler. This was Father Charles E. Coughlin, a Catholic priest who was broadcasting over a 47-station radio network and became known as the "radio priest." Coughlin's radio program every Sunday was reaching 30 million listeners, as many as some television programs reach today. This audience was proportionately much greater than most audiences reached by mass communication today. Coughlin was apparently a colorful individual: his church in Royal Oak, Michigan, was called the Shrine of the Little Flower, and he had set up on the corner of the property the Shrine Super-Service and Hot Dog Stand. His radio talks, however, seemed to present a fascist philosophy. In fact, his magazine, *Social Justice,* was eventually banned from the U.S. mail because it mirrored the Nazi propaganda line. Coughlin's radio career finally came to a stop when he was reprimanded by the Church.

Perhaps the most famous publication of the Institute for Propaganda Analysis was a book edited by Alfred McClung Lee and Elizabeth Briant Lee (1939) called *The Fine Art of Propaganda.* The book presented seven common devices of propaganda, and it used examples from Coughlin's speeches to illustrate the devices. These devices were given catchy names and were simple enough to be taught in the public schools.

The Propaganda Devices

The seven propaganda devices are name calling, glittering generality, transfer, testimonial, plain folks, card stacking, and band wagon. Each will be defined and discussed with examples from contemporary society—political campaigns, advertisements, newspaper columns, and statements by extremist groups.

Name Calling

"Name calling—giving an idea a bad label—is used to make us reject and condemn the idea without examining the evidence" (Lee & Lee, 1939, p. 26).

Name calling doesn't appear much in advertising, probably because there is a reluctance to mention a competing product, even by calling it a name. Its use in politics and other areas of public discourse is more common, however.

During the 1988 presidential campaign Michael Dukakis was called *a card-carrying member of the ACLU,* a *bleeding heart,* a *wild-eyed liberal,* a *far-left liberal,* and an *ultra liberal.* The then vice president, George Bush, was called a *wimp,* and during the Reagan presidency, "Reaganomics" was called *voodoo economics.*

President George Bush, replying to a question concerning his China policy, said, "there's some politics involved . . . when you hear *name calling* . . . when you hear people saying 'kowtow' " (January 24, 1990, press conference).

During a press conference in Chicago on August 12, 1986, President Reagan said that only radicals support sanctions against South Africa. When a reporter asked Reagan if Bishop Desmond Tutu—leader of the Anglican Church in South Africa and an outspoken advocate of foreign sanctions against the apartheid government in South Africa—was a radical, Reagan was forced to backpedal.

The White Knights of the Ku Klux Klan of Mississippi were using name calling in their publication *The Klan Ledger* when they referred to civil rights demonstrators as "Communist-led black savages." No evidence was presented linking the demonstrators to communism.

Terrorism   Two current examples of name calling are *terrorist* and *terrorism.* As the old maxim goes, "One person's terrorist is another person's freedom fighter." General semanticists point out that what we call a person will depend upon our purposes, our projections, and our evaluations, yet the person does not change when we change the label.

Terrorist and *terrorism* have been called clichés in search of meanings. Christopher Hitchens (1989) asked if an "act of terrorism" always refers to the kind of action taken or whether its use sometimes depends on who takes the action. He quoted a consultant to the U.S. State Department on terrorism, who is also the executive director of the Institute on Terrorism and Subnational Conflict and coeditor of *Fighting Back: Winning the War Against Terrorism,* as having said:

> Can I provide a universally acceptable definition of terrorism? I fear I have to say I cannot." (p. 148)

Hitchens cites two associates of the Center for Strategic and International Studies in Washington, D.C., in their book, *Terrorism as State-Sponsored Warfare*, as saying:

> There is no universal agreement about who is a terrorist because the political and strategic goals affect different states differently. There is no value-free definition. (p. 148)

Hitchens then cites the introduction of a Rand Corporation publication:

> What do we mean by terrorism? The term, unfortunately, has no precise or widely accepted definition. The problem of definition is compounded by the fact that *terrorism* has become a fad word that is applied to all sorts of violence. (p. 149) (italics in original)

Hitchens adds:

> My initial question is a simple one. How can a word with no meaning and no definition . . . have become the political and media buzzword of the '80s? How can it have become a course credit at colleges, an engine of pelf in the think tanks, and a subject in its own right in the press, on television, and at the movies? (p. 149)
>
> It disguises reality and impoverishes language and makes a banality out of the discussion of war and revolution and politics. It's the perfect instrument for the cheapening of public opinion and for the intimidation of dissent. (p. 150)
>
> What is frightening and depressing is that a pseudoscientific propaganda word like "terrorism" has come to have such a hypnotic effect on public debate in the United States. . . . Should we not be wary of a term with which rulers fool themselves and by which history is abolished and language debased? (p. 151)

A "freedom fighter" to one person may be a "terrorist" to another. At the end of World War II, when Great Britain still held a mandate over Palestine, many of Israel's leaders of today were conducting guerrilla warfare against the British. Yitzhak Shamir, later to become Israel's prime minister, had been a member of *Irgun* and then became one of the three top commanders of *Lehi* (or LHY, *Lohamei Herut Yisrael*, or Fighters for the Freedom of Israel), also known as the Stern Gang, after its first leader. As one writer points out:

> Under his (Shamir's) leadership, the group undertook a campaign of "personal terror," assassinating top British military and government officers, often gunning them down in the street. . . . Ironically, it was a guerrilla act by the Lehi's chief rival, the Irgun headed by Menachem Begin, that got Shamir in trouble. In 1946, Irgun guerrillas bombed the King David Hotel; a total of 91 people were killed, including British citizens, Jews and Arabs. . . . Was Yitzhak Shamir a terrorist? "Yes" Johnson (a former member of the Palestine Police) said, "to the British Government. But to the Jews, the Stern Gang were freedom fighters. But that is the same as the P.L.O., who are terrorists to the Israelis and freedom fighters to the Arabs." (Brinkley, 1988, p. 68)

Ezer Weizman, a senior Labor Party member and former Israeli Defense Minister, also was a member of the *Irgun* group, which blew up Jerusalem's King David Hotel in 1946 (Brooks, 1988).

Some highly respected members of our society today were once "underground" soldiers or "freedom fighters." To their enemies, as with the former police official quoted above, they were "terrorists."

The noted psychosexual therapist Dr. Ruth Westheimer, in an article arguing for women to be assigned combat duty, wrote:

At the age of 16 I immigrated to Palestine from Europe, where I became a member of the Haganah, the main underground army of the Jews . . . and was trained as a sniper so that I could hit the center of the target time after time. . . . I almost lost both my feet as a result of a bombing attack on Jerusalem (Westheimer, 1990).

Whether a person is called an "underground" soldier or "freedom fighter," or is called a "terrorist," depends on the viewpoint of the person assigning the label, or the side the person assigning the label supports. Often the *activities* of an "underground" soldier or "freedom fighter" and those of a "terrorist" *are identical*—only the *label* changes.

Sometimes name calling can affect the destinies of nations and millions of people. One notable case probably deserves more than passing attention, since it involves one of the pioneers of the public relations industry.

United Fruit Company   In the early 1950s the United Fruit Company was faced with the expropriation of its vast uncultivated land holdings in Guatemala for redistribution to landless peasants by the new Arbenz government. In his book *An American Company* (1976), the former vice president for corporate public relations of the United Fruit Company, Thomas P. McCann, tells how the company circulated the rumor that the move was Communist inspired. He tells how press junkets to Guatemala were run for leading U.S. journalists, how "Communist demonstrations" were arranged upon the journalists' arrival, and how public opinion in the United States was turned against the Guatemalan government. This was name calling with a vengeance for the sake of future hundreds-of-millions of dollars of corporate profits. McCann says, "It is difficult to make a convincing case for manipulation of the press when the victims proved so eager for the experience" (p. 47). The compensation offered for the uncultivated land by the Guatemalan government, which was based on the very value placed on the land by the United Fruit Company for purposes of taxation, was rejected as totally inadequate. The U.S. State Department was convinced of the "Communist threat." Secretary of State John Foster Dulles had been a member of the New York law firm Sullivan and Cromwell, which represented United Fruit in Central America. The legitimately elected government of Guatemala was overthrown by a CIA-mounted invasion that used United Fruit Company facilities as a base of operations (Chapter 4). Today Guatemala has the oldest and most violent civil war in Central America, as a result of repression by the extreme rightist oligarchy and the rigid concentration of wealth (Gruson, 1990a). Guatemala is the world's sixth largest producer of opium poppies and has become a major transshipment point for cocaine (Gruson, 1990b).

McCann says, "Responsible for putting the best face on corporate strategy was Edward L. Bernays, the 'father of public relations,' the biggest name in the field" (p. 45).

In his 1928 book *Propaganda,* Bernays said:

The conscious and intelligent manipulation of the organized habits and opinions of the masses is an important element in democratic society. Those who manipulate this unseen mechanism of society constitute an invisible government which is the true ruling power of our country. . . .

It has been found possible so to mold the mind of the masses that they will throw their newly gained strength in the desired direction. . . . But clearly it is the intelligent minorities which need to make use of propaganda continuously and systematically. In the active proselytizing minorities in whom *selfish* interests and public interests coincide lie the progress and development of America. (pp. 9, 19, 31)

Another well-known book by Bernays is titled *The Engineering of Consent.*

Dow Chemical Company engaged in name calling when it spread incorrect confidential medical reports claiming that a young woman Greenpeace environmental protester had syphilis. She was one of five protesters arrested during a demonstration against the Midland, Michigan-based chemical giant. They were charged with trespassing when they tried to block Dow's chemical discharge pipes into the river that flows through Midland. Dow is considered by many to be a major polluter of the river. When the charge that the woman had syphilis was proved false, the company was forced to publish a full-page newspaper ad in apology. The president of Dow U.S.A., Hunter Henry, said, "A serious error in judgment was made by several Michigan division personnel in passing along personal information which reached them about a Greenpeace member" (*Austin American-Statesman,* Oct. 19, 1985, p. A9).

It should be noted that the alleged medical condition of the Greenpeace protester had no connection whatsoever with the reason for the protest (pollution of the river), but was simply an attempt to discredit her. This is a common propaganda method used to *divert attention* from the issue and discredit the credibility of the communicator. (We will return to this topic in later chapters.)

Glittering Generality

"*Glittering generality*—associating something with a 'virtue word'—is used to make us accept and approve the thing without examining the evidence" (Lee & Lee, 1939, p. 47).

The use of glittering generalities is so pervasive that we hardly notice it.

Product Names and Promotion   One of the common uses of virtue words is in the very names of products, such as Gold Medal flour, Imperial margarine, Wonder bread, Southern Comfort, Super Shell, and Superior Dairy. Some cereals are given names that will particularly appeal to children—Cheerios, Cap'n Crunch, Froot Loops. A new cigarette that was going to be made from lettuce and therefore nicotine free was to be called Long Life.

Or the glittering generality can appear in a statement about the product. Commercials for Kellogg's cereals say they bring "the best to you each morning"—quite a glowing phrase for a bowl of cold cereal. Commercials for United Airlines invite people to "fly the friendly skies" of United, but they don't offer any evidence that the skies of United are any more friendly than the skies of any other airline. Another claim of the same type is the statement "Coke adds life." It sounds as if they've found the fountain of youth and started bottling it.

Sometimes the glittering generalities used by advertisers can involve deception to such a degree that legal action is taken. Some shampoo manufacturers were requested by the Federal Trade Commission to document the statement that their products contained "natural ingredients," a claim played up in advertising. The "natural ingredients" turned out to be things like coconut oil and plain water.

Wheaties has for a long time been advertised as the "breakfast of champions." The claim was finally challenged in a lawsuit after the company started using Olympic decathlon champion Bruce Jenner in commercials in which he said he "downed a lot of Wheaties" on his way to winning the gold medal. The suit was brought by the consumer fraud crime unit of the district attorney's office in San Francisco, which charged false advertising. In a later press conference, Jenner indicated that he had eaten Wheaties for breakfast for many years, but that he often supplemented the cereal with steak and homemade granola.

The makers of Listerine got into trouble for stating on the bottle label: "For relief of cold symptoms and minor sore throats due to colds." The Federal Trade Commission found that research on the product did not substantiate that claim and ordered the company to run corrective advertising.

Politics and Business The glittering generality device shows up in areas other than advertising, such as politics. Calling a proposed law a "right to work" law might be an effective way to get the law passed; who would oppose the right to work? In a similar use, the members of Congress who toured the United States to speak against the Panama Canal treaty called themselves a "truth squad." Franklin D. Roosevelt's decision to call his program the New Deal was an effective choice of a glittering generality; it sounded good, and it suggested that he was correcting a misdeal.

Economist Daniel Bell (1976) has brought out what a tricky public relations job it was to introduce installment buying in the United States, where the Protestant ethic, with its emphasis on saving and abstinence, prevailed. The key to the campaign was to avoid the word *debt* and emphasize the word *credit*.

The lexicon of the business world is full of glittering generalities. For example, businesses that incur annual losses now show *negative income*. Public relations releases are now sometimes called *directed communications*.

After a nationwide survey of 1,200 persons indicated that they consider *capitalism* to be associated with certain negative aspects of big business, a business research institute recommended that the term *private enterprise* be substituted by candidates for public office. The researchers found the latter term tends to be associated in most people's minds with small businesses, particularly the "mom and pop stores" of which they hold an overwhelmingly favorable impression (Tindol, 1988).

As almost everyone knows, medical insurance premiums have been increasing rapidly while benefits have been restricted. When the University of Texas at Austin concluded negotiations to renew faculty and staff health insurance a brochure titled "Your Benefits Package Just Got Bigger and Better!," subtitled "Now you can call Aetna's healthline," was circulated. Some of the added and changed provisions included: precertification requirement for hospital admissions; with "disincentives" (not *penalties*) of paying only 60 percent of covered hospital expense benefits if precertification was not obtained, and the unreimbursed 40 percent not counted toward satisfaction of coinsurance. These were called "a positive step" toward controlling medical costs that "we're happy to provide." At the same time the coinsurance limits were increased by 60 percent on one plan and 30 percent on the other, the annual medical deductible was no longer waived for accidental injury, and individual premiums increased far more than the university's contribution. Many faculty and staff could not see the "bigger and *better*" benefits package.

A glittering generality was used to persuade the citizens of Wilsonville, Illinois, to allow in their town a waste disposal center for PCB-contaminated sludge and other poisons. They were told only that "industrial residues" would be kept there.

International Relations The U.S. government invaded Panama in December 1989 under the name "Operation Just Cause." After General Manuel Antonio Noriega was brought to the United States, several legal scholars said the apprehension was basically a blunt political act with only after-the-fact legal rationale. A senior lawyer at the World

Court said the closest parallel may lie in ancient Rome when defeated leaders were taken to the circus and displayed (Lewis, 1990).

While Dow was engaged in the name calling of the Greenpeace demonstrator, it was also mounting a $60 million advertising campaign ("Dow lets you do great things") to improve its corporate image (Bussey, 1987). The campaign was filled with what many would call glittering generalities. The commercials depicted recent college grads, in conversation with friends, families, and fiancees, who had chosen to accept employment with Dow because of its international humanitarian concerns. Those who do not know or remember the recent past history of Dow may wonder why it felt compelled to spend $60 million a year on advertising to improve its corporate image.

Dow, until that time primarily a manufacturer of chemicals for resale to other manufacturers, had a serious public relations problem. It made napalm, the jellied gasoline that kills in an especially painful way, and the defoliant Agent Orange, both widely used in Vietnam; it refused to make public to disabled Vietnam veterans its data on the biological effects of dioxin (a component of Agent Orange); it cancelled contributions to a college that had a speaker who attacked its corporate policies; and it refused to allow EPA inspectors to fly over its plants to collect air samples, an issue that Dow fought to the U.S. Supreme Court and lost (Deutsch, 1987). Because of Dow's falling profits from industrial chemicals the company moved heavily into consumer products, an area where Dow's public image was more important. A few months after beginning the advertising and public relations campaign containing many glittering generalities, the company raised positive reaction to its image by 6 points to 29 percent (Bussey, 1987).

Transfer

"Transfer carries the authority, sanction, and prestige of something respected and revered over to something else in order to make the latter more acceptable" (Lee & Lee, 1939, p. 69).

Transfer works through a process of association, but instead of guilt by association it's usually something more like "admiration by association." The communicator's goal is to link an idea or product or cause with something that people like or have favorable attitudes toward.

In the 1988 vice presidential debate Dan Quayle compared himself with former president John Kennedy, calling him by the more familiar "Jack," although there is no evidence that he ever knew him.

Transfer can take place through the use of symbolic objects. Ku Klux Klan rallies feature the burning of a cross, a Christian symbol. A minor presidential candidate from Chicago named Lar Daley used to campaign in an Uncle Sam suit.

Commercial Uses   During the celebration marking the centennial of the Statue of Liberty in 1986, it was common to link the statue with all kinds of products, from plastic knickknacks to boxer shorts and G-strings.

Often the association is designed to be longer lasting than a fleeting commercial. Sears featured the Statue of Liberty on the cover of its 1986 Fall-Winter Centennial Edition catalog along with the words "Celebrating Sears New Century." Included with the catalog was a small bronze coin depicting on the face the head of the statue above the word *Liberty* and the words *Contains Authentic Material* (recovered during the restoration of the statue). The reverse of the coin carries the message "Celebrating Sears New Century."

One report commenting on commercial ties with Lady Liberty observed, "It gives Corporate America a chance to use the festivities to do some image polishing of its own—and maybe to make a little money, too" (Henriques, 1986). Another writer noted, "Lee Iacocca, the head of the fund-raising effort to restore the statue, sold it as a marketing symbol to bring in millions of dollars from big U.S. corporations" (Maclean, 1986).

Music Sometimes the transfer takes place through the use of music. Father Coughlin used to begin his Sunday radio broadcasts with churchlike music from an organ, thus transferring to himself and his message the prestige of the church. The Ku Klux Klan plays the hymn "The Old Rugged Cross" at its rallies, thus associating itself with Christianity. Music also appears in a television commercial for the telephone company. The words are "Hello, America, how are you?" but the tune, written by Steve Goodman and made popular by Arlo Guthrie, is the song "The City of New Orleans," a tribute to a train with that name. This allows the telephone company to associate itself with the nostalgia for the vanishing railroads as well as with youth.

Sometimes the transfer can take place just through two people appearing together. This kind of transfer can reach a large number of people through a news photograph, film clip, or videotape of the event showing the two people together.

Advertising Many advertisements and commercials are built primarily around the transfer device. The Marlboro cigarette campaign, thought by some experts to be the most successful advertising campaign in 40 years, was designed to transfer the ruggedness and virility of the cowboys in the ads to the cigarette and to the people who smoke Marlboros. In a Vantage cigarette commercial a skier races down a slope, associating the cigarette with health, fitness, ruggedness, and fun.

Many liquor ads around Christmas are designed to build strong associations between Christmas and the use of liquor. J&B scotch has used the song title "Jingle Bells" in ads of this type with the J and the B in the title emphasized in such a way that there appears to be an intimate connection between the old familiar song and their product. The goal seems to be to make it so you can't think of "Jingle Bells" without thinking of their product. A Seagram's 7 advertisement in magazines showed a young couple baking Christmas cookies. A couple of glasses of whiskey were prominent in the picture. If one looked more closely, there was an even more subtle tie-in between Christmas and their product—each of the cookies being baked was in the shape of a 7 with a crown on it. Commercials for Michelob beer associate their beer with the night and good times.

Sometimes the transfer is from a prestige personality that is in itself manufactured. Betty Crocker, a figment of General Mills's corporate public relations imagination since the 1920s, has sold more than 22 million cookbooks and billions of packages of General Mills products. She has gotten progressively younger with age and has now been made over from a homespun, grandmotherly housewife into a dressed-for-success yuppie. Today the sexagenarian Betty Crocker doesn't look a day over 35, just in from a day at the office and ready to whip up something for dinner with the food processor and the microwave.

Testimonial

"Testimonial consists in having some respected or hated person say that a given idea or program or product or person is good or bad" (Lee & Lee, 1939, p. 74).

Testimonial is a common technique in advertising and political campaigning. The national investment company E. F. Hutton hired the popular comedian Bill Cosby for

$3 million to act as its spokesman on television. Cosby, who did an outstanding job for Jell-O, Texas Instruments, Ford Motor Company, and Coca-Cola, did not have the public image of a financial wizard. But, Hutton hired Cosby with the hope that he could improve the company's image, which was badly tarnished by its guilty plea in 1985 to charges of mail and wire fraud (Scott, 1986).

How true are testimonials? Writer Barry Farrell (1975) did some checking on Peter Ustinov's commercials for Gallo wines. Ustinov was praising the company's new line of varietal wines, but Gallo also makes Ripple, Boone's Farm, and Thunderbird—wines unlikely to appear on Peter Ustinov's table. In the commercials, Ustinov speaks of "my friends Ernest and Julio Gallo" and their passion for making fine wines. Farrell found out that Ustinov never knew the Gallos until he was hired to do the commercials.

Plain Folks

"Plain folks is the method by which a speaker attempts to convince his audience that he and his ideas are good because they are 'of the people,' the 'plain folks'" (Lee & Lee, 1939, p. 92).

Advertising The "plain folks" device used to be more common in politics than it was in advertising, although such campaigns for commercial products have increased in recent years. Bartles and James wine cooler commercials clearly use that approach. So do the Wilfred Brimley television commercials for oatmeal, the Orville Redenbacher popcorn ads, and Charlie Welch playing "Mr. Titus" in Pepperidge Farm television commercials. A model in a television commercial promoting beauty aids says, "Don't hate me because I'm beautiful. First thing in the morning, I look just like you." Commercials for a regional brand of baked goods feature "down-home" scenes and a jingle about a "land of gingham blue," while a series for a regional brand of ice cream depicts cows that think a small town is heaven, and rural individuals give testimonials for the ice cream.

Politics During a vice presidential debate in 1988, Dan Quayle invoked "plain folks" when he said of ordinary voters, "I know them and they know me." In other debates Michael Dukakis repeatedly referred to himself as the "son of immigrants." During the 1988 campaign, then vice president George Bush appeared in oilfields wearing a hard hat and rolled-up sleeves. While campaigning in Iowa, Bush said he was a farmer, just like those in his audience. Vice presidential candidate Lloyd Bentsen was shown tossing a football, George Bush was shown jogging with citizens, and Michael Dukakis was shown mowing his own lawn, all plain folks.

A good example of the "plain folks" approach in politics appeared in television spots shown in Arkansas when Senator J. William Fulbright was running for reelection. The ads showed Fulbright without a necktie, and whittling a piece of wood. This was an unlikely image for Fulbright, a Rhodes scholar with a degree from Oxford University in England, a former president of the University of Arkansas, and for 30 years, probably one of the most erudite persons who ever served in the Senate, but it was an image that would be appealing in rural Arkansas.

A television spot in one gubernatorial campaign went like this:

> *Woman, raking leaves:* "Buddy Temple lives down the street. He's a good neighbor and he's a good friend."
> *Man, fishing:* "Buddy Temple and I have been fishing partners for many, many years. He loves the land and he loves the outdoors."

Children, in unison: "Buddy Temple is our dad!"
Woman: "He's my husband!"
Man: "Hi, I'm Buddy Temple. I'm running for governor. I'll sure appreciate your support."
Voice-over: "Who's Buddy Temple? He's our next governor!"

Note the "plain folks" identifications with the woman raking and man fishing, the emphasis on being a family man, and the implied band wagon, in the statement "He's our next governor!" But the "plain folks" approach wasn't enough—he wasn't the next governor.

Card Stacking

"Card stacking involves the selection and use of facts or falsehoods, illustrations or distractions, and logical or illogical statements in order to give the best or worst possible case for an idea, program, person, or product" (Lee & Lee, 1939, p. 95).

Card stacking is basically identical to the general semantics technique of *slanting* (see Chapter 5). It is a selecting of the arguments or evidence that support a position and ignoring the arguments or evidence that do not support the position. The arguments that are selected can be true or false. The device probably operates most effectively when the arguments are true, but other equally true arguments are ignored, because then it is hardest to detect.

Some of the clearest examples of card stacking can be found in movie ads that present quotations from movie reviews. These quotations are carefully selected to be only the most favorable. The critics no doubt said the things used in the ads, but they probably said some negative or less positive things also, and these were not brought out.

Television Commercials   Many television commercials that show interviews with ordinary citizens are also using card stacking. This is the type of commercial in which a television interviewer comes across a woman in a shopping center and asks if she would like a free cup of coffee. After she tastes it, she is asked, "Would you say it tastes as rich as it looks?" The person then says "It tastes as rich as it looks," or perhaps something even more favorable. These commercials show the people who were interviewed who praised the product, but they don't show or even report the number of interviews in which people did not praise the product. One interviewer for this kind of commercial has said, "The bulk of the answers in those things is indifference. People will say, 'Oh, it's all right'" (Grant, 1978, p. 65).

International Affairs   When General Noriega was brought to the United States in January 1990, a mug shot of him in color wearing a green T-shirt and holding an identification board in front of him was released by the U.S. government. It was widely used in newspapers, television, and magazines, including one newsweekly cover. Lawyers for the ousted Panamanian leader filed a motion saying that it prejudiced any potential juror and dashed all hope of a fair trial. (Berke, 1990).

One writer (Foot, 1987), reviewing a book, *The Korean War,* wrote:

> The Communist treatment of prisoners became a dominant theme of press coverage in the United States during the immediate postwar years. What is less well-known is the similarly appalling conditions within the United Nations camps and the parallel behavior of many United Nations soldiers. One medic describes the widespread incidence of pneumonia, malaria, dysentery and tuberculosis among men held in United Nations compounds.

Many American officers and men interviewed for the book "admitted knowledge of, or participation in, the shooting of Communist prisoners when it was inconvenient to keep them alive."

The reviewer goes on to say,

He (the author) also refers to "Communist terrorization within the compounds," but does not describe the activities of the hundreds of anti-Communist organizations that were set up in the United Nations camps, which had links with the South Korean and Chinese Nationalist Governments.

The author unfortunately neglects the diary of Adm. Turner Joy (the chief United Nations Command negotiator during the first year of the armistice talks) which records a mock screening that took place in a Chinese compound before the official polling of prisoners. Those who announced their wish to return to the People's Republic of China were horribly beaten or killed.

A use of card stacking in wartime communication occurred during an Israeli attack on Palestine guerrilla bases in Lebanon in 1978. Dr. Fathi Arafat, the brother of PLO commander Yasir Arafat, showed an Associated Press reporter sacks containing the bodies of two children killed in rocket attacks by the Israelis. There was undoubtedly a lot of information Arafat could have made available to the reporter; he selected the information that would make the Israelis look bad in the eyes of the world. This incident was strikingly similar to the use of atrocity stories in World War I, although in this case the information was probably true.

Historical Cases   Several historical cases of card stacking with wide-ranging implications have come to light in recent years.

1. The *Lusitania*

On May 7, 1915, at a time when the United States was maintaining a strong neutral position under President Woodrow Wilson, the British passenger liner *Lusitania,* which had sailed from New York, was sunk by a German submarine off the Irish coast. It went down with a loss of 1,200 men, women, and children, many of them American. German agents in New York knew that the ship was loading thousands of tons of military materials, including munitions. Prior to the sailing the Germans, in statements published in American newspapers, warned passengers not to take passage on the ship, foretelling the sinking of the liner.

The *Lusitania* was one of several ships that had been built eight years earlier under a secret agreement between the British Admiralty and the Cunard Lines and was, in actuality, an armed auxiliary cruiser of the Royal Navy, a fact that, after the sinking, both England and America vehemently denied.

Before the sinking, Winston Churchill, then first lord of the admiralty, commissioned a report to speculate about what would happen if a passenger ship with powerful neutrals aboard were sunk by Germans.

World War I naval warfare was conducted according to the internationally recognized "cruiser rules," under which noncombatant ships were boarded and searched for military contraband. If found, passengers were given time to debark before their ship was sunk, so long as that ship posed no direct threat to its attacker. Churchill issued orders to his ships, instructing them to threaten at all times and to ram any submarine that surfaced to send aboard search parties, thereby depriving them of any benefit under the cruiser rules.

The English had broken the German naval code and knew the approximate locations of all German U-boats operating around the British Isles. The Germans had information, which many now believe was planted, that military ships would be in the Irish Sea the first week of May. The British ship assigned to guide the *Lusitania* to safety was suddenly and without explanation recalled. These and many other facts were never revealed—they were kept secret for 50 years. The world raged at the barbarity of the kaiser and the German people, and the act did much to precipitate the later entrance of the United States into World War I (Simpson, 1972).

2. Gulf of Tonkin

In 1964 President Lyndon Johnson got the U.S. Congress to pass the Gulf of Tonkin resolution, which set into motion military action against North Vietnam. The claim was made that the U.S. destroyers *Maddox* and *Turner Joy,* operating in international waters, had come under unprovoked night attack from North Vietnamese patrol boats on August 2 and 4, and was so portrayed to the American people, who were outraged at the attack. It was not disclosed that in that area at that time, South Vietnamese commandos, trained and supported by the United States, were carrying out seaborne raids against North Vietnamese installations under naval cover supplied by the United States. Not disclosed at the time the Gulf of Tonkin resolution passed was the fact that there was no evidence that either of the two U.S. ships had ever been fired upon. There were no casualties, neither ship was hit, and there were no reports of fire from the North Vietnamese ships (Stone, 1966, 1968a, 1968b).

Band Wagon

"Band wagon has as its theme, 'Everybody—at least all of *us*—is doing it'; with it, the propagandist attempts to convince us that all members of a group to which we belong are accepting his program and that we must therefore follow our crowd and 'jump on the band wagon'" (Lee & Lee, 1939, p. 105).

Advertising Many examples of band wagon appeals appear in advertising. A deodorant is described as "the people's choice." A recruitment ad for the U.S. Army shows a group of smiling young people in uniform and says, "Join the people who've joined the Army." A jingle for Sara Lee baked goods states, "Nobody doesn't like Sara Lee." McDonald's brags about the billions of hamburgers sold. A soft drink refers to "the Pepsi generation," suggesting that a whole generation is drinking the product.

Wartime Use The band wagon is often used in wartime to convince people that everybody is making sacrifices for the war effort, even to the extent of sacrificing their lives. Nations involved in combat need heroes to build morale. If they do not yet have a hero, they can pick a likely candidate and exaggerate his deeds.

The United States was badly in need of a propaganda shot in the arm in the dark days following Pearl Harbor. It was announced that Army Air Force Captain Colin Kelly had sunk the Japanese battleship *Haruna* when, on December 10, 1941, he gave his own life by dropping a bomb down the ship's smokestack, thereby sinking the ship only three days after Pearl Harbor. He became the first American hero of the war, and a song using his name became a national hit in 1942. In truth, no Japanese warship of the *Haruna*'s size was in that area, and the *Haruna* survived until it was sunk in Kure Harbor, near Hiroshima, more than three years later (Scott, 1982).

During the Falkland Islands war, 22-year-old Sublieutenant Prince Andrew of Great Britain was depicted as a heroic helicopter pilot, hovering above his ship, HMS *Invincible*, willing to sacrifice himself as a decoy for Exocet missiles fired by Argentine aircraft. According to later press reports, he piloted his helicopter only once, during practice, and "never saw one of the sea-skimming missiles heading straight for him," as was splashed on the front pages, and that "the new nickname for Randy Andy among his mates is Prince BS" (Scott, 1982).

Government Propaganda   On the home front, governments often need models of production for others to emulate. In China, Chairman Mao touted the Tachai (Dazhai) Production Brigade as a model of self-reliance, saying in 1964, "In agriculture, learn from Tachai." It was then copied on walls across China. The brigade was reputed to have increased its grain yield eightfold from 1949 to 1971, despite its being located in an area of rocky soil, erosion, and poor agriculture. In 1980 the Chinese government claimed that the grain yields of Tachai brigade had been falsified and that the "self-reliant" brigade had accepted millions of yuan in government subsidies and help from army labor battalions (Rogers, 1983, pp. 339–340; Butterfield, 1982, pp. 403–404).

Effectiveness of the Propaganda Devices

The Institute for Propaganda Analysis identified the seven propaganda devices, but it did not research their effectiveness. The institute seemed to assume that the devices were effective.

Scientific evidence is now available on the effectiveness of some of the propaganda devices. Most of it comes from experiments done by social psychologists investigating how attitudes can be changed. Several of these experiments are essentially tests of the propaganda devices of card stacking, testimonial, and band wagon (Brown, 1958). These experiments are discussed briefly here and in greater detail in later chapters on attitude change and the role of groups in communication (Chapters 9, 10, and 11).

Evidence on the effectiveness of card stacking comes from experiments on the effectiveness of one-sided versus two-sided messages (Hovland, Lumsdaine, & Sheffield, 1949; Lumsdaine & Janis, 1953). The one-sided message is essentially a card-stacking message. Only the arguments on one side of a controversy are presented. In the two-sided message, some of the arguments that can be raised on the other side are mentioned briefly. In general, this research has shown that the one-sided messages work best on some kinds of people (those initially tending to agree with the argument of the message or those lower in education), and two-sided messages work best on other kinds of people (those initially tending to oppose the argument of the message or those higher in education).

Evidence on the effectiveness of testimonials comes from experiments on the effects of the credibility of the source (Hovland & Weiss, 1951). In general, these experiments show that a high-credibility source produces more attitude change than a low-credibility source but that even the high-credibility source typically changes the attitudes of fewer than half the people who receive messages attributed to that source.

Evidence on the effectiveness of band wagon appeals comes from experiments on the effects of group pressure and conformity (Asch, 1958; Sherif, 1958). These experiments demonstrate that in a rather contrived situation, most people can be influenced in their judgment when a group of other people present a different view. This effect is strongest when there is a unanimous majority against the person. If one other person breaks the unanimous majority, the influence is not nearly as strong. And even with a unanimous majority against them, one-third of the people put through these experiments remained independent in their judgments.

This evidence on three of the propaganda devices indicates that in general the devices can be effective, *but only on some people.* And whether a device will be effective or not depends on some other factors. These include characteristics of the person getting the message, such as education level and initial attitude toward the topic. They also include characteristics of the setting, such as whether the group holding a view different from a person's is unanimous or not. Psychologist Roger Brown summed up this research by saying that the evidence indicates that the propaganda devices are "contingently rather than invariably effective" (1958, p. 306).

It appears from the scientific evidence that the Institute for Propaganda Analysis exaggerated the effectiveness of these devices. Nevertheless, they can be effective enough to increase the sales of a product by a meaningful amount, and that is why they are so widespread in advertising. The seven propaganda devices are also important because they can be viewed as an early attempt to state a theory of attitude change. Some of the devices that the institute was only guessing about have turned out to be key variables in later attitude-change experiments.

Effectiveness of Nazi Propaganda

The Institute for Propaganda Analysis and others who were concerned may have over-reacted when they began flooding the country with pamphlets presenting the seven propaganda devices. It now appears unlikely that a person using these methods could have successfully introduced Nazism to the United States and become an American Hitler. But if this is the case, how does one explain the apparent success of Nazi propaganda in Germany prior to World War II?

There were important differences in the situations in the United States and Germany before World War II. For one thing, the Nazis in Germany had essentially a communication monopoly (Bramsted, 1965). Dissenting views were not permitted, and that is very different from the situation in the United States. Perhaps the most important difference, however, is that propaganda in Germany was wedded to terror and backed up by force. If your neighbor expressed a dissenting view, he could disappear from his home during the middle of the night, never to be seen again. Joseph Goebbels, the Nazi minister of propaganda, is reported to have said that "a sharp sword must always stand behind propaganda, if it is to be really effective" (Bramsted, 1965, p. 450). A book on Nazi radio propaganda written during World War II expressed a similar thought:

> Political propaganda in Nazi Germany is a form of coercion; while it lacks the bluntness and irrevocability of physical violence, it derives its ultimate efficacy from the power of those who may, at any moment, cease talking and start killing. (Kris & Speier, 1944, p. 3)

The Bullet Theory

The idea that mass communication has great power can be considered one of the first general theories of the effects of mass communication. Sometimes this theory is known as the "bullet theory" (Schramm, 1971), the "hypodermic-needle" theory (Berlo, 1960), or the "stimulus-response" theory (DeFleur & Ball-Rokeach, 1989, pp. 163–165). The theory suggests that people are extremely vulnerable to mass communication messages. It suggests that if the message "hits the target," it will have its desired effect.

We now know that this theory of mass communication is oversimplified. A mass communication message does not have the same effect on everyone. Its effect on anyone is dependent on a number of things, including personality characteristics of the person and various aspects of the situation and the context. Nevertheless, the "bullet theory" is a conceivable theory of mass communication: it seemed borne out by the apparent effectiveness of propaganda after World War I. This was partly because people were naive and believed lies. The theory will probably never work as well again, but at the time it was accurate.

The "bullet theory" may not be dead yet, however. It appears in a somewhat revised form in the writings of the French philosopher Jacques Ellul (1973). Ellul argues that propaganda is much more effective than analysis by Americans had shown (pp. 287–294). He particularly rejects the evidence from experiments, stating that propaganda is part of a total environment and cannot be duplicated in a laboratory setting (pp. 250–286). Ellul argues that propaganda is so pervasive in American life that most of us are not even aware of it, yet it is controlling our values (p. 65). The central one of these values is, of course, the "American way of life" (p. 252). This thinking is not completely different from the ideas of some American communication scholars. As we shall see, sociologists Paul Lazarsfeld and Robert Merton have discussed the tendency of mass communication to reinforce the economic and social status quo, and communication theorist Joseph Klapper has suggested that the general effect of mass communication is reinforcement of attitudes.

Conclusions

The analysis of propaganda after World War I expressed certain thinking about the effects of mass communication that we can regard as one of the first general theories about the effects of mass communication. In essence, this theory was what has come to be known as the "bullet theory," which we discuss further in Chapter 14.

The work of the Institute for Propaganda Analysis led to what we can consider a primitive theory of attitude change. Several of the propaganda devices the institute identified are quite similar to techniques later studied more carefully in scientific research on persuasion. Scientific research shows that these devices have some ability to change attitudes but that they don't work on everyone.

Even though their effectiveness is limited, the seven propaganda devices can still serve their initial purpose of providing a checklist of techniques commonly used in mass communication. In one way or another, all the propaganda devices represent faulty arguments. Knowledge of the devices can make people, including professional communicators, better consumers of information.

References

Asch, S. E. (1958). Effects of group pressure upon the modification and distortion of judgments. In E. E. Maccoby, T. M. Newcomb, and E. L. Hartley (eds.), *Readings in Social Psychology*, 3rd ed., pp. 174–183. New York: Holt, Rinehart, and Winston.
Bell, D. (1976). *The Cultural Contradictions of Capitalism*. New York: Basic Books.

Berke, R. L. (1990). Noriega lawyers object to photo. *New York Times,* January 15, p. 8.

Berlo, D. (1960). *The Process of Communication: An Introduction to Theory and Practice.* San Francisco: Rinehart Press.

Bernays, E. L. (1928). *Propaganda.* New York: Liveright.

Bramsted, E. K. (1965). *Goebbels and National Socialist Propaganda: 1925-1945.* East Lansing: Michigan State University Press.

Brinkley, J. (1988). The stubborn strength of Yitzhak Shamir. *New York Times Magazine,* August 21, pp. 27-29; 68-77.

Brooks, G. (1988). Israelis are divided over the meetings between U.S., PLO. *Wall Street Journal,* Dec. 12, pp. A1, A8.

Brown, R. (1958). *Words and Things.* New York: Free Press.

Bussey, J. (1987). Dow Chemical tries to shed tough image and court the public. *Wall Street Journal,* Nov. 20, pp. 1, 18.

Butterfield, F. (1982). *China: Alive in a Bitter Sea.* New York: Bantam.

Cantril, H. (1965). Foreword. In M. Choukas, *Propaganda Comes of Age.* Washington, D.C.: Public Affairs Press.

DeFleur, M., and S. Ball-Rokeach (1989). *Theories of Mass Communication.* 5th ed. New York: Longman.

Deutsch, C. (1987). Dow Chemical want to be your friend. *New York Times.* Nov. 22, Sect. F, p. 6.

Dulles, F. R. (1928). Problems of war and peace. *Bookman* 67: 105-107.

Ellul, J. (1973). *Propaganda: The Formation of Men's Attitudes.* New York: Vintage.

Farrell, B. (1975). Celebrity market. *Harper's,* Dec., pp. 108-110.

Fleming, L. (1980). Pope considers clearing Galileo of heresy. *Austin American-Statesman,* Oct. 26, p. A10.

Foot, R. (1987). Pointing toward Vietnam. *New York Times Book Review,* Nov. 29, p. 18.

Grant, M. N. (1978). I got my swimming pool by choosing Prell over brand X. In R. Atwan, B. Orton, and W. Vesterman (eds.), *American Mass Media: Industries and Issues,* pp. 61-67. New York: Random House.

Gruson, L. (1990a). Guerrilla war in Guatemala heats up, fueling criticism of civilian rule. *New York Times,* June 3, Sect. 1, p. 4.

——— (1990b). Voting isn't helping in Guatemala. *New York Times,* June 3, Sect. 4, p. 5.

Henriques, D. (1986). Statue of invitation: Corporate America cashes in on celebrations for Lady Liberty. *Austin American-Statesman,* May 30, pp. 1, F8.

Hitchens, C. (1989). Terrorism: A cliche in search of a meaning. *Et cetera* 45: (Summer) 147-152.

Hovland, C. I., A. A. Lumsdaine, and F. D. Sheffield (1949). *Experiments on Mass Communication.* New York: John Wiley.

Hovland, C. I., and W. Weiss (1951). The influence of source credibility on communication effectiveness. *Public Opinion Quarterly* 15: 635-650.

Kris, E., and H. Speier (1944). *German Radio Propaganda: Report on Home Broadcasts During the War.* London: Oxford University Press.

Lasswell, H. D. (1927). *Propaganda Technique in the World War.* New York: Peter Smith.

——— (1937). Propaganda. In E. R. A. Seligman and A. Johnson (eds.), *Encyclopedia of the Social Sciences,* vol. 12, pp. 521-528. New York: Macmillan.

Lee, A. M., and E. B. Lee (eds.) (1939). *The Fine Art of Propaganda: A Study of Father Coughlin's Speeches.* New York: Harcourt, Brace, and Company.

Lewis, N. (1990). Scholars say the arrest of Noriega has little legal justification. *New York Times,* Jan. 10, p. 8.

Lumsdaine, A. A., and I. L. Janis (1953). Resistance to "counterpropaganda" produced by one-sided and two-sided "propaganda" presentations. *Public Opinion Quarterly* 17: 311-318.

Maclean, J. (1986). Opportunism flickers in Lady Liberty's torch: Statue's history shadowed by personal gain. *Austin American-Statesman,* June 29, pp. 1, 14.

McCann, T. (1976). *An American Company: The Tragedy of United Fruit.* New York: Crown.

Mock, J. R., and C. Larson (1939). *Words that Won the War: The Story of the Committee on Public Information 1917-1919.* Princeton, N.J.: Princeton University Press.

Read, J. M. (1941). *Atrocity Propaganda, 1914-1919.* New Haven, Conn.: Yale University Press.

Rogers, E. (1983). *Diffusion of Innovations*, 3rd ed. New York: Free Press.

Schramm, W. (1971). The nature of communication between humans. In W. Schramm and D. Roberts (eds.), *The Process and Effects of Mass Communication*, rev. ed., pp. 3–53. Urbana: University of Illinois Press.

Scott, W. (1982). Personality parade. *Parade*, Nov. 14, p. 9.

—— (1986). Personality parade. *Parade*, June 15, p. 2.

Sherif, M. (1958). Group influences upon the formation of norms and attitudes. In E. E. Maccoby, T. M. Newcomb, and E. L. Hartley (eds.), *Readings in Social Psychology*, 3rd ed., pp. 219–232. New York: Holt, Rinehart, and Winston.

Simpson, C. (1972). *The Lusitania*. Boston: Little, Brown.

Stone, I. F. (1966). The provocations behind the Tonkin Gulf clash two years ago. *I. F. Stone's Weekly*, Sept. 12, p. 3.

—— (1968a). Special 8-page issue documenting the Tonkin Gulf fraud. *I. F. Stone's Weekly*, Mar. 4.

—— (1968b). *In a Time of Torment*. New York: Random House, Vintage Books.

Tindol, R. (1988). Capitalism by any other name. . . . *On Campus* (The University of Texas at Austin), June, p. 22.

Westheimer, R. (1990). Women know how to fight. *New York Times*, Feb. 10, p. 15.

7
The Measurement of Readability

Mass communication, which by definition attempts to reach the largest audience possible, should be committed to writing and other forms of expression that are as easy to understand as possible.

A newspaper editorial might be making the most important statement in the world, but if it is written so that a person needs a college education to understand it, it will go over the head of 80 percent of the population. The same principles apply to a magazine advertisement, a news story, an editorial page column, even the spoken messages on the broadcast media, although the evidence is less clear here.

What factors make writing easy to understand or difficult to understand? Can a method be developed to measure how easy or difficult it is to understand a piece of writing? The area of research that attempts to answer these questions is known as readability research.

The study of readability is important for two reasons. First, it may give us a way to measure the readability of written material. Readability refers to "ease of understanding or comprehension due to the style of writing" (Klare, 1963, p. 1). Ideally, one would like to find a simple formula for measuring readability. A useful formula of this type might involve making some simple counts in a book or news story and then doing some simple computations to get some kind of score. Of course, such a formula should be *reliable* and *valid*. There should be evidence that different applications of the formula (by different people, for instance) would give the same readability score, and there should be evidence that the score really measures ease or difficulty of understanding.

Second, the search for a formula could provide some information about the most important aspects of style influencing ease of understanding. This could lead to some helpful advice for writers. We would be in a position to say that we know certain factors make a real difference in understanding, and therefore a writer should pay some attention to them in his or her writing.

Some researchers have also been interested in measuring whether or not a piece of writing is interesting, but that turns out to be a different question from whether or not a piece of writing is easy to understand. For a while, researchers were trying to deal with both of these aspects, usually at the same time, but eventually they sorted them out. In the end, separate formulas were developed for measuring readability and interest.

The History of Readability Measurement

The term *readability formula* is used here, following Klare (1963), to mean "a method of estimating the probable success a reader will have in reading and understanding a piece of writing" (p. 34).

Although some interest in counting words can be traced back to biblical times, the first attempts to develop a readability formula were by educators involved in selecting reading material for both children and adults.

The first readability formula is usually attributed to Lively and Pressey (1923), although some earlier work by Sherman (1888) and Kitson (1921) dealt with factors that would later be important in formulas. Sherman and Kitson did not take the step of constructing a predictive formula, however.

Sherman published what appears to be the first investigation of sentence length, one of the elements often included in later readability formulas. He pointed out an interesting decline in the average sentence length of authors as one moves through the centuries from Chaucer to Emerson. Sherman did not relate sentence length to difficulty of understanding, however.

Kitson's work is significant because he came up with the very same two elements later used by Flesch and others in the modern readability formulas. Kitson was writing an advertising textbook, and he presented a measure of the "psychological differences" between periodicals. He compared publications on number of syllables per word and sentence length, the elements later used by Flesch and others. Kitson found that the percentage of words over two syllables long was 13.2 in the *Chicago Evening Post*, 7.7 in the *Chicago American*, 13.5 in *Century* magazine, and 9.9 in *American* magazine. He found that the percentage of sentences longer than 20 words was 49.0 for the *Post*, 43.4 for the *Chicago American*, 45.4 for *Century* magazine, and 33.5 for *American* magazine. Kitson was primarily interested in estimating the intellectual level of the public that a periodical served in order to help an advertiser choose a medium. He was not interested in measuring the reading difficulty of the material except as that was a measure of something else, and he did not develop a predictive formula.

The Lively and Pressey study—a frequent choice for the first readability formula—was based on the assumption, which was common among educators at that time, that vocabulary difficulty was a key factor in determining the difficulty of understanding for written material. They were concerned with the practical problem of selecting junior high school science textbooks. Many of these textbooks were so heavily laden with technical vocabulary that the teaching of the course almost became the teaching of vocabulary. They argued that it would be useful to have a means of measuring this "vocabulary burden." They also suggested that such a technique might be useful in measuring the vocabulary difficulty of supplementary reading, such as novels that might be assigned in addition to texts.

The Lively and Pressey formula rests on the key assumption that word difficulty is directly related to word frequency, with the most frequent words in the English language being the easiest to understand. The technique is based on E. L. Thorndike's *Teacher's Word Book* (1975), which rests on the same key assumption. Thorndike's book lists the 10,000 most common words in the English language with an index number beside each one. The more common the word, the higher the index number. For instance, the word *and* had an index number of 210 and the word *atom* had an index number of 4. Words that are so rare that they did not appear in the 10,000 most common are considered zero-value words.

The Lively and Pressey method was a good beginning, but it rested on the assumption that word frequency was the key element in determining difficulty of reading, and it did not provide much of a scale for interpreting scores. The scores were mostly interpretable in relation to other scores. If you studied two or more books, you could show that one scored as more difficult than another, but you couldn't give much meaning to a single score taken alone.

A more comprehensive look at the elements that might influence readability was published in 1935 by Gray and Leary under the title *What Makes a Book Readable*. These authors were particularly interested in the problem that many American adults were not reading widely and apparently found much of the available reading material too difficult.

Rather than assume that any one element was an adequate measure of difficulty of understanding of writing, Gray and Leary began their research with an exhaustive search aimed at finding all the possible elements that might influence readability. They began by surveying a number of librarians, publishers, and other persons interested in adult education. These experts were asked what elements they thought contributed to readability for adults of limited education. This produced a list of 289 elements. Some of these had to do with format, content, and general organization rather than style. When these were eliminated, the list had been pared down to 82 style elements. Some of these, such as "poetic and highly literary words," could not be objectively measured. When these were eliminated, 64 elements remained on the list. A preliminary investigation showed that only 44 of these occurred frequently enough to appear at least once in half the passages studied.

The next step of the research was to see which of these 44 elements correlated with a measure of the difficulty of various passages. Measures of the difficulty of several passages were available from paragraph meaning comprehension tests given to adults. These tests involve giving a person a paragraph to read and then immediately asking multiple-choice questions about the paragraph. If a paragraph is easy to read, more people will give the correct answer. This procedure can be used to assign a difficulty score to each paragraph. The correlations would show which of the 44 style elements vary systematically with the difficulty of the paragraph. For example, a correlation coefficient would express in one number whether or not there was a tendency for longer sentences to appear in paragraphs that were more difficult to understand. This stage of the research showed that 21 of the elements had significant correlations with difficulty as measured by paragraph meaning comprehension scores.

The final step was to boil these 21 down to a few that could be used in a mathematical formula that would measure difficulty. The most useful elements were selected on this basis: they had to correlate closely with average reading score, correlate relatively little among themselves, be readily recognizable, and give an adequate representation of known measures of difficulty.

The final Gray and Leary formula used five elements and looked like this:

$$X_1 = -.01029 \, X_2 + .009012 \, X_5 - .02094 \, X_6 - .03313 \, X_7 - .01485 \, X_8 + 3.774$$

where X_1 = reading score
       X_2 = number of different hard words (words not on a list of 756 easy words) in a passage of 100 words
       X_5 = number of first-, second-, and third-person pronouns
       X_6 = average sentence length in words
       X_7 = percentage of different words
       X_8 = number of prepositional phrases

The Readability Laboratory of Teachers College, Columbia University, became the scene of the next two important developments in readability measurement. This lab was set up by the American Association for Adult Education and focused on the problem of assessing reading materials for adults. Two of the researchers who worked there were Irving Lorge and Rudolf Flesch.

Lorge (1939) paved the way for the modern, streamlined formulas by suggesting that a two-element formula might work. He studied a number of two-element combinations and found a higher multiple correlation with reading comprehension scores for some of them than Gray and Leary had with their five-element formula. Combinations that worked well included number of prepositional phrases and number of different hard words (giving a multiple correlation of .7456), average sentence length and number of different hard words (.7406), and number of prepositional phrases and average sentence length (.6949).

Flesch set forth in his doctoral dissertation to develop a still better formula. He took as his starting point the finding that the Gray and Leary formula failed to indicate clear differences in readability beyond a certain level of difficulty. Research at the Readability Laboratory found that the Gray and Leary formula could not distinguish between mature English prose and what is known as "light reading." Flesch undoubtedly was influenced also by the finding of Lorge that a formula using only two elements could predict difficulty as accurately as a formula with five or more elements.

Flesch (1943) reasoned that the Gray and Leary formula did not measure readability at the adult level better because it relied too heavily on the use of uncommon words as a measure and that this element is really not that important with adults. Flesch turned to linguistic theory and other research on reading ability for some clues about other elements that might be important. These theories suggested that "seeing verbal relationships, logic, ideas, meaning" might be an important element in adult reading that was left out of earlier formulas. Flesch interpreted this as "abstract reasoning," and tried to find a way to measure it. One method he tried was to count the number of abstract words. Gray and Leary had considered this factor but had dropped it because of the difficulty of getting agreement on whether or not a word is abstract. Flesch came up with a solution by creating his own list of 13,918 abstract words. However, he found in further research that counting the number of affixes (additions placed at the beginning or end of words) was just as good a measure of abstraction, so he dropped the abstract word count.

Flesch kept the sentence length measure that had been used by Gray and Leary and others because it appeared to be a good measure of readability at both the children's level and the adult level. And he included a count of personal words because Lyman Bryson, the director of the Readability Laboratory, said that "appeal" was an important part of readability. Gray and Leary had included a count of personal pronouns in their formula. Flesch decided to disregard all neuter pronouns and count all words referring to people either by names or by words meaning people. He was assuming that human interest was the most important part of appeal and that the types of words he classified as "personal references" would correlate with human interest.

The result of this research was the first Flesch readability formula:

$$X = .133 \, X_S + .0645 \, X_M - .0659 \, X_H - .7502$$

where X = reading score
       X_S = average sentence length in words
       X_M = number of affixes within a 100-word sample
       X_H = number of personal references within a 100-word sample

The resulting score could be looked up on a chart that would supply either a verbal description of style such as "very easy" or a school grade level of the potential audience.

Flesch showed that his formula produced a multiple correlation coefficient of .7358 with paragraph meaning comprehension test scores, an improvement over the multiple correlation coefficient of .6435 that Gray and Leary obtained with five elements.

Flesch went on to popularize and publicize his formula probably more than any other readability researcher. His dissertation, *Marks of a Readable Style,* was published as a book. Flesch himself said that since it was a Ph.D. dissertation it "was not a very readable book." He rewrote it in a simplified version, and the result was published in 1946 as *The Art of Plain Talk.*

Soon after the publication of *The Art of Plain Talk,* two psychologists applied the Flesch readability formula to a group of standard psychology textbooks (Stevens & Stone, 1947a). Their results indicated an unexpectedly high readability score for Kurt Koffka's *Principles of Gestalt Psychology,* a book regarded by graduate students as notoriously difficult. In fact, Koffka scored higher than William James, a textbook author that students thought relatively easy. Stevens and Stone explained that this appeared to be true because of the high number of personal pronouns Koffka used. Flesch was apparently provoked to action by the results concerning Koffka and James, for he wrote Stevens and Stone that he was working on a revision of his formula (Stevens & Stone, 1947b).

The Flesch Formulas

Flesch indicated that he was working on a new formula element that was the "percentage of nondeclarative sentences," and that this element correctly indicated that James was more readable than Koffka. Flesch did come out with a revised formula the following year, but it did not contain the "percentage of nondeclarative sentences." Instead, Flesch (1948) had dropped the count of "personal references" from the readability formula and used it to create a new "human interest" formula. Another change was that the count of affixes in the readability formula had been replaced by a measure of word length, the number of syllables per 100 words. The results were two formulas, the reading ease formula and the human interest formula, both still in use today.

The reading ease formula is as follows:

$$R.E. = 206.835 - .846 \, wl - 1.015 \, sl$$

where   R.E. = reading ease score
   wl = number of syllables per 100 words
   sl = average number of words per sentence

The resulting score should range between 0 and 100 and can be looked up in a chart such as the one presented in Table 7.1.

The human interest formula is as follows:

$$H.I. = 3.635 \, pw + .314 \, ps$$

where   H.I. = human interest score
   pw = number of personal words per 100 words
   ps = number of personal sentences per 100 sentences

The resulting score should fall between 0 and 100 and can be looked up in a chart such as the one in Table 7.2.

The Flesch reading ease formula has proved to be the most widely used readability formula (Klare, 1963). It was popularized in a book published in 1949—*The Art of Readable Writing.*

The Flesch reading ease formula has produced a number of useful offshoots. The Gunning fog index, developed by Robert Gunning (1952), is based on two elements: average sentence length in words and number of words of three syllables or more per 100 words. These two numbers are added and multiplied by .4, and the resulting number is the approximate grade level at which the material can be read. When Gunning began his consulting work with newspapers, he was using the original Flesch formula that counted affixes (Gunning, 1945), and the formula that he later developed resembles the reading ease formula. At the earlier stage in Gunning's career, the term *fog index* also had a different meaning—it referred to a "measure of uselessly long and complex words" (p. 12). The main advantage of the Gunning fog index over the Flesch reading ease formula is that the former

Table 7.1
CHART FOR INTERPRETING FLESCH READING EASE SCORES

Reading Ease Score	Description of Style	Estimated Reading Grade
90–100	Very easy	5th grade
80–90	Easy	6th grade
70–80	Fairly easy	7th grade
60–70	Standard	8th and 9th grade
50–60	Fairly difficult	10th to 12th grade
30–50	Difficult	college
0–30	Very difficult	college graduate

Table 7.2

CHART FOR INTERPRETING FLESCH HUMAN INTEREST SCORES

Human Interest Score	*Description of Style*
0–10	Dull
10–20	Mildly interesting
20–40	Interesting
40–60	Highly interesting
60–100	Dramatic

Table (Page 179) from *The Art of Readable Writing* by Rudolf Flesch. Copyright 1949, 1974 by Rudolf Flesch. Reprinted by permission of HarperCollins Publishers Inc.

gives a grade level immediately while a reading ease score has to be looked up in a table to produce a grade level.

In another step of simplification, Wayne Danielson and Sam Dunn Bryan (1963) developed a computerized readability formula in which the computer does the counts and the computations and gives a readability score. The formula is based on two elements that are similar to the two in the Flesch reading ease formula except that they are defined in units that the computer can recognize easily. They are: average number of characters per space (essentially a measure of word length) and average number of characters per sentence (essentially a measure of sentence length). The resulting score is very much like a reading ease score and in fact can be looked up on the Flesch reading ease chart.

Initially, in order to use the Danielson and Bryan computerized formula, you had to have the written material you wanted to analyze punched on cards, paper tape, or some other means of input that the computer could read. In some cases, this required keyboarding by hand. But in the case of wire copy such as that provided by the Associated Press, the hand keyboarding was not necessary. Wire copy is normally available in the form of punched paper tapes that can be used to operate a typesetting machine in a newspaper building. Danielson discovered that it was necessary to modify the tape punching machine only slightly for the paper tapes to be read directly into a computer. This allowed him to study the readability of the Associated Press output for a week without keyboarding the material. Today most wire service copy is transmitted as electrical impulses to be stored in computer memory banks, making it easy to apply computerized readability formulas to it.

Also available are tables that eliminate the computation necessary to apply the Flesch reading ease and human interest formulas (Farr & Jenkins, 1949). To determine the reading ease score of a sample, you simply look up the average sentence length at the side of the table and the number of syllables per 100 words across the top of the table. Where the row and the column intersect can be found the reading ease score. A similar table for the human interest score has percentage of personal sentences at the side and percentage of personal words across the top.

Using a Formula

An example will help to bring out exactly how the Flesch reading ease formula can be applied to a piece of writing. We will take a sample of writing and make the necessary counts and do the computations to come up with a reading ease score.

Before we begin, we need to present exact definitions of some of the things we will be counting. Flesch defines a word as a letter, number, symbol, or group of letters, numbers, or symbols surrounded by white space. Thus, *1949, C.O.D.,* and *unself-conscious* would all be counted as words. Flesch defines a sentence as a unit of thought that is grammatically independent and is usually marked by a period, question mark, exclamation point, semi-colon, colon, or dash. Syllables are counted the way you would pronounce the word. For example, *1916* would count as a four-syllable word. Since you need to find the number of syllables per 100 words, one shortcut that is sometimes useful is to start by writing down 100 and then count only the words of two syllables or more, writing down a 1 for a two-syllable word, a 2 for a three-syllable word, and so forth. Then you simply add all the numbers you have written down, including the 100. This can often save time because many words have only one syllable. Writing down the number of syllables for each word permits you to go back and check your work.

Now we are ready to apply the reading ease formula to the following sample—the beginning paragraphs of a news story written by a student.

> The Texas Water Rights Commission (TWRC) voted Tuesday to allow the South Texas Nuclear Project the use of Colorado River water despite a warning from Atty. Gen. John Hill that such action could result in state instituted court proceedings against TWRC.
>
> Hill's warning came at the commission's meeting, after he advised it that the Lower Colorado River Authority (LCRA) had no control over the unallocated waters involved in a debate between LCRA and TWRC and should not be paid for the use of them.
>
> The debate stemmed from a dispute between TWRC, which controls all the unallocated water in the state, and LCRA, which has power over all Colorado River water within a 10-county area, over who would profit from sale of the water.

This sample is more than 100 words long, so it is adequate to illustrate the workings of the formula, although you would probably measure the entire story if you were seriously attempting to determine its readability.

First, it is necessary to determine the average sentence length (sl). Remember that *LCRA, TWRC* and *10-county* should count as one word each. The sample contains 3 sentences and 124 words. Dividing 124 by 3 gives an average sentence length of 41.33 words.

Next, it is necessary to determine the number of syllables per 100 words (wl). The easiest way to determine this is to count the syllables in the first 100 words. The 100th word is the word *the* before the word *state* in the third paragraph. The only tricky parts in counting the syllables might be the word *TWRC,* which includes six syllables when it is pronounced, and the words *Atty.* and *Gen.,* which include three syllables each when pronounced in full. The number of syllables in the first 100 words is 189.

Next, we substitute these numbers for *sl* and *wl* in the reading ease formula, and obtain the following:

R.E. = 206.835 − .846 (189) − 1.015 (41.33)

Performing the two multiplications gives the following:

R.E. = 206.835 − 159.894 − 41.950

And doing the final subtractions gives 4.991, the reading ease score. This is a very low reading ease score. In the reading ease chart in Table 7.1, it falls in the "very difficult" category, where the estimated reading grade is "college graduate." This is understandable when we look at the long sentences used, the acronyms (*LCRA* and *TWRC*), and the use of complicated terms (*unallocated water*). Of course, if the entire story had been analyzed, the reading ease score might have been higher. News writers often attempt to pack a great deal of information into the beginning of a news story, and this can make the beginning less readable than the rest of the story. This practice can be questioned, however; if the beginning of the story is not readable, people might not get to the later sections.

Applications of Readability Formulas

Readability measurement has been used in a number of areas, including textbook evaluation, analysis of mass communication, writing for new literates, and improving corporate and government documents. We turn now to some of these applications.

Textbook Evaluation

The main reason Lively and Pressey and some of the other pioneers developed their measures of readability was to help in textbook selection. Gray and Leary had a similar purpose—the selection of suitable books for adult readers.

Extending the idea of textbook evaluation to college texts, Stevens and Stone (1947a, 1947b) used Flesch's first formula to study 18 psychology textbooks. They found that most of the ratings agreed pretty well with student assessments of difficulty, except for the problem we have discussed—Koffka's book received a score of higher readability than William James's.

Researchers following in the footsteps of Stevens and Stone have used Flesch formulas to study the readability of psychology texts (Gillen, 1973; Cone, 1976), educational psychology texts (Hofmann & Vyhonsky, 1975), and journalism texts (Tankard & Tankard, 1977). The latter study of nine books using the reading ease formula showed five were in the "difficult" range, two were in the "fairly difficult" range, and two were in the "standard" range. The human interest formula placed one journalism text in the "dull" category, three in the "mildly interesting" category, and five in the "interesting" category.

One professor using the first edition of this book selected 50 random samples of 100 words each and had 50 students apply the Flesch reading ease formula to them. The results, for the total sample, indicated a mean sentence length of 23.73 words, 168.15 syllables per 100 words, and a reading ease score of 40.49. As Table 7.1 indicates, this puts the score in the middle of the college level.

Readability formulas are also being used by a number of college textbook publishers to make sure texts are not being written at too difficult a level. Some of these publishers have recently been criticized for placing too much reliance on readability formulas to make texts easy to understand (Fiske, 1987). Critics say the formulas encourage choppy writing that fails to challenge students. Readability formulas, like any tool, can be misused. It seems clear that the mechanical application of a formula can never take away the need for human judgment and will never solve all the problems of textbook development.

Newspapers and Wire Services

Soon after Flesch's first formula was published in 1943, Robert Gunning began applying it in consulting work for newspapers (Gunning, 1945). He studied the readability of eight newspapers in 1944 and concluded, "Today's newspapers are offering the public some of the most difficult reading material published" (p. 2).

Several readability experts—including Gunning, Flesch, and Danielson—have served as consultants to the major wire services. Gunning worked with United Press in the 1940s and reported that "within three weeks the reading difficulty of U.P. copy had been cut by five grade levels" (1945, p. 2).

Flesch and Danielson have served at different times as consultants to the Associated Press. Flesch studied the AP news report from 1948 to 1950. In keeping with his formulas, Flesch recommended that AP writers use short sentences, short words, and human interest writing.

Readability studies going back to some of the earliest (Lively & Pressey, 1923; Gray & Leary, 1935) have often included newspapers as a base of comparison. Typically the newspapers have not scored as the easiest material being considered. In the Lively and Pressey study, for instance, the newspaper studied had the largest vocabulary range of all materials studied. Gray and Leary found that newspapers contained a longer median sentence length (measured in syllables) than general magazines or books.

Charles Seib, the ombudsman of the *Washington Post,* conducted a nonscholarly but informative study of sentence length, one of the two elements in the popular readability formulas. Seib (1976) found the average sentence length on the front pages of three newspapers on a Sunday to be as follows: *Washington Star,* 31 words; *New York Times,* 33 words; *Washington Post,* 38 words. By contrast, he found the average sentence length for several popular books to be as follows: Saul Bellow's *Humbolt's Gift,* just under 12 words; Woody Allen's *Without Feathers,* just over 12 words; Jimmy Breslin's *How the Good Guys Won,* under 11 words. Seib concluded, "News stories can't be judged on the same basis as fiction or even Breslin's free-style journalism. But an average of over 30 words per sentence is too much for comfortable reading. Particularly when the tube is waiting just across the room" (p. B25).

As Seib's analysis points out, readability research can be used to formulate some advice for journalists. That advice would be to use short sentences and short words. Flesch has been even more specific in his advice about sentence length: he has recommended to the AP that newswriters use an average sentence length of 19 words. Several popular magazines are already doing a good job of following his advice—the average sentence length a number of years ago in *Time* and *Reader's Digest* was 17 words or less (Gunning, 1952).

Research has also shown that the readability level of a newspaper article has a definite effect on how much of the article will be read. Swanson (1948) conducted a controlled field experiment to determine the effect of readability on readership. Two versions of the same story were produced—one with a Flesch reading ease score of 49.84 (difficult) and the other with a reading ease score of 84.94 (easy). Then two versions of an experimental campus newspaper were produced—one with the difficult story and one with the easy story. In a "trailer village" where married students lived, one version was delivered to odd-numbered trailers and the other to even-numbered trailers. Interviewers arrived within 30 hours to ask the adult male at each trailer about his readership of every paragraph in the paper. The mean number of paragraphs read was 13 for the "difficult" story and 24 for the "easy" story. The story with the greatest reading ease had nearly twice as many paragraphs read, on the average, as the story with the difficult readability.

240 Years of Novels

Danielson and Lasorsa (1989) studied stylistic variables in 240 novels covering a 240-year time span, and found a definite relationship between four stylistic factors and the passage of time. They found a tendency for more recent novels to have fewer words per sentence (see Figure 7.1), a smaller percentage of long words, a smaller percentage of rare punctuation, and a greater degree of informality (as measured by number of contractions using apostrophes). At least two of these factors, average sentence length and average word length, are typically found in readability formulas, and therefore the results suggest that novels are becoming more readable. Danielson and Lasorsa (1989) offer the following speculation as to why this might have occurred:

> Does our faster paced life demand shorter sentences? Has the rise of photography, motion pictures, and television influenced prose styles? Are writers today less capable of producing elaborate, detailed sentences than were their literary forebears? Are today's readers less skilled in decoding extended and involved expressions than were their grandparents or their great-grandparents? Is modern style a reflection of the democratization of society and the decline of class distinctions in the written word? We tend toward the latter interpretation, but realize the difficulty of establishing anything resembling proof. (p. 197)

News Releases

Thomas Haven Miller (1984) used computerized Flesch reading ease and Danielson-Bryan formulas to study the readability of computer industry news releases. The average

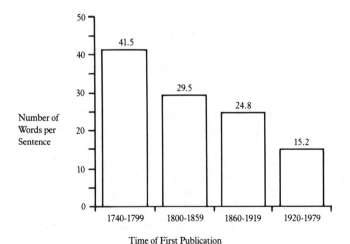

Time of First Publication

FIGURE 7.1 • AVERAGE SENTENCE LENGTH IN NOVELS FOR FOUR TIME PERIODS

Adapted from W. A. Danielson and D. L. Lasorsa, "A New Readability Formula Based on the Stylistic Age of Novels," *Journal of Reading* 33, no. 3 (1989): 194–197.

reading ease score for releases was 25.5 on Flesch's 100-point scale—a score in the "very difficult" range. Releases from computer hardware companies (with a reading ease score of 31.8) were slightly more readable than those from companies making peripherals (27.9), companies making software (27.3), or a category of "other" companies (16.8), which were involved in fiberoptic cable, office equipment, training manuals, copiers, and accounting machines. Miller found no relationship between size of the company and readability of the news release.

Advertising Copy

A study of the readability of advertisements found a relationship between readability score of the ad copy and how many people recalled seeing the ad. Wesson (1989) acquired recall measures obtained by Starch-Hooper research for all the advertisements in selected issues of *Sports Illustrated, Woman's Day,* and *Reader's Digest.* He then computed Gunning fog index scores for the copy in the advertisements. Finally, he looked at the relationship between the recall measures and the readability scores. The relationship he found was a curvilinear one in the form of a U-shaped curve, with the greatest recall for low readability scores and high readability scores. Wesson expected to find the greatest recall for low readability scores, but he did not expect that recall would also be high for high readability scores. He speculated that reading the more difficult text required greater cognitive involvement in the form of attention in processing the message.

Broadcast News

Leonard Arthur Stevens (1949) wanted to know whether readability formulas were also applicable to material that was going to be spoken, as in a radio news broadcast. He conducted an investigation of the "hearability" of written prose. Stevens conducted an experiment in which two groups of subjects were each exposed to six news stories. One group read the stories from written pages, while the other group heard recordings of the stories with a competent newscaster doing the reading. Subjects in each condition were then tested for comprehension with a set of multiple-choice test questions that covered the six stories. Overall, Stevens found no significant differences in comprehension between the two modes—reading and hearing. Stevens concluded that these findings indicate that the Flesch reading ease formula can be used to measure "hearability" as well as readability.

Corporate Annual Reports

Several researchers have examined the readability of corporate annual reports. One study examined the annual reports produced by the 24 top corporations in the *Fortune* 500 directory (Hoskins, 1984). The Flesch reading ease formula was applied to three samples of 100 words taken from the "overview section" of each report. This should be the most readable since it is intended for a wide and varied audience. Four were rated "very difficult," 19 rated "difficult," and only 1 fell into the "fairly difficult" category. The researcher concluded that the general overview section of the corporate annual reports was "not more readable than the annual report as a whole, including the complicated financial section."

However, an oil company official, when asked to comment on the findings, said of his own company's annual report, "The portfolio managers and investment counselors who make these large investment decisions and the institutional and brokerage analysts who closely follow the petroleum industry constitute the real readership for this report." He added that he hoped the individual shareholder would read "the chairman's report."

The researcher then drew additional 200-word samples from the chairman's letter from each of the annual reports. They were found to be somewhat more readable than the general overview sections, but nevertheless 3 were still rated "very difficult," 16 "difficult," 2 "fairly difficult," and only 3 were rated "standard" on the Flesch scale.

Two other researchers (Heath & Phelps, 1984) compared the readability of annual reports with the business press. They argue that annual reports should help raise slumping public confidence in corporate leadership and ethical performance. The annual report should, according to them, remind "shareholders of the virtues of free enterprise and the pitfalls of unwise regulation."

They cited a Bureau of Census report that of the nearly 30 million people who are shareholders, 65 percent have not completed college and 34 percent have no college education. The authors say these 30 million shareholders and the people they influence are a sizable population with a vested interest in the success of corporations.

Annual reports of 20 companies randomly selected from the *Fortune* 500 list were used. Samples of 200 words from each of three sections (president's letter, general text, and notes on the financial statement) were measured with Gunning's fog index. The researchers found that the readability of the "reports exceeds the level appropriate for a majority of the shareholders, based on Bureau of Census data. . . . the level of even the most readable section would be difficult for at least 50 percent of the readers. In contrast, the readability level of business publications corresponds to that of a high school junior. . . . " The researchers conclude, "At a time when several billion dollars are spent annually on corporate image and issue campaigns, the least that can be done is to create a readable report" (p. 61).

Readability of Documents

Collective Bargaining Agreements   Two researchers (Suchan & Scott, 1986) examined three clauses from each of 196 collective bargaining agreements. Five variables used to measure readability were taken from the Flesch reading ease score, the Farr-Jenkins-Patterson (1951) reading ease index, and the Gunning fog index.

Suchan and Scott found that 95 to 99 percent of the agreements would be either "difficult" or "very difficult" for the rank and file to understand, according to the Flesch and Farr-Jenkins-Paterson formulas. According to the Gunning fog index the score was 18.73, meaning it would take nearly 19 years of education, a college degree and three years of graduate school, to unscramble a typical union-management agreement.

The researchers observe, "Most negotiators inhabit a semantic world different from that of the rank and file's." They go on to say:

> Is it any wonder that workers are often suspicious of the contracts they've ratified, the contracts that control many of their job rights and working conditions? They are probably unsure of what the contracts mean and angered at having to rely on union or management representatives to explain contract provisions. . . . The tangled language in the agreements we examined undercuts rather than aids the formation or maintenance of a coherent company value system. Instead of feeling a shared purpose with management, workers, confronted with unreadable agreements, feel cut off, isolated from management, and ultimately distrustful of those who wear white collars. (pp. 22–23)

The researchers conclude:

A contract written in plain English could save management money by avoiding unnecessary grievances, costly arbitration hearings, and even work stoppages caused by worker discontent over a misinterpreted contract provision. (p. 25)

Homeowner's Insurance Policies   The Texas State Board of Insurance put a task force to work to simplify its standard insurance form (Hight, 1990). The old form, unchanged for 30 years, required at least a ninth grade education. It had an average sentence length of 46 words. Task force chairman Don Olsen said it took "a country lawyer to interpret (p. A6)." The task force simplified the vocabulary and grammatical structure and reduced the length of sentences. The new version had an average sentence length of fewer than 20 words and was readable with a seventh grade education.

Adult Literacy in the United States   A national survey indicated how difficult documents such as income tax forms and insurance policies must be for a majority of the population. In 1986 the Department of Education released the findings of a study dealing with U.S. literacy, called "the most comprehensive of its kind ever undertaken." The random sample of 3,600 subjects was drawn from the population aged 21 to 25 years old. The subjects were asked to perform a variety of tasks requiring increasing levels of comprehension and sophistication during a 90-minute examination in each home.

It was concluded that 95 percent of all young adults can read as well as the average fourth grader. However, one-fifth of all young adults could not read beyond the eighth grade level, and the proportion for minority group members was far higher.

In the area of prose literacy (for example, reading and interpreting news reports, magazines, and books), less than 40 percent could understand a "somewhat difficult" newspaper article and fewer than 11 out of 100 young adults could deal with the most demanding material. For blacks the figure drops to less than 1 in 100, and is only about 3 in 100 for Hispanics.

In using information in documents such as charts, maps, and tables, less than 60 percent could read a paragraph in the documents and the "most challenging" tasks were accomplished by fewer than 25 in 100 young adults. The survey found that only one out of five young adults can use a bus schedule and select correct departures and arrivals (Werner, 1986).

While the survey showed that much remains to be done regarding literacy education, it also provides valuable information for communicators. Material written beyond the eighth grade level is above that of 20 percent of the adult population and "somewhat difficult" newspaper articles will probably exclude more than 60 percent of the adult population. The percentages are far higher for some of the groups in the population a communicator may wish to reach.

The "most challenging" tasks in using documents were found to be beyond the capabilities of 75 percent of the adult white population, 93 percent of the Hispanic population, and 99 percent of the black population. It is clear that communicators must take extreme care when designing maps, charts, tables, and other materials, including income tax forms and insurance policies, for mass audiences.

Cloze Procedure

A very different approach to measuring readability has been introduced by communication scholar Wilson L. Taylor (1953). He noticed that readability formulas had a weakness in that their basic assumptions could be contradicted. Most of the formulas are based on the assumption that a short word is easier to understand than a long word. Yet anyone can think of examples in which that would not be true. The word *erg* is shorter than the word *respectability,* but most people would not know the meaning of *erg* while they would know the meaning of *respectability.* If a sample of writing had a lot of words of this type that violated the assumptions of the formulas, the formulas would give very misleading readability scores.

Taylor invented another procedure for measuring readability that he says measures *all* the potential elements influencing readability. He called this method "cloze procedure." The name is based on the word *closure,* which stands for the human tendency to complete a familiar but incomplete pattern.

To use cloze procedure, you take the sample of writing you are interested in and "mutilate" it by replacing some of the words with blanks. This can be done in different ways, but a common way is just to replace every fifth word with a blank. Then the mutilated passage is given to a test group of subjects who are asked to fill in the missing words. The cloze score becomes the number or percentage of blanks that are filled in correctly. The simplest scoring procedure is to count only the exact word and not synonyms. Attempting to count synonyms introduces a subjective element into the scoring and slows it down considerably.

The theory behind cloze procedure is, in its most basic form, the notion that the simpler a piece of writing is, the easier it will be for a test reader to replace the missing words. Putting it another way, cloze procedure measures the extent to which a sample of prose is written in the patterns that a reader is naturally anticipating. And these patterns can involve all the different factors that might influence readability—overall organization, sentence structure, appropriateness of vocabulary, simplicity of vocabulary, and so forth.

We can also think of cloze procedure as a measure of *redundancy* (see Chapter 3). The more redundant a piece of writing is, the easier it will be for someone to fill in the blanks. Two communication scholars, in an article about information theory, recently commented that cloze procedure "is also an ingenious method to distinguish highly informative words (those that are difficult to predict) from highly redundant ones (those that are easily guessed)." They added, "Thus, cloze scores have come to be used not only as an indication of the readability of a prose passage relative to a particular audience, but also as an indication of comprehension for individuals within that audience" (Finn & Roberts, 1984, p. 464).

Taylor did not just assume that his method measured readability, but provided some evidence of its validity. First he showed that his procedure ranked passages very similarly to the Flesch reading ease formula and other orthodox formulas when the passages studied were "standard."

Then Taylor devised an "acid test" for cloze procedure: could it give a more trustworthy rating of readability for material that might fool the readability formulas? The kind of material he needed was written prose that might violate a lot of the assumptions basic to the formulas. Taylor decided that this kind of material could be found in two novels recognized by literary critics as being highly experimental—James Joyce's *Finnegans Wake* and Gertrude Stein's *Geography and Plays.* Taylor set up a test in which both Flesch reading ease scores and cloze procedure scores would be determined for passages from these two experimental novels and six other, more standard books. Taylor predicted that the reading ease scores would indicate that the Joyce and Stein were easy reading because they contain short words and short sentences, even though critics find both books difficult to read.

Cloze procedure, in contrast, was expected to rank the two experimental novels as more difficult than the other six books. In the cloze procedure for this test, Taylor deleted every seventh word in a passage from each book until he had 25 deletions for each book. Each passage was read by 18 subjects, giving a possible total cloze score for each book of 18 × 25, or 450. The results of the test are summarized in Table 7.3.

The Flesch reading ease scores indicate that the Stein passage is the easiest of the eight, and that the Joyce is somewhere in the middle. These scores fall in the "very easy" and "fairly easy" categories. In contrast, the cloze scores rank the Stein and Joyce selections seventh and eighth in difficulty. This supports Taylor's argument that in the case of written material that violates the assumptions of the formulas, cloze procedure would give a truer indication of reading difficulty than the formulas.

Cloze scores are probably easiest to interpret when two or more samples of writing are being compared. Then the several passages can be tested on the same group of subjects, and the passages can be ranked according to difficulty. The passages with the highest average cloze scores are the easiest ones and the passages with the lowest cloze scores are the most difficult.

Meaning can also be assigned to individual cloze scores. Rankin and Culhane (1969), extending earlier work by Bormuth (1968), have developed a scale for interpreting cloze scores. Their research indicates that a cloze score of 61 percent or higher shows the material is at the "independent level" of reading, a score of 41 percent or higher shows the material is at the "instructional level" of reading, and a score below 41 percent indicates the material is too difficult to be used with that particular class.

Cloze procedure is coming into some general use, although it is not yet being used as widely as the formulas. Kincaid and Gamble (1977) used cloze to study automobile insurance policies rewritten by the Nationwide and Sentry companies to be more readable. The cloze scores showed that the rewritten policies were easier to understand than standard policies used by the same companies.

Table 7.3

COMPARISONS OF FLESCH READING EASE SCORES AND
CLOZE PROCEDURE SCORES FOR SAMPLES FROM EIGHT BOOKS

Work	Reading Ease Score	Rank by Reading Ease Score	Cloze Score	Rank by Cloze Score
Stein, *Geography and Plays*	96	1	123	7
Boswell, *Life of Johnson*	89	2	186	3
Swift, *Gulliver's Travels*	80	3	170	4
Caldwell, *Georgia Boy*	79	4.5	336	1
Joyce, *Finnegans Wake*	79	4.5	49	8
Dickens, *Bleak House*	69	6	263	2
Huxley, *Man Stands Alone*	68	7	155	5
James, *The Ambassadors*	47	8	135	6

Adapted from W. L. Taylor, "'Cloze Procedure': A New Tool for Measuring Readability," *Journalism Quarterly* 30 (1953): 428. Reprinted by permission.

Seth Finn (1985) applied cloze procedure and Shannon's entropy formula to test unpredictability in news articles as a correlate of reader enjoyment. Nine articles (taken from five magazines, three newspapers, and one wire service), all dealing with the Apollo moonwalk of July 20, 1969, were rated by 144 college students. Each student read one article and indicated reader enjoyment on a seven-point scale. Another group of 144 comparable students then filled in blanks in a cloze procedure test of the same articles (with every eighth word deleted). He concluded that reader enjoyment of the articles related to both syntactic and semantic unpredictability (see Table 7.4).

Zinkhan and Blair (1984), two marketing researchers, applied cloze procedure to copy-test advertising. In six separate applications they tested two print advertisements, one for a brand of ice cream and another for a brand of camera; two promotional letters, one for a hotel and one for a trade show; and two radio commercials, one for a mayoral candidate and one for a cola drink. They concluded that cloze procedure is able to discriminate between two relatively effective messages aimed at a given target audience. They add, "The versatility and uniqueness of this instrument make it attractive. No other readability measure so effectively captures the interaction of the reader with passage as does the cloze procedure" (p. 408).

Cloze procedure has also been used in a group setting as a method of reading and language instruction. With this approach, a small group of students discusses a cloze passage and tries to work together to fill in the blanks. Working with language in the cloze format can help elementary students develop more precise understanding of words and concepts. Jacobson (1990) gave a cloze passage to students during one class period to fill in the blanks individually, and then at the following class period gave them the same passage to work on in cooperative learning groups. Group scores were overwhelmingly higher than scores of any individuals in the group. Perhaps more surprisingly, groups were sometimes able to correctly fill in a blank that no member of the group had been able to fill in correctly while

Table 7.4

RATINGS OF READER ENJOYMENT AND UNPREDICTABILITY
SCORES FOR NINE SAMPLE ARTICLES

Publication or Source	Reader Enjoyment	Function-Word Unpredictability	Content-Word Unpredictability
Time	5.69	1.08	2.42
Associated Press	5.38	1.05	1.89
New York Times	5.25	.98	2.00
Newsweek	5.19	1.11	2.29
Reader's Digest	5.19	1.04	2.12
Life (Edwin Aldrin)	5.13	1.32	2.28
Life (Neil Armstrong)	4.38	1.17	2.00
St. Louis Post-Dispatch	4.25	1.25	1.88
San Francisco Examiner	4.19	1.54	2.31

From Seth Finn, "Unpredictability as a Correlate of Reader Enjoyment of News Articles," *Journalism Quarterly* 62, no. 2 (1985): 334–339, 345. Reprinted with permission.

working individually. This finding illustrates the effectiveness of the group cloze procedure technique in sharpening the precision of student understanding of words and concepts.

Conclusions

The most obvious use for readability formulas is in measuring the difficulty of samples of writing. They do this quickly and with a fairly high degree of accuracy, and they are being used in many different fields.

The following general guidelines might help in selecting a readability formula. The Flesch reading ease formula is the most widely used. The easiest formula to apply, according to Klare (1963), is that of Farr, Jenkins, and Paterson (1951). This formula is based on average sentence length and number of one-syllable words per 100 words. The most accurate formula, also according to Klare, is the Dale and Chall (1948). This formula is based on average sentence length and the percentage of words outside the Dale list of 3,000 easy words. Klare reports that the Dale and Chall formula predicts reading comprehension scores more reliably than any of the other popular formulas.

Readability formulas are also useful in providing us with some solid evidence about which elements make writing easy or difficult to understand. The two most important elements, identified through a series of studies building on one another, are vocabulary burden and sentence complexity. We can translate this into advice for writers and editors and recommend that they use short words and short sentences.

Flesch has recommended that newswriters use an average sentence length of 19 words. That does not mean that every sentence has to be exactly that length. Some variety in sentence length is usually more pleasing than having all sentences the same length. But it means that in newswriting, 19 words is a good average length to aim for over a number of sentences.

Not everyone who reads this chapter has to become a champion of readability formulas. But we hope that not many readers will take on the attitude of the distinguished newspaper writer who bragged that he used to write 70-word sentences as a protest because the newspaper he worked for "was enamored of this guy Rudolf Flesch." This kind of attitude may be appropriate if you are interested in writing only for a small minority of the elite in our society, but if you are attempting to reach the largest audience possible, it is foolhardy.

References

Bormuth, J. R. (1968). Cloze test readability: Criterion reference scores. *Journal of Educational Measurement* 5: 190–196.

Cone, A. L. (1976). Six luxury models. *Contemporary Psychology* 21: 544–548.

Dale, E., and J. S. Chall (1948). A formula for predicting readability. *Educational Research Bulletin* 27: 11–20, 37–54.

Danielson, W. A., and S. D. Bryan (1963). Computer automation of two readability formulas. *Journalism Quarterly* 40: 201–206.

Danielson, W. A., and D. L. Lasorsa (1989). A new readability formula based on the stylistic age of novels. *Journal of Reading* 33, no. 3: 194–197.

Farr, J. N., and J. J. Jenkins (1949). Tables for use with the Flesch readability formulas. *Journal of Applied Psychology* 33: 275–278.

Farr, J. N., J. J. Jenkins, and D. G. Paterson (1951). Simplification of Flesch reading ease formula. *Journal of Applied Psychology* 35: 333–337.

Finn, S. (1985). Unpredictability as a correlate of reader enjoyment of news articles. *Journalism Quarterly* 62: 334–339, 345.

Finn, S., and D. F. Roberts (1984). Source, destination, and entropy: Reassessing the role of information theory in communication research. *Communication Research* 11: 453–476.

Fiske, E. B. (1987). The push for smarter schoolbooks. *New York Times*, Aug. 2, education supplement, pp. 20–23.

Flesch, R. (1943). *Marks of a Readable Style: A Study in Adult Education*. New York: Teachers College, Columbia University.

——— (1946). *The Art of Plain Talk*. New York: Harper & Row.

——— (1948). A New Readability Yardstick. *Journal of Applied Psychology* 32: 221–233.

——— (1974). *The Art of Readable Writing*. Rev. ed. New York: Harper & Row.

Gillen, B. (1973). Readability and human interest scores of thirty-four current introductory psychology texts. *American Psychologist* 28: 1010–1011.

Gray, W. S., and B. E. Leary (1935). *What Makes a Book Readable with Special Reference to Adults of Limited Reading Ability: An Initial Study*. Chicago: University of Chicago Press.

Gunning, R. (1945). Gunning finds papers too hard to read. *Editor & Publisher*, May 19, p. 12.

——— (1952). *The Technique of Clear Writing*. New York: McGraw-Hill.

Heath, R., and G. Phelps (1984). Annual reports II: Readability of reports vs. business press. *Public Relations Review*, Summer, pp. 56–62.

Hight, B. (1990). Legal ease: New homeowners' insurance policy reduces overwritten underwriting. *Austin American-Statesman*, Feb. 20, pp. A1, A6.

Hofmann, R. J., and R. J. Vyhonsky (1975). Readability and human interest scores of thirty-six recently published introductory educational psychology texts. *American Psychologist* 30: 790–792.

Hoskins, R. (1984). Annual reports I: Difficult reading and getting more so. *Public Relations Review*, Summer, pp. 49–55.

Jacobson, J. M. (1990). Group vs. individual completion of a cloze passage. *Journal of Reading* 33: 244–250.

Kincaid, J. P., and L. G. Gamble. (1977). Ease of comprehension of standard and readable automobile insurance policies as a function of reading ability. *Journal of Reading Behavior* 9: 85–87.

Kitson, H. D. (1921). *The Mind of the Buyer: A Psychology of Selling*. New York: Macmillan.

Klare, G. R. (1963). *The Measurement of Readability*. Ames: Iowa State University Press.

Lively, B. A., and S. L. Pressey (1923). A method for measuring the "vocabulary burden" of textbooks. *Educational Administration and Supervision* 9: 389–398.

Lorge, I. (1939). Predicting reading difficulty of selections for children. *Elementary English Review* 16: 229–233.

Miller, T. H. (1984). *A readability study of computer industry news releases*. Unpublished master's thesis, University of Texas at Austin.

Rankin, E. F., and J. W. Culhane (1969). Comparable cloze and multiple-choice comprehension test scores. *Journal of Reading* 13: 193–198.

Seib, C. (1976). Papers need to work on handling the English language. *Austin American-Statesman*, Feb. 29, p. B25.

Sherman, L. A. (1888). Some observations upon the sentence-length in English prose. *University Studies of the University of Nebraska* 1, no. 2: 119–130.

Stevens, L. A. (1949). *Reliability of readability formulas as applied to listener comprehension of radio newscasts*. Unpublished master's thesis, Iowa State University.

Stevens, S. S., and G. Stone (1947a). Psychological writing, easy and hard. *American Psychologist* 2: 230–235.

——— (1947b). Further comment. *American Psychologist* 2: 524–525.

Suchan, J., and C. Scott (1986). Unclear contract language and its effect on corporate culture. *Business Horizons*, Jan.-Feb., pp. 20–25.

Swanson, C. (1948). Readability and readership: A controlled experiment. *Journalism Quarterly* 25: 339–345.

Tankard, J. W., and E. F. Tankard (1977). Comparison of readability of basic reporting texts. *Journalism Quarterly* 54: 794–797.

Taylor, W. L. (1953). "Cloze procedure": A new tool for measuring readability. *Journalism Quarterly* 30: 415–433.

Thorndike, E. L. (1975). *A Teacher's Word Book of the Twenty Thousand Words Found Most Frequently and Widely in General Reading for Children and Young People.* Rev. ed. Detroit, Mich.: Gale. (Reprint of 1932 edition)

Werner, L. M. (1986). U.S. literacy survey shows mixed results. *New York Times,* Sept. 25, pp. 1, 11.

Wesson, D. A. (1989). Readability as a factor in magazine ad copy recall. *Journalism Quarterly* 66: 715–718.

Zinkhan, G., and E. Blair (1984). An assessment of the cloze procedure as an advertising copy test. *Journalism Quarterly* 61: 404–408.

P A R T IV

The Social-Psychological Approach

Communication is obviously a social act, and we can go only so far in understanding it by approaching it at the individual level, as we did in Part III. In approaching communication as a social act, it is useful to draw upon theories that have been developed and research that has been conducted in the field of social psychology.

A number of theories have been developed around the idea that individuals strive for consistency between their attitudes, beliefs, values, and behaviors. This striving for consistency has a social aspect because it is often the perception of others that puts pressure on people to be consistent, and also because the source of much of our inconsistency comes through communication with others. The various theories of cognitive consistency are discussed in Chapter 8.

One of the primary functions of communication is persuasion, or the influencing of others through the use of symbols. Many researchers have been interested in the process of persuasion, and a number of theories have been proposed to explain persuasion. These theories are discussed in Chapter 9.

A fundamental lesson of social psychology is that people often act and think as members of groups rather than as individuals. This impact of groups on individuals applies to the reception of messages, and to other aspects of communication. Chapter 10 describes the role of groups in the communication process.

The social aspect of communication shows up in another way—it is getting more and more difficult to draw a sharp line between mass communication and interpersonal communication. Mass communication often depends on interpersonal communication to extend its reach, and research on adoption of innovations has shown that people at certain stages of the adoption process are more dependent on interpersonal communication than mass communication. The relationship between mass communication and interpersonal communication is explored in Chapter 11.

8

Cognitive Consistency
and Mass Communication

The general notion of consistency underlies all of science. It is the notion that phenomena are ordered (or consistent) that allows predictability. Predictability, in turn, allows the scientist to formulate and test hypotheses, make generalizations from them, build theory, and predict future outcomes. The purpose of the communication researcher and theorist is, to a great measure, to predict the effect or future outcomes of messages.

The concept of consistency in human behavior is an extension of the general notion from the physical world to the area of human behavior. Various theorists contend that humans strive for consistency in a number of ways—between attitudes, between behaviors, between attitudes and behaviors, in our perception of the world, and even in the development of personality. In short, we try to organize our world in ways that seem to us to be meaningful and sensible.

The concepts of human consistency are based on the notion that human beings act in rational ways. However, we also use *rationalization*—the attempt to explain irrational behavior in a rational or consistent way. Rationalization emphasizes that in our desire to appear rational or consistent to ourselves we often employ means that may seem irrational or inconsistent to others.

The notions of consistency assume that inconsistency generates "psychological tension" or discomfort within human beings, which results in internal pressure to eliminate or reduce the inconsistency and, if possible, achieve consistency.

Examples of the consistency principles in everyday affairs are widespread. Militant defenders of American involvement in Vietnam were often forced to resort to a number of psychological mechanisms to reduce inconsistency when they were confronted with such statements as these:

> I want to tell you, I don't think the whole of South East Asia, as related to the present and future safety and freedom of the people of this country, is worth the life or limb of a single American. But maybe the people are and maybe the people of South America are, too. And maybe that's confusing.
>
> I believe that if we had and would keep our dirty, bloody, dollar-crooked fingers out of the business of these nations so full of depressed, exploited people, they will arrive at a solution of their own. That they design and want. That they fight and work for. And if unfortunately their revolution must be of the violent type because the "haves" refuse to share with the "have-nots" by any peaceful method, at least what they get will be their own, and not the American style, which they don't want crammed down their throats by Americans. (Shoup, 1967, p. S2280)

131

For many people who were militant supporters of America's role in Vietnam that quotation created considerable psychological tension, especially when they were told the source. The speaker, General David M. Shoup, served as commandant of the U.S. Marine Corps from 1959 to 1963, was a member of the Joint Chiefs of Staff, and was a holder of the nation's highest military decoration, the Congressional Medal of Honor. The quotation was part of a much longer speech he made in May 1966 in Los Angeles as the American participation in the Vietnam War was rapidly escalating. In 1962, while commandant of the Marine Corps, he testified before a U.S. Senate subcommittee formed to investigate anticommunist indoctrination in the armed services and criticized the panel for sending investigators to question Marine Corps enlisted men. He said that the Marine Corps should not be teaching hate but should be teaching men how to defend themselves and their country (Daley, 1983).

Many also find it hard to believe that the most decorated officer of the Vietnam War, Colonel David H. Hackworth, took early retirement at age 41 to work as a waiter in a resort cafe on the "Gold Coast" of Australia. Hackworth won 91 medals before he retired, including 8 Purple Hearts (he was wounded four times in Korea and four more times during his 5½ years in Vietnam), 10 Silver Stars, 8 Bronze Stars, and 8 Vietnamese medals for bravery. He authored the classic infantry handbook *Vietnam Primer*. Hackworth joined the Army in 1944, at the age of 14, altering his birth certificate. In Korea he was awarded a battlefield commission. He said he went to Australia to lead "a more creative, truthful and worthwhile life than I have been living for the last 25 years" (*New York Times*, Jan. 5, 1973, p. 6; see also Hackworth, 1973).

Students at a large southern university resorted to rationalization when confronted with the information that executives of 134 national companies rated the locally highly touted business school only 19th nationally. One department chair was quoted as saying, "Surveys are a pool of collective ignorance. It means nothing" (Schnitt, 1985). However, administrators of the same school, in an interview published four days later on the same topic, were quick to cite another survey, which ranked the school 5th among public institutions and 14th with public and private schools combined (Edwards, 1985). Apparently, this survey was not "a pool of collective ignorance."

When *Business Week* magazine published its 1988 graduate business school rankings, low-ranked schools immediately set out to discredit the survey, some might say by rationalizing. Some schools attacked its methodology, one sponsored a survey ranking schools by quality of research (one of the sponsoring school's strengths), one explained that recruiters downgraded a school because its students command high salaries and recruiters don't like to pay top dollar, one suggested that New York schools were downgraded because "New Yorkers love to trash themselves"; and another claimed that its students' happiness quotient was low because the students were facing exam and job pressures (Deutsch, 1990).

A university board of regents rejected a three-semester appointment of a visiting professor and the gift of a collection of personal papers. The individual was a high-ranking member of Marshal Tito's Communist government. The rejection by the regents came after the appointment was approved by the departments of history and comparative studies and by the university provost (*New York Times*, June 20, 1971, p. 19).

A first-ranked football team in an area where football reigns supreme suffered a humiliating defeat at the hands of a long-standing rival. The following day both the media and individual conversations were filled with rationalizations and justifications.

As noted, consistency theories recognize human attempts at rationality, but in achieving it we often display striking irrationality. The concept of rationalization assumes both rationality and irrationality—we often use irrational means to achieve understanding, to justify painful experiences, or to make the world fit our "frame of reference."

Mass communication research is concerned, in part, with how individuals deal with discrepant or inconsistent information, which is often presented with the purpose of bringing about attitude change. This attitude change is one of the many ways in which we can reduce or eliminate the discomfort or psychological pressure of inconsistency.

Although a number of consistency theories are of interest to behavioral scientists (Kiesler, Collins, & Miller, 1969; Abelson et al., 1968), for the purposes of this book only four major ones will be discussed.

Heider's Balance Theory

Most writers usually credit Fritz Heider (1946) with the earliest articulation of a consistency theory, although the informal concept can be traced back to earlier work (see Kiesler et al., 1969, p. 157). As a psychologist, Heider was concerned with the way an individual organizes attitudes toward people and objects in relation to one another within that individual's own cognitive structure. Heider postulated that unbalanced states produce tension and generate forces to restore balance. He says that "the concept of a balanced state designates a situation in which the perceived units and the experienced sentiments co-exist without stress" (1958, p. 176).

Heider's paradigm focused on two individuals, a person (P), the object of the analysis, some other person (O), and a physical object, idea, or event (X). Heider's concern was with how relationships among these three entities are organized in the mind of one individual (P). Heider distinguished two types of relationships among these three entities, liking (L) and unit (U) relations (cause, possession, similarity, etc.). In Heider's paradigm, "a balanced state exists if all three relations are positive in all respects or if two are negative and one is positive" (1946, p. 110). All other combinations are unbalanced.

In Heider's conception, degrees of liking cannot be represented; a relation is either positive or negative (Figure 8.1). It is assumed that a balanced state is stable and resists outside influences. An unbalanced state is assumed to be unstable and is assumed to produce psychological tension within an individual. This tension "becomes relieved only when change within the situation takes place in such a way that a state of balance is achieved" (Heider, 1958, p. 180). This pinpoints the communicator's interest in the theory for it implies a model of attitude change and resistance to attitude change. Unbalanced states, being unstable states, are susceptible to change toward balance. Balanced states, being stable states, resist change. Data supporting Heider's balance theory are discussed in Zajonc (1960), Kiesler et al. (1969), and Abelson et al. (1968).

Newcomb's Symmetry Theory

Social psychologist Theodore M. Newcomb took Heider's idea of balance out of the head of one person and applied it to communication between people. He uses the term symmetry to distinguish it from balance theory and contends that we attempt to influence one another to bring about symmetry (or balance or equilibrium). As discussed in some detail

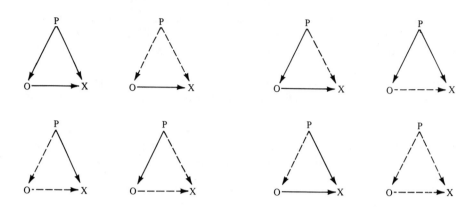

Balanced States   Unbalanced states

FIGURE 8.1 • EXAMPLES OF BALANCED AND UNBALANCED STATES ACCORDING TO HEIDER'S DEFINITION OF BALANCE (SOLID LINES REPRESENT POSITIVE RELATIONS; BROKEN LINES, NEGATIVE RELATIONS.)

From R. B. Zajonc, "The Concepts of Balance, Congruity, and Dissonance," *Public Opinion Quarterly* 24 (1960): 283. Copyright 1960 by Princeton University. Reprinted by permission of University of Chicago Press.

in Chapter 3, Newcomb postulates that attempts to influence another person are a function of the attraction one person has for another. In this respect Newcomb's theory is more of a theory of interpersonal attraction than one of attitude change. If we fail to achieve symmetry through communication with another person about an object important to both of us, we may then change our attitude toward either the other person or the object in question in order to establish symmetry.

Because Newcomb's model (see Chapter 3) deals with two people and the communication between them, he labels them A and B (rather than Heider's P and O) and retains X to represent the object of their attitudes. As with Heider, he assumes a human need for consistency, which he calls a "persistent strain toward symmetry." If A and B disagree about X, the amount of this strain toward symmetry will depend on the intensity of A's attitude toward X and A's attraction for B. An increase in A's attraction for B and an increase in A's intensity of attitude toward X will result in (1) an increased strain toward symmetry on the part of A toward B about their attitudes toward X, (2) the likelihood that symmetry will be achieved, and (3) the probability of a communication by A to B about X. The last item, of course, is the focus of our concern.

Newcomb says, "The likelihood of a symmetry-directed A to B re X varies as a multiple function of the perceived discrepancy (i.e., inversely with perceived symmetry), with valence toward B and with valence toward X" (Newcomb, 1953, p. 398).

Newcomb, in contrast to Heider, stresses communication. The less the symmetry between A and B about X, the more probable that A will communicate with B regarding X. Symmetry predicts that people associate with or become friends of people with whom they agree ("Birds of a feather flock together").

However, for attitude change to take place, a person must come into contact with information that differs from his or her present attitudes. Newcomb's symmetry model predicts that the more A is attracted to B (a person or a group), the greater the opinion change on the part of A toward the position of B.

Osgood's Congruity Theory

The congruity model is a special case of Heider's balance theory. Though similar to balance theory, it deals specifically with the attitudes persons hold toward sources of information and the objects of the source's assertions. Congruity theory has several advantages over balance theory, including the ability to make predictions about both the direction and the degree of attitude change. The congruity model assumes that "judgmental frames of reference tend toward maximal simplicity." Because extreme judgments are easier to make than refined ones (see discussion of either-or thinking and two valued evaluation in Chapter 5), valuations tend to move toward the extremes, or there is "a continuing pressure toward polarization." In addition to this maximization of simplicity, the assumption is also made that identity is less complex than discrimination of fine differences (either-or thinking and categorization). Because of this, related "concepts" are evaluated in a similar manner.

In the congruity paradigm a person (P) receives an assertion from a source (S), toward which he has an attitude, about an object (O), toward which he also has an attitude. In Osgood's model, how much P likes S and O will determine if a state of congruity or consistency exists (Figure 8.2).

According to congruity theory, when a change occurs, it is always toward greater congruity with prevailing frames of reference. Osgood uses his semantic differential to measure the amount of liking a person may have for a source and the object of an assertion.

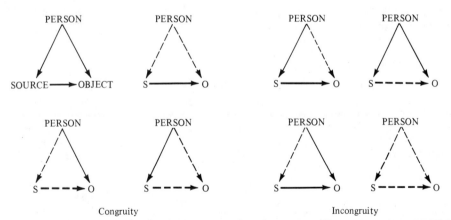

FIGURE 8.2 • EXAMPLES OF CONGRUITY AND INCONGRUITY (HEAVY LINES REPRESENT ASSERTIONS; LIGHT LINES, ATTITUDES. SOLID HEAVY LINES REPRESENT ASSERTIONS THAT IMPLY A POSITIVE ATTITUDE ON THE PART OF THE SOURCE, AND BROKEN HEAVY LINES IMPLY NEGATIVE ATTITUDES. SOLID LIGHT LINES REPRESENT POSITIVE ATTITUDES, AND BROKEN LIGHT LINES REPRESENT NEGATIVE ATTITUDES.)

From R. B. Zajonc, "The Concepts of Balance, Congruity, and Dissonance," *Public Opinion Quarterly* 24 (1960): 287. Copyright 1960 by Princeton University. Reprinted by permission of University of Chicago Press.

In essence, the definitions of balance and congruity are identical. Incongruity exists when the attitudes toward the source and the object are similar and the assertion is negative or when they are dissimilar and the assertion is positive. An unbalanced state has either one or all negative relations.

Percy Tannenbaum had 405 college students evaluate three sources—labor leaders, the *Chicago Tribune,* and Senator Robert Taft—and three objects—gambling, abstract art, and accelerated college programs. Some time later the students were presented with newspaper clippings that contained assertions attributed to the sources about the objects. The entire range of predicted changes was supported by Tannenbaum's data, as summarized in Table 8.1. The direction of change is indicated by either a plus or a minus sign, while the extent of change is indicated by one or two such signs.

Incongruity and the Media

A graphic example of this phenomenon in the media world occurred when Walter Cronkite and CBS covered the Democratic National Convention in Chicago in August 1968. CBS News reported at the time what the Walker Commission later called a "police riot" on the streets of Chicago. Walter Cronkite expressed the opinion on the air that the convention floor seemed to be under the control of a "bunch of thugs" after Dan Rather was "decked" while "on camera" when he attempted to interview delegates from a southern state being removed from the convention floor. CBS News (the source) had made negative assertions about objects (Mayor Richard Daley and the Chicago police) that apparently were held in high esteem by many persons in the television audience. Feedback to CBS News expressed considerable dissatisfaction on the part of audience members with the news coverage. Presumably their attitude toward the source, Walter Cronkite and CBS News, became more negative. If, in a democracy, we cannot behead the messenger who brings unpleasant news (that does not agree with our "prevailing frame of reference" of reality), as was the case in ancient Persia, congruity theory predicts that we come to dislike the bearer of information that does not agree with our view of the world. We have incorpo-

Table 8.1

CHANGE OF ATTITUDE TOWARD THE SOURCE AND THE OBJECT

WHEN POSITIVE AND NEGATIVE ASSERTIONS ARE MADE BY THE SOURCE

Original Attitude toward the Source	Positive Assertion about an Object toward Which the Attitude is		Negative Assertion about an Object toward Which the Attitude is	
	Positive	*Negative*	*Positive*	*Negative*
	Change of Attitude toward the Source			
Positive	+	− −	− −	+
Negative	+ +	−	−	+ +
	Change of Attitude toward the Object			
Positive	+	+ +	− −	−
Negative	− −	−	+	+ +

From R. B. Zajonc, "The Concepts of Balance, Congruity and Dissonance," *Public Opinion Quarterly* 24 (1960): 288. Reprinted with permission of the publisher.

rated this into the folk saying, "Don't confuse me with the facts, I have already made up my mind."

Incongruity does not always produce attitude change. There is some basis for the belief that much material in the media that would produce incongruity in an individual never does so. In the process of selecting what we will pay attention to, we may avoid messages that we suspect will not agree with our concept of the world (selective exposure) or perhaps pay attention to only the parts of a message that agree with our "prevailing frame of reference" (selective attention).

If we do receive a message that causes incongruity, we may misperceive the message (*selective perception*) to make it fit our view of reality. Two articles treated the same report about a university quite differently. The first cited the report as identifying a number of problems keeping the university from becoming "first class," including overly flexible admissions standards, pressure from politicians, and meddling from regents (McNamara, 1982). The second, published four days later in a different newspaper, said the report noted that the university ranked higher than Harvard in academics and social life (Gunnels, 1982).

Two daily newspapers in the same city, reporting a visit by President Reagan to Moscow, headlined their stories "Reagan tells dissidents future looking brighter," and "Things aren't better, refuseniks tell Reagan." Each saw a different aspect of the same story as the most newsworthy (*Houston Chronicle* and *Houston Post,* both May 31, 1988, p. 1).

When an American navy ship shot down an Iranian airliner over the Persian Gulf, one news account related:

> The inquiry found that in the stress of battle, radar operators . . . mistakenly convinced themselves that the aircraft they had spotted . . . was hostile and intended to attack the Vincennes. . . . With the perceived threat fast approaching, they wrongly interpreted what they saw on their radar screens in a way that reinforced this preconceived notion . . . all radars and records showed the aircraft to be at the higher altitude, even though the radar operators reported that the plane was diving at the Vincennes. (Trainor, 1988)

When the *New York Times,* in an article titled "Debt-policy shift set on 3d world," used a table "Ranking the World's debtors, By external debt to public and private entities," it listed 17 nations, but excluded the United States, which had become the world's largest debtor nation one year earlier (*New York Times,* March 11, 1989, p. 19).

News items that refute public opinion, which presumably cause psychological discomfort, are relatively uncommon. One study pointed out that contrary to popular opinion, households with incomes below $10,000 give away an average of 2.8 percent of their incomes, nearly twice as much as the 1.5 percent donated by households with income between $50,000 and $100,000. Even those with incomes of more than $100,000 at 2.1 percent were still below the lowest income group (Cox, 1988).

When President Reagan visited a sixth grade civics class in Columbia, Missouri, a student asked him, "All this publicity and the press and stuff, they like to drive me out of my mind. I just wonder what is it that made it worthwhile to you?" Reagan said that he was convinced that the 11-year-old had asked him about arms sales to Iran. After he left the girl said to reporters, "He never did answer my question," and Reagan, when questioned, said, "As a matter of fact, I heard the word 'Iran' " (*New York Times,* March 28, 1987, p. 7).

If we are unable to misperceive the message, we may attack the credibility of the communicator. Credibility is, after all, the most important thing a communicator has. A communicator in the news media who lacks credibility probably also has no audience. When it was discovered that the publisher of the two largest dailies in one state and president of the Associated Press Association of four western states had, for more than 30 years, lied about having a heroic military record, he promptly resigned, saying, "I am sorry for the shame I have brought upon the newspapers. I believe the integrity of what the newspapers do is paramount and to compromise that integrity is unacceptable" (Greene, 1985).

Denial or incredulity is another means of dealing with incongruity. Many individuals simply do not believe that a former Marine Corps commandant, holder of the Congressional Medal of Honor and member of the Joint Chiefs of Staff, made such strong public statements against our Vietnam intervention as early as 1966, even when copies of the *Congressional Record* in which those remarks were reprinted at the time are shown to them.

When in 1967 President Lyndon B. Johnson received a top secret report from then director of the Central Intelligence Agency Richard Helms stating that there was no Communist-controlled or foreign-inspired link to the protests against the Vietnam War, he refused to believe it. The report concluded, "On the basis of what we now know, we see no significant evidence that would prove Communist control or direction of the U.S. peace movement or its leaders." A historian who later examined the report and Johnson's reaction to it said that Johnson "ignored it because it did not suit his political purpose, which was to establish foreign control of the antiwar movement" (*New York Times,* Aug. 8, 1982, p. 13).

The New York City health commissioner, speaking of the AIDS epidemic, said, "The way mankind responds to crisis is first disbelief, then denial, then the third stage is mobilization, and we're at that horizon now" (*New York Times,* Feb. 14, 1988, p. 1).

If, indeed, an incongruous message does reach an individual, there is still no guarantee of attitude change. *Selective retention* may enter the picture, and we may well remember only points that support our "prevailing frame of reference."

The Role of Media Gatekeepers

According to many reports, the Japanese are not taught in school about the surprise attack on Pearl Harbor. Some Japanese see in their nation a sort of collective amnesia. A professor of Japanese intellectual and social history in Tokyo said, "In general, Japanese tend to forget the past, thinking that it can be washed away" (Chira, 1985). One Japanese textbook publisher deleted a description of Japanese brutality in World War II as the result of protests from politicians (Chira, 1988b). As one writer pointed out, "as Japan wields more power in the world, the question of how the Japanese see their past—and how they teach it—looms more important." She quotes a historian and professor emeritus at Tokyo University of Education as saying, "There is the inclination in teaching children to avoid the bad sides, and there isn't a willingness to learn a lesson from past mistakes" (Chira, 1988a). One former Japanese naval officer who took part in the attack on Pearl Harbor and later spent 13 years as a government military historian says, "I have studied history, I have lived through the flow of this history, and I don't think that what Japan did before and during the war was aggression" (Lehner, 1988). When the epic film *The Last Emperor* was shown in Japan a part showing Japanese soldiers committing atrocities in Nanjing in 1938, the six-week orgy of murder, rape, and mayhem known as the "Rape of Nanjing," was cut out (Haberman, 1988).

It has been pointed out that Americans hold a highly ethnocentric view of Columbus. One lecturer in psychology wrote:

> Most school history texts do not tell that Columbus was the first European to bring slavery to the New World. Two days after he "discovered" America, Columbus wrote in his journal that with 50 men he could force "the entire population be taken to Castile, or be held captive." On his second voyage, in December 1494, Columbus captured 1,500 Tainos on the island of Hispaniola and herded them to Isabela, where 550 of the "best males and females" were forced aboard ships bound for the slave markets of Seville.
> Under Columbus's leadership, the Spanish attacked the Taino, sparing neither men, women nor children. Warfare, forced labor, starvation and disease reduced Hispaniola's Taino population (estimated at one million to two million in 1492) to extinction within 30 years.
> Until the European discovery of America, there was only a relatively small slave trade between Africa and Europe. Needing labor to replace the rapidly declining Taino, the Spanish introduced African slaves to Hispaniola in 1502; by 1510, the trade was important to the Caribbean economy.
> When the Duvalier regime was overthrown in Haiti, demonstrators, descended from African slaves, tossed the great statue of Columbus into the bay. Attempts in the United Nations to pass resolutions celebrating the anniversary of the "discovery" have been defeated, largely by protests from third world countries that view Columbus not as a discoverer, but as an invader. (Strong, 1989)

College seniors in the United States often claim that little or nothing is said in high school or college about the Vietnam War, the Pentagon Papers, or Watergate, all having taken place before they were born or during their childhood and all, apparently, to be collectively forgotten.

A study done in a graduate school of education found that of seven social studies textbooks examined, four contained no coverage of Watergate, two had what was called minimal coverage, and only one was termed adequate. The writer wonders whether the lessons of Watergate have been forgotten for a generation of schoolchildren (Woodward, 1987).

One researcher (Ehrenhaus, 1989) points out that for more than a decade the Vietnam War was collectively forgotten. He asks, how does a society commemorate its failures? When faced with the obligation to commemorate Vietnam and its veterans the United States chose not to remember. The author says:

> The end of war brings with it the obligation to remember. . . . Remembrance entails reaffirming the legitimacy of purpose for which a community has issued its call for sacrifice. . . . the significance of commemoration lies not in the occurrence of events; it lies in the fact that certain events are remembered while others are not. . . .(pp.97–98)

Ehrenhaus adds:

> How does remembrance in the wake of war serve the interests of those whose right and obligation it is to commemorate? Because acts of closure represent the particular interests of those empowered to commemorate, narrative is selective and distortive; it privileges and advances certain world views over alternative ones. . . . no acceptable narrative structure could give meaning to the deaths of more than 58,000 Americans; most Americans simply no longer accepted as legitimate the premises upon which their call to sacrifice was based. . . . with its political leadership unwilling to be held accountable for the human tragedy and political travesty of Vietnam, and with a public unprepared to accept the challenge of

confronting what that experience might reveal about themselves and their national community, the United States shook off its long national nightmare of Vietnam and turned away. . . . (pp. 99–100)

Ehrenhaus points out that President Ford urged Americans not to reflect upon the meaning of the past. Ehrenhaus argues that such reflection might challenge the assumptions of the relationships between individuals and the state. He says that "fundamental belief in U.S. righteousness was confronted by revelations of political cowardice and lies at home . . . " (p. 104). For these and other reasons, Ehrenhaus contends the society and its leaders chose to "forget" Vietnam for more than a decade.

And, of the millions of Vietnamese, Cambodian, and Laotian civilian casualties, little or nothing is ever said in the United States, other than a few references to widespread birth defects as the result of the massive spraying of Agent Orange.

Festinger's Theory of Cognitive Dissonance

The most general of all the consistency theories and, as one might expect, the one that has generated the largest body of empirical data is Leon Festinger's theory of cognitive dissonance. It is also a theory that has generated considerable controversy in the field of social psychology.

Dissonance theory holds that two elements of knowledge "are in dissonant relation if, considering these two alone, the obverse of one element would follow from the other" (Festinger, 1957, p. 13). As with other consistency theories, it holds that dissonance, "being psychologically uncomfortable, will motivate the person to try to reduce dissonance and achieve consonance" and "in addition to trying to reduce it the person will actively avoid situations and information which would likely increase the dissonance" (p. 3).

In cognitive dissonance the elements in question may be (1) irrelevant to one another, (2) consistent with one another (in Festinger's terms, consonant), or (3) inconsistent with one another (dissonant in Festinger's terms). Relationships need not be logically related for consistency or inconsistency.

A relationship may be logically inconsistent to an observer while psychologically consistent to an individual who holds these obverse beliefs. In the earlier example of the university board of regents' refusal of a visiting professorship for a former high government official from a Communist country, the decision was probably logically inconsistent with what most people would regard as the duty of a university to deal openly with all ideas. However, since the individual was obviously a staunch Communist, the refusal was probably psychologically consistent with the beliefs of a majority of the board of regents and perhaps many of their constituency.

Several rather interesting consequences follow from dissonance theory, especially in the areas of decision making and role playing. The focus of this book is on how people use information, and dissonance theory is important in that respect.

Decision Making

Upon making a decision, dissonance is predicted to follow to the extent that the rejected alternative contains features that would have resulted in its acceptance and that the chosen alternative contains features that could have caused its rejection. In other words, the more difficult a decision is to make, the greater the predicted dissonance after the decision (postdecision dissonance). It also follows that postdecision dissonance is greater for more important decisions. A number of studies report evidence to support these hypotheses.

One researcher reports that purchasers of new cars were more apt to notice and read ads about the cars they had just bought than about other cars (Ehrlich, Guttman, Schonbach, & Mills, 1957). Since ads are supposed to stress "benefits" of the products they promote, presumably the new car buyers were seeking reinforcement for their decisions by reading ads for the cars they had just purchased.

Evidence has also been cited for a change in the attractiveness of alternatives once a decision has been made. In other words, after a decision has been made between alternatives ranked as nearly equal in desirability, the chosen alternative is later seen as more desirable than it had been before the decision, and the rejected alternative is ranked as less desirable than it was before the decision was made (Brehm, 1956). The authors of one book on attitude change state, "The postdecision process involves cognitive change not unlike that of attitude change; indeed the effects of this process may legitimately be referred to as attitude change" (Kiesler, Collins, & Miller, 1969, p. 205).

An article about computer owners resolving postdecision dissonance put it this way:

> For some inexplicable reason, people who would not ordinarily think of criticizing your preferences in automobiles, underwear or religion, for example, feel justified in castigating you on a personal level for your choice of computer. Dr. Mark Spiegel, a psychiatrist in Manhattan, was asked to fathom the thinking of such computer zealotry. "Rational human beings don't do that," he said. Granted. So what explains all the irrational behavior of computer owners? "It could be a number of things," he suggested, "but cognitive dissonance is a psychological mechanism in which the individual, finding that his actions don't necessarily coincide with his ideas or psychological precepts, has to find some way to make them correlate, or bring them into assonance. If you spend a lot of money on a computer, you have to justify it," explained Dr. Spiegel. . . . (Lewis, 1987)

Forced Compliance

An interesting area, even if not directly related to the mass media, is attitude change following forced compliance. Dissonance theory postulates that when an individual is placed in a situation where he or she must behave publicly in a way that is contrary to that individual's privately held beliefs or attitudes, the individual experiences dissonance from knowledge of that fact. Such situations often occur as the result of a promise of a reward or the threat of punishment, but sometimes it may be simply as the result of group pressure to conform to a norm an individual does not privately agree with. Role playing is one such example.

If a person performs a public act inconsistent with his or her beliefs, it is predicted that dissonance will follow. One way of resolving this dissonance is to change the privately held beliefs to conform with the public act. The least amount of pressure necessary (promise of reward or threat of punishment) to induce an individual to act publicly in a way contrary to his or her privately held beliefs will result in the greatest dissonance. The greater the dissonance, the greater the pressure to reduce it, hence the greater the chance for attitude change in the direction of the public act or behavior. In the case of a relatively large promised reward or threatened punishment, the individual can always rationalize the public behavior that was contrary to the privately held beliefs or attitudes (e.g., "I did it for the money" or "Anybody would do the same under such a threat").

One foreign teacher at the Shanghai Institute of Foreign Trade said in an interview that her students were given summer assignments to write essays about the student demonstrations in China in 1989. She reported that their scholarships depended on what they wrote (National Public Radio, Oct. 14, 1989).

Selective Exposure and Selective Attention

Dissonance theory is of greatest interest to us in the areas of information seeking and avoidance, often called *selective exposure* and *selective attention.* Dissonance theory predicts that individuals will avoid dissonance-producing information, and there is considerable evidence indicating that media personnel are acutely aware of this.

ABC-TV's "Primetime" aired an interview (October 25, 1990) by Diane Sawyer done in Moscow with Edward Lee Howard, the only CIA agent ever to defect to the Soviet Union. Although Howard is a graduate of the University of Texas at Austin, and was an honor student and a member of the ROTC, neither the city nor campus media commented on her interview or Howard's defection.

In recent years some attention has been given to the effects of Agent Orange on Vietnam veterans, but almost no attention has been given to its effects on the Vietnamese people. One Vietnam combat veteran, now an Emmy and Peabody Award–winning television producer, who recently returned to Vietnam, says,

> We saw the lunarlike landscape near the Cambodian border which had been defoliated by Agent Orange. We met disabled veterans, war widows, orphans and deformed children in desperate need. . . . Isn't there a studio in Hollywood today that will buck the system and make a movie about the Vietnamese? . . . We need a movie or movies in which the Vietnamese are in the forefront. We still owe them a peace. (Bird, 1990, p. 16)

Some researchers have contended that individuals do not ordinarily select or reject entire messages (*selective exposure*) because we often cannot judge the message content beforehand. Others have observed that usually we are surrounded by people and media that agree with us on the major issues (McGuire, 1968). Some researchers argue that more typically individuals will pay attention to the parts of a message that are not contrary to their strongly held attitudes, beliefs, or behaviors (*selective attention*) and not pay attention to the parts of a message that are counter to strongly held positions and might cause psychological discomfort or dissonance. There is some evidence that people will pay attention to material that does not support their position if they believe it will be easy to refute, but they will avoid information that is supportive of their position if it is weak. The latter may cause them to lose confidence in their initial position (Brock & Balloun, 1967; Lowin, 1969; Kleinhesselink & Edwards, 1975).

In a summary of research, several authors concluded that there is little evidence to support the hypothesis that individuals will avoid entire messages (*selective exposure*) that are contrary to their beliefs (Brehm & Cohen, 1962; Freedman & Sears, 1965; Sears, 1968). Researchers have found that individuals seeking novelty will not necessarily avoid dissonance-producing information. The perceived utility of information (e.g., the learning of "implausible" counterarguments to one's position cited in Chapter 4) may impel an individual to pay attention to dissonance-producing information. Contradictory information that is new, interesting, salient, personally relevant, or entertaining will probably not be avoided. Contradictory information that is useful in learning a skill or solving a problem will probably be attended to. In other words, if the message contains rewards that exceed the psychological discomfort or dissonance it may generate, the message will probably not be avoided. Individuals are more apt to pay attention to material that is contradictory to their beliefs, behaviors, or choices if they are ones not strongly held. With strongly held beliefs, people who are highly confident of their views will not avoid contradictory material because they believe they can easily refute it. For differing positions on this issue, see Freedman and Sears (1965), who concluded people do not avoid dissonant information, and Mills (1968), who argued that under some circumstances they do. Both are included in Abelson et al. (1968), which provides an extended, in-depth treatment of consistency theories.

However, Cotton (1985), in an exhaustive review of research dealing with selective exposure, concluded that the earlier studies suffered from a variety of methodological flaws. He believes that earlier studies contained a variety of artifacts that may have affected their findings. Cotton concludes, "Later research on selective exposure, generally more carefully controlled, has produced more positive results. Almost every study found significant selective-exposure effects" (p. 25).

At this point we can say only that the jury is still out on the question of selective exposure and the final verdict is yet to come.

Entertainment Choices

There is some evidence that choices in entertainment are made "on impulse," or spontaneously, rather than with deliberate *selective exposure* (Zillmann & Bryant, 1986). However, research (Bryant & Zillmann, 1984) has shown that people seem to select entertainment intuitively, depending upon their mood. The researchers say:

> The data revealed that exciting programs attracted bored subjects significantly more than stressed subjects and that relaxing programs attracted stressed subjects significantly more than bored subjects. . . . it was found that almost all subjects had chosen materials that helped them to escape effectively from undesirable excitatory states. In fact almost all subjects overcorrected, that is, bored subjects ended up above base levels and stressed ones below base levels of excitation. (pp. 307–308)

Other studies (Zillmann & Bryant, 1985) suggest that "all people who are down on their luck may be expected to seek, and obtain, mood lifts from comedy" (p. 309). However, "provoked, angry persons were found to refrain from watching hostile comedy and turn to alternative offerings" (Zillmann, Hezel, & Medoff, 1980).

Crime-apprehensive people selected drama that was lower in violent victimization and higher in justice restoration than did nonapprehensive counterparts. Apprehensive persons exhibited a tendency to expose themselves to information capable of reducing their apprehensions. One researcher (Zillmann, 1980) concludes that "the main message of television crime drama—namely, that criminals are being caught and put away, which should make the streets safer—apparently holds great appeal for those who worry about crime" (p. 311).

Selective Retention

Earlier several studies were cited in support of the concept of *selective retention*, that people tend to remember material that agrees with their "prevailing frame of reference" or attitudes, beliefs, and behaviors and forget material that disagrees with them. More recent research has tended to cast some doubt on these findings. One study concluded that neither prior attitudes nor prior familiarity was related to learning of material and that novelty enhances learning of propagandistic information (Greenwald & Sakamura, 1967). Another study, which tested the hypotheses of both the Levine and Murphy study and the Jones and Kohler study (cited in Chapter 4), concluded that only under certain conditions does an attitude-memory relationship exist, if at all, and that "the specific nature of these conditions is not as yet understood" (Brigham & Cook, 1969, p. 243). As with all scientific research, this is an area in which theory is being refined and sharpened. Recent studies are applying more rigid controls and investigating alternative explanations. At this point we can say only that the factors that influence selective retention of information are yet to be determined, and much work remains to be done concerning the selective retention of information.

Conclusions

As should be obvious by now, consistency theories have many implications for how humans perceive the world, communicate, and use, distort, ignore, or forget the contents of the mass media. In their generality and scope they apply to both media practitioners and media consumers—from the reporter at the scene of the news or the producer of an advertisement to the final destination of the message.

As we have seen, nations can selectively forget unpleasant past events and deny current problems, individuals can selectively perceive objective data, even from highly sophisticated electronic instruments, and presidents can and do selectively misperceive questions and data. People reduce postdecision dissonance with selective retention of facts and nations attempt to change attitudes through forced role playing. The media not only vary in their perceptions of an event, but often also ignore unpleasant facts about their own societies.

References

Abelson, R. P., E. Aronson, W. J. McGuire, T. M. Newcomb, M. H. Rosenberg, and P. H. Tannenbaum (eds.) (1968). *Theories of Cognitive Consistency: A Sourcebook*. Skokie, Ill.: Rand-McNally.

Bird, T. (1990). Man and boy confront the images of war. *New York Times,* May 27, Sect. 2, pp. 11, 16.

Brehm, J. W. (1956). Post-decision changes in the desirability of alternatives. *Journal of Abnormal and Social Psychology* 52: 384–389.

Brehm, J. W., and A. R. Cohen (1962). *Explorations in Cognitive Dissonance*. New York: John Wiley.

Brigham, J., and S. Cook (1969). The influence of attitude on the recall of controversial material: A failure to confirm. *Journal of Experimental Social Psychology* 5: 240–243.

Brock, T. C., and J. L. Balloun (1967). Behavioral receptivity to dissonant information. *Journal of Personality and Social Psychology* 6: 413–428.

Bryant, J., and D. Zillmann (1984). Using television to alleviate boredom and stress: Selective exposure as a function of induced excitational states. *Journal of Broadcasting* 28: 1–20.

Chira, S. (1985). Japanese confront history at Pearl Harbor attack site. *Austin American-Statesman,* Dec. 8, p. A16.

——— (1988a). Despite new efforts, Japan avoids making peace with the war. New York Times, Dec. 25, p. E12.

——— (1988b). For Japanese, textbook drops a lesson on war. New York Times, Oct. 5, p. 19.

Cotton, J. L. (1985). Cognitive dissonance in selective exposure. In D. Zillmann and J. Bryant (eds.), *Selective Exposure to Communication*, pp. 11–33. Hillsdale, N.J.: Lawrence Erlbaum.

Cox, M. (1988). Poorer households lead in rate of charitable giving. *Wall Street Journal*, Oct. 19, p. B1.

Daley, S. (1983). Gen. David M. Shoup dead at 78; ex-commandant of Marine Corps. *New York Times Biographical Service*, Jan., p. 111.

Deutsch, C. (1990). The M.B.A. Rat Race. *New York Times*, Nov. 4, Education (Special section), pp. 50–51.

Edwards, B. (1985). Survey indicates business program ranks 19th in U.S. *The Daily Texan*, Oct. 16, p. 6.

Ehrenhaus, P. (1989). Commemorating the unwon war: On *not* remembering Vietnam. *Journal of Communication* 39: 96–107.

Ehrlich, D., I. Guttman, P. Schonbach, and J. Mills (1957). Post-decision to relevant information. *Journal of Abnormal and Social Psychology* 54: 98–102.

Festinger, L. A. (1957). *A Theory of Cognitive Dissonance*. Stanford, Cal.: Stanford University Press.

Freedman, J. L., and D. Sears (1965). Selective exposure. In L. Berkowitz (ed.), *Advances in Experimental Social Psychology*, pp. 57–97. New York: Academic Press.

Greene, T. (1985). Fabricated military record leads Arizona newspaper publisher to quit. *Austin American-Statesman*, Dec. 28, p. C4.

Greenwald, A., and J. Sakamura (1967). Attitude and selective learning: Where are the phenomena of yesteryear? *Journal of Personality and Social Psychology* 7: 387–397.

Gunnels, K. (1982). Guide rates UT ahead of Harvard. *Austin American-Statesman*, Feb. 8, p. 1.

Haberman, C. (1988). Japanese remove sequence from film 'Last Emperor.' *New York Times*, Jan. 21, p. 8.

Hackworth, D. H. (1973). You have become someone else. *New York Times*, Feb. 21, p. 43.

Heider, F. (1946). Attitudes and cognitive organization. *Journal of Psychology* 21: 107–112.

Heider, F. (1958). *The Psychology of Interpersonal Relations*. New York: John Wiley.

Kiesler, C. A., B. E. Collins, and N. Miller (1969). *Attitude Change*. New York: John Wiley.

Kleinhesselink, R., and R. Edwards (1975). Seeking and avoiding belief-discrepant information as a function of its perceived refutability. *Journal of Personality and Social Psychology* 31: 787–790.

Lehner, U. (1988). More Japanese deny nation was aggressor during World War II. *Wall Street Journal*, Sept. 8, p. 1.

Lewis, P. (1987). I.B.M.? Mac? Feelings may prevent cool look. *New York Times*, Dec. 1, p. 19.

Lowin, A. (1969). Further evidence for an approach-avoidance interpretation of selective exposure. *Journal of Experimental Social Psychology* 5: 265–271.

McGuire, W. J. (1968). Selective exposure: A summing up. In R. Abelson et al. (eds.), *Theories of Cognitive Consistency: A Sourcebook*, pp. 797–800. Skokie, Ill.: Rand-McNally.

McNamara, C. (1982). Good ol' boys stunt UT, guide says. *Daily Texan*, Feb. 4, p. 1.

Mills, J. (1968). Interest in supporting and discrepant information. In R. Abelson et al. (eds.), *Theories of Cognitive Consistency: A Sourcebook*, pp. 771–776. Skokie, Ill.: Rand-McNally.

Newcomb, T. M. (1953). An approach to the study of communicative acts. *Psychological Review* 60: 393–404.

Schnitt, P. (1985). Business ranks academia. *Austin American-Statesman*, Oct. 12, p. C1.

Sears, D. O. (1968). The paradox of de facto selective exposure without preferences for supportive information. In R. Abelson et al. (eds.), *Theories of Cognitive Consistency: A Sourcebook*, pp. 777–787. Skokie, Ill.: Rand-McNally.

Shoup, D. M. (1967). Former Marine Corps commandant questions Vietnam. Speech delivered May 14, 1966. *Congressional Record—Senate*, Feb. 20, pp. S2279–S2282.

Strong, B. (1989). Slavery and colonialism make up the true legacy of Columbus. *New York Times*, Nov. 4, p. 14.

Trainor, B. (1988). Errors by a tense U.S. crew led to downing of Iran jet, inquiry is reported to find. *New York Times*, Aug. 3, p. 1.

Woodward, A. (1987). In search of Watergate in the textbooks. *New York Times*, Mar. 11, p. 26.

Zajonc, R. B. (1960). The concepts of balance, congruity and dissonance. *Public Opinion Quarterly* 24: 280–296.

Zillmann, D. (1980). Anatomy of suspense. In P. H. Tannenbaum (ed.), *The Entertainment Functions of Television,* pp. 133–163. Hillsdale, N.J.: Lawrence Erlbaum.

———, R. T. Hezel, and N. J. Medoff (1980). The effect of affective states on selective exposure to televised entertainment fare. *Journal of Applied Social Psychology* 10: 323–339.

———, and J. Bryant (1985). Affect, mood, and emotion as determinants of selective exposure. In D. Zillmann and J. Bryant (eds.), *Selective Exposure to Communication,* pp. 157–190. Hillsdale, N.J.: Lawrence Erlbaum.

———, and J. Bryant (1986). "Exploring the entertainment experience." In J. Bryant and D. Zillmann (eds.), *Perspectives on Media Effects,* pp. 303–324. Hillsdale, N.J.: Lawrence Erlbaum.

9

Theories of Persuasion

Persuasion is only one type of mass communication, but it is a type in which many people are interested. The advertiser using mass communication to sell soft drinks, headache remedies, or automobiles is engaged in persuasion. So is the nuclear power industry when it hires public relations experts to help it convince the public that nuclear power is safe. So are the political candidate who buys newspaper ads, the public health organization that prepares radio spots to encourage people to stop smoking, and the religious organization that puts evangelical messages on television. All of these people are attempting to use mass communication messages to produce some kind of change in other people.

Persuasion has probably always been a part of human life. It seems inevitable that people will try to influence other people, even their closest friends and family members. For centuries people must have operated on the basis of intuition and common sense in their attempts to persuade. Aristotle was one of the first to try to analyze and write about persuasion, in his classic works on rhetoric. Years later, particularly when mass communication became more widespread, people began to study persuasion even more systematically. The Institute for Propaganda Analysis, with its identification of seven techniques of propaganda, was doing some of this early work. Part of the motive for this more careful study of persuasion was obviously fear—the war-inspired fear that propaganda could win the hearts and minds of people. The institute was operating in that panicky period just before World War II. A few years later, the same war was to produce the first careful scientific studies of persuasion, or attitude change, as it became known. This work was done by a psychologist named Carl Hovland and his associates, all of whom were working for the Research Branch of the U.S. Army's Information and Education Division. This work was so original and influential that it has been called "the most important fountainhead of contemporary research on attitude change" (Insko, 1967, p. 1). The Hovland work was based on controlled experiments in which variables were carefully manipulated in order to observe their effects.

Some earlier work on attitude change was done before Hovland, but rather poorly. A study sometimes cited as the first attitude change study was an investigation by Rice and Willey of the effects of William Jennings Bryan's address on evolution at Dartmouth College in 1923 (described in Chen, 1933). A group of 175 students indicated their acceptance or rejection of evolution on a five-point scale. The students were asked to give their attitudes after hearing the speech, and, from retrospection, their attitudes before hearing the

147

speech. They found that more than one-quarter of the students showed substantial change in attitude, but the use of the retrospective report makes the finding highly questionable.

The Concept of Attitude

The concept of attitude has been described by psychologist Gordon Allport (1954) as "probably the most distinctive and indispensable in contemporary American social psychology" (p. 43). Allport points out that the term came to replace in psychology such vague terms as *instinct, custom, social force,* and *sentiment.*

A number of investigators agree that the concept of attitude was first used in a scientific way in 1918 in a study by Thomas and Znaniecki (1927). They defined the concept this way: "By attitude we understand a process of individual consciousness which determines real or possible activity of the individual in the social world" (p. 22). This is not too different from more recent definitions, such as the following:

> Attitude is primarily a way of being "set" toward or against certain things. (Murphy, Murphy, & Newcomb, 1937, p. 889)

> A mental and neural state of readiness, organized through experience, exerting a directive or dynamic influence upon the individuals' responses to all objects and situations with which it is related. (Allport, 1954, p. 45)

> An enduring, learned predisposition to behave in a consistent way toward a given class of objects. (English & English, 1958, p. 50)

> An enduring system of positive or negative evaluations, emotional feelings and pro or con action tendencies with respect to a social object. (Krech, Crutchfield, & Ballachey, 1962, p. 177)

Some other scholars, such as Rosenberg and Hovland (1960), have suggested that an attitude has three components: an affective component (evaluation of something or feeling toward something), a cognitive component (perceptual responses or verbal statements of belief), and a behavioral component (overt actions). This approach is logical, since most of us would agree that an attitude can manifest itself in several different ways. This approach may be unnecessarily complicated, however, and it may be blurring the distinction between attitude and behavior in an unfortunate way. Other scholars say it is best to restrict attitude to the affective component and leave the relationship between attitude and behavior open for investigation through research.

Part of the problem in defining attitude is that it is basically an internal state, and thus not available for direct observation. This leads to some obvious difficulties in measuring attitudes.

Hovland's Army Research

Hovland's approach to attitude change was essentially a learning theory or reinforcement theory approach. He believed that attitudes were learned, and that they were changed through the same processes that occurred when learning took place. Hovland had studied and worked at Yale with Clark Hull, whose theory was probably the most influential theory of learning between 1930 and 1950 (Hilgard & Bower, 1966).

During World War II, the U.S. Army began using films and other forms of mass communication on an unprecedented scale. Most of this material was used in the training and motivation of U.S. soldiers. The Experimental Section of the Research Branch of the War Department's Information and Education Division was given the task of evaluating the effectiveness of these materials. This section was directed by Carl Hovland and was made up mostly of psychologists, including Irving Janis, Nathan Maccoby, Arthur A. Lumsdaine, and Fred D. Sheffield. Other prominent names in psychology were also involved. Samuel Stouffer was civilian head of the Research Branch professional staff, and Lieutenant Colonel Charles Dollard was one of the officers in charge of the branch. This bringing together of some of the brightest people in psychology in a large-scale program is generally recognized as the beginning of modern attitude change research, and as the source of some of the classic contributions to mass communication theory.

Much of the research of the Experimental Section is reported in the volume *Experiments on Mass Communication,* first published in 1949 (Hovland, Lumsdaine, & Sheffield, 1965). The section did two basic types of research: evaluation studies of existing films and experimental studies in which two different versions of the same film (or message) were compared. The section had to do much of the first type of research because it suited the practical purposes of the Army. The researchers felt, however, that the second type of research was really more useful because it could lead to general principles of attitude change. These experimental studies, in which certain variables were manipulated, really constituted the beginning of attitude change research. The evaluation studies of existing films also made some useful contributions to communication theory, however.

One of the first tasks the section took on was to evaluate the first four films of a series of films called "Why We Fight." This series was produced by Frank Capra, the famous Hollywood filmmaker who would later direct *It's A Wonderful Life.* The "Why We Fight" films were designed as motivational films to be used in the training and orientation of American soldiers. They were based on the assumptions that many draftees did not know the national and international events that led to America's entrance into World War II and that a knowledge of these events would lead men to accept more easily the transition from civilian life to that of a soldier.

One of the films studied in great detail was *The Battle of Britain,* a 50-minute film that had the purpose of instilling greater confidence in America's British allies. Hovland and his associates designed research to determine the film's impact in three main areas: specific factual knowledge gained from the film, specific opinions concerning the Battle of Britain, and acceptance of the military role and willingness to fight. The research procedure was simply to have an experimental group that saw the film and a control group that did not, and then one week later to give both groups a questionnaire that appeared unrelated but measured knowledge and opinions on subjects related to the film. These Army studies were conducted with military units and therefore ended up with large sample sizes—the *Battle of Britain* study involved 2,100 people.

The results showed the film was quite effective in conveying factual information about the air war over Britain in 1940, that it was somewhat effective in changing specific opinions about the conduct of the air war, and that it had essentially no effect at all on motivation to serve or in building increased resentment of the enemy. Thus the film failed in its ultimate objective, increasing soldiers' motivations. Similar results showed up for the other "Why We Fight" films studied.

This research on the "Why We Fight" series became part of the growing body of evidence indicating that a single mass communication message is unlikely to change strongly held attitudes. Similar evidence comes from other studies as different as the Cooper and Jahoda investigation of antiprejudice cartoons and research by Lazarsfeld and his associates on political campaigns.

The research on *The Battle of Britain* produced another curious result. In one study subjects were tested for opinion change five days after seeing the film and then again nine weeks later. On some opinion items there was a greater amount of opinion change after nine weeks than there had been after five days. The authors called this a "sleeper" effect. They suggested a number of possible explanations for this effect, none of which they were really able to test. One possible explanation was that the source for the items that showed the sleeper effect might have been one that was regarded as untrustworthy but that this source could have been forgotten after the passage of time.

One-Sided and Two-Sided Messages

Hovland and his associates turned to the second type of research, in which the same message is produced in two versions that differ in only one variable, in an experiment on the effectiveness of one-sided and two-sided messages. On many issues there are arguments on both sides. Which is the better strategy—to mention only the arguments on the side you are pushing or to mention the arguments on both sides but focus on the ones on the side you are pushing? This is essentially the old question of the effectiveness of card stacking, one of the propaganda devices identified by the Institute for Propaganda Analysis.

Hovland and his associates were trying to answer this question because they faced a real communication dilemma. After the defeat of Germany in 1945, many soldiers apparently felt the war was almost over. The Army wanted to get across the idea that there was still a tough job ahead in defeating the Japanese.

The researchers realized that there were arguments for each strategy. A one-sided presentation can be defended on the basis that a two-sided presentation raises doubts in the minds of people unfamiliar with the opposing arguments. A two-sided presentation can be defended on the basis that it is more fair and that it will help prevent people who are opposed to a message from rehearsing counterarguments while being exposed to the message. A specific purpose of the study was to measure the effectiveness of the two kinds of message presentation on two kinds of audience members—those initially opposed to the message and those initially sympathetic to the message.

Two versions of a radio message were prepared. Both presented the general argument that the war would take at least two more years. The one-sided message was 15 minutes long and brought out arguments such as the size of the Japanese army and the determination of the Japanese people. The two-sided message was 19 minutes long and brought out arguments on the other side, such as the advantage of fighting only one enemy, but it focused mostly on the arguments that the war would be a long one.

One week before the presentation of the radio message, subjects were given a preliminary questionnaire on which they expressed their estimates of how long the war in the Pacific would take. Then one group made up of eight platoons heard the one-sided message, a second group of eight platoons heard the two-sided message, and a third group heard neither message and served as the control group. Then all three groups received another questionnaire differing from the first one in its form and its announced purpose, but again asking for an estimate of how long the war in the Pacific would take. All questionnaires were anonymous, but the before and after questionnaires for the same person could be matched on the basis of the answers to questions about date of birth, schooling, and so forth.

Looked at in general for all groups, the results (Table 9.1) indicated that both kinds of presentations produced clear opinion change in comparison with the control group, but that neither presentation was more effective than the other.

The researchers had anticipated that the two-sided presentation might work better with an audience initially opposed to the message, however, and so they proceeded to check out this possibility. They did this by dividing each test group into subjects initially opposed to the message and subjects initially favorable to the message. The men who had given initial estimates that the war would take 1½ years or less were considered to be initially opposed to the message, while those who gave initial estimates of more than 1½ years were considered to be initially favorable to the message. Results of this analysis are shown in Table 9.2. Results are presented in terms of *net effect*, or the percentage in a group who increased their estimate minus the percentage in that group who decreased their estimate.

This examination of results according to initial attitude shows the one-sided message is most effective with persons initially favorable to the message and the two-sided message is most effective with persons initially opposed to the message. This is what the researchers had predicted.

Hovland and his associates also investigated whether one type of message—one-sided or two-sided—might work better with a more educated or a less educated audience. One might expect that better-educated audience members would be less affected by a clearly one-sided presentation. To check out this possibility, the researchers divided each test group into those subjects who graduated from high school and those who did not (see Table 9.3). The results of the analysis by education level showed that the one-sided message is most effective with people of less education and the two-sided message is most effective with people of greater education.

Both additional analyses—the one by initial opinion and the one by education level—show that the kind of presentation that is most effective depends on the characteristics of

Table 9.1

SOLDIERS WHO ESTIMATED A WAR OF MORE THAN 1 1/2 YEARS
AFTER HEARING ONE-SIDED AND TWO-SIDED MESSAGES

	Group 1 (8 platoons)	Group 2 (8 platoons)	Control Group (8 platoons)
Preliminary survey	37%	38%	36%
Exposure to message	one-sided	two-sided	none
Follow-up survey	59%	59%	34%

Adapted from C. I. Hovland, A. A. Lumsdaine, and F. D. Sheffield, *Experiments on Mass Communication* (New York: Wiley, 1965), Vol. III, Studies in Social Psychology in World War II, p. 210. Copyright 1949, © renewed 1977 by Princeton University Press. Reprinted by permission of Princeton University Press.

Table 9.2

EFFECTS OF ONE-SIDED AND TWO-SIDED MESSAGES ON MEN WHO
WERE INITIALLY EITHER OPPOSED OR FAVORABLE TO THE MESSAGE

	Initially Opposed (%)	Initially Favorable (%)
One-sided	36	52
Two-sided	48	23

Note: The number in the table is the *net effect,* or the percentage in a group who increased their estimate minus the percentage in that group who decreased their estimate.
Adapted from C. I. Hovland, A. A. Lumsdaine, and F. D. Sheffield, *Experiments on Mass Communication* (New York: Wiley, 1965), Vol. III, Studies in Social Psychology in World War II, p. 213. Copyright 1949, © renewed 1977 by Princeton University Press. Reprinted by permission of Princeton University Press.

in the message sometimes interact with other variables, such as personal characteristics of the audience. This is part of the evidence that led psychologist Roger Brown (1958), in his analysis of propaganda, to conclude that the propaganda devices are "contingently effective rather than invariably effective" (p. 306).

The Yale Communication Research Program

After the war, Hovland returned to Yale University, where he had been a faculty member, and continued his research on attitude change. A number of his fellow workers in the research for the Army, including Irving Janis, Arthur Lumsdaine, and Fred Sheffield, also went to work at Yale. The researchers received funding from the Rockefeller Foundation and set up the Yale Communication Research Program. This program had the purpose of "developing scientific propositions which specify the conditions under which the effectiveness of one or another type of persuasive communication is increased or decreased" (Hovland, Janis, & Kelley, 1953, p. v). The project had three characteristics: (1) It was primarily concerned with theoretical issues and basic research; (2) It drew upon theoretical

Table 9.3

EFFECTS OF THE ONE-SIDED AND TWO-SIDED MESSAGES ON MEN
WHO GRADUATED FROM HIGH SCHOOL AND MEN WHO DID NOT

	Didn't Graduate (%)	Did Graduate (%)
One-sided	46	35
Two-sided	31	49

Note: The number in the table is the *net effect,* or the percentage in a group who increased their estimate minus the percentage in that group who decreased their estimate.
Adapted from C. I. Hovland, A. A. Lumsdaine, and F. D. Sheffield, *Experiments on Mass Communication* (New York: Wiley, 1965), Vol. III, Studies in Social Psychology in World War II, p. 214. Copyright 1949, © renewed 1977 by Princeton University Press. Reprinted by permission of Princeton University Press.

developments from diverse sources, both within psychology and related fields; and (3) It emphasized testing propositions by controlled experiment (Hovland, Janis, & Kelley, 1953).

This program was to produce a number of important volumes on attitude change, which are sometimes known as "the Yale series." It included these books:

Communication and Persuasion (Hovland, Janis, & Kelley, 1953)

The Order of Presentation in Persuasion (Hovland et al., 1957)

Personality and Persuasibility (Janis et al., 1959)

Attitude Organization and Change (Rosenberg, Hovland, McGuire, Abelson, & Brehm, 1960)

Social Judgment (Sherif & Hovland, 1961)

The first volume, *Communication and Persuasion,* was the most general. It dealt with a number of topics that would later receive entire volumes in the Yale series or else become topics investigated extensively by later researchers. Two of these topics—source credibility and fear appeals—are particularly important because they led to many later studies. The book also reported some further research on one-sided and two-sided messages.

Source Credibility

One of the variables in a communication situation that the communicator typically has some control over is the choice of the source. And, judging from many day-to-day examples of communication campaigns, there appears to be a widespread belief that having the right source can increase the effectiveness of your message. For instance, the Earth Day celebration in Washington, D.C., in 1990 was addressed by popular actors Tom Cruise and Richard Gere, as well as actress Olivia Newton-John. Similarly, a program that night on ABC television titled "The Earth Day Special" featured appearances by Bette Midler, Meryl Streep, Dustin Hoffman, Robin Williams, Barbra Streisand, and E. T. in what *USA Today* called a "glut of celebrities" (Roush, 1990, p. 1D). In a different example, when the federal government sent a booklet on "Understanding AIDS" to every U.S. household in 1988, they put on the cover a message from C. Everett Koop, the surgeon general. Clearly, the planners of many communication efforts are putting some thought into the choice of the message source.

The selection of an effective source to speak for your idea or product is essentially the propaganda device of the testimonial. But the effectiveness of this technique was not really investigated by the Institute for Propaganda Analysis. Hovland and Weiss (1951) designed an experiment to test the effectiveness of source credibility.

Hovland and Weiss apparently became interested in the possible impact of source credibility after learning of a phenomenal radio program involving entertainer Kate Smith. In an 18-hour program during World War II, Kate Smith received pledges for an astounding $39 million worth of war bonds. To get an idea of how much money that was, 80 percent of the families in the United States earned less than $5,000 in 1947 (U.S. Bureau of the Census, 1975, p. 289). In comparison, the Jerry Lewis muscular dystrophy telethon for 1977 was on the air for 20 hours and received pledges for $27 million. Researchers who studied the Kate Smith broadcast concluded that key elements in her success were her perceived *sincerity* and *trustworthiness*.

Hovland and Weiss designed an experiment in which the same messages would be presented to some people as coming from a high-credibility source and to other people as coming from a low-credibility source. This would allow them to determine the effect of the source variable alone.

The experiment was done with four messages on four different topics. Each subject received a booklet containing four articles. Each article was on a different topic. The subjects' opinions on the four topics were measured with questionnaires before getting the communication, immediately after getting it, and four weeks after getting it. Each article was presented with a high-credibility source for half the subjects and a low-credibility source for the other half.

The four topics were controversial ones at the time and revolved around the following opinion questions:

1. "Should antihistamine drugs continue to be sold without a doctor's prescription?" The high-credibility source on this issue was the *New England Journal of Biology and Medicine*. The low-credibility source is identified in the research report as "a mass circulation monthly pictorial magazine."

2. "Can a practicable atomic-powered submarine be built at the present time?" The high-credibility source was J. Robert Oppenheimer, the head of the team of scientists that developed the atomic bomb. (This was before Oppenheimer's security clearance investigation, which undoubtedly damaged his credibility.) The low-credibility source was *Pravda*, the Russian newspaper.

3. "Is the steel industry to blame for the current shortage of steel?" The high-credibility source was the *Bulletin of National Resources Planning Board*. The low-credibility source is identified as an "anti-labor, anti–New Deal, 'rightist' newspaper columnist."

4. "As a result of TV, will there be a decrease in the number of movie theaters in operation by 1955?" The high-credibility source was *Fortune* magazine. The low-credibility source was identified as "a woman movie-gossip columnist."

The design was counterbalanced so that every source argued both pro and con on his or her topic, although each subject would see only the pro or the con message.

The results for the immediate aftertest (see Table 9.4) show that the high-credibility source did produce more opinion change on three of the four topics. The exception was the topic of the future of movies, where the results show slightly more opinion change for the low-credibility source.

The retest of opinion after four weeks produced a striking finding. Results for this retest are presented in Figure 9.1 for all four topics combined.

The figure shows that when the subjects were retested after four weeks, the amount of opinion change retained was approximately equal for the high-credibility and low-credibility sources. But for the low-credibility source, there appeared to be *greater* opinion change after four weeks than there was immediately after receiving the communication. This was the second occurrence of what Hovland, Lumsdaine, and Sheffield earlier had called a "sleeper" effect. Hovland and Weiss did some further research and found that this was not due to the forgetting of the source, as Hovland, Lumsdaine, and Sheffield had suggested, but to a tendency after the passage of time to dissociate the source and the opinion.

Table 9.4
SUBJECTS WHO CHANGED THEIR OPINION IN DIRECTION OF
COMMUNICATION FOR HIGH- AND LOW-CREDIBILITY SOURCES

	High-Credibility Source (%)	Low-Credibility Source (%)
Antihistamines	23	13
Atomic submarines	36	0
Steel shortage	23	−4
Future of movies	13	17

Note: The number in the table is the net percentage of subjects who changed their opinions in the direction of the communication, or the percentage who changed in the direction of the communication minus the percentage who changed in the opposite direction.
Adapted from C. I. Hovland, I. L. Janis, and H. H. Kelley, *Communication and Persuasion* (New Haven, Conn.: Yale University Press, 1953), p. 30. Copyright © 1953 by Yale University Press. Reprinted by permission.

Several other studies since the original Hovland and Weiss study have also supported the effectiveness of source credibility. McGinnies and Ward (1974) examined the effectiveness of source credibility in five countries—the United States, Japan, New Zealand, Australia, and Sweden. Subjects read a message arguing for the extension of international maritime boundaries. For some subjects, the message was attributed to a highly credible communicator—Dr. Paul Horst, a West German expert on international law. For others,

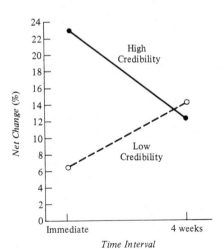

FIGURE 9.1 • CHANGES IN EXTENT OF AGREEMENT WITH HIGH-CREDIBILITY AND LOW-CREDIBILITY SOURCES AFTER FOUR WEEKS

From C. I. Hovland and W. Weiss, "The Influence of Source Credibility on Communication Effectiveness," *Public Opinion Quarterly* 15 (1951): 646. Copyright 1951 by Princeton University Press. Reprinted by permission of the University of Chicago Press.

the message was attributed to a less credible source—Mr. Paul Horst, a writer for a West German newspaper accused of having a neo-Nazi editorial policy. Source credibility had a significant effect on attitude change in three of the countries—the United States, Australia, and Sweden.

Horai, Naccari, and Fatoullah (1974) conducted an experiment varying source expertise (high, low, or no information) and physical attractiveness (high, low, or no photograph). Subjects were presented with a booklet arguing for the value of receiving a broad, general education in high school. On the cover of the booklet was a picture of an attractive or an unattractive male or no photograph. The source was identified as either a professor of education at a university or a teacher's aide at a high school, or no information was given about the source. Agreement with the message was greater for the high-expertise source than for either the low-expertise source or the source about which no information was given. Agreement with the message was also greater for the physically attractive source than for the unattractive source or the unpictured source.

Much research since the Hovland and Weiss experiment has gone into attempting to find the dimensions of source credibility. Hovland and Weiss had suggested that the dimensions of *expertness* and *trustworthiness* might be important. Many of these studies use factor analysis of rating scales applied to speakers to try to find the common dimensions used in the ratings. In one of the more comprehensive of these studies, Whitehead had subjects rate two speakers on 65 semantic differential scales solely on the basis of tape-recorded introductions (Whitehead, 1968). Whitehead found four dominant factors: trustworthiness, professionalism or competence, dynamism, and objectivity. The trustworthiness factor was based on the scales *right-wrong, honest-dishonest, trustworthy-untrustworthy,* and *just-unjust.* The professionalism or competence factor was based on the scales *experienced-inexperienced* and *has professional manner–lacks professional manner.* The dynamism factor was based on the scales *aggressive-meek* and *active-passive.* The objectivity factor was based on the scales *open minded–closed minded* and *objective-subjective.*

Whitehead's results are similar to the suggestions of Hovland and Weiss, in that they showed trustworthiness to be an important dimension. The professionalism or competence dimension is also similar to Hovland and Weiss's dimension of expertness, although it differs in dealing more with manner of presentation than with the actual knowledge that a person might possess. Whitehead's research suggests that source credibility is more complicated than that, however, with dynamism and objectivity being important components.

Anderson (1971) has provided a theoretical basis for thinking about source credibility and its components. Anderson has suggested that source credibility can be thought of as a "weight" that amplifies the value of information in a message. The weight is determined by the various characteristics of the source. Anderson argues that the status, reliability, and expertness of the source will all affect the weight. Anderson also speculates about the process by which the various factors might be combined in determining the weight. He says the most plausible hypothesis might be a multiplicative model. That is, the values on different dimensions of source credibility might not merely add up, but might multiply one another. This might help explain that special skill at communication that is sometimes given the name *charisma.* Perhaps a communicator with charisma has extremely high scores on all or nearly all the dimensions of source credibility, and these scores are combined to arrive at a final weighting by multiplying them by each other.

Other researchers have found evidence that the credibility of sources plays an important role in determining whether mass communication has an effect on public opinion. Page, Shapiro, and Dempsey (1984) studied the effect of the content of television newscasts on public opinion concerning questions of national policy. They found that news coming from different sources can have quite different effects. They found that media editorials and statements by experts (such as SALT II negotiators) had the greatest positive effect on public opinion. In contrast, many prominent political figures, including presidents, members of their administration, members of the opposition party, and interest groups, had little if any positive effect on public opinion. These authors concluded:

> For this reason it is probably misleading to talk about "media effects" per se; it is much better to deal with the effects of the statements and actions of particular kinds of political actors, as reported in the mass media. (p. 31)

Still other research has been done on source credibility since the original Hovland and Weiss study. Some researchers have challenged the existence of a sleeper effect. Gillig and Greenwald (1974) were unable to produce a sleeper effect—that is, a statistically significant increase in opinion change for a group exposed to a low-credibility source—in seven replications of an experiment designed to show the effect. Furthermore, their review of the literature indicated no previous study had really shown that kind of sleeper effect. What the earlier studies, including that of Hovland and Weiss, had shown was a significant difference in the effects of high- and low-credibility sources over time, but that is not the same as a significant increase in opinion change for a group exposed to a low-credibility source.

Other research has shown additional support for a sleeper effect, however. Cook and Flay (1978) have used the term *absolute sleeper effect* to refer to the kind of change mentioned above—a statistically significant increase in attitude change over time for a group exposed to a low-credibility source. They report that "*demonstrably* strong tests of the absolute sleeper effect have recently been conducted, and they repeatedly result in absolute sleeper effects" (p. 19).

Fear Appeals

Another common tactic in mass communication is to threaten or arouse some fear in the audience. Films shown to teenagers to promote safe driving sometimes show terrible traffic accidents and what they do to people. A television commercial for an insurance company arouses fear by saying, "You need something to help keep these promises, even if you're not there."

An example of the use of fear to achieve persuasion was described in the Oscar-winning film *Scared Straight,* which has also been shown on public television. The film describes a program developed at Rahway State Prison in New Jersey aimed at scaring youthful offenders out of future criminal behavior by exposing them to the brutality of prison life (Finckenauer, 1979). The method involves having prison inmates who are serving long sentences badger the youths and threaten them with stories of what happens in prison, including extortion, homosexual rape, and murder. The film claims that the program achieved a 90 percent success rate, with 16 of the 17 youthful offenders in the film free of further trouble three months after participating in the Rahway program. But later research, as we shall see, has raised questions about this apparent high success rate.

The book *Communication and Persuasion* (Hovland et al., 1953) describes a classic experiment by Janis and Feshbach aimed at investigating the effectiveness of fear appeals in producing attitude change. On the basis of learning theory, a key element in the Hovland approach, it can be predicted that a strong fear appeal would lead to increased attitude change because it would increase arousal and bring about greater attention and comprehension. Motivation to accept the recommendations of the communication would also be increased. In reinforcement theory terms, learning and practicing the recommended practices should become associated with the reinforcement of reduced fear and anxiety. On the other hand, the researchers realized that a high degree of emotional tension could lead to spontaneous defensive reactions and the possibility of the audience distorting the meaning of what is being said. Part of their research purpose was to investigate this potentially adverse effect of a strong fear appeal.

Janis and Feshbach designed an experiment that was based on three different messages with three different levels of fear appeal. They selected dental hygiene as their topic. The subjects were the entire freshman class of a large Connecticut high school. The class was randomly divided into four groups, three of which were to get the different fear messages and one of which was to be a control group.

The basic message, common to all three fear levels, was a standard lecture on dental hygiene. The level of fear was varied primarily through changing the material used to illustrate the lecture. In the minimal fear appeal message, the illustrative material used X rays and drawings to represent cavities, and any photographs used were of completely healthy teeth. In the moderate fear appeal version, photographs of mild cases of tooth decay and oral diseases were used. In the strong fear appeal version, the slides used to illustrate the lecture included very realistic photographs of advanced tooth decay and gum diseases. The strong fear condition also contained some personalized threats, such as the statement, "This can happen to you." The control group received a lecture on the structure and function of the human eye.

Subjects were given a questionnaire asking specific questions about their dental hygiene practices one week before the lecture and one week after. Comparison of these questionnaires would show whether subjects changed their dental hygiene behavior after being exposed to the various types of messages.

The results in Table 9.5 show that the minimal fear appeal was the most effective in getting the students to follow the dental hygiene recommendations in the lecture. The strong fear appeal was the least effective. This was definite evidence that a fear appeal can be too strong and can evoke some form of interference that reduces the effectiveness of the communication. This experiment had several strengths that have not always been present in later attitude change studies. One is that the message was shown to have an effect on reported behavior, and not just on a paper and pencil measure of a hypothetical attitude. The field of attitude change research was involved in a controversy a few years later in which many studies were criticized for producing slight changes in unimportant attitudes. Second, the persuasive messages used by Janis and Feshbach were shown to have produced long-term attitude change. Another criticism of some later attitude change studies is that they dealt only with short-term attitude change, often measured immediately after the message. Janis and Feshbach went back to their subjects a year later and still found the differences in attitude change between their experimental groups.

The Janis and Feshbach study was the first of a number of studies on fear appeals. Not all these studies have agreed with the finding that strong fear produces less attitude change.

Table 9.5
CONFORMITY TO DENTAL HYGIENE RECOMMENDATIONS IN SUBJECTS
WHO RECEIVED MESSAGES WITH DIFFERENT LEVELS OF FEAR

	Strong Fear Appeal (%)	Moderate Fear Appeal (%)	Minimal Fear Appeal (%)	Control Group (%)
Increased conformity	28	44	50	22
Decreased conformity	20	22	14	22
No change	52	34	36	56

Adapted from C. I. Hovland, I. L. Janis, and H. H. Kelley, *Communication and Persuasion* (New Haven, Conn.: Yale University Press, 1953), p. 80. Copyright © 1953 by Yale University Press. Reprinted by permission.

One possible explanation for the findings of Janis and Feshbach is that the recommendation of brushing your teeth properly was not seen as a believable recommendation for preventing the kinds of horrible consequences presented in the strong fear appeal message. Other studies have shed some light on this possibility. Leventhal and Niles (1964) presented a message to audiences at a New York City health exposition recommending that they get a chest X ray and that they stop smoking. The message was presented to different groups with differing levels of fear: high fear (featuring a color movie of removal of a lung), medium fear (featuring the same color movie but without the graphic scene of a lung removal), and low fear (with no movie). They found that the amount of reported fear in audience members was correlated with stated intentions to stop smoking and to get a chest X ray. These results suggest that fear facilitates attitude change—the opposite of the Janis and Feshbach finding. What could account for this difference? Possibly the difference was due to the degree to which the recommendations appeared to be effective. Toothbrushing may not have seemed adequate to prevent the rotted teeth and bloody gums seen in the Janis and Feshbach experiment. In contrast, stopping smoking may appear to be a believable recommendation for preventing lung cancer.

Building on the Leventhal and Niles research as well as some other research of his own, Rogers (1975) developed a model that summarizes three key elements in the operation of a fear appeal: (1) the magnitude of noxiousness of a depicted event, (2) the probability of that event's occurrence, and (3) the efficacy of a protective response. Each component brings about a process of cognitive appraisal, and these cognitive appraisal processes then determine the amount of attitude change (see Figure 9.2). That is, when audience members receive a fear appeal, they weigh it in their minds. If the portrayed noxiousness or horribleness of the event is not believed, or the event is thought not to be likely, or the recommended actions are not believed to be adequate to deal with the threat, then attitude change is not likely. Rogers calls his model a protection motivation theory of fear appeals and attitude change. Attitude change is said to be a function of the amount of protection motivation aroused by the cognitive appraisal that the audience member goes through.

The protection motivation theory model has received some support in a study by Rogers and Mewborn (1976). Results from an experiment they conducted on the dangers of vene-

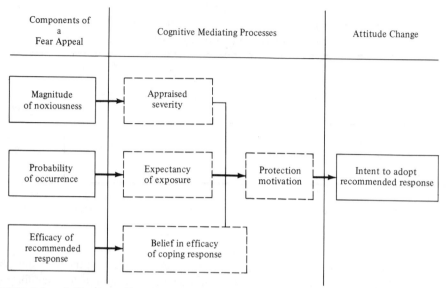

FIGURE 9.2 • A MODEL OF PROTECTION MOTIVATION THEORY

From R. W. Rogers, "A Protection Motivation Theory of Fear Appeals and Attitude Change," *Journal of Psychology* 91 (1975): 99. Reprinted with permission of the Helen Dwight Reid Educational Foundation. Published by Heldref Publications, 4000 Albemarle St., N.W., Washington, D.C. 20016. Copyright © 1975.

real disease are presented in Figure 9.3. The graph shows that when a recommendation is given that is seen to be low in efficacy, then neither low noxiousness nor high noxiousness in the message leads to a high score on intent to adopt the recommended response. When the recommendation is seen as high in efficacy, however, then the high noxiousness message leads to a higher score on intent to adopt the recommended response than the low noxiousness message.

Some research on the effectiveness of the antidelinquency program described in the film *Scared Straight* also supports the conclusion that a strong fear appeal may not be effective in achieving attitude change. J. O. Finckenauer (1979) did a study in which some juveniles were randomly assigned to the Rahway "scared straight" treatment or to a control group that received no special treatment. The rate of getting into further trouble was 11 percent for the control group and 41 percent for those exposed to the "scared straight" treatment. The researcher concluded, "Results from a six-month follow-up study of both samples showed that the project was worse than ineffective in deterring future delinquent behavior" (Finckenauer, 1979, p. 6).

It is not clear why the "scared straight" program had an effect that was opposite the one intended. Perhaps specific recommendations that were believable and that would help the youngsters stay out of trouble were not provided—a step that protection motivation theory would suggest is necessary. For instance, it is possible that the causes in society that lead to crime, such as poverty, were basically untouched by the Rahway program and were still operating after the youths left the program. This should not lead to a greater likelihood of

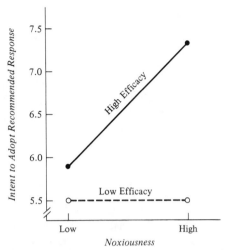

FIGURE 9.3 • INTERACTION OF MAGNITUDE OF NOXIOUSNESS AND EFFICACY OF COPING RE-
SPONSE IN INFLUENCING INTENT TO ADOPT THE RECOMMENDED RESPONSE

From R. W. Rogers and C. R. Mewborn, "Fear Appeals and Attitude Change: Effects of a Threat's Noxiousness,
Probability of Occurrence, and the Efficacy of Coping Responses," *Journal of Personality and Social Psychology*
34 (1976): 58. Copyright 1976 by the American Psychological Association. Reprinted by permission of the
author.

getting into trouble than the control group, however. Another possibility is that the youths
actually began to identify with the convicts who were giving them a rough time, and
wanted to be like them.

Reardon (1989) has discussed how fear appeals might best be used in a communication
about AIDS addressed to teenagers, who typically perceive the threat of death as remote.
She suggested that mass media messages aimed at adolescents emphasize the more immediate consequences of the disease, including mental problems, skin rashes and sores, and
the negative effect on a teenager's social life. She suggested, furthermore, that the media
campaigns be combined with interpersonal question-and-answer sessions in which discussion can bring out information regarding methods for avoiding the problems described or
depicted in the media messages.

The effectiveness of fear appeals in condom advertisements stressing the prevention of
AIDS was studied by Hill (1988). He found that subjects had more positive attitudes toward a moderate fear appeal commercial (stating that sex can be a risky business) than
either a nonfear appeal (stressing the sensitivity of the condom and saying nothing about
AIDS) or high fear appeal (mentioning the possibility of death). Hill speculated that a
nonfear appeal may appear inappropriate in an AIDS environment, but that a high fear
appeal may be viewed as too threatening when it is combined with the individual's existing
level of AIDS-related anxiety.

Fear appeals are attempting to bring about changes in people's motivations, a tricky
enterprise at best. As Ross (1985) has noted, "Audience motivation through symbolic interaction is terribly complex; we should be wary of 'infallible' motive appeals" (p. 48).

Resistance to Counterpropaganda

With so much energy being devoted to changing attitudes, it might be extremely useful to discover some methods of making attitudes resistant to change. Lumsdaine and Janis report a study in *Communication and Persuasion* (Hovland et al., 1953) that deals with building resistance of an attitude to change. Their experiment follows up on the earlier work on one-sided and two-sided messages by Hovland, Lumsdaine, and Sheffield.

Lumsdaine and Janis produced one-sided and two-sided messages arguing that Russia would be unable to produce large numbers of atomic bombs for at least five years. This was a realistic issue for differences of opinion in the early 1950s. The one-sided message argued that the Russians lacked some crucial secrets, that their espionage was not effective, and that Russia was lacking in industry. The two-sided message added brief mentions of the arguments that Russia had uranium mines in Siberia, that it had many top scientists, and that its industry had grown since the war. Several weeks before the messages were presented, all subjects were given a questionnaire to determine their initial opinions. One group received the one-sided message and another received the two-sided message. A week later, half of each group was exposed to an opposing communication from a different communicator arguing that Russia had probably already developed the atomic bomb. This counterpropaganda brought out some new arguments not included in the two-sided message. Both the initial messages and the counterpropaganda were presented in the form of recorded radio programs. Finally, all subjects were given another questionnaire.

The key question, asked in both the initial and final questionnaires, was this: "About how long from now do you think it will be before the Russians are really producing *large numbers* of atomic bombs?"

The net opinion change from initial to final questionnaire for those who received counterpropaganda and those who did not in both the one-sided and two-sided conditions is

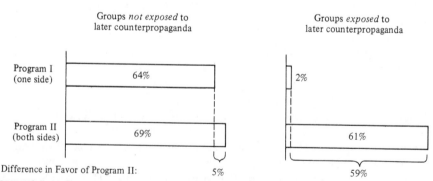

Net Change in the Positive Direction

FIGURE 9.4 • COMPARISON OF THE EFFECTIVENESS OF PROGRAMS I AND II: CHANGES IN OPINIONS CONCERNING THE LENGTH OF TIME BEFORE RUSSIA PRODUCES LARGE NUMBERS OF A-BOMBS

From A. Lumsdaine and I. Janis, "Resistance to 'Counterpropaganda' Produced by One-Sided and Two-Sided 'Propaganda' Presentations," *Public Opinion Quarterly* 17 (1953): 316. Copyright 1953 by Princeton University. Reprinted by permission of the University of Chicago Press.

presented in Figure 9.4. The results show that for those receiving no counterpropaganda, the one-sided and two-sided messages were about equally effective. This replicates the finding of the earlier study by Hovland, Lumsdaine, and Sheffield. The results show a striking difference for those receiving counterpropaganda, however. Those receiving a one-sided message showed almost no remaining attitude change after they were exposed to counterpropaganda. In contrast, those receiving a two-sided message showed almost as much attitude change remaining after counterpropaganda as they did when they weren't exposed to counterpropaganda.

One of the advantages of the two-sided message over the one-sided message, then, is that it is more effective in building resistance to later persuasive efforts.

Lumsdaine and Janis speak of the recipient of the two-sided message as becoming "inoculated." This is a medical analogy that William McGuire and Demetrios Papageorgis drew upon later in developing their "inoculation theory."

Inoculation Theory

McGuire and Papageorgis's theory rests on the medical analogy that is suggested by its name. They point out that most people have many unchallenged beliefs, and that these beliefs can often be easily swayed once they are attacked because the person is not used to defending them. The situation is similar to that in the medical field when a person is brought up in a germ-free environment and is suddenly exposed to germs. That person's body is vulnerable to infection because it has not developed any resistance. Such a person can be given resistance either by supportive treatment—good diet, exercise, rest, and so forth—or by inoculation, a deliberate exposure to a weakened form of the germ that stimulates the development of defenses. In the medical area the inoculation approach has been more effective than supportive treatment in producing resistance. The word *immunization* can be applied to either of these methods of building immunity—the supportive approach or the inoculation approach.

McGuire and Papageorgis have conducted a number of experiments to test this theory. One of the first (McGuire & Papageorgis, 1961) tested the basic prediction that the supportive approach of preexposing a person to arguments supporting basic beliefs would have less immunizing effectiveness than the inoculation approach of preexposing the person to weakened, defense-stimulating forms of arguments attacking the beliefs. It also tested a second hypothesis that active participation during exposure to a defense should be less effective than passive participation in producing immunity to later persuasion. The researchers made this prediction because they theorized that subjects would not be accustomed to active participation in defending their basic beliefs and so would not do it very well. Furthermore, they thought that active participation might interfere with the reception of any defensive material presented. (There was also a complicated third hypothesis that need not concern us here.)

McGuire and Papageorgis selected for their study some beliefs that were hardly ever attacked in our culture, which they called "cultural truisms." The four beliefs were these: "Everyone should get a chest X-ray each year in order to detect any possible tuberculosis symptoms at an early stage." "The effects of penicillin have been, almost without exception, of great benefit to mankind." "Most forms of mental illness are not contagious."

"Everyone should brush his teeth after every meal if at all possible." These cultural truisms were so widely believed that control groups of subjects rated them at an average level of 13.26 on a scale ranging from 1 for "definitely false" to 15 for "definitely true."

Subjects took part in two one-hour experimental sessions held two days apart. The first exposed subjects to the two types of immunizing material designed to make the basic beliefs ("cultural truisms") more resistant to change; the second exposed subjects to strong counterarguments attacking the basic beliefs. Questionnaires were administered at the end of each session to measure strength of acceptance of beliefs.

The two major types of immunizing material presented to subjects were "supportive" and "refutational." The supportive material was made up of arguments supporting the cultural truisms. The refutational material consisted of possible counterarguments against the cultural truisms together with refutations of these counterarguments. The amount of participation in the defense was varied primarily by having subjects write in a high participation condition and read in a low participation condition. Each subject was tested on one cultural truism for which he or she received no immunization but did receive the later counterarguments. The average scale position for these beliefs after they were attacked was 6.64, compared with the average level of 13.26 prior to attack. This result shows that the cultural truisms were highly vulnerable to attack if no immunization was given.

McGuire and Papageorgis found, as they had predicted, that the refutational defenses were more effective in making the cultural truisms resistant to change than were the supportive defenses. After the supportive defenses, the counterarguments were able to reduce the belief in the cultural truisms to an average rating of 7.39, only slightly better than the 6.64 level achieved when there was no prior preparation at all. After the inoculation defenses the counterarguments were able to reduce the beliefs in the cultural truisms only to an average scale rating of 10.33. The authors also found support for their second hypothesis: the passive (reading) conditions had a greater effect in making beliefs resistant to persuasion than did the active (writing) conditions.

The McGuire and Papageorgis experiment was limited in one respect that needed further investigation. The attacks on the cultural truisms that were presented and then refuted in the inoculation were the same attacks that were presented in the next session when the cultural truisms were assailed. It was not clear whether presenting and refuting one set of attacks would also provide later immunity to a different set of attacks. This question was investigated in another experiment by Papageorgis and McGuire (1961).

Papageorgis and McGuire predicted that a kind of generalized immunity would develop when people were exposed to attacks on basic beliefs and refutations of those attacks. That is, they predicted that this procedure would develop a general resistance that would make the basic belief unlikely to change even when it was exposed to attacks that were not the same. They expected this result for two reasons: (1) The experience of seeing the first attacks refuted could lower the credibility of the later attacks. (2) Preexposure to attacks may make a person more aware that his or her beliefs are indeed vulnerable and motivate the person to develop additional supporting arguments.

Their results showed inoculation led to an immunity to differing counterarguments that was almost as strong as the immunity to the same counterarguments. In fact, the final attitude positions in these two conditions were not significantly different. This, of course, increases the potency of an inoculation—the developers of the inoculation program do not have to anticipate all the attacks on a belief that a person might later be exposed to.

Katz's Functional Approach

The two major theoretical approaches to attitude change—the learning theory approach, primarily associated with Hovland, and the consistency theory approach, primarily associated with Festinger, Newcomb, Heider, and Osgood and Tannenbaum—existed side by side with little apparent relation to one another for some time. But eventually researchers became interested in reconciling these rather different ways of dealing with attitude change. Daniel Katz and his colleagues Irving Sarnoff and Charles McClintock tackled this problem, and it led them to develop the functional approach to attitude change.

These authors were trying to bring together two different models of human behavior that have been presented over the years—the rational model and the irrational model. The irrational model suggests that human beings are nonthinking creatures whose beliefs are easily influenced by people around them and who even can have their perception of reality influenced by their own desires. The rational model suggests that human beings are intelligent and critical thinkers who can make wise decisions when given ample information. How can both of these models be true? Katz and his associates suggest that the answer to this dilemma is that human beings are both rational and irrational, depending on the situation, the motivations operating at the time, and so forth. And they argue that this tendency for people to operate with different ways of thinking has important implications for understanding attitude change.

Katz argues that both attitude formation and change must be understood in terms of the functions that attitudes serve for the personality. As these functions differ, so will the conditions and techniques of attitude change. Katz points out that much of the earlier research on mass communication dealt with factors that are not really psychological variables, such as exposure to a motion picture. Since being exposed to a motion picture can serve different functions for different individuals, Katz argues that the researcher dealing only with exposure to a film is not really able to understand or predict attitude change. Katz makes the key point that the same attitude can have a different motivational basis in different people. He suggests that "unless we know the psychological need which is met by the holding of an attitude we are in a poor position to predict when and how it will change" (Katz, 1960, p. 170).

Katz identifies the following four major functions that attitudes can serve for the personality:

1. *The instrumental, adjustive, or utilitarian function.* Some attitudes are held because people are striving to maximize the rewards in their external environments and minimize the penalties. For instance, a voter who thinks taxes are too high might favor a political candidate because that candidate promises to reduce taxes.

2. *The ego-defensive function.* Some attitudes are held because people are protecting their egos from their own unacceptable impulses or from knowledge of threatening forces without. Feelings of inferiority are often projected onto a minority group as a means of bolstering the ego. This would be an example of an attitude of prejudice serving the ego-defensive function.

3. *The value-expressive function.* Some attitudes are held because they allow a person to give positive expression to central values and to the kind of person the individual feels he or she is. For instance, a teenager who likes a particular rock and roll group is expressing his or her individuality through this attitude.

4. *The knowledge function.* Some attitudes are held because they satisfy a desire for knowledge or provide structure and meaning in what would otherwise be a chaotic world. Many religious beliefs serve this function, as do other attitudes such as the shared norms of a culture. Katz has presented a table (see Table 9.6) summarizing the origin and dynamics, the arousal conditions, and the change conditions for attitudes serving each of the four functions.

Katz warns that an attempt to change an attitude may backfire if it is not based on an understanding of the functions the attitude is serving. For instance, an attempt to change attitudes of prejudice by presenting factual information on the accomplishments of minority group members would be attempting to change the attitudes as if they were serving the knowledge function. It is not likely to succeed if the attitudes of prejudice are held for ego-defense reasons.

Attitudes and Behavior

Despite all the research on attitude change, researchers for a long time neglected an important question. In its more general form, the question is whether attitudes as they are measured by social science methods have any real relation to behavior. In its more specific form, the question is whether attitude change produced by persuasive messages is accompanied by any meaningful change in behavior.

One early study had indicated that attitudes might not bear much of a relationship to behavior. A social scientist named Richard LaPiere traveled in the early 1930s around the United States with a young Chinese couple. They made 251 visits to hotels and restaurants, and in only one case were they refused service. Six months later, LaPiere sent a questionnaire to each establishment asking: "Will you accept members of the Chinese race as guests in your establishment?" He received replies from 128 of these businesses. The responses from 92 percent of the restaurants and 91 percent of the hotels were no. Only one person gave a definite yes (LaPiere, 1934). This classic study, then, provided some evidence that people's verbal reports of their attitudes might not be very good predictors of their actual behavior.

Leon Festinger, the psychologist who developed the theory of cognitive dissonance, raised some basic questions about attitude change experiments and subsequent behavior in an address he gave in 1963. Festinger (1964) said he had been reading a manuscript by Arthur R. Cohen when he came across the statement that very little work on attitude change had dealt explicitly with the behavior that may follow a change in attitude. Festinger was intrigued by this notion and attempted to find as many studies as he could that showed an effect of attitude change on subsequent behavior change. He found only three. One of these was the Janis and Feshbach study of fear appeals. Their study did not investigate actual behavior change, but it did look at verbal reports of toothbrushing behavior and other dental hygiene behavior. Festinger was willing to accept this verbal report since it did purportedly deal with actual behavior. In all three of the studies Festinger found, there seemed to be a slight inverse relationship between attitude change and behavior change. For instance, in the Janis and Feshbach study, the individuals who indicated the most concern about their teeth after receiving the persuasive messages showed the least

Table 9.6

DETERMINANTS OF ATTITUDE FORMATION, AROUSAL,
AND CHANCE IN RELATION TO TYPE OF FUNCTION

Function	Origin and Dynamics	Arousal Conditions	Change Conditions
Adjustment	Utility of attitudinal object in need satisfaction. Maximizing external rewards and minimizing punishments	1. Activation of needs 2. Salience of cues associated with need satisfaction	1. Need deprivation 2. Creation of new needs and new levels of aspiration 3. Shifting rewards and punishments 4. Emphasis on new and better paths for need satisfaction
Ego defense	Protecting against internal conflicts and external dangers	1. Posing of threats 2. Appeals to hatred and repressed impulses 3. Rise in frustrations 4. Use of authoritarian suggestion	1. Removal of threats 2. Catharsis 3. Development of self-insight
Value expression	Maintaining self-identity; enhancing favorable self-image; self-expression and self-determination	1. Salience of cues associated with values 2. Appeals to individual to reassert self-image 3. Ambiguities which threaten self-concept	1. Some degree of dissatisfaction with self 2. Greater appropriateness of new attitude for the self 3. Control of all environmental supports to undermine old values
Knowledge	Need for understanding, for meaningful cognitive organization, for consistency and clarity	1. Reinstatement of cues associated with old problem or of old problem itself	1. Ambiguity created by new information or change in environment 2. More meaningful information about problems

From D. Katz, "The Functional Approach to the Study of Attitudes," *Public Opinion Quarterly* 24 (1960): 192. Copyright 1960 by Princeton University. Reprinted by permission of the University of Chicago Press.

change in their reported behavior. Festinger argued that this inverse relationship indicates that the relationship between attitude change and behavior is not a simple one.

One reason attitude change might not be automatically followed by behavior change, Festinger (1964) suggested, is that the environmental factors that had produced an original attitude would usually still be operating after that attitude was changed. Thus there would be a tendency for an attitude to revert to its original position after exposure to a persuasive message. Festinger noted:

> I want to suggest that when opinions or attitudes are changed through the momentary impact of a persuasive communication, this change, all by itself, is inherently unstable and will disappear or remain isolated unless an environmental or behavioral change can be brought about to support and maintain it. (p. 415)

Festinger was suggesting to attitude change theorists the disturbing possibility that they had conducted hundreds of experiments on variables that make very little difference in terms of human behavior.

Wicker (1969) brought up again the more general issue of whether attitudes are related to behavior. He looked at more than 30 studies of attitude and behavior and reported that attitude-behavior correlations are "rarely above .30, and often are near zero" (p. 65). Wicker concluded, "Taken as a whole, these studies suggest that it is considerably more likely that attitudes will be unrelated or only slightly related to overt behaviors than that attitudes will be closely related to actions" (p. 65).

A number of other studies after Wicker's review article also indicated little relationship between attitude and behavior. At this point, some researchers were beginning to suggest that the concept of attitude was proving to be worthless and should be thrown out. Others suggested that the prediction of behavior from attitudes could be improved if other crucial variables were considered. For instance, in certain cases, the situation can have a greater role in determining behavior than a person's attitude. One obvious example of this is the presence of a mob, which can cause many people to become caught up in behavior they might say was wrong at another time. This is a common phenomenon—in almost any case in which other people are present, the situation itself can play a great role in influencing behavior. Perhaps the prediction of behavior from attitudes could be improved if situational variables could also be taken into account.

Still other thinkers (Gross & Niman, 1975) pointed out that past studies have often been limited in that they attempted to use an attitude measurement to predict a single act of behavior. Perhaps the predictions would be improved if an attitude-measuring instrument using a range of questions were then related to a range of behaviors.

These two lines of thinking have led to some of the recent research on the attitude-behavior question.

Realizing that the prediction of a specific behavior depends on a number of factors in addition to some kind of measure of attitude, Martin Fishbein attempted to develop a model that would include all the important factors. The model (see Ajzen & Fishbein, 1970) takes the form of the following equation:

$$B \sim BI = [A_{act}]w_0 + [NB(M_c)]w_1$$

Although the model looks complicated, it becomes easier to understand when it is put into words. The letters in the equation can be translated as follows:

B   = overt behavior

BI   = the behavioral intention to perform that behavior

A_{act} = attitude toward performing a given behavior in a given act situation

NB   = normative beliefs, or beliefs that significant others think one should or should not perform the behavior

M_c = motivation to comply with the norm C

w_0 and w_1 = regression weights to be determined empirically

The equation can be rephrased in the following English sentence: A person's intention to perform a given behavior is a function of (1) the person's attitude toward performing that behavior and (2) the person's perception of the norms governing that behavior and the individual's motivation to comply with those norms.

This model brings in some of the key situational factors, particularly the beliefs that other people have about the behavior and the individual's motivation to conform to those beliefs. If precise measurements could be made of all the variable quantities in the model, it should be possible to make rather exact predictions of behavioral intention and then of actual behavior. Fishbein (1973) reports that a number of experiments using the model to predict behavioral intention have produced multiple correlations of about .80, which are quite high. These experiments also found correlations between behavioral intention and overt behavior of .70, so all the key parts have been supported. In a continuation of the Fishbein research, Ajzen (1971) has used the Fishbein model to demonstrate behavioral change as the result of persuasive communication, the phenomenon that Festinger had difficulty finding in 1963.

Weigel and Newman (1976) took the second line of thinking mentioned above. That is, they conducted a study designed to overcome the limitation of most studies of attitude and behavior that had attempted to use a general attitude measure to predict a single specific behavior. They conducted a field study of attitudes on environmental issues using a random sample of residents of a community. People were first given an attitude scale measuring environmental concern. Then, over the next eight months, their behavior in the environmental area was determined with regard to 14 separate acts. The opportunities to engage in these acts were presented by people who knocked on their doors but did not identify themselves with the earlier administration of the attitude questionnaire. The 14 acts included signing of three petitions on environmental issues (1–3), circulating these petitions to others (4), participating in a litter pickup (5), recruiting a friend to pick up litter (6), and participating in a recycling program in eight different weeks (7–14). Correlations between attitude scale scores and these single behaviors ranged from .12 to .57. When the behaviors were summed into one index, however, the correlation was .62. The authors suggest that the comprehensive behavioral measure produces a higher correlation because it is broader and provides an adequate range of the universe of actions implied in the attitude measure.

These are two recent lines of research on attitude-behavior consistency—the Fishbein approach that incorporates norms and other relevant variables in a predictive model, and the Weigel and Newman approach that attempts to predict from attitude to a range of behaviors rather than a single act of behavior.

Another important development, which seems to have come about particularly because of Festinger's address, is that many more researchers are now including behavioral measures in their studies of attitude change. For instance, many fear appeal studies now include behavioral measures such as the "disclosing wafer" test of how well teeth are actually cleaned (Evans, Rozelle, Lasater, Dembroski, & Allen, 1970) or the actual act of going to get a shot or vaccination (Krisher, Darley, & Darley, 1973). Similarly, the Stanford project aimed at reducing heart disease through communication used such behavioral measures as blood pressure, cholesterol level, weight, and number of cigarettes smoked (Maccoby & Farquhar, 1975).

Classical Conditioning of Attitudes

Some other researchers besides Hovland have also attempted to apply learning theory to attitude change. In particular, Staats and Staats have applied classical conditioning to the learning of attitudes (Staats, 1968).

Staats and Staats begin by demonstrating the application of classical conditioning to the learning of the emotional meaning of language. They point out that in our everyday experience certain words are systematically paired with certain emotional experiences. For instance, words like *joy, happy, play, dinner, pretty,* and *good* are typically paired with positive emotions, while words like *angry, hurt, dirty, awful, sick, sad,* and *ugly* are typically paired with negative emotions. In the terms of classical conditioning, the emotional stimuli can be considered the unconditioned stimuli that elicit emotional responses. When a word stimulus is systematically paired with such an unconditioned stimulus, the word should become a conditioned stimulus and also elicit the emotional responses.

In an experiment to test this possibility, researchers exposed two groups of subjects to a list of spoken words (Staats, Staats, & Crawford, 1962). For the experimental group, 9 of the 14 times a subject was presented with the word *large,* it was followed by a negative stimulus—either a loud noise delivered by earphone or a shock to the right forearm. Both noise and shock were set at a level where they were "uncomfortable" but not "painful." Members of the control group also received the negative stimuli 9 times, but they were paired with different "filler" words other than *large.* Results showed that those subjects who experienced the word *large* being paired with the aversive stimulus came to display an emotional reaction, as measured by the galvanic skin response (GSR), when presented with the word *large.* This was not true for the control group. Furthermore, measurements with semantic differential scales showed that *large* had acquired a negative rating on the evaluative scale for the experimental group that it did not have for the control group.

Staats and Staats (1957) went on to hypothesize that this conditioning of meaning should work from word to word as well as from a physical stimulus to a word. In another experiment, nonsense syllables such as *yof, laj, xeh, wuh, giw,* and *qug* were presented visually on a screen while words were presented aurally. For one group of subjects, two of the nonsense syllables were always paired with words that had high loadings on evaluative meaning, such as *beauty, win, gift, sweet,* and *honest.* A different high evaluation word was used in every pairing, so that subjects would not associate particular pairs of words. The other four nonsense syllables were paired with words that had no systematic meaning. For another group of subjects, the procedures were identical except that the two nonsense syllables were always paired with words with negative emotional meaning, such as *thief, bit-*

ter, ugly, sad, and *worthless.* Subjects were later given semantic differential scales to measure their evaluative meanings for the nonsense syllables, and those scales showed positive ratings in general for the group receiving positive stimulus words and negative ratings in general for the group receiving negative stimulus words.

Staats and Staats argue that attitude is nothing more than this kind of emotional meaning for a word that has been established by classical conditioning. In another experiment (Staats & Staats, 1958), names of nations and familiar masculine names were used as the conditioned stimulus rather than nonsense syllables. The national names were *Dutch* or *Swedish,* and the masculine names were *Tom* and *Bill.* For all four of these, subjects would be expected to have existing attitudes on the basis of prior experience. Thus, the experiment was really a study of attitude change. The experiment showed that pairing any of the four words with either positive or negative words could condition the subjects' attitudes in either a positive or a negative direction.

The Staats and Staats research provides a theoretical explanation for some of the propaganda devices, such as "glittering generality," which attempts to link a person or idea to a virtue word, or "name calling," which attempts to associate a person or idea with a bad label.

This conditioning of attitudes also seems to be related to much of what goes on in advertising. Many product names, such as Ipana or Qantas, are essentially nonsense syllables to the public when they are first introduced. A major goal of advertising is to associate them with positive words or experiences, which, through conditioning, might give them a positive meaning. A slogan such as "Coke is the real thing" is attempting to transfer positive associations to Coke. In the cases of some other products, such as Fab or Sprite, the product name might be chosen because of positive associations that it already has.

The Theory of Low Involvement

The normal idea of attitude change preceding behavior change has been reversed in one theory dealing particularly with the effects of television advertising. Herbert Krugman, manager of public opinion research for General Electric, has developed a theory that says that people process messages on television differently from messages in the print media (Krugman, 1965, 1972, 1977). He argues that the familiar AIETA model—awareness, interest, evaluation, trial, adoption—applies primarily to the print media. He calls this the left-brain, verbal, "look before you leap," reasonable, or "rational" model. Television, he argues, is processed by the right hemisphere of the brain rather than the left hemisphere. This kind of processing of information takes place with low involvement or no involvement. Krugman says messages processed in this way are stored in memory but cannot be recalled. Krugman states, "The theory of low involvement asserts that repetition of exposure has an effect which is not readily apparent until a behavioral trigger comes along" (1977, p. 9). That is, a person might see a television commercial for Coors beer, store the message in some form through right-brain processing, go to the grocery store, see Coors beer on display, purchase some Coors beer, and then formulate a favorable attitude toward Coors beer.

Krugman's theory, if it is correct, might apply to much of the other content of television as well as commercials. The effect of entertainment programs on clothing styles, fads, language (including slang), and even values might be explained by this kind of effect taking place through right-hemisphere processing.

In fact, the Krugman theory starts to sound quite a bit like subliminal perception (see Chapter 4). Research on subliminal perception, however, has generally not shown this technique to be effective in persuasion. Further research is needed to clear up this discrepancy.

Techniques of Persuasion

We now turn to three important techniques commonly used in persuasion: appeals to humor, appeals to sex, and extensive repetition of an advertising message. Audiences and communicators need to understand their applications—and their potential misuse.

Appeals to Humor

The use of humor is a popular technique in communication. Many public speakers obviously believe in the importance of beginning their talks with a humorous story. Studies have suggested that 15 to 20 percent of television commercials contain some element of humor (Kelly & Solomon, 1975; Duncan & Nelson, 1985).

In the typical study of the effects of humor on attitude change or other variables in the hierarchy of effects, different groups are exposed to different versions of the same message—one with humor and one without. For instance, Brooker (1981) examined the effects of humor in two commercials—one for a toothpaste and one for a flu vaccine. Examples of the humorous appeals used in his study appear in Table 9.7.

When attitude change or persuasion is the dependent variable of interest, most studies have not found a significant effect due to humor (Gruner, 1965, 1967, 1970, 1972; Brooker, 1981).

Other studies of the effectiveness of humor indicate that it has more of an effect on lower-order communication effects (responses lower in the response hierarchy) than on higher-order communication effects (Gelb & Pickett, 1983; Duncan & Nelson, 1985). That is, humor is more effective in attracting attention, generating liking for the communicator, and so forth, than it is in producing attitude change or changes in behavior.

Not all studies agree, however, that humor is even effective in generating liking for the communicator. One study showed that a woman speaker was liked less when she used humor than when she did not (Taylor, 1974). The author suggests that the speaker was perceived as "trying too hard to curry favor." Similarly, another study showed that college teachers who use humor are perceived with "suspicion and hostility" because they are acting contrary to student expectations that a teacher's behavior will be controlling and evaluative (Darling & Civikly, 1984).

The research on the effectiveness of humor that has been conducted so far should be interpreted in light of its limitations, however. One limitation is that the settings of the studies have often been classrooms or laboratories, which might not be representative of the settings where humor is expected. Another limitation is that the research has tended to be nontheoretical, with little discussion of why humor might or might not be effective in achieving various effects. Markiewicz (1974) has suggested that learning theory and distraction theory are two promising theories for understanding the relationship of humor to persuasion. A learning theory approach might suggest that humor would provide reinforcement and thus lead to greater attitude change. A distraction theory approach might

Table 9.7

HUMOR APPEALS USED IN BROOKER'S EXPERIMENT

Pun

Toothbrush: Here's an idea with some "teeth" in it.

Vaccine: Song of the spring camper: "We're tenting tonight on the old damp ground."

Limerick

Toothbrush: If your lady friend turns aside her nose
Whenever you begin to propose
The halitosis demon
Might be what sends her screamin'
And your toothbrush could help to solve your woes.

Vaccine: There was an old lady of Crewe
Who was horribly frightened of flu.
She spoilt her complexion
Through fear of infection
Having fixed on her gas mask with glue.

Joke

Toothbrush: Detecting decay in the tooth of a beautiful young woman, the dentist said, "What's a place like this doing in a girl like you?"

Vaccine: A little boy was found watching a movie by the manager in the morning. "Why aren't you in school?" he asked the boy. "It's O.K., mister, I'm just getting over the flu."

One-liner

Toothbrush: Oscar Levant once said, "The first thing I do in the morning is brush my teeth and sharpen my tongue."

Vaccine: Many flu sufferers have said, "I hope I'm really sick. I'd hate to feel like this if I'm well."

From G. W. Brooker, "A Comparison of the Persuasive Effects of Mild Humor and Mild Fear Appeals," *Journal of Advertising* 10, no. 4 (1981): 32. Used by permission.

make the prediction that humor would be distracting. This distraction, in turn, might lead to greater attitude change by preventing counterarguing (Festinger & Maccoby, 1964). Or distraction might lead to less attitude change by interfering with attentiveness to the message.

It has also been suggested that the use of humor needs to be studied in relation to other variables (Kelly & Solomon, 1975). For instance, in advertising, is the humor more effective when it relates to the topic or when it does not? In a commercial, should the humor come at the beginning, at the end, or all through the commercial?

Appeals to Sex

The use of sexy models and other sexual appeals is a common technique in advertising. One study has indicated that more than one-fourth of magazine ads contain "obviously alluring" female models (Sexton & Haberman, 1974). Furthermore, these kinds of ads are on the increase. The same study showed the ads with "obviously alluring" models increased from 10 percent in 1951 to 27 percent in 1971. Many advertisers apparently believe that "sex sells." But does it?

At least one study suggests that a sexy model can affect the perception or image of a product, even if there is very little logical connection between the model and the product. Smith and Engel (1968) prepared a print ad for an automobile in two versions. In one version, a female model clad in black lace panties and a simple sleeveless sweater stood in front of the car. She held a spear—on the assumption that the spear might be regarded as a phallic symbol and might lead the model to be seen as more aggressively seductive. In the other version, there was no model. When the car was pictured with the woman, subjects rated it as more appealing, more youthful, more lively, and better designed. Even objective characteristics were affected. When the car appeared with the woman, it was rated as higher in horsepower, less safe, more expensive by $340, and able to move an average 7.3 miles per hour faster. In general, male and female subjects responded the same way to the ads.

In contrast to the Smith and Engel study, however, a number of studies investigating the effects of sexy models on brand recall have shown either no effect or less recall with the sexy model (Chestnut, LaChance, & Lubitz, 1977; Alexander & Judd, 1978). It appears that the sexy models distract the viewers' attention away from the portion of the ad presenting the product or company name.

One study suggests that for certain products, an attractive female might not be as effective in stimulating sales as an attractive male (Caballero & Solomon, 1984). This study changed the displays for a brand of beer and a brand of tissue that appeared at the end of an aisle in a Tom Thumb supermarket. They found that overall, the male models tended to stimulate more beer sales among both male and female customers than either the female stimulus or the control (no model) treatment.

Another study indicates that response to sex in advertising is not a simple variable (Morrison & Sherman, 1972). The study had a number of subjects look at ads from magazines and express their reaction to them on rating scales. They then used cluster analysis to look for different patterns of response. For the males, they identified three dimensions of response as important: (1) the "Tom Jones" dimension, (2) the intellectualizing dimension, and (3) the fetishism dimension. For females, they identified four dimensions: (1) sensualism, (2) love/sexism, (3) romanticism, and (4) fantasism. Not only do different ads emphasize some of these dimensions and not others, but different people respond to some dimensions favorably while ignoring others completely. The authors also found that, contrary to their expectation, women were more quick to pick up on suggestiveness in copy than men.

There are also some clear-cut age differences in responses to sex appeals in advertising, with younger people approving of them more than older people (Wise, King, & Merenski, 1974).

Even though sex in advertising is common, it appears that there are some risks in using it. Appeals to sex might be disapproved of by some audience members, might be misperceived or missed by others, and might distract still others from the real purpose of the ad. Few, if any, studies exist that show a positive effect of sex in advertising on brand recall or product sales. While the Smith and Engel study shows a sexy model having the effect of increasing the favorable evaluation of an automobile in an ad, it did not test for brand recall after seeing the ad. It is possible that the subjects did not recall the name of the kind of automobile any better with the sexy model than without, and this would defeat the purpose of the ad.

Jib Fowles, the author of an article titled "Advertising's Fifteen Basic Appeals," draws this conclusion about appeals to the need for sex: "As a rule, though, advertisers have found sex to be a tricky appeal, to be used sparingly. Less controversial and equally fetching are the appeals to our need for affectionate human contact" (1982, p. 278).

Effects of Repetition

Many mass communication messages—particularly advertisements, whether commercial or political—are repeated extensively. There are a number of reasons why this might be a good idea. Not all audience members will be watching at the same time, or, in the print media, not all readers will see a single printing of an advertisement. Another advantage of repetition is that it might remind the audience of a source for a message from a high-credibility source, and thus prevent the drop-off in attitude change from a high-credibility source found over time by Hovland and Weiss. Repeating a message might help the learning of attitudes and emotional meanings for words discussed by Staats and Staats, since a repeated association of the two stimuli is part of the process of conditioning. Repetition might help the audience remember the message itself. Zielske (1959) showed that advertising is quickly forgotten if not continuously exposed.

Krugman (1972) has presented the intriguing argument that three exposures might be all that are needed for a television advertisement to have its desired effect. But he adds the important qualification that it might take 23 exposures to get the three that produce the particular responses that are needed. Krugman suggests that the first exposure to an ad is dominated by a cognitive "What is it?" response. The second exposure is dominated by an evaluative "What of it?" response. And the third exposure is a reminder, but also the beginning of disengagement. Krugman points out a fundamental difficulty, however, in that people can screen out television ads by stopping at the "What is it?" response without further involvement. Then, on perhaps the 23rd exposure, they might, or might not, move on to the "What of it?" response. Thus, Krugman's analysis is stating that three exposures to an advertisement might be enough under ideal circumstances, but that it might take a number of repetitions to achieve those three.

Too much repetition can also have some undesirable effects, however. In one study, three groups of subjects were presented with one, three, or five repetitions of a persuasive message (Cacioppo & Petty, 1979). The researchers found that the message repetition led at first to increasing agreement with the advocated position, but that after a certain point it led to decreasing agreement with the advocated position. They found repetition led to decreasing, then increasing, counterarguing against the message by the recipient of the message. And they found that any amount of repetition led to increasing topic-irrelevant thinking. This kind of curvilinear relationship between repetition and communication effects was also found in a study of political advertising. Becker and Doolittle (1975) found that both liking for a candidate and seeking of information about a candidate were highest with a moderate amount of repetition but declined with high repetition.

Another study found that humor ratings declined steadily with repetition of ads (Gelb & Zinkham, 1985). A change in the creative execution of the ad was found to boost the humor ratings back up, though.

New Directions in Persuasion Theory

Probably the major change in the field of persuasion theory in recent years has been a move away from a mechanistic stimulus-response view of persuasion to a view that recognizes the active role of the receiver. As Raymond S. Ross puts it, "In our view, persuasive messages attempt to influence *how* receivers choose or decide which information to process. This implies the utility of strategy and theory and the criticality of audience analysis" (1985, p. 3).

Taking essentially the same view, Mary John Smith has stated, "A process of persuasion has occurred when people internalize the meanings they assign to messages in an atmosphere of perceived choice" (1982, p. 7).

This approach is sometimes called a transactional approach to persuasion. It emphasizes the choice of the receiver.

One point at which we see the active role of the receiver is when *counterarguing* takes place. Counterarguing is the disagreeing with a message that takes place in people's minds during exposure to the message. Of course, the opposite—supportive argumentation—can also occur (Smith, 1982, p. 17).

One example of the new approach to persuasion theory is the information integration theory developed by Norman Anderson (1971, 1981), among others. This approach postulates that attitude change is a result of the way individuals combine or integrate all the information available relevant to a given attitude object. As a person receives a new piece of information judged to be relevant to the attitude object, the person assigns a *weight* and a *value* to that information. The weight is the person's subjective belief in the truth of the information. The value is defined as the person's affective evaluation of the piece of information, and it may range from extremely positive to extremely negative. The weight rating and the value rating can be multiplied to obtain the *importance* rating for the piece of information.

The person's attitude is made up of a composite of the importance ratings of all pieces of information received that are relevant to the attitude object. A person who is forming an attitude toward another person, for instance, might take into account a diverse collection of pieces of information, including the statements the person makes, the position or role of the person, the statements made about the person by other people, the way the person dresses, and even the person's gestures and body language.

It is not clear yet how the various pieces of information (or ratings) are combined to arrive at a final attitude. Some scholars have argued for a model in which the ratings are added, while others have argued for a model in which the ratings are averaged.

It is apparent that information integration theory gives a much more active role to the receiver than many of the older models of persuasion. The individual receiver determines the weights and values to be assigned to incoming information—vital stages in determining the final attitude. This theory also presents a more complex conception of attitude. In fact, attitude as viewed in this theory becomes very much like *schema*, a concept discussed in Chapter 4.

Conclusions

The field of attitude change research has expanded greatly since the early days when the learning theory approach and the consistency theory approach were dominant. Katz's functional approach was developed specifically to reconcile these two divergent views and fit them both into a larger picture. The Katz approach has drawn particular attention to the problem of changing attitudes serving the ego-defensive function—not an easy kind of attitude to change.

McGuire and Papageorgis's inoculation theory provides a nice kind of balance to the many studies of attitude change. While others have been trying to discover the best means of persuading people, McGuire and Papageorgis have been investigating the best means of making people resistant to persuasion.

Festinger raised the important issue of whether attitude change produced by persuasive messages was accompanied by any real behavior change. About the same time, researchers began a serious study of whether attitudes in general as they were measured by researchers were useful in predicting behavior. One of the beneficial results of all this questioning is that many attitude change studies now incorporate behavioral measures as well as attitude measures.

Staats and Staats's theory that attitudes are learned through classical conditioning suggests a strategy for use in advertising and other persuasive efforts. Under this theory, the goal of a persuasive message is to cause the learning of a positive or negative response to a word.

Krugman's theory of low involvement suggests that messages, particularly on television, can produce a kind of low-level, latent learning, and that this learning might not have an effect until the person has to act, as in making a purchase. The messages that appear to be useful for this kind of learning are primarily nonverbal ones.

We have discussed three techniques that are common in persuasive communication—humor, sex, and repetition. The research on the first two suggests that they be used carefully, because they can be misunderstood or can distract from the message, and there is little evidence that they actually bring about attitude change. Repetition has its pros and cons and should also be used carefully. It increases the chances of penetrating through audience indifference or resistance, and it can lead to greater learning—of a message, of a relationship between a product name and positive associations, or of the connection between a credible source and particular message. But it can also lead to increased counterarguing and increased thinking about other, irrelevant topics.

Finally, we have seen that newer theories of persuasion grant a more active role to the receiver; information-integration theory is one of the more popular of these new theories.

References

Ajzen, I. (1971). Attitudinal vs. normative messages: An investigation of the differential effects of persuasive communications on behavior. *Sociometry* 34: 263–280.

Ajzen, I., and M. Fishbein (1970). The prediction of behavior from attitudinal and normative variables. *Journal of Experimental Social Psychology* 6: 466–487.

Alexander, M. W., and B. Judd (1978). Do nudes in ads enhance brand recall? *Journal of Advertising Research* 18, no. 1: 47–50.

Allport, G. W. (1954). The historical background of modern social psychology. In G. Lindzey (ed.), *Handbook of Social Psychology*, vol. 1, pp. 3–56. Reading, Mass.: Addison-Wesley.

Anderson, N. H. (1971). Integration theory and attitude change. *Psychological Review* 78: 171–206.

———— (1981). Integration theory applied to cognitive responses and attitudes. In R. E. Petty, T. M. Ostrom, and T. C. Brock (eds.), Cognitive Responses in Persuasion, pp. 361–397. Hillsdale, N.J.: Lawrence Erlbaum.

Becker, L. B., and J. C. Doolittle (1975). How repetition affects evaluations of and information seeking about candidates. *Journalism Quarterly* 52: 611–617.

Brooker, G. W. (1981). A comparison of the persuasive effects of mild humor and mild fear appeals. *Journal of Advertising* 10, no. 4: 29–40.

Brown, R. (1958). *Words and Things.* New York: Free Press.

Caballero, M. J., and P. J. Solomon (1984). Effects of model attractiveness on sales response. *Journal of Advertising* 13, no. 1: 17–23.

Cacioppo, J. T., and R. E. Petty (1979). Effects of message repetition and position on cognitive responses, recall, and persuasion. *Journal of Personality and Social Psychology* 37: 97–109.

Chen, W. (1933). The influence of oral propaganda material upon students' attitudes. *Archives of Psychology* 150: 1–43.

Chestnut, R. W., C. C. LaChance, and A. Lubitz (1977). The "decorative" female model: Sexual stimuli and the recognition of advertisements. *Journal of Advertising* 6, no. 4: 11–14.

Cook, T. D., and B. R. Flay (1978). The persistence of experimentally induced attitude change. In L. Berkowitz (ed.), *Advances in Experimental Social Psychology,* Vol. 11, pp. 2–57. New York: Academic Press.

Darling, A. L., and J. M. Civikly (1984). The effect of teacher humor on classroom climate. *Proceedings of the Tenth International Conference on Improving University Teaching,* pp. 798–806.

Duncan, C. P., and J. E. Nelson (1985). Effects of humor in a radio advertising experiment. *Journal of Advertising* 14, no. 2: 33–40, 64.

English, H. B., and A. C. English (1958). *A Comprehensive Dictionary of Psychological and Psychoanalytical Terms: A Guide to Usage.* New York: Longmans, Green.

Evans, R. I., R. R. Rozelle, T. M. Lasater, T. M. Dembroski, and B. P. Allen (1970). Fear arousal, persuasion and actual versus implied behavioral change: New perspective utilizing a real-life dental hygiene program. *Journal of Personality and Social Psychology* 16: 220–227.

Festinger, L. (1964). Behavioral support for opinion change. *Public Opinion Quarterly* 28: 404–417.

Festinger, L., and N. Maccoby (1964). On resistance to persuasive communications. *Journal of Abnormal and Social Psychology* 68: 359–366.

Finckenauer, J. O. (1979). Scared crooked. *Psychology Today,* August, pp. 6–11.

Fishbein, M. (1973). Introduction: The prediction of behaviors from attitudinal variables. In C. D. Mortensen and K. K. Sereno (eds.), *Advances in Communication Research,* pp. 3–31. New York: Harper & Row.

Fowles, J. (1982). Advertising's fifteen basic appeals. *ETC* 39: 273–290.

Gelb, B. D., and C. M. Pickett (1983). Attitude toward the ad: Links to humor and to advertising effectiveness. *Journal of Advertising* 12, no. 2: 34–42.

Gelb, B. D., and G. M. Zinkham (1985). The effect of repetition on humor in a radio advertising study. *Journal of Advertising* 14, no. 4: 13–20, 68.

Gillig, P. M., and A. G. Greenwald (1974). Is it time to lay the sleeper effect to rest? *Journal of Personality and Social Psychology* 29: 132–139.

Gross, S. J., and C. M. Niman (1975). Attitude-behavior consistency: A review. *Public Opinion Quarterly* 39: 358–368.

Gruner, C. R. (1965). An experimental study of satire as persuasion. *Speech Monographs* 32: 149–153.

——— (1967). Effect of humor on speaker ethos and audience information gain. Journal of Communication 17, no. 3: 228–233.

——— (1970). The effect of humor in dull and interesting informative speeches. Central States Speech Journal 21: 160–166.

——— (1972). Effects of including humorous material in a persuasive sermon. Southern Speech Communication Journal 38: 188–196.

Hilgard, E. R., and G. H. Bower (1966). *Theories of Learning.* New York: Appleton-Century-Crofts.

Hill, R. P. (1988). An exploration of the relationship between AIDS related anxiety and the evaluation of condom advertisements. *Journal of Advertising* 17: 35–42.

Horai, J., N. Naccari, and E. Fatoullah (1974). The effects of expertise and physical attractiveness upon opinion agreement and liking. *Sociometry* 37: 601–606.

Hovland, C. I., I. L. Janis, and H. H. Kelley (1953). *Communication and Persuasion.* New Haven, Conn.: Yale University Press.

Hovland, C. I., A. A. Lumsdaine, and F. D. Sheffield (1965). *Experiments on Mass Communication.* New York: John Wiley.

Hovland, C. I., W. Mandell, E. H. Campbell, T. Brock, A. S. Luchins, A. R. Cohen, W. J. McGuire, I. Janis, R. L. Feirabend, and N. H. Anderson (1957). *The Order of presentation in Persuasion* New Haven, Conn.: Yale University Press.

Hovland, C. I., and W. Weiss (1951). The influence of source credibility on communication effectiveness. *Public Opinion Quarterly* 15: 633–650.

Insko, C. A. (1967). *Theories of Attitude Change.* New York: Appleton-Century-Crofts.

Janis, I., C. I. Hovland, P. B. Field, H. Linton, E. Graham, A. R. Cohen, D. Rife, R. P. Abelson, G. S. Lesser, and B. T. King (1959). *Personality and Persuasibility.* New Haven: Yale University Press.

Katz, D. (1960). The functional approach to the study of attitudes. *Public Opinion Quarterly* 24: 163–204.

Kelly, J. P., and P. J. Solomon (1975). Humor in television advertising. *Journal of Advertising* 4, no. 3: 31–35.

Krech, D., R. S. Crutchfield, and E. L. Ballachey (1962). *Individual in Society: A Textbook of Social Psychology.* New York: McGraw-Hill.

Krisher, H. P. III, S. A. Darley, and J. M. Darley (1973). Fear-provoking recommendations, intentions to take preventive actions, and actual preventive actions. *Journal of Personality and Social Psychology* 26: 301–308.

Krugman, H. E. (1965). The impact of television advertising: Learning without involvement. *Public Opinion Quarterly* 24: 349–356.

—— (1972). Why three exposures may be enough. Journal of Advertising Research 12, no. 6: 11–14.

—— (1977). Memory without recall, exposure without perception. Journal of Advertising Research 17, no. 4: 7–12.

LaPiere, R. T. (1934). Attitudes vs. actions. *Social Forces* 13: 230–237.

Leventhal, H., and P. Niles (1964). A field experiment on fear arousal with data on the validity of questionnaire measures. *Journal of Personality* 32: 459–479.

Maccoby, N., and J. W. Farquhar (1975). Communicating for health: Unselling heart disease. *Journal of Communication* 25, no. 3: 114–126.

Markiewicz, D. (1974). Effects of humor on persuasion. *Sociometry* 37: 407–422.

McGinnies, E., and C. D. Ward (1974). Persuasibility as a function of source credibility and locus of control. *Journal of Personality* 42: 360–371.

McGuire, W., and D. Papageorgis (1961). The relative efficacy of various types of prior belief-defense in producing immunity against persuasion. *Journal of Abnormal and Social Psychology* 62: 327–337.

Morrison, B. J., and R. C. Sherman (1972). Who responds to sex in advertising? *Journal of Advertising Research* 12, no. 2: 15–19.

Murphy, G., L. B. Murphy, and T. M. Newcomb (1937). *Experimental Social Psychology: An Interpretation of Research upon the Socialization of the Individual.* Rev. ed. New York: Harper and Brothers.

Page, B. I., R. Y. Shapiro, and G. R. Dempsey (1984). *Television news and changes in Americans' policy preferences.* Paper presented at the annual meeting of the Midwest Political Science Association, Chicago, Ill.

Papageorgis, D., and W. McGuire (1961). The generality of immunity to persuasion produced by pre-exposure to weakened counterarguments. *Journal of Abnormal and Social Psychology* 62: 475–481.

Reardon, K. K. (1989). The potential role of persuasion in adolescent AIDS prevention. In R. E. Rice and C. K. Atkin (eds.), *Public Communication Campaigns.* 2nd ed., pp. 273–289. Newbury Park, Cal.: Sage.

Rogers, R. W. (1975). A protection motivation theory of fear appeals and attitude change. *Journal of Psychology* 91: 93–114.

Rogers, R. W., and C. R. Mewborn (1976). Fear appeals and attitude change: Effects of a threat's noxiousness, probability of occurrence, and the efficacy of coping responses. *Journal of Personality and Social Psychology* 34: 54–61.

Rosenberg, M. J., and C. I. Hovland (1960). Cognitive, affective and behavioral components of attitudes. In M. Rosenberg, C. Hovland, W. McGuire, R. Abelson, and J. Brehm, *Attitude Organization and Change: An Analysis of Consistency Among Attitude Components,* pp. 1–14. New Haven, Conn.: Yale University Press.

Rosenberg, M. J., C. I. Hovland, W. J. McGuire, R. P. Abelson, and J. Brehm (1960). *Attitude Organization and Change: An Analysis of Consistency Among Attitude Components.* New Haven, Conn.: Yale University Press.

Ross, R. S. (1985). *Understanding Persuasion: Foundations and Practices.* 2nd. ed. Englewood Cliffs, N.J.: Prentice-Hall.

Roush, M. (1990). "Earth Day" squanders its glut of celebrities. *USA Today,* April 20, p. 1D.

Sexton, D. E., and P. Haberman (1974). Women in magazine advertisements. *Journal of Advertising Research* 14, no. 4: 41–46.

Sherif, M., and C. I. Hovland (1961). *Social Judgment: Assimilation and Contrast Effects in Communication and Attitude Change.* New Haven, Conn.: Yale University Press.

Smith, G. H., and R. Engel (1968). Influence of a female model on perceived characteristics of an automobile. *Proceedings of the 76th Annual Convention of the American Psychological Association* 3: 681–682.

Smith, M. J. (1982). *Persuasion and Human Action: A Review and Critique of Social Influence Theories.* Belmont, Cal.: Wadsworth.

Staats, A. W. (1968). *Learning, Language, and Cognition.* New York: Holt, Rinehart, and Winston.

Staats, A. W., and C. K. Staats (1958). Attitudes established by classical conditioning. *Journal of Abnormal and Social Psychology* 57: 37–40.

Staats, A. W., C. K. Staats, and H. L. Crawford (1962). First-order conditioning of meaning and the parallel conditioning of a GSR. *Journal of General Psychology* 67: 159–167.

Staats, C. K., and A. W. Staats (1957). Meaning established by classical conditioning. *Journal of Experimental Psychology* 54: 74–80.

Taylor, P. M. (1974). An experimental study of humor and ethos. *Southern Speech Communication Journal* 39: 359–366.

Thomas, W. I., and F. Znaniecki (1927). *The Polish Peasant in Europe and America,* vol. 1. 2nd ed., New York: Alfred A. Knopf.

U.S. Bureau of the Census (1975). *Historical Statistics of the United States, Colonial Times to 1970,* pt. 1. Bicentennial ed., Washington, D.C.: U.S. Government Printing Office.

Weigel, R. H., and L. S. Newman (1976). Increasing attitude-behavior correspondence by broadening the scope of the behavioral measure. *Journal of Personality and Social Psychology* 33: 793–802.

Whitehead, J. L. (1968). Factors of source credibility. *Quarterly Journal of Speech* 54: 59–63.

Wicker, A. W. (1969). Attitudes versus actions: The relationship of verbal and overt behavioral responses to attitude objects. *Journal of Social Issues* 25, no. 4: 41–78.

Wise, G. L., A. L. King, and J. P. Merenski (1974). Reactions to sexy ads vary with age. *Journal of Advertising Research* 14, no. 4: 11–16.

Zielske, H. A. (1959). The remembering and forgetting of advertising. *Journal of Marketing* 23, no. 3: 239–243.

10
Groups and Communication

The Dutch philosopher Baruch Spinoza pointed out 300 years ago that human beings are social animals. His statement has been strongly reinforced by modern psychology, which has shown that other people have a great influence on our attitudes, our behavior, and even our perceptions.

The other people that influence us are in the groups that we belong to, large or small, formal or informal. These groups can have a great influence on the way we receive a mass communication message. This was hinted at in Chapter 4 in which we reported Cooper and Jahoda's suggestion that group membership can make attitudes of prejudice hard to change. Groups influence people's communication behavior in other ways, as we shall see.

The scientific study of the influence of groups on human behavior began in the 1930s, primarily with the work of social psychologist Muzafer Sherif. Solomon Asch, another social psychologist, did some noteworthy work on group pressures and conformity. Another important name in the study of groups was Kurt Lewin, the founder of the field known as group dynamics. The importance of groups in the formation of political attitudes and the making of voting decisions was brought out in some classic election studies conducted in the 1940s by sociologist Paul Lazarsfeld and his associates.

Three of the most important types of groups are the following. A *primary group* is a group (two or more persons) involving long-standing, intimate, face-to-face association. Examples are a family, a work group, a team, a fraternity, and a military unit. A *reference group* is a group identified with and used as a standard of reference, but not necessarily belonged to. For instance, a student wishing to belong to a certain fraternity might begin to dress like members and adopt their attitudes even though he is not a member. A *casual group* is a one-time group of people who didn't know each other before they were brought together. Examples are people riding in an elevator, people riding a bus, or strangers sitting together at a football game.

Sherif's Research on Group Norms

Groups often share certain rules or standards, and these can be referred to as *norms*. Norms operate in almost every area of human behavior. Some everyday examples of areas for the operation of norms are hair style, skirt length, taste in popular music, courtship behavior (such as whether or not to kiss on the first date), style of greeting, and form of handshake. Some norms are shared by an entire society. Many people may not realize that the norms

181

of their society are basically arbitrary until they see that different norms operate in a different culture. In some countries, the evening meal is served much later than it is in the United States. In some countries, it is customary to take a midday siesta—not an American habit. Many other differences in food preferences and habits, sexual mores, conversational styles, gestures, clothing choices, and even values show up between cultures. All these things can be thought of as norms.

Sherif (1936, 1937) wanted to study the process of the formation of norms. He found a laboratory situation that was ideal for this purpose. Sherif built his research around a phenomenon known as the *autokinetic light effect*. When a person is seated in a completely darkened room and a tiny stationary point of light is made to appear, the person usually sees the light begin to move. The light appears to move because the nervous system is overcompensating for the dim light, and in doing so it sends the same type of impulses to the brain that are normally sent when the eye is following a moving object (McBurney & Collings, 1977). This gave Sherif a situation that was high in ambiguity and would therefore work well for the study of norms. Almost everyone sees the light move, but since it really isn't moving, no one can really know how far it moves.

Sherif set up an experimental situation in which a subject was placed in a darkened room with a telegraph key in a convenient place. Five meters away was a device for presenting a point of light. The person was given these instructions: "When the room is completely dark, I shall give you the signal *ready*, and then show you a point of light. After a short time the light will start to move. As soon as you see it move, press the key. A few seconds later the light will disappear. Then tell me the distance it moved. Try to make your estimates as accurate as possible." When the subject pressed the key, a timer began ticking off. It ticked for two seconds, and then the light went off.

Sherif first ran this experiment with an individual alone in the room. After repeated trials, a person usually settles on a personal standard. The estimates might range between 4 and 6 inches but would generally be around 5 inches. Other people would settle on very different personal ranges, however. One person might have a personal standard of 1/2 inch and another might have a standard of 2 feet.

In the next stage of the experiment, Sherif took several people who had been in the room alone and had established their own standards and put them in the room together. They went through the experiment together and could hear one another giving their estimates. The usual finding in this situation was that as trials were repeated, the different estimates became closer and closer together. Eventually the group adopted a norm of its own, which often would be somewhere around the average of the separate standards of the individuals.

In the third stage of the experiment, Sherif took individuals who had been in the group situation and put them back in the room alone for further trials. In this situation, the individual usually stayed with the norm that he or she had formed in the group.

Sherif's experiment shows that in a situation of uncertainty, people are dependent on other people for guidance. It also shows that the influence of the group can extend to situations in which the group is not present. Many norms in society must develop through the process that Sherif has isolated. After all, many situations in life are full of uncertainty. In some of the most important areas of human concern—politics, religion, morality—there is little that is certain. On the basis of Sherif's work, we might expect to find that groups have a great deal of influence on attitudes in these and other ambiguous areas.

Asch's Research on Group Pressure

Sherif's research dealt with groups in a situation with high ambiguity. Asch (1955; 1956) investigated similar forces at work in a situation with little ambiguity. Asch wanted to investigate group pressure and the tendency for people to either conform to the pressure or be independent of it.

Asch set up an experimental situation that appeared to be an investigation of a subject's ability to judge the length of some drawn lines. Subjects were shown two cards. One of them had a single line. The other card had three lines of different lengths labeled 1, 2, and 3. The task for the subject was to call out the number for the one of the three that was the same length as the single line. There were 12 different sets of cards. This is a relatively easy perceptual task that people can do quite well in the absence of group pressure. A control group of 37 included 35 people who made no errors, one who made one error, and one who made two errors.

Asch was really interested in what happens when group pressure is introduced into the situation. In this phase of the experiment, he had subjects participating in the line-judging task in groups of eight. Actually only one of these eight was a true subject, and the others were allies of the experimenter who were instructed to begin giving wrong answers after a couple of trials with correct answers. They all would give the same incorrect answer, so the subject would hear everyone else appear to agree on a single answer, but one that his or her senses indicated was the wrong one. What would a person do in this situation?

The results for 123 subjects (Table 10.1) showed 76 percent of them yielding to the group pressure and giving the wrong answer at least once. In the total number of answers given, the subjects were influenced by group pressure to give the wrong answer in 36.8 percent of their answers.

Asch modified his experiment in several ways and came up with additional findings of interest. The size of the group giving the incorrect judgment was varied from 1 to 15. The striking finding here was that a group of 3 giving a unanimous opinion was essentially as effective in producing conformity to wrong answers as were larger groups.

Asch also investigated the effect of having one other person give the correct answer in addition to the subject. He found that having one lone supporting partner of this type eliminates much of the power of group pressure. Subjects answered incorrectly only one-fourth as often as they did when confronted with a unanimous majority.

Asch also attempted to make the physical difference in the length of lines so great that no one would still be susceptible to group pressure. He was not able to do this. Even with

Table 10.1
ERROR RATES ON 12 TRIALS FOR 123 SUBJECTS IN THE ASCH EXPERIMENT

Error Rate	Number of Subjects	Percentage of Subjects
0 errors	29	24
1–7 errors	59	49
8–12 errors	35	27
	123	100

a difference of 7 inches between the correct and incorrect lines, some people still gave in to the group response.

Asch's research gives a striking demonstration that some people will go along with the group even when it means contradicting information derived from their own senses.

Group pressures have also been shown to have strong effects in decision making in politics and government. Psychologist Bertram H. Raven has described how a particular kind of group pressure called the "risky-shift" led former president Richard Nixon and his aides to questionable actions (*Austin American-Statesman*, Sept. 1, 1974, p. A12). The "risky-shift" refers to the tendency for a group to take greater risks than any of its members would endorse individually. This can happen in a group like the Nixon inner circle, which shared norms of being tough and taking bold positions. Raven points out as an example the meeting in which G. Gordon Liddy presented a plan of using highly paid prostitutes, kidnappings, blackmail, and burglaries to help defeat the Democrats. Even though people were apparently shocked at this plan, no one said anything stronger than indicating that it was "not exactly what I had in mind."

One further point should be made about the Sherif and Asch studies. Their experiments show that even casual groups, people who had never seen each other before, exert a strong influence. It seems likely that the power of groups would be even greater when we are dealing with primary groups such as families or work groups.

Lewin's Food Habits Studies

Kurt Lewin made a number of contributions that have been important in the study of communication, including the idea of the gatekeeper, the statement that "there is nothing so practical as a good theory," and the founding of the group dynamics movement. Lewin was a brilliant scholar and teacher whose students, including Leon Festinger, Alex Bavelas, Ron Lippitt, and Dorwin Cartwright, went on to make additional major contributions to psychology.

During World War II, Lewin participated in a program designed to use communication to get people to change some of their food habits. He became involved in this work through his friendship with anthropologist Margaret Mead. Mead was helping M. L. Wilson, director of extension in the U.S. Department of Agriculture. Wilson wanted to apply social science to problems of social change. He appointed Mead secretary for the Committee on Food Habits of the National Research Council (Marrow, 1977).

In one group of experiments, Lewin (1958) and his associates were attempting to get housewives as part of the war effort to increase their use of beef hearts, sweetbreads, and kidneys—cuts of meat not frequently served. Assisted by Bavelas, Lewin set up two experimental conditions—a lecture condition and a group decision condition. In the three groups in the lecture condition, oral presentations were given describing the nutrition, economics, and methods of preparation of the unpopular cuts of meat, and mimeographed recipes were handed out. In the three groups in the group decision conditions, people were given some initial information but then a discussion was begun on the problems "housewives like themselves" would face in serving these cuts of meat. Techniques and recipes were offered, but only after the groups became sufficiently involved to want to know whether some of the problems could be solved.

At the end of the meeting, the women were asked to indicate by a show of hands who was willing to try one of the cuts of meat in the next week. A follow-up showed that only 3 percent of the women who heard the lectures served one of the meats they hadn't served before, while 32 percent of the women in the group decision condition served one of them.

A number of factors were at work in this experiment, including group discussion, public commitment, coming to a decision on future action, and perception of group consensus. A subsequent experiment by Edith Bennett Pelz (1958) indicates that the first two did not have much of an impact and that the latter two alone were sufficient to cause differences as large as those found by Lewin and his associates.

Groups and Political Attitudes

In the 1940s, researchers carried out some of the first careful studies of how people decide whom to vote for in an election. These studies were conducted by Paul Lazarsfeld and his associates at the Bureau of Applied Social Research at Columbia University. They studied voters in Erie County, Ohio, during the 1940 election between Roosevelt and Willkie (Lazarsfeld, Berelson, & Gaudet, 1968), and voters in Elmira, New York, during the 1948 election between Truman and Dewey (Berelson, Lazarsfeld, & McPhee, 1954). Both studies were sample surveys of the panel type, in which the same respondents are interviewed several times.

Both studies made a point of looking at the mass media as important factors in the election decision-making process. Both studies came up with the surprising finding that the mass media played a weak role in election decisions compared with personal influence, or the influence of other people. In fact, it is sometimes said that these studies rediscovered personal influence, a factor communication researchers had tended to overlook as they began to think along the lines of the "bullet theory."

These studies showed a strong tendency for people to vote the same way the members of their primary groups voted. The family is one of the most important of these primary groups. The influence of the family is indicated by the fact that 75 percent of the first voters in the Elmira study voted the same way their fathers did. People also tend to vote like their friends and coworkers. Table 10.2 reports data from the Elmira study that show a strong tendency for people to vote like their three best friends, particularly when the three best friends are unanimous.

Table 10.3 reports additional data from the Elmira study showing a strong tendency for people to vote like their three closest coworkers. Berelson, Lazarsfeld, and McPhee refer to this strong consistency as the "political homogeneity of the primary group" (1954, p. 88). The findings are strikingly parallel to the Asch research on group pressure, which showed that a unanimous majority of three was sufficient to influence many people's judgments.

This homogeneity of opinion in the political area could be explained by two different processes. One is that the group exerts pressure on and influences the individual's judgment, just as it did in the Asch experiments. The other is that people might select friends whose political attitudes agree with their own. Both are probably true to some extent. But the second explanation would not be sufficient alone. People have a great deal of choice in selecting their friends. But they have less choice in selecting their coworkers, and often no choice in selecting their families.

Table 10.2

RESPONDENTS WHO INTENDED TO VOTE REPUBLICAN AND
THE VOTE INTENTIONS OF THEIR THREE CLOSEST FRIENDS

	Vote Intentions of Their Three Closest Friends			
	Republican *Republican* *Republican*	*Republican* *Republican* *Democrat*	*Republican* *Democrat* *Democrat*	*Democrat* *Democrat* *Democrat*
Respondents who intended to vote Republican (%)	88	74	48	15

Adapted from B. R. Berelson, P. F. Lazarsfeld, and W. N. McPhee, *Voting: A Study of Opinion Formation in a Presidential Campaign* (Chicago: University of Chicago Press). Copyright © 1954 by the University of Chicago. Reprinted by permission.

People also belong to certain larger groups just because of their sex, age, race, occupation, religious preference, and other serendipitous criteria. People in these types of very broad groups also tend to vote alike. This similarity in voting is shown in Table 10.4, based on data from the Elmira study. Knowledge of just two factors—religion and socioeconomic status—makes a person's vote predictable with a fairly high degree of accuracy. Using several more factors—say five or six—makes a person's vote even more predictable. This tendency of people in certain broad categories to vote alike is also the basis of the election night projections that the television networks use to announce the winners of elections on the basis of as little as 5 percent of the vote (Skedgell, 1966).

The recognition that people are influenced by their membership in broad categories has led to a refinement of thinking about the psychology of groups. Several researchers, including particularly psychologists John C. Turner and Henri Tajfel, have developed what they

Table 10.3

RESPONDENTS WHO INTENDED TO VOTE REPUBLICAN AND
THE VOTE INTENTIONS OF THEIR THREE CLOSEST COWORKERS

	Vote Intentions of Their Three Closest Coworkers			
	Republican *Republican* *Republican*	*Republican* *Republican* *Democrat*	*Republican* *Democrat* *Democrat*	*Democrat* *Democrat* *Democrat*
Respondents who intended to vote Republican (%)	86	75	53	19

Adapted from B. R. Berelson, P. F. Lazarsfeld, and W. N. McPhee, *Voting: A Study of Opinion Formation in a Presidential Campaign* (Chicago: University of Chicago Press). Copyright © 1954 by the University of Chicago. Reprinted by permission.

Table 10.4

RESPONDENTS WHO VOTED REPUBLICAN, TABULATED
BY RELIGIOUS AFFILIATION AND SOCIOECONOMIC STATUS

	High Status		Middle Status		Low Status	
	Protestant	*Catholic*	*Protestant*	*Catholic*	*Protestant*	*Catholic*
Respondents who voted Republican (%)	98	50	83	31	66	31

Adapted from B. R. Berelson, P. F. Lazarsfeld, and W. N. McPhee, *Voting: A Study of Opinion Formation in a Presidential Campaign* (Chicago: University of Chicago Press). Copyright © 1954 by the University of Chicago. Reprinted by permission.

call the *social identification* model of group influence. This model proposes that a social group be defined as two or more individuals who share a common social identification or perceive themselves to be members of the same social category (Turner, 1982). Under this view, group members do not have to relate to each other face to face, nor does the group require a structure. Group membership is seen primarily as a cognitive process, often resulting from attempts of the person to answer the question, "Who am I?" This question can be answered in terms of the groups that a person belongs to or identifies with. Thus, a person gets a sense of *social identity* from the groups that are admired and identified with. Furthermore, this sense of social identity does not appear to be operating all the time but seems to be switched on and off by certain situations. Once it is switched on, the individual attempts to behave in accordance with the norms of the social categories that he or she belongs to and that are relevant to the situation.

The social identification model alters our thinking about groups in some significant ways. First, it suggests that an important kind of group membership is based on cognitive responses ("Who am I?") rather than emotional responses ("Do I like these people?"). Second, it suggests that the social categories that people assign themselves to are not just weak associations but are an important kind of group membership in themselves. Third, it suggests that this process of identification with social categories might have important consequences. Individuals take these category memberships seriously because they are related to their concept of who they are.

Communication scholar Vincent Price has suggested that the social identification model is useful for helping us understand the formation of public opinion and the role the mass media play in that process. Price (1988) argues that the mass media play an important role in bringing social identification processes to bear on the formation of public opinion. First, the mass media depict which groups are at odds over a particular issue, therefore signaling which group identities are relevant to that issue. Second, by depicting how the groups are responding to the issue, the media can indicate the opinions that are being held by each group and thus the norms that should be followed by people identifying with that group. Third, the opinion norms of the group are likely to become perceptually exaggerated in the minds of audience members. Fourth, people impute their group's perceived opinion norm to themselves and become more likely to express this exaggerated norm. It is at this point that public opinion on various issues might appear to solidify or crystallize.

Groups as Instruments of Change

Because of the power of social influence, groups can sometimes be used as agents or instruments of change. Group structure and group dynamics are very much a part of the process at work in organizations such as Alcoholics Anonymous, Weight Watchers, and some groups that help people to stop smoking. The principles of group norms and group pressure can often be seen at work in these kinds of efforts. Alcoholics Anonymous, for instance, has a group norm that permits and encourages people to talk about their problems with alcohol. This is a reversal of the norm in the culture at large, which discourages talking about an individual's alcohol problem and almost makes such discussion a taboo. AA members also share other norms, such as the willingness to be available to talk to another member any time of night or day. Similar forces are at work in stop-smoking groups, whose members often are encouraged to select a "Quit Day" and publicly announce it to the group. This then generates group pressure for the individual actually to quit on that day and then stick by the decision.

The writings of Alcoholics Anonymous (1967), which describe the 12 steps and the 12 traditions of AA, bring out the importance of the group as part of the process. Bill W., one of the founders of AA, wrote in *The A.A. Way of Life:*

> The moment Twelfth-Step work forms a group, a discovery is made—that most individuals cannot recover unless there is a group. Realization dawns on each member that he is but a small part of a great whole; that no personal sacrifice is too great for preservation of the Fellowship. He learns that the clamor of desires and ambitions within him must be silenced whenever these could damage the group.
>
> It becomes plain that the group must survive or the individual will not. (p. 9)

Bill W.'s belief that the group was more important than the individual was once put to a severe test—he was offered a chance to have his picture on the cover of *Time* magazine as the cofounder of Alcoholics Anonymous. He thought about it a while and turned it down.

Group dynamics can also be applied to fund drives, such as the United Way or United Fund. DeFleur and Ball-Rokeach (1982, pp. 227–228) have described the way this process often works. First a quota is set for the community as a whole. This quota is sometimes displayed in the middle of town on a big thermometer so that everyone can see it. This quota is in fact somewhat arbitrary, being set by the fund drive organizers, but it begins to take on the appearance of a community norm. This approach is carried further by distributing pledge cards to individuals that indicate the "fair share" that they are supposed to pay for the community to meet the quota. This is a tactic of group pressure, in that the individual is made to feel that he or she will be letting others down if a donation is not made. Personal influence is also brought into the process. Often the pledge cards are distributed and collected by an important coworker, such as the boss's secretary. Some of these fund drives also use door-to-door collections, in which the person doing the collecting is a neighbor or a person living on the same block—an effective use of social influence.

A kind of social influence within the primary group of the family appears to have been taking place lately in the revival of the ecology movement. Youngsters have been learning about threats to the environment from school, television, and rock stars, and have been exerting pressure on their parents to act in more ecologically sound ways. Often the children are more aware of environmental issues than their parents. Cases have been reported of children urging parents to avoid purchasing aerosol sprays; to recycle cans, bottles, plastic, and paper; and to use waxed paper instead of plastic sandwich bags (Manning, 1990).

Groups and Mass Communication

The importance of group influence has been well understood by many people involved in mass communication. Father Coughlin, the "radio priest" who was such a skillful user of propaganda, would ask his audience to listen to him in groups. He also began his broadcasts with music and told audience members to take that time to call a friend and ask the person to listen to the program.

Many advertisements and commercials attempt to incorporate some form of group influence. For instance, a television commercial for a dye for gray hair makes the statement, "I bet a lot of your friends are using it and you don't even know it." Basically, this type of commercial is using the old propaganda device of band wagon.

Another promising idea is to use mass communication channels to attempt to stimulate interpersonal discussion. For instance, one California grocery chain's campaign theme was "Tell a Friend" (Solomon, 1989, p. 100).

Researchers working in the field of health communication have found an approach based on group influence to be an effective one. One example of this work is the Stanford Heart Disease Prevention Program, a joint effort by Stanford's Department of Communication and School of Medicine (Maccoby & Farquhar, 1975, 1976). The purposes of the program were to apply communication theory to the development of a health communication campaign and to use evaluation research to measure change due to the campaign. The campaign was intended to change people's habits relating to the three leading risk factors in heart disease—diet, smoking, and lack of exercise. The researchers picked three California towns that were as alike as possible to test their approaches. The first was given an eight-month media campaign involving local TV and radio spots, a newspaper tabloid, billboards, and direct mail. The second town was given the same media campaign but selected groups of high-risk people were also given intensive group instruction in reducing risks. The third town served as a control group and received no campaign or instruction.

The results showed some effect of the media-only campaign in changing attitudes and behavior related to heart disease risk, but much greater effect with the people receiving the media campaign plus the intensive group instruction. Cholesterol level was down 1 percent in the media-only town, down 5 percent in the media-plus-group-instruction town, and up 2 percent in the town receiving no campaign.

The Stanford Heart Disease Prevention Program also found that using mass mailings to send nutrition tip sheets and refrigerator magnets to hold them was effective in stimulating some discussion of nutrition issues (Solomon, 1989, p. 100).

Flay (1987), in a summary of research on mass media programs designed to help people stop smoking, found that television self-help clinics that included social support in the form of group discussion were particularly effective. The studies examined by Flay suggested that making written materials available to accompany a television program will double its effectiveness, and that adding group discussions can triple it. Flay estimates that television self-help clinics are able to help 5–15 percent of participating smokers to quit permanently. Although this may sound like a small effect, if such a clinic were conducted once nationally, it could help between 2.5 million and 7.5 million of the nation's 50 million smokers to quit. It has been suggested that the same kind of television self-help clinic might be useful in getting people to modify other health-related behaviors such as alcohol and drug abuse, or sexual practices increasing the risk of AIDS and other sexually transmitted diseases (McAlister, Ramirez, Galavotti, & Gallion, 1989).

In politics, the mass media campaigns are often supplemented by various types of interpersonal communication, including door-to-door visits, telephone calls, and neighborhood coffees.

Rogers and Storey identify interpersonal communication as one of the important factors that contribute to the success of a communication campaign. They wrote, "Interpersonal communication through peer networks is very important in leading to and maintaining behavior change" (Rogers & Storey, 1987, p. 837).

Reardon and Rogers (1988) have suggested that the common division in academic circles between mass communication and interpersonal communication is a false dichotomy, and that the strongest possible communication theory will be developed only when researchers integrate the two.

Conclusions

Groups have impact on mass communication in a number of ways:

1. Groups serve to anchor attitudes and make them hard to change. This was suggested by the Cooper and Jahoda study of the Mr. Biggott cartoons and also documented in the area of politics by the election studies of Lazarsfeld and his associates.

2. Knowledge of the groups that a person belongs to or identifies with can often help us predict the person's behavior. This is particularly true in the area of political preferences, where knowledge of five or six broad group categorizations about a person will often give a high degree of accuracy in predicting an election vote.

3. Effective programs of communication often involve a combination of mass communication and interpersonal communication. This is true of many of the well-organized charity fund drives and many election campaigns. Programs aimed at reducing the risk of heart disease or helping people stop smoking suggest that a combination of mass media and interpersonal communication is also an effective approach in the health area.

4. Sometimes ways can be found to obtain some of the advantages of interpersonal communication *through* mass communication. Television programs in which a candidate answers questions telephoned in by viewers would be an example. So would presidential "citizens press conferences," in which the president answered questions phoned in by citizens during a national radio broadcast. Some of the same advantages can be obtained by having a panel of typical citizens in the studio to question a political candidate in a kind of "town meeting" format.

References

Alcoholics Anonymous World Services, Inc. (1967). *The A.A. Way of Life: A Reader by Bill.* New York: Author.

Asch, S. E. (1955). Opinions and social pressure. *Scientific American,* Nov., 31–35.

——— (1956). Studies of independence and conformity: I. A minority of one against a unanimous majority. *Psychological Monographs* 70, no. 9: 1–70.

Berelson, B. R., P. F. Lazarsfeld, and W. N. McPhee (1954). *Voting: A Study of Opinion Formation in a Presidential Campaign.* Chicago: University of Chicago Press.

DeFleur, M., and S. Ball-Rokeach (1982). *Theories of Mass Communication.* 4th ed. White Plains, N.Y.: Longman.

Flay, B. R. (1987). *Selling the Smokeless Society: Fifty-Six Evaluated Mass Media Programs and Campaigns Worldwide.* Washington, D.C.: American Public Health Association.

Lazarsfeld, P. F., B. Berelson, and H. Gaudet (1968). *The People's Choice: How the Voter Makes Up His Mind in a Presidential Campaign.* 3rd ed. New York: Columbia University Press.

Lewin, K. (1958). Group decision and social change. In E. E. Maccoby, T. M. Newcomb, and E. L. Hartley (eds.), *Readings in Social Psychology.* 3rd ed., pp. 197–211. New York: Holt, Rinehart, and Winston.

Maccoby, N., and J. W. Farquhar (1975). Communicating for health: Unselling heart disease. *Journal of Communication* 25, no. 3: 114–126.

———(1976). Bringing the California health report up to date. *Journal of Communication* 26, no. 1: 56–57.

Manning, A. (1990). Kids push parents to try conservation. *USA Today,* Feb. 27, p. 1D.

Marrow, A. J. (1977). *The Practical Theorist: The Life and Work of Kurt Lewin.* New York: Teachers College Press.

McAlister, A., A. G. Ramirez, C. Galavotti, and K. J. Gallion (1989). Antismoking campaigns: Progress in the application of social learning theory. In R. E. Rice and C. K. Atkin (eds.), *Public Communication Campaigns.* 2nd ed., pp. 291–307. Newbury Park, Cal.: Sage.

McBurney, D. H., and V. B. Collings (1977). *Introduction to Sensation/Perception.* Englewood Cliffs, N.J.: Prentice-Hall.

Pelz, E. B. (1958). Some factors in "group decision." In E. E. Maccoby, T. M. Newcomb, and E. L. Hartley (eds.), *Readings in Social Psychology.* 3rd ed., pp. 212–219. New York: Holt, Rinehart, and Winston.

Price, V. (1988). On the public aspects of opinion: Linking levels of analysis in public opinion research. *Communication Research* 15, no. 6: 659–679.

Reardon, K. K., and E. M. Rogers (1988). Interpersonal versus mass media communication: A false dichotomy. *Human Communication Research* 15, no 2: 284–303.

Rogers, E. M., and J. D. Storey (1987). Communication campaigns. In C. R. Berger and S. H. Chaffee (eds.), *Handbook of Communication Science,* pp. 817–846. Newbury Park, Cal.: Sage.

Sherif, M. (1936). *The Psychology of Social Norms.* New York: Harper & Brothers.

———(1937). An experimental approach to the study of attitudes. *Sociometry* 1: 90–98.

Skedgell, R. A. (1966). How computers pick an election winner. *Transaction* 4, no. 1: 42–46.

Solomon, D. S. (1989). A social marketing perspective on communication campaigns. In R. E. Rice and C. K. Atkin (eds.), *Public Communication Campaigns,* 2nd ed., pp. 87–104. Newbury Park, Cal.: Sage.

Turner, J. C. (1982). Towards a cognitive redefinition of the social group. In H. Tajfel (ed.), *Social Identity and Intergroup Relations,* pp. 15–40. Cambridge: Cambridge University Press.

11 Mass Media and Interpersonal Communication

The decades between the two world wars saw an increasing concern with and a fear of the all-powerful nature of the mass media. During the decade of the 1920s many people became aware of how widespread and effective had been the use of propaganda during the First World War. After the war the use of advertising increased dramatically. The decade of the 1930s saw the rising use of radio to address huge audiences on both sides of the Atlantic. In the United States President Franklin Roosevelt overcame both a hostile press and a hostile Congress by going over their heads directly to the American people with his "fireside chats" on the radio. The impact of radio on the general public can be illustrated by the effect of a 1938 Halloween radio broadcast, Orson Welles's "War of the Worlds," which caused panic in some communities. In Europe radio was put to far different and more sustained and dangerous uses by Adolf Hitler in his attempt to conquer the world.

Under these conditions it is no surprise that the prevalent image of the mass media was that of a hypodermic needle or a bullet. This was a concept of the media with direct, immediate, and powerful effects on any individual they reached. It was parallel to the stimulus-response principle that characterized much of psychological research in the 1930s and 1940s.

The decade of the 1940s began with both Europe and Asia at war. Japanese armies were deep in China. Hitler's blitzkrieg had overrun Poland in a few weeks, then turned west, invaded Denmark and Norway, defeated France in six weeks, and forced the British to evacuate the remains of their army from the beaches of Dunkirk to defend their home islands. Under these circumstances President Roosevelt announced that he would run for a third term—a move unprecedented in American history.

At Columbia University a group of social scientists at the Bureau of Applied Social Research became concerned about the apparently all-pervasive direct effects of the media on individuals and what this might imply for the give and take of the democratic process.

The Mass Media and Voting Behavior

To investigate the effects of the mass media on political behavior, the researchers from the Columbia Bureau of Applied Social Research selected four groups of registered voters from Erie County, Ohio. This was a typical county in that it had voted in every presidential election as the nation had voted up to that time. These voters were then interviewed at intervals throughout the campaign to determine what factors had the greatest influence in their decision making regarding the election.

The design used three control groups to check on any effects of the seven monthly interviews of the main panel. All four groups (with 600 registered voters in each) were interviewed in May. The panel was interviewed every month after the May interview up to the November election and then immediately after it. Each of the three control groups was interviewed once after the initial interview—one in July, one in August, and one in October (Lazarsfeld, Berelson, & Gaudet, 1948).

Because the hypodermic model of the effects of mass media prevailed among communication researchers at the time, the 1940 Erie County study was designed to demonstrate the power of the mass media in affecting voting decisions. Two researchers said, "This study went to great lengths to determine how the mass media brought about such changes" (Lazarsfeld & Menzel, 1963, p. 96).

What the researchers found was that "personal contacts appear to have been both more frequent and more effective than the mass media in influencing voting decision" (Katz, 1957, p. 63). However, only 8 percent of the respondents actually switched from one candidate to another between the first interview in May and the last one in November. The researchers proposed that messages from the media first reach opinion leaders, who then pass on what they read or hear to associates or followers who look to them as influentials. This process was named the *two-step* flow of communication.

Because the design of the study did not anticipate the importance of interpersonal relations, the two-step flow concept was the one least well documented by the data. As a result, a number of other studies were later done to verify and refine the concept.

Among the conclusions of the 1940 voting study were the following:

> 1. Voters who decided late in the campaign or changed their minds during the campaign were more likely than others to cite personal influence as having figured in their decisions
> 2. Opinion leaders were found at every social level and were presumed to be very much like the people they influenced
> 3. Opinion leaders were found to be more exposed to the mass media than people who were not designated opinion leaders. (Katz, 1957, p. 63)

In the 1940 voting study, a panel of voters was drawn at random. Respondents were asked if they had tried to convince anyone of their political ideas or if anyone had asked their advice on political matters. Besides the question of the validity of designating opinion leaders by this method there is also another problem. The data result in only two subgroups, those who report themselves to be opinion leaders and those who do not. There is no way to compare individual opinion leaders with the specific individuals who look to them for advice.

As the 1940 voting study was being completed, another study in a small New Jersey town (Rovere) was begun. A sample of 86 persons was asked to name the people from whom they sought information and advice. Individuals named four or more times were considered opinion leaders and were interviewed in depth. In Rovere there was certainly greater validity in designating individuals as opinion leaders than in the Erie County study, and they were no doubt influential with a greater number of people. In the Rovere study the original sample was used only to identify the opinion leaders. After that all of the attention was focused on the attributes of the opinion leaders.

When the war ended, the researchers were able to resume their work on opinion leadership with a study in Decatur, Illinois. Here the research was able to compare the leader with the person who named the leader or, more technically, to examine the adviser-advisee dyad. Do the adviser and advisee tend to be of the same social class, age, and sex? Is the leader more exposed to the mass media than the follower? Is the leader more interested in the topic of influence than the follower?

It was during the Decatur research that the investigators saw the need to examine chains of influence longer than a dyad. Opinion leaders were reporting that they had been influenced by other opinion leaders. Also, opinion leaders were found to be influential only at certain times and only on certain issues. Opinion leaders are influential not only because of who they are (social status, age, sex, etc.) but also because of the structure and values of the groups they are members of.

The Role of the Community in Decision Making

It also became clear that although the earlier research had allowed for the study of individual decisions, it did not permit study of decision making on a community level. The next study introduced the notion of *diffusion,* or widening communication of a new idea, over time through the social structure of a community (Katz, 1957).

The diffusion study examined how medical doctors make decisions to adopt new drugs. All doctors in several specialties in four midwestern cities were interviewed. Besides the usual demographic data (age, medical school attended, etc.) and data about attitudes, prescription of drugs, exposure to information sources and influence, and other details, the doctors were asked to name the three colleagues they were most apt to talk with about cases, the three they were most apt to seek information and advice from, and the three they were most likely to socialize with.

These questions regarding a doctor's interactions with colleagues allowed the researchers to "map" the interpersonal relations in the medical communities. The study also allowed focus on a specific item (a new drug) as it gained acceptance and a record over time (through prescriptions on file at pharmacies).

In the drug study, an objective record of decision making (the prescriptions) was available as an additional source of information (along with the self-report of the doctor). Also, inferences could be drawn about the different influences on the making of a decision. For example, early adopters were more likely to attend out-of-town medical meetings in their specialties. The mapping of interpersonal relations made possible inferences regarding the effect of social relations in decision making.

Findings about Opinion Leadership

The following conclusions were reached from the series of studies after the 1940 voting study:

1. Personal influence was both more frequent and more effective than any of the mass media, not only in politics but also in marketing, fashion decisions, and movie attendance (these last three were investigated in the Decatur study). In the case of the drug diffusion study, the doctors most integrated in the medical community were the ones most likely to

be early adopters of the innovation. The doctors most frequently named as discussion partners were most apt to be innovators. Extent of integration proved more important than the doctor's age, medical school, income of patients, readership of medical journals, or any other factor examined.

The researchers attributed the innovativeness of doctors who are integrated in their respective medical communities to their being in touch and up to date with medical developments. They also noted that these were the doctors who could count on social support from their colleagues when facing the risks of innovation in medicine.

2. Interpersonal influence in primary groups is effective in maintaining a high degree of homogeneity of opinions and actions within a group. In the voting studies, voters who changed their minds reported initially that they had intended to vote differently from their families or friends. Medical doctors tended to prescribe the same drugs as their closest colleagues, especially when treating the more puzzling diseases.

3. In the decision-making process, different media play different roles. Some media inform about or announce the existence of an item, while others legitimate or make acceptable a given course of action.

Who will lead and who will follow is determined, to a large extent, by the subject matter under consideration. In the area of marketing, opinion leadership was concentrated among older women with larger families. In the Rovere study, some individuals were opinion leaders in "local" affairs while others were influential in "cosmopolitan" affairs. In the areas of fashion and movie attendance the young unmarried woman was most often the opinion leader. The researchers found that an opinion leader in one area is unlikely to be an opinion leader in another, unrelated area.

But people talk most often to others like themselves. In marketing, fashions, movie attendance, and public affairs, opinion leaders were found at every socioeconomic and occupational level.

If opinion leaders are found at all levels, what distinguishes the leaders from their followers?

The researchers concluded that the following factors differentiate leaders from their followers:

1. Personification of values (who one is)
2. Competence (what one knows)
3. Strategic social location (whom one knows)

Strategic social location actually involves two sets of contacts: whom one knows within the group in which opinion leadership is exercised and whom one knows outside of the group for information on topics salient to the group.

Personification of values is another way of saying that the influential person is someone that followers wish to emulate. The "influencee" admires the influential and wishes to become as similar as possible. However, the opinion leader must also be regarded as knowledgeable or competent in the area in which leadership is sought. We seldom pay attention to the opinions of people who don't seem to know what they are talking about.

Even if one is both the type of person others want to emulate and is competent, one must also be accessible to the people who are interested in the area in which leadership is sought. To be a leader one must have followers. As mentioned, an individual is also most apt to be an opinion leader if he or she maintains contacts outside the group who in turn provide information and opinions of interest to the group members. This was found to be true in many diverse areas of opinion leadership (politics, medicine, and farming, among others).

Opinion leaders were found to be more exposed to media appropriate to their sphere of influence than their followers. The Rovere study found that opinion leaders on "cosmopolitan" matters were more likely to read national news magazines than people who were influential on "local" matters. In the drug study the influential medical doctors were more likely to read a large number of professional journals and value them more highly than their less influential colleagues. They also attended more out-of-town meetings and had more out-of-town contacts as well. One researcher observed, "the greater exposure of the opinion leader to the mass media may only be a special case of the more general proposition that opinion leaders serve to relate their groups to relevant parts of the environment through whatever media happen to be appropriate" (Katz, 1957, p. 76).

The Interpersonal Environment

Opinion leaders and their followers are very similar and usually belong to the same groups. It is highly unlikely that the opinion leader will be very far ahead of followers in level of interest in a given topic. Interpersonal relations are not only networks of communication but also sources of social pressure to conform to the group's norms and sources of social support for the values and opinions an individual holds.

Two other authors, in discussing this interaction of media, social, and psychological variables in the communication process, have written:

> In more recent times it has been realized that mass media information is received, passed on, distorted, assimilated, rejected, or acted upon in ways which are in part determined by the operation of various social and social-psychological systems at various points of transmission and reception as the flow of information takes place. Therefore, for the student of mass communication the operation of primary groups, role structures, voluntary associations, personality variables, and vast complexes of other variables related to the operation of "diffusion networks" have become a new research domain. The developing model of the operation of the mass media couples the mass communication process to the social networks of family, work, play, school and community. (De Fleur & Larsen, 1958, p. xiii)

As pointed out at the beginning of this chapter, most media researchers during the 1930s and even the 1940s employed the hypodermic needle model of communication in their thinking of media effects—direct, immediate, and powerful. As more sophisticated methods were employed by media researchers, the hypodermic model was recognized as far too simplistic. Throughout the 1940s and 1950s communication researchers began to recognize many psychological and sociological variables that intervene between the media and the mind of the receiver (selective exposure, attention, perception, and retention; group memberships, norms, and salience; opinion leadership, etc.).

Two of the researchers involved in the series of studies done at Columbia concluded, "The whole moral . . . is that knowledge of an individual's interpersonal environment is basic to an understanding of his exposure and reactions to the mass media" (Katz & Lazarsfeld, 1955, p. 133).

Criticisms of the Two-Step Flow

Numerous criticisms have been made of the two-step flow model. Here is a review of some of them.

1. Many studies indicate that major news stories are spread directly by the mass media to a far greater extent than by personal sources. Westley (1971, p. 726) cites several studies supporting this and discusses them briefly.

2. Findings show that opinions on public affairs are reciprocal or that often there is "opinion sharing rather than opinion giving." Troldahl and Van Dam (1965, p. 633) say that opinion givers "were not significantly different [from seekers] in their exposure to relevant media content, their information level on national news, their occupational prestige, and four of five attributes of gregariousness."

3. Related to point 2 is the observation by Lin (1971, p. 203) that "the definition of the opinion leader versus non–opinion leader dichotomy is also unclear and the problem is further confounded by varying operationalizing methods." He adds that opinion leadership has been determined by both self-designation and nomination and has been applied to both specific topics and general activities.

4. Empirical definitions of *mass media* vary. In some instances specialized media (special bulletins, medical journals, farm journals) have been used; in other instances they have not been part of the definition of the mass media (Lin, 1971, p. 204).

5. Other investigators (Rogers & Shoemaker, 1971, p. 206) have pointed out that opinion leaders can be either active or passive whereas the two-step flow model implies a dichotomy between active information-seeking opinion leaders and a mass audience of passive individuals who then rely on the opinion leaders for guidance.

6. The original model is limited to two steps, whereas the process may involve more or even fewer. As already mentioned, however, the Columbia group saw the need to investigate longer chains of influence during the Decatur study and followed this line of study in the drug diffusion research.

7. It is implied that opinion leaders rely on mass media channels only. Sometimes, especially in developing countries without extensive networks of mass media, personal trips and conversations with change agents assume the information role that mass media might normally play.

8. Early knowers and late knowers of the same information behave differently. It was found that early knowers of information more often rely on media sources and late knowers more on interpersonal sources (Rogers & Shoemaker, 1971, pp. 259, 348).

9. In the diffusion of an innovation it was found that mass media serve primarily to inform whereas interpersonal channels are most important at persuading. Rogers and Shoemaker (1971, p. 208) contended that these differences applied to both opinion leaders and followers.

The criticisms of the two-step flow model are mainly that it originally did not explain enough. As we shall see, subsequent work has considerably expanded and refined the model—as one would expect in the case of any cumulative research.

Diffusion of Innovations

The two-step flow model has evolved gradually into a multistep flow model that is often used in *diffusion research*, the study of the social process of how innovations (new ideas, practices, objects, etc.) become known and are spread throughout a social system. The two-step flow model is mainly concerned with how an individual receives information and passes it along to others; the diffusion process concentrates on the *final stage* of the adoption or rejection of an innovation.

Probably the best-known and most widely respected researcher in diffusion research today is Everett Rogers. In his book *Diffusion of Innovations* (third edition published in 1983), he examines more than 2,000 empirical diffusion research reports and 3,000 publications to revise earlier theory about the innovation decision process, a result of the vast increase in diffusion research in recent years. Rogers defines an innovation as "an idea, practice, or object that is perceived as new by an individual or another unit of adoption" (pp. xviii, 11).

One of the most influential diffusion studies of all time dealt with the diffusion of hybrid seed corn among Iowa farmers (Ryan & Gross, 1943). The innovation, released to Iowa farmers in 1928, resulted in agricultural innovations for more than 20 years and a revolution in farm productivity. The Ryan and Gross study formed the classical diffusion paradigm. The investigation included each of the four main elements of diffusion: (1) an innovation, (2) communicated through certain channels, (3) over time, and (4) among the members of a social system. The following steps were taken:

1. Some 259 farmers were interviewed to ascertain when and how they adopted hybrid seed corn and to obtain information about them and their farm operations.

2. The rate of adoption was plotted over time (resulting in the familiar S curve).

3. Farmers were assigned to adopter categories based on time of adoption of the new seed corn.

4. Various communication channels were identified as playing different roles in the innovation decision process. (See Rogers, 1983, pp. 32–34; 54–56.)

In his third edition Rogers shifts emphasis from a unidirectional communication activity to information exchange among participants in a communication process. As a theoretical framework Rogers uses the concepts of uncertainty and information of Shannon and Weaver. An innovation generates a kind of uncertainty in that it provides an alternative to present methods or ideas.

Rogers categorizes the characteristics of an innovation that affect their rate of adoption as follows:

1. *Relative advantage*—the degree to which an innovation is perceived as better than the idea it supersedes

2. *Compatibility*—the degree to which an innovation is perceived as being consistent with the existing values, past experiences, and needs of potential adopters

3. *Complexity*—the degree to which an innovation is perceived as difficult to understand and use

4. *Trialability*—the degree to which an innovation may be experimented with on a limited basis

5. *Observability*—the degree to which the results of an innovation are visible to others (1983, pp. 15–16, ch. 6)

Rogers adds that "in general, innovations that are perceived by receivers as having greater relative advantage, compatibility, trialability, observability, and less complexity will be adopted more rapidly than other innovations" (1983, p. 16).

Heterophily and Homophily

Diffusion is defined as a special type of communication concerned with the *spread* of innovations. In the discussion of the two-step flow model we have seen that opinion leaders and their followers are remarkably similar in many attributes. Diffusion research calls this similarity *homophily,* or the degree to which pairs of individuals who interact are similar in certain attributes such as beliefs, values, education, or social status. However, in the diffusion of an innovation, *heterophily* is most often present. Heterophily is the degree to which pairs of individuals who interact are different in certain attributes (the mirror opposite of homophily). A high degree of source-receiver heterophily, often present in the diffusion of innovations since new ideas often come from people who are quite different from the receiver, creates unique problems in obtaining effective communication.

The Innovation Decision Process

The innovation decision process is a mental process through which an individual or other unit making decisions passes. The process consists of five stages:

1. *Knowledge*—exposure to an innovation and some understanding of how it functions
2. *Persuasion*—formation of an attitude toward the innovation
3. *Decision*—activity resulting in a choice to adopt or reject the innovation
4. *Implementation*—putting the innovation into use
5. *Confirmation*—reinforcement or reversal of the innovation decision made (see Rogers, 1983, ch. 5)

Rogers specifies five adapter categories, classifying individuals or other decision-making units in their rate of adoption of an innovation:

1. *Innovators*—venturesome; eager to try new ideas, more cosmopolite relationships than their peers
2. *Early adopters*—respectable localities, usually highest degree of opinion leadership within social system
3. *Early majority*—deliberate, interact frequently with their peers but seldom hold leadership positions
4. *Late majority*—skeptical; often adopt an innovation because of economic necessity or increasing network pressure
5. *Laggards*—traditionals; most localite; many are near-isolates; point of reference is the past (see Rogers, 1983, ch. 7)

Consequences are the changes that occur to an individual or to a social system as a result of the adoption or rejection of an innovation (Rogers, 1983, p. 31). Rogers lists three classifications of consequences:

1. *Desirable* versus *undesirable* consequences, depending on whether the effects of an innovation in a social system are functional or dysfunctional
2. *Direct* versus *indirect* consequences, depending on whether the changes to an individual or to a social system occur in immediate response to an innovation or as a second-order result of the direct consequences of an innovation
3. *Anticipated* versus *unanticipated* consequences, depending on whether the changes

are recognized and intended by the members of a social system or not (see Rogers, 1983, pp. 31–32, ch. 11)

Communication *channels* may either be interpersonal or mass media in nature or may originate from either localite or cosmopolite sources (Rogers, 1983, p. 198). Cosmopolite communication channels are those from outside the social system being investigated; localite channels are from inside the social system being investigated (p. 200). Research shows that these channels play different roles in the diffusion process. Mass media channels reach large audiences rapidly, spread information, and change weakly held attitudes. Interpersonal channels provide a two-way exchange of information and are more effective than the mass media in dealing with resistance or apathy on the part of the receiver. An interpersonal source can add information or clarify points and perhaps surmount psychological and social barriers (selective exposure, attention, perception, retention; group norms, values, etc.). In the process of diffusion of an innovation, the mass media channels and the cosmopolite channels are relatively more important at the knowledge stage, whereas the interpersonal channels and local channels are more effective at the persuasion stage. Mass media channels and cosmopolite channels are relatively more important than interpersonal channels and localite channels for earlier adopters than for late adopters (Rogers, 1983, pp. 197–201).

Change Agents

In the diffusion of innovation, *change agents* play key roles in the evaluation and trial stages. A change agent is a professional person who attempts to influence adoption decisions in a direction that he or she feels desirable. Often a change agent will use local opinion leaders to assist in diffusing an innovation or to prevent the adoption of what may be seen as a harmful innovation. Change agents usually have more education and status than the individuals they are trying to influence, making them heterophilous from their clients. To overcome this they frequently use aides, often recruited from the local population, who are usually more homophilous with the people they are trying to reach. Change agents can be salespeople and dealers in new products (e.g., hybrid seed corn), representatives of pharmaceutical companies promoting new drugs to medical doctors, technical assistance workers in developing nations, and many others who serve to link individual social systems together. The role of change agents in the evaluation and trial of innovations is especially important to advertising and public relations (see Rogers, ch. 9).

One author points out that

> when a gatekeeper is a commercial change agent, his integrity is questioned by the people he seeks to change. His vulnerability is best understood by seeing him in a conflict situation: he is responsible to the bureaucracy that pays him, but he must simultaneously satisfy the need of the so-called client system—the people he seeks to influence. His credibility is impaired if he appears to execute the demands of the bureaucracy while disregarding the expectations of the client system. This happens to a commercial change agent when people feel that he promotes the over-adoption of new ideas to secure higher sales. These findings suggest that a public communicator's credibility will be low when he is seen as ignoring the interests of a public in favor of his employer's interests. (Lerbinger, 1972, p. 197)

In an earlier edition Rogers and Shoemaker (1971) contended that a "combination of mass media and interpersonal communication is the most effective way of reaching people with new ideas and persuading them to utilize these innovations" (p. 260). They cite and discuss the use of *media forums* (organized small groups of individuals who meet regularly to receive a mass media program, broadcast or print, and then discuss its content) in Canada, India, Africa, China, Latin America, and Italy. Father Coughlin apparently used media forums in the United States in the 1930s. We have also seen the use of discussion groups in Kurt Lewin's efforts to change housewives' attitudes toward less desirable cuts of meat during World War II.

Diffusion of News

One of the subcategories within diffusion research is news diffusion. Melvin L. De Fleur (1988) summarized four decades of research about the flow of news from media sources through a population. We have already cited the Erie County study of the presidential election of 1944. Now we shall note briefly a few of the studies that followed the Erie County study.

A classic work, *The Psychology of Rumor*, by Gordon W. Allport and Leo Postman (1947), describes the process of leveling, sharpening, and assimilation as information is passed along by a series of individuals. They demonstrated processes that distort information as it is passed on through a population, important for anyone working in the mass media.

Wayne Danielson (1956) did a study that investigated, among other things, how the news of President Eisenhower's decision to seek reelection reached 198 residents of Palo Alto, California. He found that direct contact with a medium was the major news source, and the principal medium of first contact was the radio.

Richard J. Hill and Charles M. Bonjean (1964) investigated the diffusion of news of the assassination of President John F. Kennedy in Dallas. More than half the subjects interviewed in Dallas learned of the assassination by word of mouth, only one-fourth by television, and one-sixth by radio.

Another study of the same event, in San Jose, California, was conducted by Bradley S. Greenberg (1964a, 1964b). Greenberg also found that half the 419 adults he contacted first learned the news of the assassination from other people.

A few years later, the flow of information about President Lyndon Johnson's decision not to run for office again was investigated by Irvin L. Allen and J. David Colfax (1968). Because the announcement was made on a Sunday evening when a large proportion of the population were at home, these researchers found that nearly three-fourths of the respondents learned of the decision from the original television broadcast.

In his 1988 summary, De Fleur concluded that the 1960s were the most active period for news diffusion research.

From more than two dozen studies of the diffusion of information conducted since the Erie County study of 1944, De Fleur makes the following generalizations:

> 1. Changing media technologies in the United States have led to changes in the way people receive their first information about important news events. Television has become the most frequently cited source, followed by radio. Newspapers have become, for the most part, suppliers of greater detail at a later time. Word of mouth remains important in some cases.
>
> 2. Most people get most of their news directly from a medium, rather than from other people. The two-step flow model does not describe the pattern by which most of the daily

news reaches the public. The majority have firsthand contact with television or radio, and, on some occasions, with a newspaper for their first exposure to a story.

3. News events of deep concern to large numbers of people will move faster and farther within a population, whatever the first source, than stories of less emotional nature. This generalization refers to the so-called news value of a story. It remains a poorly defined, if intuitively understood, concept. The uses and gratifications provided by news stories of high versus low news values are largely unknown.

De Fleur adds that word of mouth may still be the most significant source of learning about an event for stories of very high news value. But even then, truly urgent news travels between all kinds of people, rather than only from opinion leaders as described by the two-step flow.

Patterns of first exposure to sources of news and later diffusion vary depending on the time of day. Different sources (media and interpersonal) are used at different times of the day.

Individual differences and social categories shape people's interest in a news item and the social networks from which they get information. Different types of people use different ways to learn about a particular event (1988, p. 81).

De Fleur concludes with the statement:

> The news industry may have a special responsibility to support research on the diffusion of news. The industry often claims that it enjoys a privileged status within our society, protected and guaranteed by constitutional law. Traditionally, the press has justified those claims by maintaining that it serves the needs of citizens in a democracy, by providing them with accurate information about what is really going on. This is supposed to provide the basis for intelligent decision making, which leads to better government, and so forth. But there appear to be real questions as to whether these claims have a solid foundation in fact. Does the present system that our society uses to disseminate the news actually keep citizens informed, thereby achieving those cherished democratic ideals? From the research evidence already accumulated, even with all of its warts, there are grounds to suspect that the system does not work all that well. (p. 81)

De Fleur concludes with a series of unanswered questions about the diffusion of information in our society. He raises questions about who is informed by which medium, with what completeness and how much distortion. He also asks what media people rely on for confirmation and interpretation, how this information shapes their view of reality, and whether these views differ from the actual events reported in the media. De Fleur wonders how the system can be redesigned to improve its quality and thoroughness and ends by asking if the press is "forever beyond accountability in assessments of its performance?" (p. 81).

Conclusions

The available evidence indicates that the greatest effect is achieved when media messages advocating innovation or attitude change are coupled with small group discussion. Among the reasons given are social expectations and the pressures applied by the group on individuals to attend and participate and the effects of group pressures on attitude change. As Rogers and Shoemaker pointed out, "Media forums serve to heighten the impact of change-oriented messages by reducing the possibility of selective exposure and selective perception" (1971, p. 264).

As the De Fleur review of research about diffusion of information demonstrated, we have much to learn about how various types of news are diffused and what can be done to improve the diffusion of information. These are important questions for our form of government.

References

Allen, I. L., and J. D. Colfax (1968). The diffusion of news of LBJ's decision. *Journalism Quarterly* 45: 321–324.

Allport, G. W., and L. Postman (1947). *The Psychology of Rumor.* New York: Henry Holt.

Danielson, W. A. (1956). Eisenhower's February decision: A study of news impact. *Journalism Quarterly* 33: 433–441.

De Fleur, M. L. (1988). Diffusing information. *Society* 25: 72–81.

———— and O. Larsen (1958). *The Flow of Information.* New York: Harper.

Greenberg, B. S. (1964a). Diffusion of news about the Kennedy assassination. *Public Opinion Quarterly* 28: 225–232.

———— (1964b). Person-to-person communication in the diffusion of news events. *Journalism Quarterly* 41: 489–494.

Hill, R. J., and C. M. Bonjean (1964). News diffusion: A test of the regularity hypothesis. *Journalism Quarterly* 41: 336–342.

Katz, E. (1957). The two-step flow of communication: An up-to-date report of an hypothesis. *Public Opinion Quarterly* 21: 61–78. Also in W. Schramm (ed.) (1960), *Mass Communications.* Urbana: University of Illinois Press.

Katz, E., and P. F. Lazarsfeld (1955). *Personal Influence: The Part Played by People in the Flow of Mass Communications.* Glencoe, Ill.: Free Press.

Lazarsfeld, P. F., B. R. Berelson, and H. Gaudet (1948). *The People's Choice.* New York: Columbia University Press.

Lazarsfeld, P. F., and H. Menzel (1963). Mass media and personal influence. In W. Schramm (ed.), *The Science of Human Communication.* New York: Basic Books.

Lerbinger, O. (1972). *Designs for Persuasive Communication.* Englewood Cliffs, N.J.: Prentice-Hall.

Lin, N. (1971). *The Study of Human Communication.* Indianapolis: Bobbs-Merrill.

Rogers, E. (1983). *Diffusion of Innovations.* 3rd ed. New York: Free Press.

Rogers, E., and F. Shoemaker (1971). *Communication of Innovations.* New York: Free Press.

Ryan, B., and N. Gross (1943). The diffusion of hybrid seed corn in two Iowa communities. *Rural Sociology* 8: 15–24.

Troldahl, V., and R. Van Dam (1965). Face-to-face communication about major topics in the news. *Public Opinion Quarterly* 29: 626–634.

Westley, B. (1971). Communication and social change. *American Behavioral Scientist* 14: 719–742.

PART V

Mass Media Effects and Uses

A major concern of communication theory for years—and probably rightfully so—has been to investigate the effects of mass communication. The mass media have become a major force in society, and it is reasonable to wonder about the effects that this force is producing. Are the effects of mass communication large or small? Are they malevolent or benign? Are they obvious or subtle? Communication theorists have tried to answer these questions, as well as others about the effects of mass communication.

One of the effects of mass communication seems to be to direct our attention to certain problems or issues. This effect is called the agenda-setting function of the mass media, and it is described in Chapter 12.

Information is sometimes thought of as the cure for many problems, and there is undoubtedly some truth in that idea. But if information is thought of as a method of reducing the social inequality gap between the rich and the poor in society, the cure may not work the way it is expected to. Recent research has indicated that an increased flow of information can lead to the widening of a knowledge gap between the well-off and the not-so-well-off. Chapter 13 takes an in-depth look at this knowledge gap hypothesis.

There are a number of other possible effects of mass communication besides the agenda-setting function and the knowledge gap. These range from Marshall McLuhan's visionary thinking about the effects of new communication technology on our very thought processes to Elisabeth Noelle-Neumann's spiral of silence, a theory of the formation of public opinion that draws heavily on earlier research on the power of social groups. Chapter 14 is devoted to these and a number of other theories of the effects of mass communication.

Focusing on the effects of mass communication can have its drawbacks, however. This approach to theory can cause us to view the audience as a passive target that is vulnerable and inactive in the communication process. It can cause theorists—and those of us reading their theories—to overlook the active role of the communication receiver. The active role of the communication receiver is a basic premise of the uses and gratifications approach to the study of mass communication, an approach that is described in Chapter 15.

12
Agenda Setting

A few days before the 1980 presidential election between Jimmy Carter and Ronald Reagan, most public opinion polls said the race was too close to call. Two days before the election, the news media played up a story that the American hostages being held in Iran might be released. As it turned out, they were not. When the election results were known a few days later, Reagan had won an overwhelming victory, carrying all but six states and the District of Columbia.

One possible explanation for this outcome lies in the concept of agenda setting. By playing up the hostage release story, the news media increased the public's awareness of the Iranian hostage issue. That is, for many members of the public, the hostage issue might have moved from a low position on a list of issues that concerned them to a high position on the list, as in Figure 12.1. Of course, it is very likely that raising the hostage issue on people's agendas would work against Carter, because many people might have regarded the hostage crisis as one of the great failures of his administration. This explanation is only hypothetical; however, it has been suggested as a possibility by social psychologist Donald Kinder and political scientist Shanto Iyengar (Cordes, 1984).

Agenda setting is one of the possible ways that the mass media can have an effect on the public. Agenda setting is the idea that the news media, by their display of news, come to determine the issues the public thinks about and talks about.

Another example of agenda setting comes from the muckraking period of American journalism. Lincoln Steffens describes it in a chapter of his autobiography titled "I Make

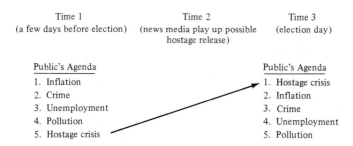

FIGURE 12.1 • A HYPOTHETICAL CASE OF AGENDA SETTING

a Crime Wave." Steffens was working for a New York newspaper, the *Evening Post*. He says that there were always a lot of crime stories being told in the basement of the police station that were not reported in the newspapers. One day he decided to report one of these stories because it involved a well-known family. When the story came out, Jake Riis, the police reporter for the *Evening Sun*, was asked by his newspaper why he didn't have the story. Riis had to find another crime story to make up for it. Soon, all the New York papers were working to find crimes of their own to keep up with the others. They would even rewrite each other's, adding still more. The result was a sudden increase in crimes reported in the newspaper, which was perceived as a "crime wave." Teddy Roosevelt, who was police commissioner, personally looked into the "crime wave," and also took credit for stopping it once he found out it was really caused by Steffens and Riis (Steffens, 1931).

In the Steffens example, the public, and public officials, came to see crime as an important issue simply because crime stories were getting more play in the newspapers. That is agenda setting at work.

A third example of agenda setting also comes from the 1980 presidential election. Edward ("Ted") Kennedy was challenging President Carter for the Democratic nomination. About the time Kennedy began his campaign, Roger Mudd interviewed him on television and brought up the Chappaquiddick incident, in which a young woman was drowned in an automobile accident while riding with Kennedy. A few months after the interview, *Reader's Digest* featured a story titled "Chappaquiddick: The Still Unanswered Questions" on its front page. Kennedy later lost the nomination to Carter. The media attention given to Chappaquiddick during the campaign may have raised this issue in the public's mind, to Kennedy's disadvantage. The Mudd interview was broadcast on November 4, 1979. Harris polls showed Kennedy's ratings dropping seven points between November 10 and November 26 (Robinson, 1981). Between November 1979 and April 1980, the percentage of the public thinking that Kennedy lied about Chappaquiddick virtually doubled (Robinson, 1981). Without the news coverage focusing on Chappaquiddick, these changes in public opinion toward Kennedy probably would not have occurred. Kennedy's decision not to be a candidate in 1984 and the later announcement that he would not be a candidate in 1988 might have also been related to the news media's highlighting of Chappaquiddick.

In all three of these examples, we see the possible action of agenda setting—mass media attention to an issue causing that issue to be elevated in importance to the public.

The Chapel Hill Study

The first systematic study of the agenda-setting hypothesis was reported in 1972 by McCombs and Shaw (1972). They studied agenda setting in the presidential campaign of 1968 and hypothesized that the mass media set the agenda for each political campaign, influencing the salience of attitudes toward the political issues. They conducted their study by focusing on undecided voters in Chapel Hill, North Carolina, because "undecideds" should be most susceptible to agenda-setting effects. The researchers interviewed a sample of 100 respondents and simultaneously conducted a content analysis of the mass media serving these voters—five newspapers, two newsmagazines, and two television network evening news broadcasts. Respondents were asked to cite the major problems in the country, as they saw them. These responses were coded into 15 categories representing the major issues, as well as other types of campaign news. The news media content dealing with the election was also sorted into these 15 categories, by amount. News media content was also divided into "major" and "minor" categories.

The findings supported an agenda-setting effect. For major items, the correlation between emphasis in the media on an issue and voter perception of that issue as important was .967. For minor items, the correlation was .979. As the authors point out, these data suggest a very strong relationship between the emphasis placed on different campaign issues by the media and the judgments of voters as to the salience and importance of various campaign topics.

Precursors of the Hypothesis

Researchers before McCombs and Shaw had stated some ideas that were very similar to the agenda-setting hypothesis. A rather direct statement of the agenda-setting idea appears in a 1958 article by Norton Long:

> In a sense, the newspaper is the prime mover in setting the territorial agenda. It has a great part in determining what most people will be talking about, what most people will think the facts are, and what most people will regard as the way problems are to be dealt with. (Long, 1958, p. 260)

Kurt Lang and Gladys Engel Lang also came up with an early statement of the agenda-setting idea:

> The mass media force attention to certain issues. They build up public images of political figures. They are constantly presenting objects suggesting what individuals in the mass should think about, know about, have feelings about. (Lang & Lang, 1959, p. 232)

Another statement of the agenda-setting idea that is repeated in almost every book or article on the topic is this statement by Bernard Cohen about the power of the press:

> It may not be successful much of the time in telling people what to think, but it is stunningly successful in telling its readers what to think about. (Cohen, 1963, p. 13)

A Change in Thinking

The agenda-setting hypothesis came about when researchers became dissatisfied with the dominant theoretical position in mass communication research during the 1950s and 1960s—the limited effects model. Joseph Klapper stated this model well in his book *The Effects of Mass Communication* (1960) when he wrote, "Mass communication *ordinarily* does not serve as a necessary and sufficient cause of audience effects, but rather functions among and through a nexus of mediating factors and influences" (p. 8). To some people, the idea that the mass media ordinarily did not have any effects just did not seem very reasonable. Researchers also began to consider the possibility that they might have been looking for effects in the wrong places. For many years, the approach used in communication research was to look for *attitude change* and most of the research had found that the mass media have little effect in this area. But perhaps researchers were looking at the wrong target. Maybe the mass media had their effects on people's perceptions—their views of the world—rather than their attitudes.

This change in thinking by communication researchers might also have been reinforced by a change taking place at the same time in the field of psychology. The 1950s marked the emergence of cognitive psychology as a rival to the then dominant approach, behaviorism. Behaviorism stressed the importance of reinforcement, rewards and punishments, and conditioning in shaping behavior, and attempted to use these concepts to explain even human thought and language (Skinner, 1957).

Cognitive psychology, in contrast, saw men and women as active seekers of knowledge who function in the world on the basis of this knowledge (Neisser, 1967). In this view, people are seen as "problem solvers" rather than as objects of conditioning or manipulation. Cognitive psychology is concerned with the "representations" of the world people build in their heads and how they go about building them.

The agenda-setting hypothesis, by investigating the salience or importance that people assign to certain issues and how these saliences are arrived at, is very compatible with cognitive psychology.

The Media Agenda and Reality

Shortly after the McCombs and Shaw study on agenda setting appeared in *Public Opinion Quarterly,* another study, by G. Ray Funkhouser, was published in the same journal. Funkhouser, apparently unaware of the McCombs and Shaw research, was also interested in the relationship between news coverage and public perception of the importance of issues. Funkhouser also brought in another aspect, however—the actual prominence of the specific issues in reality.

Funkhouser focused his study on the 1960s, an active decade in which many issues were prominent. To get his measure of public opinion about what issues were important, Funkhouser used Gallup polls in which people were asked about "the most important problem facing America." He obtained his measures of media content by counting the numbers of articles on each issue appearing in the three weekly newsmagazines (*Time, Newsweek,* and *U.S. News and World Report*) for each year in the decade. Articles on each issue were located by looking under appropriate headings in the *Readers' Guide to Periodical Literature.* The measure of the importance of an issue in reality was based on statistics taken from *Statistical Abstracts of the United States* and other sources. For instance, the number of U.S. troops in Vietnam was taken as a measure of U.S. involvement in Vietnam, and examining this number from year to year showed the trend in our involvement. For the few issues where no statistics were available (such as student unrest and ecology), he had to deal with apparent trends in events.

Funkhouser then looked at the relationship between public opinion and media content, and the relationship between media content and reality. The first relationship—the relationship between public rating of the importance of issues and media content—is shown in Table 12.1.

The table shows a strong correspondence between public ranking of an issue as important and the amount of coverage given the issue by the media. The issues that the public gave a high ranking to were also the issues that the mass media (or, at least, the three newsmagazines) were giving a lot of coverage to. These results are very much in line with the agenda-setting hypothesis, although they leave open the important question of causal direction (perhaps the interests of the public are setting the media agenda).

In the second part of his study, Funkhouser looked at the relationship between media coverage and reality. This analysis is not one that can be summarized easily in a table. The

Table 12.1

AMOUNT OF COVERAGE GIVEN BY NATIONAL NEWS MAGAZINES TO
VARIOUS ISSUES DURING THE 1960s, AND RANK SCORES OF THE ISSUES
AS "MOST IMPORTANT PROBLEM FACING AMERICA" DURING THAT PERIOD

Issue	Number of Articles	Coverage Rank	Importance Rank
Vietnam War	861	1	1
Race relations (and urban riots)	687	2	2
Campus unrest	267	3	4
Inflation	234	4	5
Television and mass media	218	5	12[a]
Crime	203	6	3
Drugs	173	7	9
Environment and pollution	109	8	6
Smoking	99	9	12[a]
Poverty	74	10	7
Sex (declining morality)	62	11	8
Women's rights	47	12	12[a]
Science and society	37	13	12[a]
Population	36	14	12[a]

Rank-order correlation between coverage and importance = .78 (p = .001).
[a] These items were never noted as "the most important problem" in the Gallup findings, so they are ranked equally below the items that did.
From G. R. Funkhouser, "The Issues of the Sixties: An Exploratory Study in the Dynamics of Public Opinion," *Public Opinion Quarterly* 37 (1973): 66. Copyright 1973 by Columbia University Press. Reprinted by permission of the University of Chicago Press.

pattern that Funkhouser found, however, seemed to be that media coverage did not correspond very well to the realities of the issues. For instance, media coverage of the Vietnam War, campus unrest, and urban riots peaked a year or two before these happenings reached their climaxes in reality. Coverage of drugs and inflation was somewhat in line with reality, but coverage of race relations, crime, poverty, and pollution bore little, if any, relation to actuality.

Funkhouser's study suggests that the news media did not give a very accurate picture of what was going on in the nation during the 1960s. Funkhouser concludes, "The news media are believed by many people (including many policymakers) to be reliable information sources, but the data presented here indicate that this is not necessarily the case" (1973a, p. 75).

The Charlotte Study

An important question left open by the original McCombs and Shaw study of agenda setting is the question of causal order. The original Chapel Hill study found strong correlations between the media agenda and the public agenda during the 1968 election campaign, but it could not show which was influencing which. It is possible that the media agenda was influencing the public agenda, as the hypothesis suggests, but it is also plausible that the public agenda may have been influencing the media agenda.

As their next step in exploring agenda setting, McCombs and Shaw planned an additional study focusing on the 1972 presidential election campaign (Shaw & McCombs, 1977). This study was set in Charlotte, North Carolina. It used a larger sample than the Chapel Hill study, and it was a panel design, with respondents being interviewed at several points throughout the campaign. One of the specific purposes of this study was to obtain evidence concerning the causal direction of agenda setting. The use of a panel design, with several measures repeated through time, would allow some investigation of the causal sequence.

In the Charlotte survey, the same random sample of voters was interviewed during June prior to the national political conventions, again in October during the height of the campaign, and finally in November when the election returns were in. In order to investigate the causal direction of agenda setting, the authors focused on the two time periods of June and October. For each time period, they also had a measure of the media agenda, based on content analysis of the Charlotte newspaper and the evening newscasts of two television networks (CBS and NBC). These data for the two time periods were looked at with a technique known as cross-lagged correlation. The results—for newspapers only—are presented in Figure 12.2.

The key correlations to look at in the diagram are those on the two diagonals. Comparing these correlations gives us an indication of the causal sequence. Which correlation is larger, the correlation between newspaper agenda at time 1 and public agenda at time 2, or the correlation between newspaper agenda at time 2 and public agenda at time 1? If the first correlation—the correlation between newspaper agenda at time 1 and public agenda at time 2—is larger, that would provide support for agenda setting. And that is indeed what the figure shows.

The results are not as clear-cut as we might wish. For instance, the high correlation of

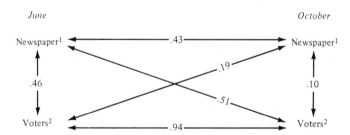

[1]Correlations are based on the "official" newspaper agenda.
[2]Analysis is based on panel members who read *only* the Charlotte *Observer*
(*N* = 178).

FIGURE 12.2 • CROSS-LAGGED CORRELATION COMPARISON OF CHARLOTTE VOTERS AND THE CHARLOTTE *OBSERVER* IN JUNE AND OCTOBER 1972

From D. L. Shaw and M. E. McCombs (eds.), *The Emergence of American Political Issues: The Agenda Setting Function of the Press* (St. Paul, Minn.: West, 1977), p. 91. Reprinted by permission. Copyright © 1977 by West Publishing Co. All rights reserved.

.94 between public agenda at time 1 and public agenda at time 2 is troublesome, as researcher Bruce Westley has pointed out (Westley, 1978). How can there be an agenda-setting effect when the public's agenda essentially remains unchanged? Furthermore, the cross-lagged correlation analysis for television does not show the support for agenda setting that Figure 12.2 does for newspapers. Nevertheless, the results of the Charlotte study do provide some evidence for causal direction—that it is likely that the media (or newspapers, at least) do have a causal effect in shaping the public's agenda, rather than vice versa.

Experimental Evidence

How could investigators obtain more powerful evidence regarding causality? We pointed out in Chapter 2 that the most effective method for showing a causal relationship is the experiment. Is it possible that an experiment could be conducted to investigate the effects of agenda setting?

Researcher Shanto Iyengar of Yale University and two colleagues conducted several experiments just for this purpose (Iyengar, Peters, & Kinder, 1982). In general, their approach was to take videotapes of television network newscasts and alter them by editing out some stories and replacing them with others. This allowed them to manipulate the content of the news media in such a way that certain issues were played up and others were played down. Subjects in various experimental conditions were then exposed to these altered newscasts and were later questioned about their rankings of the importance of various issues, including those manipulated in the newscasts.

In both experiments, participants came to offices at Yale University and were told they were taking part in a study of television newscasts. On the first day, they filled out a questionnaire that included questions on a number of political matters, including their ratings of the importance of various issues. On days 2 through 5, participants viewed what they thought were regular television newscasts of the day. What they did not know was that the newscasts had been altered to provide heavier coverage of some issues than others. On the sixth day, subjects filled out another questionnaire that repeated the questions about the importance of various issues.

Their first experiment involved only two conditions. One group of respondents saw newscasts that had been modified by inserting additional stories dealing with weaknesses in U.S. defense capability. The other group of respondents saw newscasts with no defense stories. The respondents' perceptions of the importance of eight problems was measured before and after exposure to the newscasts. Participants rated each problem on four questions. Ratings were summed, so that each problem could range in score from a 4 for lowest importance to a 20 for highest importance. The effect of the newscasts was examined by looking at adjusted changes scores, or scores comparing the pretest score and the posttest score. A positive change score indicates an increase in importance. Results of the first experiment are presented in Table 12.2. The table shows a positive change score of .90 for the defense issue for those exposed to the "defense-emphasizing" condition. In comparison, the control group, which saw no defense stories, showed a decreased rating of the importance of the defense issue ($-.79$). This is a statistically significant difference, while none of the other seven issues shows a significant difference.

The second experiment by Iyengar and his associates involved three issues and three experimental conditions. One group saw newscasts emphasizing inadequacies in U.S. de-

Table 12.2

ADJUSTED CHANGE SCORES FOR PROBLEM IMPORTANCE IN EXPERIMENT 1

	Condition	
Problem	Defense	Control
Defense*	.90	−.79
Inflation	−.49	.23
Energy	−.40	.22
Drug addiction	−.19	−.48
Corruption	−.67	.05
Pollution	−.58	.60
Unemployment	.28	.54
Civil rights	−.27	−.27

*p< .05, one-tailed test.
From S. Iyengar, M. D. Peters, and D. R. Kinder, "Experimental Demonstrations of the 'Not-So-Minimal' Consequences of Television News Programs," *American Political Science Review* 76 (1982): 852. Reprinted by permission.

fense preparedness. A second group saw newscasts emphasizing pollution of the environment. A third group saw newscasts that emphasized inflation. The newscasts for each condition also deliberately omitted any stories dealing with the topics emphasized in the other two conditions. As before, analysis of the experiment involved looking at change scores in ratings of the importance of various issues before and after exposure to the experimentally manipulated newscasts. The results of the second experiment are presented in Table 12.3. The table shows a positive change score of 1.53 on the pollution issue for those exposed to the pollution-emphasizing newscast. In contrast, the two groups who did not see pollution-emphasizing newscasts show negative change scores of −.71 and −.23, indicating they are rating pollution as less important than they did before. A similar pattern of results appears in the table for the defense issue. The issue for which the pattern does not show up is inflation. But the authors give a rather compelling explanation for this discrepancy. Exam-

Table 12.3

ADJUSTED CHANGE SCORES FOR PROBLEM IMPORTANCE IN EXPERIMENT 2

Problem	Pollution	Inflation	Defense
Pollution	1.53**	−.71	−.23
Inflation	− .11	.11	−.06
Defense	− .44	−.34	.76*

*p < . 05.
**p < .01.
From S. Iyengar, M. D. Peters, and D. R. Kinder, "Experimental Demonstrations of the 'Not-So-Minimal' Consequences of Television News Programs," *American Political Science Review* 76 (1982): 852. Reprinted by permission.

ination of the questionnaires showed that respondents were rating inflation as so important before the experiment (a mean rating of 18.5 out of a possible 20) that they didn't really have much room to increase its rating of importance.

In a later book, Iyengar and Kinder (1987) reported a series of additional experiments that provided further evidence for agenda setting. In some of these experiments, viewers' perceptions of whether a problem was one of the country's most important were significantly affected by exposure to a single television news story.

Wanta (1988) conducted a similar experiment testing agenda setting except that he used newspapers instead of television news broadcasts. Wanta designed a study to investigate the effects of the size of photographs accompanying a story on audience salience assigned to issues. He had copies of an actual newspaper printed with different front pages. In the dominant condition, the crucial story was accompanied by one large photo. In the balanced condition, the crucial story was accompanied with one small photo and there were other photos on the same page. In the third condition, no photo accompanied the crucial story. Three groups of subjects were presented with the altered newspapers. The three photo conditions were combined with three different stories, so that each subject saw one story with a dominant photo, one story with a balanced photo, and one story with no photo. Stories dealt with national defense, the plight of the American farmers, and pollution. Subjects were given a pretest to assess their importance rankings of 12 issues, including the three in the experimental stories. Then, over a period of several days, they were exposed to the experimental newspapers. Finally, they were given another questionnaire to assess their importance ratings for the issues after exposure to the newspapers.

Results showed the use of a dominant photo with a story increased the audience's importance rating of the issue covered in the accompanying story. The balanced photo had the same effect, although not as strongly. The story without a photo did not have an effect on audience issue importance rating. Besides proving some additional support for agenda setting in general, the Wanta experiment also identifies a particular cue with some ability to influence agenda setting—the size of photographs accompanying stories in newspapers.

Priming

Iyengar and his associates also discovered a special way that television newscasts might be having an impact on presidential elections. By setting the agenda for an election campaign, the media also determine the criteria by which presidential candidates will be evaluated. We have already discussed this possibility in our two examples taken from the 1980 presidential election. By raising the hostage crisis situation on the public's agenda right before the election, the media might have lowered the public's evaluation of President Carter. Or by raising the Chappaquiddick issue, the media might have lowered the public's evaluation of Ted Kennedy. Iyengar and his associates call this process *priming*. Priming is the process in which the media attend to some issues and not others and thereby alter the standards by which people evaluate election candidates.

The researchers found some evidence of priming in their experiments. Subjects in the experiments, in addition to the measures we have already discussed, also rated President Carter as to his performance in the three specific problem areas—defense, pollution, and inflation. They also gave general ratings of Carter's overall performance, competence, and integrity. As predicted by the concept of priming, the correlation between the overall rating and the rating in a specific problem area was greater for respondents who saw coverage emphasizing that problem area than it was for respondents who saw coverage neglecting that problem area. For example, when respondents saw coverage emphasizing inflation, the correlation between Carter's performance rating on inflation and his overall performance rating was .63. But when respondents saw coverage neglecting inflation, the correlation between Carter's performance rating on inflation and his overall performance rating was .39.

In other words, respondents were evaluating President Carter in terms of topics they had seen emphasized in the news recently. This is a rather subtle but powerful way that agenda setting could be influencing our most important elections.

Agenda Setting in Television

A massive study of the agenda-setting function of television news was conducted in West Germany (Brosius & Kepplinger, 1990). These researchers studied weekly surveys of public awareness of 16 issues, and conducted a content analysis of the main German television news shows in which they looked for the same issues. Both types of data were collected for the entire year of 1986. They found that television coverage influenced problem awareness for four issues—energy supply, defense, environmental protection, and European politics. But problem awareness influenced television coverage on three other issues—pensions, public debt, and public security. The researchers suggested that television coverage is likely to shape public awareness of a problem when the coverage is intensive (more than 30 items per month) and increases suddenly. They suggested that public awareness is likely to boost media coverage when problem awareness showed a long-term steady increase with little variation.

Presidential Agendas

One question of interest to researchers has been: Who sets the agenda for the media? This might be a particularly important question if, as Funkhouser's study suggested, the media agenda differs somewhat from reality.

One very likely choice for an influence on the media agenda is the president of the United States. He is the number one newsmaker in the country, and has access to mass communication not available to many others.

One of the places where the president presents a fairly explicit agenda of issues, as he sees it, is in the State of the Union address. If the president has the capability to influence the media agenda, one of the instances where this influence might show up clearly is in this annual address. Although ostensibly for the benefit of Congress, the address is also broadcast on radio and television to the nation as a whole.

To investigate the possible influence of the State of the Union address on the media agenda, Gilberg, Eyal, McCombs, and Nicholas (1980) conducted a study of President Carter's second State of the Union address. They performed a content analysis of the address to identify the issues mentioned and then ranked the eight issues on the basis of the amount of the address spent dealing with each one. They then looked at press coverage in two major newspapers and the three television networks for four weeks prior to the State of the Union address and for four weeks after. Four weeks before was included as a control—it could help in interpreting the correlations between the president's agenda and the subsequent press agenda.

Contrary to their hypothesis, the correlations between the president's agenda and the subsequent media agenda were weaker than the correlations between the president's agenda and the prior media agenda. That is, the evidence from the study suggested not that President Carter was setting the press's agenda, but that the press was setting President Carter's agenda.

In order to understand this surprising outcome better, McCombs, Gilbert, and Eyal (1982) attempted to replicate the study with Richard Nixon's 1970 State of the Union address. This changed the study to a president with a different style and to an earlier period in history when the issues were different. In both cases, the studies dealt with a president's second State of the Union address.

Content analysis of Nixon's address produced a list of 15 issues, compared with 8 from Carter's address. As in the first study, the authors then examined press coverage in two major newspapers and the three television networks for the four weeks prior to the address and the four weeks after.

The results showed stronger support for the original hypothesis of presidential agenda setting than for the revised hypothesis that the press influences the presidential agenda. In all five comparisons (for the two newspapers and the three networks), the correlations between the presidential agenda and the postspeech media agenda were stronger than the correlations between the presidential agenda and the prespeech media agenda.

McCombs and his colleagues also found that correlations between the prespeech media agenda and the postspeech media agenda were even stronger than either of the correlations between the presidential agenda and pre- or postspeech media agendas. This suggests a kind of stability or consistency of news coverage—probably due to news routines, news values used by journalists, and other factors in journalism itself.

The different outcome of these two studies of presidential State of the Union addresses suggests that situational factors need to be taken into account when trying to understand agenda setting. In this particular area, presidential influence on an agenda, factors such as difference in presidential leadership style and the number and nature of the issues being dealt with played a role in determining the direction of an agenda-setting effect.

"The Day After"

The ABC television network broke new ground in television drama in 1983 when it presented the fictional program "The Day After." The drama gave a realistic depiction of a nuclear missile attack on the United States and its aftermath. Could such a program, with its dramatic message, have an agenda-setting effect all by itself?

M. Mark Miller and Jan P. Quarles of the University of Tennessee at Knoxville conducted a before-and-after study of the effects of this program on public opinion (1984). The researchers were aware of the general finding of much prior research that mass communication does not ordinarily produce attitude change. So they designed their study to pinpoint not attitude change effects but agenda-setting effects.

They based their study on telephone interviews with a random sample of Knoxville residents. Interviews were conducted with one group prior to the telecast of "The Day After" and with another group after the telecast. This design allowed for comparison of three groups: (1) prebroadcast respondents (who did not yet have an opportunity to watch the program), (2) postbroadcast respondents who elected not to watch the program, and (3) postbroadcast respondents who elected to watch the program.

They asked questions in their interviews dealing with the perceived importance of the issue of nuclear war, how much people engaged in discussion of nuclear war, and attitudes on several nuclear weapons topics.

The results were somewhat mixed, but they do provide some support for agenda setting. The prominence of nuclear war on the public agenda was measured several ways. First, respondents were asked two open-ended questions about "the most important problem facing our country today." Their responses were coded as either mentioning nuclear war or not. The responses to these questions by each of the three groups were then looked at in a cross-tabulation table. The results of this analysis are presented in Table 12.4, which shows that the viewers were much more likely to mention nuclear war as a problem than either the prebroadcast group or the nonviewers.

Another measure of the prominence of nuclear war showed a less clear result, however. Respondents were asked to compare their concern about nuclear war with four other major issues: inflation, unemployment, U.S. military involvement in other countries, and crime. The cross-tabulation of their rankings of "nuclear war" by group is presented in Table 12.5. As the table shows, the viewer group was more likely to rank "nuclear war" number one than either the prebroadcast group or the nonviewers. The opposite result is true for ranking "nuclear war" number two, however. The authors say this pattern of results offers "only marginal support for the proposition that watching the movie increases levels of concern" (Miller & Quarles, 1984, p. 7). The support may be stronger than that, however—what the table may be showing is that watching the program has an effect primarily on those who are ranking "nuclear war" second, and that the effect was to make them move it up to the first rank.

Analysis of the attitude items showed no difference among the three groups. This supports the findings of many earlier studies that mass communication alone is seldom effective in changing attitudes. Results of the question concerning discussion were ambiguous, since it wasn't possible to determine whether discussion occurred before or after the showing of the program.

Table 12.4
MENTION OF NUCLEAR WAR BY VIEWING GROUP

	Prebroadcast (N = 92)	Nonviewers (N = 96)	Viewers (N = 144)
Percent not mentioning nuclear war	72	68	48
Percent mentioning nuclear war	28	32	52

$\chi^2 = 16.44$, df = 2, $p < .001$.
Adapted from M. Mark Miller and Jan P. Quarles, *Dramatic Television and Agenda Setting: The Case of* The Day After, paper presented to the Theory and Methodology Division, Association for Education in Journalism and Mass Communication, Gainesville, Fla., August 1984. Reprinted by permission.

Table 12.5
RANK OF NUCLEAR WAR BY VIEWING GROUP

Rank	Prebroadcast (%)	Nonviewers (%)	Viewers (%)
1	7	17	24
2	22	14	10
3	13	18	19
4	29	17	19
5	29	35	28

$\chi^2 = 21.95$, df $= 8$, $p < .01$.
Adapted from M. Mark Miller and Jan P. Quarles, *Dramatic Television and Agenda Setting: The Case of* The Day After, paper presented to the Theory and Methodology Division, Association for Education in Journalism and Mass Communication, Gainesville, Fla., August 1984. Reprinted by permission.

In general, the Miller and Quarles study provides some support for the agenda-setting hypothesis. The effects of the program appear to have been not on attitudes but on perceptions of the importance of issues. The study also extends the application of agenda setting from news presentations to dramatic or fictional television programs as well.

The Obtrusiveness of Issues

Several of the later agenda-setting studies that attempted to show causal direction by using panel studies at two points in time have shown only weak agenda-setting effects. This is true of the Charlotte study by McCombs and others, which found evidence of the proper time sequence for newspapers but not for television. It is also true of several other studies (Tipton, Haney, & Baseheart, 1975; McLeod, Becker, & Byrnes, 1974). Harold Gene Zucker hypothesized that the reason for this could be that these earlier studies were based on an incorrect assumption—that the agenda-setting effect would take place for *all* issues (Zucker, 1978). Zucker went on to suggest that the obtrusiveness of the issue may be an important factor in whether or not agenda setting takes place. Zucker argued that the less direct experience the public has with a given issue area, the more it will have to depend on the news media for information about that area. Issues that the public experiences directly, like unemployment, are obtrusive issues. Issues that the public may not experience as directly, like pollution, are unobtrusive issues.

Zucker conducted a study comparing three obtrusive issues—the cost of living, unemployment, and crime—with three issues that were unobtrusive at the time—pollution, drug abuse, and the energy crisis. The amount of coverage of the six issues over an eight-year period was taken from the *Television News Index*, a monthly publication. The measure of public opinion on the importance of the six issues was taken from a number of Gallup polls that asked, "What is the most important problem facing the country today?"

Zucker found that for the three unobtrusive issues, heavy news media coverage preceded the rise of importance of an issue in the public opinion polls. For the three obtrusive issues, however, heavy news media coverage did not precede the rise of importance to the public. Rather, the two seemed to increase together.

Zucker's research demonstrates that agenda setting may take place for unobtrusive issues but not for obtrusive issues and suggests that the obtrusiveness of issues is an important concept that should be added to the agenda-setting hypothesis.

Zucker makes another interesting suggestion. He argues that agenda-setting effects should show up for both users and nonusers of the news media. If agenda setting takes place mostly on unobtrusive issues, then the only ways people can find out about them are through the media or through talking to other people who have been exposed to the media. That is, agenda setting and the two-step flow of communication may combine in having an effect. This may help explain why some studies that looked for media effects by comparing viewers and nonviewers—such as the Miller and Quarles study of "The Day After"—did not find a strong effect due to the media.

Bias by Agenda

Conservatives have sometimes claimed that the evening television newscasts have a liberal bias. Senator Jesse Helms of North Carolina has made that accusation about CBS News. Furthermore, Fairness in Media, a group he is affiliated with, indicated that it was attempting to buy controlling stock in CBS. One of the charges the conservatives sometimes make is that the networks do not so much say liberal things as imply them by covering topics that either make conservatives look bad (such as inefficiency in the Pentagon) or make liberal causes look good (such as the plight of migrant workers). This notion is really a kind of "bias by agenda," with the issues that are being played up by the media being the ones that reflect favorably or unfavorably on a particular ideology.

Some support for bias by agenda was found in a massive study of television network news by Michael J. Robinson and his colleagues at George Washington University (Robinson, 1985; Fischman, 1985). The results showed some liberal bias by agenda for CBS and NBC but some conservative bias by agenda by ABC (see Table 12.6).

The Question of Time Lag

Agenda setting, as we have noted, is a causal hypothesis suggesting that media content has an influence on the public perception of the importance of issues. If this hypothesis is correct, an important question concerns the time lag. How long does it take for media content to have an effect on the public's subjective rankings?

Researchers Gerald Stone and Maxwell McCombs (1981) conducted a study aimed at

Table 12.6

PERCENTAGE OF NETWORK NEWS TIME
DEVOTED TO "LIBERAL" OR "CONSERVATIVE" ISSUES

	CBS	NBC	ABC
Liberal	37	21	13
Neither	40	72	56
Conservative	23	7	31

Adapted from J. F. Fischman, "Views of Network News," *Psychology Today*, July 1985, p. 16.

investigating the time lag for agenda setting. Their basic technique was to obtain data on the public's agenda from some studies done previously and then conduct an additional analysis of media content over a long period of time prior to the time the public's agenda was measured. They then looked at the correlation between the public's agenda and the media agenda (actually based on *Time* and *Newsweek*), with the media agenda entered into the analysis for a number of different time points prior to the interviews with the public. Stone and McCombs did this analysis for three different sets of survey data—the June interviews from the Charlotte survey, the October interviews from the Charlotte survey, and an additional survey of male sophomores at Syracuse University. The different data sets agreed in showing that a period ranging from two months to six months seemed to be necessary for an item to move from the media agenda to the public agenda.

In a different study, Winter and Eyal (1980) investigated time span by focusing on a single issue, civil rights. They looked at coverage in the *New York Times* of the civil rights issue from 1954 to 1976 and compared it with Gallup Poll data on the public perception of the importance of civil rights. The public agenda was based on the percentage of respondents who replied to the question "What is the most important issue facing the American public today?" with a response categorized as "civil rights." This percentage ranged from 0 to 52 percent over the 22 years.

Winter and Eyal found that the strongest correlations between the media agenda and the public agenda on the civil rights issue were for a four- to six-week span. They call this period—which might be different for other issues—the "optimal effect span."

The Winter and Eyal figure is rather different from the one obtained by Stone and Mc-Combs, but the difference could be due to some variations in the studies. One variation is that Winter and Eyal looked at only one issue. It seems quite likely that different issues will take different amounts of time to arouse a sufficient clamor to attract the public's attention. As Eyal, Winter, and DeGeorge (1981) point out, an oil embargo may suddenly thrust the issue of energy shortage onto the public agenda, while it may take years for the "honesty in government" issue to rise in public awareness.

Shoemaker, Wanta, and Leggett (1989) attempted to resolve the issue of the time span needed for agenda setting in their study of public concern about the drug problem. They found evidence that both the Stone and McCombs and the Eyal, Winter, and DeGeorge time intervals were correct. Their study revealed two time periods in which media coverage of drug issues correlates with later public concern about drugs—one to two months and four to five months.

The question of time span is important for media practitioners. Public relations professionals and other information campaign workers can plan their campaigns better if they know how long it takes to elevate an issue into public consciousness. The findings concerning time span also tell us something about how agenda setting works. It does not take place overnight, but it does not take years, either.

Agenda Building

Researchers Gladys Engel Lang and Kurt Lang (1983) studied the relationship between the press and public opinion during the Watergate crisis, and found that the original notion of agenda setting needed to be expanded in order to explain this complicated chapter of American history. They have suggested that the concept of agenda setting be expanded into the concept of agenda building, which they break down into six steps:

1. The press highlights some events or activities and makes them stand out.

2. Different kinds of issues require different kinds and amounts of news coverage to gain attention. Watergate was a high-threshold (or unobtrusive) issue, and therefore it took extensive coverage to bring it to the public's attention.

3. The events and activities in the focus of attention must be "framed," or given a field of meanings within which they can be understood. Watergate was originally framed as a partisan issue in an election campaign, and this made it difficult for it to be perceived in a different frame—as a symptom of widespread political corruption.

4. The language used by the media can affect perception of the importance of an issue. The initial references to the Watergate break-in as a "caper," which persisted for months, tended to belittle it. The later switch to the term "scandal" gave more importance to the issue.

5. The media link the activities or events that have become the focus of attention to secondary symbols whose location on the political landscape is easily recognized. People need to have a basis for taking sides on an issue. In the case of Watergate, they were aided in doing this when the issue became linked to such secondary symbols as "the need to get the facts out" and "confidence in government."

6. Agenda building is accelerated when well-known and credible individuals begin to speak out on an issue. For instance, when Judge John Sirica said the public was not being told the truth about Watergate, that had a dramatic impact on the public, as well as on other prominent persons, including some Republicans, who were then more willing to speak out.

The Langs' concept of agenda building is more complicated than the original agenda-setting hypothesis. It suggests that the process of putting an issue on the public's agenda takes time and goes through several stages. It suggests that the way the media frame an issue and the code words they use to describe it can have an impact and that the role of well-known individuals commenting on the issue can be an important one.

The importance of framing was also indicated in a study by Williams, Shapiro, and Cutbirth (1983). These authors conducted a study comparing agenda setting for television newscast and newspaper stories that explicitly linked an issue to a campaign (put the issue in a "campaign" frame) and stories that did not explicitly link an issue to a campaign (no framing). The study was conducted during the 1980 presidential campaign. Stories on the three television network newscasts and in a daily newspaper were coded as to the issue and whether the issue was framed as being related to the presidential race. The audience agenda was determined by a telephone survey in which respondents were asked what was the most important presidential campaign issue. For those stories framed in terms of the campaign, significant correlations were generally found between the media agenda and the public agenda. For those stories not framed in terms of the campaign, significant correlations between the media agenda and the public agenda generally were not found.

The Need for Orientation

Agenda setting might not take place to the same extent and in the same way for all individuals. McCombs and Weaver have suggested that individuals differ in their *need for orientation* and that this may determine whether or not agenda setting takes place (Weaver, 1977).

Need for orientation, as they conceived of it, is based on two factors: the relevance of the information (to the individual) and the degree of uncertainty concerning the subject of the message. The greater the relevance of the information and the greater the uncertainty concerning the subject, the greater the need for orientation. They hypothesized that the higher the need for orientation, the more susceptible the individual is to mass media agenda-setting effects. They found evidence in the Charlotte study that the hypothesis is true, although the evidence was stronger for newspapers than for television.

Who Sets the Media Agenda?

Many studies have been done showing the media agenda and its possible effect on the public's agenda, but until recently researchers have tended to ignore an important question: Who sets the *media* agenda? Or, as Bruce Westley has asked concerning the media agenda, "What makes it change?" (Westley, 1976).

Part of the answer lies in events occurring in reality. To some extent, the media are simply passing on issues and events that are occurring in society. This works in only a rough way, however—the Funkhouser and Zucker studies showed that news media coverage often does not correspond well to events in reality. Many other studies have suggested this same conclusion. If that is so, what does determine the media agenda? Westley has provided part of the answer himself. He suggested that in some cases pressure groups or special interest groups are able to boost an issue onto the media agenda. Examples of this would be the Student Nonviolent Coordinating Committee (SNCC) playing a part in putting racial discrimination on the public agenda in the 1960s and the National Organization for Women (NOW) and other women's groups putting women's issues on the public agenda in the 1970s.

Funkhouser (1973b) has suggested a list of five mechanisms in addition to the flow of actual events that operate to influence the amount of media attention an issue might receive:

1. Adaptation of the media to a stream of events. As the same pattern of events persists, it may be perceived as "just more of the same" and cease to be considered news.

2. Overreporting of significant but unusual events. Some events, such as the Santa Barbara oil spill, are important but receive exaggerated coverage because of their unusualness or sensationalism.

3. Selective reporting of the newsworthy aspects of otherwise nonnewsworthy situations. For instance, one well-known study has shown that television coverage of a parade honoring General MacArthur, by selecting certain details, made the event seem more exciting than it was (Lang & Lang, 1972).

4. Pseudoevents, or the manufacturing of newsworthy events. Protest marches, demonstrations, sit-ins, and publicity stunts are examples of pseudoevents that might help to move issues onto the press agenda.

5. Event summaries, or situations that portray nonnewsworthy events in a newsworthy way. An example is the release in 1964 of the surgeon general's report showing a relationship between smoking and lung cancer.

The question of who sets the media agenda really becomes the larger question of what are the influences on media content, and there are obviously many. This larger question involves the approach sometimes known as media sociology, and it has been the subject of much recent research and theorizing (Shoemaker & Reese, 1991).

One of the important influences on the media agenda suggested by recent research is the content of other media. In particular, it appears that the elite media, such as the *New York Times,* can set the agenda for other media. Danielian and Reese (1989) refer to this process as *intermedia agenda setting.* They found evidence that the prominence of the drug issue in the media in 1985 and 1986 was more a result of intermedia agenda setting than any increase in the drug problem in society. In fact, actual drug use did not rise dramatically in 1985 and 1986, although mass media coverage of the issue did. They found that "a general intermedia agenda setting influence was noted from the *New York Times* to the other media" (p. 48). In general, they found that the print media lead the television networks rather than vice versa (Reese & Danielian, 1989).

The process of intermedia agenda setting is also documented in Timothy Crouse's *The Boys on the Bus* (1973), which reports on press coverage of the 1972 presidential campaign. Crouse tells of reporters from other media looking over the shoulder of R. W. (Johnny) Apple, Jr., of the *New York Times* to see the lead of his news story so they would know what to play up in their own stories.

Other evidence suggests that newsmakers are becoming particularly savvy about placing items on the media agenda. This may happen especially with the president of the United States, who not only is the number one newsmaker but also has considerable power to bring attention to himself and shape that attention. When President Reagan was running for his second term, for instance, he took a tour to promote his administration's record on environmentalism. The tour was full of photo opportunities, including the president standing on a fishing boat in the Chesapeake Bay and the president wearing a park ranger's hat at Mammoth Cave, Kentucky. Even though environmentalists said the Reagan administration had a terrible record on the environment, many people were likely to see photos of the president in the ranger hat and make a positive link between Reagan and the environment. Reese (1990) has suggested that Larry Speakes, Reagan's press secretary, was particularly adept at dreaming up photo opportunities that encouraged favorable coverage of the president.

George Bush, during his 1988 campaign for the presidency, was also adept at manipulating his own media coverage. Bush's strategy was to concentrate on one issue a day and present it in an attractive setting so TV producers would put it on the air. In one particularly effective instance of this technique, Bush toured Boston Harbor and denounced his opponent, Michael Dukakis, for not cleaning up the waterway (Katz, 1988).

Shoemaker and Reese (1991), drawing upon work by Herbert Gans and Todd Gitlin, have proposed the following five major categories of influences on media content:

1. Influences from individual media workers. Among these influences are communication workers' characteristics, personal and professional backgrounds, personal attitudes, and professional roles.

2. Influences of media routines. What gets into the mass media is influenced by the day-to-day practices of communicators, including deadlines and other time constraints, space requirements in a publication, the inverted pyramid structure for writing a news story, news values, the standard of objectivity, and the reliance of reporters on official sources.

3. Organizational influences on content. Media organizations have goals, with making money one of the most widely shared. These goals of the media organization can have an impact on content in numerous ways.

4. Influences on content from outside of media organizations. These influences include interest groups lobbying for (or against) certain kinds of content, people creating pseudoevents in order to get media coverage, and government, which regulates content directly through libel and obscenity laws.

5. The influence of ideology. Ideology represents a society-level phenomenon. Fundamental to ideology in the United States is "a belief in the value of the capitalist economic system, private ownership, pursuit of profit by self-interested entrepreneurs, and free markets" (Shoemaker & Reese, 1991, p. 184). This all-encompassing ideology probably influences the content of the mass media in many ways.

These five categories range from individual media workers, representing the most "micro" level, to the influence of ideology, representing the most "macro" level. They make up what Shoemaker and Reese call a "hierarchy of influences," with ideology sitting at the top of the hierarchy and filtering down through all the other levels.

How Broad Is Agenda Setting?

One of the important questions about agenda setting has to do with how generally it is conceptualized.

In its original statement, the hypothesis was rather narrow. It suggested a correspondence between the media agenda and the public agenda, where agenda was conceptualized to be a rank order of political issues according to importance. The setting for this predicted correspondence was a political election.

Later researchers have broadened the idea of agenda setting, however. Weaver and colleagues, for example, broadened the focus of the agenda-setting idea beyond issues to include candidate images (Weaver, 1982). That is, they looked to see if media coverage made some candidates or certain attributes of candidates more salient than others.

Some agenda-setting researchers have related agenda setting to Lippmann's *Public Opinion* (1922/1965), in which he argued that the mass media shape the "pictures in our heads."

If it is conceived too generally, however, the idea loses much of its distinctiveness. If agenda setting is conceived of as shaping the "pictures in our heads," it becomes difficult to distinguish it from Gerbner's cultivation theory, which suggests that television watching shapes people's worldview. It may also lose much of its predictive power as it moves to this vaguer kind of statement.

Although it is useful to have agenda setting conceived very broadly—it explains more phenomena, for instance—it also makes the hypothesis less precise and therefore less testable. Somewhere between an all-encompassing statement of the effects of the media and a narrow effect on the ranking of a limited set of issues there must be a happy medium.

How Does Agenda Setting Work?

Despite all the research on agenda setting, one of the things we still don't understand very well is how agenda setting works (McCombs, 1981). That is, we still don't have a very good understanding of the process of agenda setting. What takes place when issue saliences are transferred from the media to the minds of individuals? Are some cues (headline size, front-page play, position in a news broadcast, use of photographs or visuals) more important in suggesting salience than others? Or is the important factor the accumulation of cues over time, no matter what their particular form? How does the mind store the information that it is accumulating on an issue? Is there some kind of mental score sheet or tally sheet involved? To what extent is agenda setting a conscious process in the human mind? Does it achieve some of its effectiveness by being an unconscious process? What is the role of interpersonal communication in agenda setting? Does it augment it, as Zucker suggests? Or does it serve as an anchor, as group influence often does, and thus help people resist the effects of the media?

Many of these questions focus on processing of information by the individual. It may be that we need more studies focused at this level in order to develop a full understanding of the process of agenda setting.

Manheim (1987) has done some work on the conceptualizing of agendas that has potential to aid our understanding of the process of agenda setting. Manheim proposes that agenda setting involves the interaction of three agendas—the media agenda, the public agenda, and the policy agenda. Each of these is conceptualized as involving three important dimensions:

1. For the media agenda, the three dimensions are *visibility* (the amount and prominence of coverage given an issue), *audience salience* (the relevance of news content to audience needs), and *valence* (the favorable or unfavorable coverage given to an issue).

2. For the public agenda, the three dimensions are *familiarity* (the degree of public awareness of a given topic), *personal salience* (interest or perceived relevance to one's self), and *favorability* (the favorable or unfavorable judgment on the topic).

3. For the policy agenda, the three dimensions are *support* (action more or less favorable to a given issue position), *likelihood of action* (probability that a governmental body will act on the issue), and *freedom of action* (range of possible governmental actions).

Part of the value of Manheim's conceptualization is that the three dimensions of the three agendas encompass many of the key variables that have been identified in diverse agenda-setting studies, and they do it in a systematic way. For example, Wanta's variable of dominance of photographs in newspapers can be incorporated under the media agenda dimension of visibility. Zucker's variable of the obtrusiveness of an issue can be incorporated under the public agenda dimension of familiarity. Weaver's variable of need for orientation can be incorporated under the public agenda dimension of salience.

In Manheim's conceptualization of the public (or audience) agenda as a three-dimensional concept, each issue can be represented as a point in a three-dimensional space. This is a significant conceptual advance over the idea of a public agenda as a rank-order list of issues. As Manheim notes, "None of these agendas is, in fact, merely a list. . . . Rather, each is a dynamic system in its own right" (Manheim, 1987, p. 509).

Manheim's conceptualization also lends itself to the development of hypotheses concerning the various dimensions of the three models. Hypotheses can be developed relating to the initial location of issues on the agendas or relating a position on one dimension of one agenda to a position on another dimension of a different agenda. Manheim has already suggested a number of these hypotheses. By facilitating the development of these kinds of hypotheses, the Manheim conceptualization is moving us toward the development of an overall theory of agenda setting.

Conclusions

The agenda-setting hypothesis has been one of the major concepts in communication theory since the early 1970s. The hypothesis is important because it suggests a way that the mass media can have an impact on society that is an alternative to attitude change. Furthermore, there are indications that the impact could be a significant one. There is evidence that the media are shaping people's views of the major problems facing society and that the problems emphasized in the media may not be the ones that are dominant in reality. There is also evidence that the media, while producing minimal attitude change, are still exerting an important influence on presidential elections through the concept of priming.

The evidence on agenda setting may not be conclusive, but there has been enough supporting evidence to suggest that the concept should be taken seriously.

For the practicing journalist, the concept of agenda setting raises important questions of responsibility. The labels that journalists apply to events can have an important influence on whether the public pays attention to the issues connected with the event, as the analysis of Watergate suggests. In an election campaign, the issues that the media play up can have the effect of favoring one candidate over another through the process of priming. The media can also help to create a certain image for a candidate by playing up some personal characteristics and ignoring others.

For the enterprising reporter, the findings of agenda-setting research also suggest opportunities. If the press typically does not cover significant happenings in proportion to their importance—as the Funkhouser and Zucker studies suggest—this means there are probably crucial news stories waiting to be uncovered.

For the public relations worker, agenda setting suggests the importance of framing an event in the right way in order to catch the public's attention.

Much of the research on agenda setting suggests that the press is not a mirror, reflecting the realities of society as they are (Shoemaker & Mayfield, 1984). As Lippmann (1922/1965, p. 229) suggested many years ago, it is more like a searchlight, and where the searchlight is shining can be affected by groups with special interests in an issue, by pseudoevents created to get attention, and by certain habits and rituals of journalists.

References

Brosius, H.B., and H. M. Kepplinger (1990). The agenda-setting function of television news. *Communication Research* 17: 183–211.

Cohen, B. C. (1963). *The Press and Foreign Policy.* Princeton, N.J.: Princeton University Press.

Cordes, C. (1984). Media found able to "prime" voters. *APA Monitor,* June, p. 31.

Crouse, T. (1973). *The Boys on the Bus.* New York: Random House.

Danielian, L. H., and S. D. Reese (1989). A closer look at intermedia influences on agenda setting: The cocaine issue of 1986. In P. J. Shoemaker (ed.), *Communication Campaigns about Drugs: Government, Media and the Public,* pp. 47–66. Hillsdale, N.J.: Lawrence Erlbaum.

Eyal, C. H., J. P. Winter, and W. F. DeGeorge (1981). The concept of time frame in agenda-setting. In G. C. Wilhoit and H. de Bock (eds.), *Mass Communication Review Yearbook,* vol. 2, pp. 212–218. Beverly Hills, Cal.: Sage.

Fischman, J. F. (1985). Views of network news. *Psychology Today,* July, pp. 16–17.

Funkhouser, G. R. (1973a). The issues of the sixties: An exploratory study in the dynamics of public opinion. *Public Opinion Quarterly* 37: 62–75.

——— (1973b). Trends in media coverage of the issues of the '60s. *Journalism Quarterly* 50: 533–538.

Gilberg, S., C. Eyal, M. McCombs, and D. Nicholas (1980). The State of the Union address and the press agenda. *Journalism Quarterly* 57: 584–588.

Iyengar, S., and D. R. Kinder (1987). *News That Matters: Television and American Opinion*. Chicago: The University of Chicago Press.

Iyengar, S., M. D. Peters, and D. R. Kinder (1982). Experimental demonstrations of the "not-so-minimal" consequences of television news programs. *American Political Science Review* 76: 848–858.

Katz, G. (1988). Study: GOP has taken TV initiative. *USA Today*, September 6, p. 11A.

Klapper, J. T. (1960). *The Effects of Mass Communication*. New York: Free Press.

Lang, G. E., and K. Lang (1983). *The Battle for Public Opinion: The President, the Press, and the Polls During Watergate*. New York: Columbia University Press.

Lang, K., and G. E. Lang (1959). The mass media and voting. In E. Burdick and A. J. Brodbeck (eds.), *American Voting Behavior*, pp. 217–235. Glencoe, Ill.: Free Press.

Lang, K., and G. E. Lang (1972). The unique perspective of television and its effect: A pilot study. In W. Schramm (ed.), *Mass Communications*, 2nd ed., pp. 544–560. Urbana: University of Illinois Press.

Lippmann, W. (1922, reprinted 1965). *Public Opinion*. New York: Free Press.

Long, N. E. (1958). The local community as an ecology of games. *American Journal of Sociology* 64: 251–261.

Manheim, J. B. (1987). A model of agenda dynamics. In M. L. McLaughlin (ed.), *Communication yearbook 10*, pp. 499–516. Newbury Park, Cal.: Sage.

McCombs, M. E. (1981). Setting the agenda for agenda-setting research: An assessment of the priority ideas and problems. In G. C. Wilhoit and H. de Bock (eds.), *Mass Communication Review Yearbook*, vol. 2, pp. 209–211. Beverly Hills, Cal.: Sage.

McCombs, M., S. Gilbert, and C. Eyal (1982). *The State of the Union address and the press agenda: A replication*. Paper presented at the annual meeting of the International Communication Association, Boston.

McCombs, M. E., and D. L. Shaw (1972). The agenda-setting function of mass media. *Public Opinion Quarterly* 36: 176–187.

McLeod, J. M., L. B. Becker, and J. E. Byrnes (1974). Another look at the agenda-setting function of the press. *Communication Research* 1: 131–166.

Miller, M. M., and J. P. Quarles (1984). *Dramatic television and agenda setting: The case of "The Day After."* Paper presented at the annual meeting of the Theory and Methodology Division, Association for Education in Journalism and Mass Communication, Gainesville, Fla., August.

Neisser, U. (1967). *Cognitive Psychology*. New York: Appleton-Century-Crofts.

Reese, S. D. (1990). *Setting the media's agenda: A power balance perspective*. Paper presented to the Communication Theory and Methodology Division of the Association for Education in Journalism and Mass Communication, Minneapolis, August.

Reese, S. D., and L. J. Danielian (1989). Intermedia influence and the drug issue: Converging on cocaine. In P. J. Shoemaker (ed.), *Communication Campaigns about Drugs: Government, Media and the Public*, pp. 29–45. Hillsdale, N.J.: Lawrence Erlbaum.

Robinson, M. J. (1981). The media in 1980: Was the message the message? In A. Ranney (ed.), *The American Elections of 1980*, pp. 177–211. Washington: American Enterprise Institute for Public Policy Research.

——— (1985). Jesse Helms, take stock. *Washington Journalism Review* 7, no. 4: 14–17.

Shaw, D. L., and M. E. McCombs (eds.) (1977). *The Emergence of American Political Issues: The Agenda Setting Function of the Press*. St. Paul, Minn.: West.

Shoemaker, P. J., and E. K. Mayfield (1984). *Mass media content as a dependent variable: Five media sociology theories*. Paper presented at the annual meeting of the Communication Theory and Methodology Division, Association for Education in Journalism and Mass Communication, Gainesville, Fla., August.

Shoemaker, P. J., and Reese, S. D. (1991). *Mediating the Message: Theories of Influences on Mass Media Content*. New York: Longman.

Shoemaker, P. J., W. Wanta, and D. Leggett (1989). Drug coverage and public opinion, 1972–1986. In P. J. Shoemaker (ed.), *Communication Campaigns about Drugs: Government, Media and the Public*, pp. 67–80. Hillsdale, N.J.: Lawrence Erlbaum.

Skinner, B. F. (1957). *Verbal Behavior*. New York: Appleton-Century-Crofts.

Steffens, L. (1931). *The Autobiography of Lincoln Steffens*. New York: Harcourt, Brace, and World.

Stone, G. C., and M. E. McCombs (1981). Tracing the time lag in agenda-setting. *Journalism Quarterly* 58: 51–55.

Tipton, L., R. D. Haney, and J. R. Baseheart (1975). Media agenda-setting in city and state election campaigns. *Journalism Quarterly* 52: 15–22.

Wanta, W. (1988). The effects of dominant photographs: An agenda-setting experiment. *Journalism Quarterly* 65: 107–111.

Weaver, D. H. (1977). Political issues and voter need for orientation. In D. L. Shaw and M. E. McCombs (eds.), *The Emergence of American Political Issues: The Agenda Setting Function of the Press*, pp. 107–119. St. Paul, Minn.: West.

————— (1982). Media agenda-setting and media manipulation. In D. C. Whitney, E. Wartella, and S. Windahl (eds.), *Mass communication review yearbook*, vol. 3, pp. 537–554. Beverly Hills, Cal.: Sage.

Westley, B. H. (1976). What makes it change? *Journal of Communication* 26, no. 2: 43–47.

————— (1978). Review of *The Emergence of American Political Issues: The Agenda Setting Function of the Press*. *Journalism Quarterly* 55: 172–173.

Williams, W., M. Shapiro, and C. Cutbirth (1983). The impact of campaign agendas on perceptions of issues in 1980 campaign. *Journalism Quarterly* 60: 226–231.

Winter, J. P., and C. H. Eyal (1980). *An agenda-setting time-frame for the civil rights issue*. Paper presented at the annual meeting of the International Communication Association, Acapulco.

Zucker, H. G. (1978). The variable nature of news media influence. In B. D. Ruben (ed.), *Communication Yearbook 2*, pp. 225–240. New Brunswick, N.J.: Transaction.

13

The Knowledge-Gap Hypothesis

Information is a resource. It has value, and it lets people do things that they couldn't do otherwise. An old aphorism states that knowledge is power, and this means simply that knowledge gives people the capability to do things, and to take advantage of opportunities.

It is apparent, however, that knowledge, like other kinds of wealth, is not distributed equally throughout our society. People who are struggling with financial poverty are also often information-poor. There are haves and have-nots with regard to information just as there are haves and have-nots with regard to material wealth.

The book *The Information-Poor in America* suggests the following list of questions as typical information needs of the disadvantaged adult in the United States (Childers & Post, 1975, p. 56):

> How do I get my baby into a day-care center?
>
> Whom do I talk to to get rid of rats?
>
> My husband walked out on me three weeks ago. What do I do?
>
> How do I know if I have lead-based paint on the walls?
>
> Where can I get $10 to last till my welfare check comes in?
>
> I need enough food to get us through the weekend.
>
> How do I get an abandoned car removed from in front of my house?
>
> There's a gang of kids terrorizing the neighborhood. Where do I turn?
>
> My daughter has been acting funny lately. Can anyone help?

Childers and Post also suggest the following as a "portrait of the disadvantaged American in his native information habitat." The prototypal disadvantaged American, more than his average counterpart:

> Does not know which formal channels to tap in order to solve his problems, or what specific programs exist to respond to his needs.
>
> Watches many hours of television daily, seldom reads newspapers or magazines and never reads books.
>
> Does not see his problems as information needs.
>
> Is not a very active information seeker, even when he does undertake a search.
>
> May lean heavily on formal channels of information if it becomes apparent that the informal channels are inadequate and if his need is strongly felt.

> Is locked into an informal information network that is deficient in the information that is ordinarily available to the rest of society. (p. 42)

Information is important in our society because a democracy depends on well-informed citizens. People elect public officials to run the government, and citizens vote on specific issues such as whether or not a city should participate in a nuclear power plant project. One must be well-informed to vote intelligently on such matters.

It appears certain that information will be even more important in the future, as we move into an increasingly technological age. Many modern problems, including environmental pollution, nuclear power, the dangers from various food additives, and the risk of nuclear war, will require information, and an informed public, for their solution.

One of the great promises of mass communication is that it might be able to help alleviate many of the problems mentioned above by providing people with the information they need. Mass communication has the potential of reaching people who haven't been reached by other means. These people could include the disadvantaged in the big cities of America as well as the poor in more rural areas such as Appalachia. Television sets are now present in almost all homes (about 98 percent) in America. Mass communication could also provide vital information to needy people in the many underdeveloped countries in the world, although many people in these countries have even less access to the media than the poor in the United States.

The Role of the Mass Media

One example of an attempt to use mass communication to provide information to the disadvantaged is the educational television program "Sesame Street." This program, which was first broadcast in 1969, was an attempt to achieve some of the goals of the government Head Start programs for disadvantaged preschoolers through the mass medium of television. "Sesame Street" was based on extensive research. It attempted a bold, new mission—to reach a large audience of children and hold their interest by combining information and entertainment in a new format.

Other mass communication efforts, it has been suggested, might also have the advantage of getting information to people not usually reached. For instance, televised presidential debates might take the presidential election campaign to people who would not normally be exposed to the campaign, and thus help our democracy to work more effectively.

The attempt to improve people's lives or make democracy work better by increased quantities of information from the mass media might not always work the way the planners would hope, however. An unexpected and undesired possibility is that mass communication might actually have the effect of increasing the difference or gap in knowledge between members of different social classes. This phenomenon, called the "knowledge-gap hypothesis," was first proposed in 1970 in an article titled "Mass Media Flow and Differential Growth in Knowledge" by Tichenor, Donohue, and Olien.

The authors state the knowledge-gap hypothesis this way:

> As the infusion of mass media information into a social system increases, segments of the population with higher socioeconomic status tend to acquire this information at a faster rate than the lower status segments, so that the gap in knowledge between these segments tends to increase rather than decrease. (pp. 159–160)

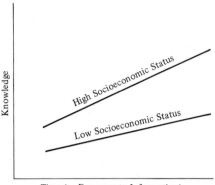

FIGURE 13.1 • THE KNOWLEDGE-GAP HYPOTHESIS

A general picture of the knowledge-gap hypothesis is presented in Figure 13.1. The dimension from the left to the right in the figure represents the passage of time and the infusion of additional information. The hypothesis predicts that people of both low and high socioeconomic status will gain in knowledge because of the additional information but that persons of higher socioeconomic status will gain more. This would mean that the relative gap in knowledge between the well-to-do and the less-well-off would increase.

Tichenor, Donohue, and Olien suggest that a knowledge gap is particularly likely to occur in such areas of general interest as public affairs and science news. It is less likely to occur in more specific areas that are related to people's particular interests—areas like sports or lawn and garden care.

Operational Forms of the Hypothesis

For purposes of testing, Tichenor, Donohue, and Olien say the knowledge-gap hypothesis can be stated in the following two ways:

1. *Over time,* acquisition of knowledge of a heavily publicized topic will proceed at a faster rate among better-educated persons than among those with less education.

2. *At a given point in time,* there should be a higher correlation between acquisition of knowledge and education for topics highly publicized in the media than for topics less highly publicized.

Tichenor and his associates present evidence supporting both of the operational forms of the hypothesis. First, they present some time trend data. Figure 13.2 summarizes some data gathered by the American Institute of Public Opinion at several times. In four different polls, respondents were asked whether they believed man would reach the moon in the foreseeable future. The increasing gap between educational levels is readily apparent, with acceptance of the belief going up much more rapidly for college-educated respondents than for persons with less education.

The researchers also present data supporting the second form of the knowledge gap hypothesis. This operational test suggests that, at a given time, there should be a higher

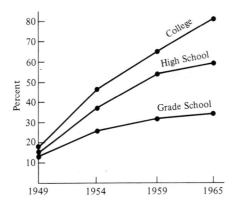

FIGURE 13.2 • Respondents in National Surveys Stating Belief That Man Will Reach the Moon, by Education and Year

From P. J. Tichenor, G. A. Donohue, and C. N. Olien, "Mass Media Flow and Differential Growth in Knowledge," *Public Opinion Quarterly* 34 (1970): 166. Copyright 1970 by Columbia University Press. Reprinted by permission of the University of Chicago Press.

correlation between acquisition of knowledge and education for highly publicized topics than for less publicized topics. Table 13.1 presents some data from a field experiment that is relevant to this test. Respondents were handed two science articles to read and then were asked to recall what the articles said. The general pattern of correlations in the table is consistent with the knowledge-gap hypothesis. That is, in each case the correlation between education and understanding of the article is higher for the more publicized topic than for the less publicized topic. An example may help to make this clear. One of the four comparisons of interest is for the first article read when the area is medicine and biology. In this comparison, the correlation for the more publicized topic is .109. This is larger than

Table 13.1

CORRELATIONS BETWEEN EDUCATION AND UNDERSTANDING OF SCIENCE ARTICLES FOR HIGH- AND LOW-PUBLICITY TOPICS IN TWO GENERAL AREAS

	First Article Read		Second Article Read	
Area	More Publicized Topics	Less Publicized Topics	More Publicized Topics	Less Publicized Topics
Medicine and biology	$r = .109$ ($N = 84$) *n.s.*	$r = .032$ ($N = 111$) *n.s.*	$r = .264$ ($N = 90$) $p < .02$	$r = .165$ ($N = 108$) *n.s.*
Social sciences	$r = .278$ ($N = 104$) $p < .01$	$r = .228$ ($N = 93$) $p < .05$	$r = .282$ ($N = 91$) $p < .01$	$r = .117$ ($N = 97$) *n.s.*

From P. J. Tichenor, G. A. Donohue, and C. N. Olien, "Mass Media Flow and Differential Growth in Knowledge," *Public Opinion Quarterly* 34 (1970): 169. Copyright 1970 by Columbia University Press. Reprinted by permission of the University of Chicago Press.

the correlation for the less publicized topic of .032, and this is what the operational form of the knowledge-gap hypothesis predicts.

Possible Reasons for a Knowledge Gap

Why should the knowledge-gap hypothesis be expected to be true? Tichenor, Donohue, and Olien (1970) present five reasons:

1. There is a difference in communication skills between those high and low in socioeconomic status. There is usually a difference in education, and education prepares one for such basic information-processing tasks as reading, comprehending, and remembering.

2. There is a difference in the amount of stored information, or previously acquired background knowledge. Those of higher socioeconomic status might already know of a topic through education, or they might know more about it through previous media exposure.

3. People of higher socioeconomic status might have more relevant social contact. That is, they might associate with people who are also exposed to public affairs and science news and might enter into discussions of such topics with them.

4. The mechanisms of selective exposure, acceptance, and retention might be operating. Persons of lower socioeconomic status might not find information concerning public affairs or science news compatible with their values or attitudes, or they just might not be interested in such information.

5. The nature of the mass media system itself is that it is geared toward persons of higher socioeconomic status. Much of the news of public affairs and science appears in print media and print media are oriented toward the interests and tastes of higher status persons.

The Knowledge Gap in Public Affairs

The knowledge-gap hypothesis is also supported by a number of other types of evidence gathered by researchers. One prediction from the knowledge-gap hypothesis is that people of higher socioeconomic status are more likely to be exposed to certain types of information (particularly, that dealing with public affairs and science) than people of lower socioeconomic status. Some research on the audiences for some major addresses delivered over the radio provides evidence relating to this question. Figure 13.3 shows the audience for a major address by Supreme Court Justice Hugo Black. The bar graph shows a definite relationship, with the audience declining regularly as one moves from high socioeconomic status to low socioeconomic status.

The audience for a major address by President Roosevelt looked at according to socioeconomic status is shown in Figure 13.4. The bar graph shows a pattern similar to Figure 13.3, with the audience declining regularly with declining socioeconomic status.

These graphs alone provide some fairly strong evidence for a knowledge gap. Persons of lower socioeconomic status were less likely to listen to the two speeches, and therefore would be less likely to know the information that was contained in the speeches.

Presidential debates, such as those in 1988 between presidential contenders George Bush and Michael Dukakis or vice presidential candidates Dan Quayle and Lloyd Bentsen,

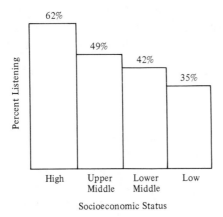

FIGURE 13.3 • RADIO AUDIENCE FOR A SPEECH BY SUPREME COURT JUSTICE HUGO BLACK, BY
SOCIOECONOMIC STATUS

Adapted from P. F. Lazarsfeld, *Radio and the Printed Page* (New York: Duell, Sloan and Pearce, 1940), p. 26.

are often among the high points of a presidential election campaign. Because of their
drama, excitement, and uniqueness, the debates offer the possibility of overcoming the
barriers of selective exposure and apathy that keep many citizens from participating in a
campaign.

The debates might have many effects, but one of the simplest would be to increase
viewers' knowledge of the positions of the candidates on various issues. Research on the
1976 presidential debates, however, suggests that the people most likely to watch the debates are those more politically involved in the first place, and that, furthermore, those
people tend to be the ones of higher education (Bishop, Oldendick, & Tuchfarber, 1978).
The findings suggest that the result of the debates was that the knowledge-rich got richer
and the knowledge-poor got poorer. In other words, the results suggested a widening of the
knowledge gap.

Evidence of a knowledge gap on the energy issue showed up in a panel study in West

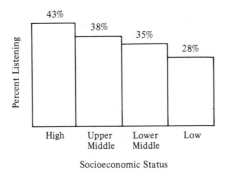

FIGURE 13.4 • RADIO AUDIENCE FOR A SPEECH BY PRESIDENT ROOSEVELT, BY SOCIOECONOMIC
STATUS

Adapted from P. F. Lazarsfeld, *Radio and the Printed Page* (New York: Duell, Sloan and Pearce, 1940), p. 28.

Allis, Wisconsin, conducted by Griffin (1987). This researcher found that knowledge of energy was related to reading of newspaper energy stories by the more educated, but to viewing televised energy commercials among the less educated. This finding suggests that the planners of information campaigns dealing with energy or similar complex issues might need to choose different media to reach different audience sectors.

"Sesame Street"

The first-year report on "Sesame Street" states that the prime target of the program was the disadvantaged inner-city child (Ball & Bogatz, 1970, p. 209). The first-year report also states that "Sesame Street" "helped to close the gap between advantaged and disadvantaged children" (Ball & Bogatz, p. 358). Other researchers who examined the test results on "Sesame Street" viewers have challenged that conclusion, however.

Perhaps the major challenge to the conclusion came in a book called *"Sesame Street" Revisited* (Cook et al., 1975). Researcher Thomas Cook and his colleagues based their challenge on extensive reanalysis of the evaluation data gathered by the producers of "Sesame Street" themselves. One set of data dealt simply with how much "Sesame Street" was watched in households in which the heads of the households had varying amounts of education. Figure 13.5 shows some 1970 data concerning the percentage of households where "Sesame Street" was viewed at least once a week in the last three months, according to education of head of household. The figure shows a regular pattern: the higher the level of education of the head of household, the more likely it was that "Sesame Street" would be watched. Figure 13.6 shows some similar results for 1971.

On the basis of the data presented above and other data, Cook and his associates concluded, "The implication of these data is that *Sesame Street* will have great difficulty in

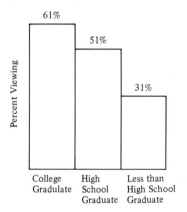

FIGURE 13.5 • HOUSEHOLDS WITH CHILDREN UNDER SIX WHERE "SESAME STREET" WAS VIEWED AT LEAST ONCE IN THE PRECEDING THREE MONTHS, BY EDUCATION OF HEAD OF HOUSEHOLD (1970)

Adapted from T. D. Cook, H. Appleton, R. F. Conner, A. Shaffer, G. Tamkin, and S. J. Weber, *"Sesame Street" Revisited: A Case Study in Evaluation Research* (New York: Russell Sage Foundation, 1975), p. 293.

narrowing any achievement gaps between groups of different income or education levels" (pp. 308–309).

The data in Figures 13.5 and 13.6 have only to do with exposure, and do not actually show a difference in the effects of viewing. Another researcher, however, reexamined some different data that were also gathered by the program producers and had to do more directly with effects (Katzman, 1974). Table 13.2 presents a comparison of achievement score results for disadvantaged and advantaged children viewing "Sesame Street." It shows a number of interesting results, but the most relevant for the present discussion comes from looking at the row for gain scores for disadvantaged and advantaged children. For the first three quartiles of viewing, this comparison shows the advantaged children in each quartile making a greater gain in achievement scores than the disadvantaged children. In other words, even when viewing is the same, the advantaged children are getting more out of "Sesame Street" than the disadvantaged children. This pattern is not observed in the fourth quartile, however. This holds out the possibility that for the heaviest viewers, the knowledge gap might be narrowed rather than widened. For the first three quartiles, however, the knowledge gap is widened by viewing the program.

In response to the criticisms of Cook and others, the creators of "Sesame Street" have said the program was not intended to reduce the gap between advantaged and disadvantaged children (Lesser, 1974, p. 186). Rather, the goal was to bring all children up to a basic level of preparation for doing well in school. "Sesame Street" has continued to be successful, of course, with 11 million U.S. households watching it every week and with 83 countries now having their own version of the show.

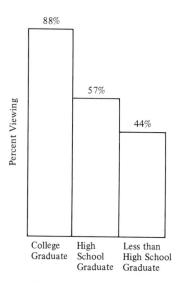

FIGURE 13.6 • HOUSEHOLDS WITH CHILDREN UNDER SIX WHERE "SESAME STREET" WAS VIEWED AT LEAST ONCE IN THE PRECEDING THREE MONTHS, BY EDUCATION OF HEAD OF HOUSEHOLD (1971)

Adapted from T. D. Cook, H. Appleton, R. F. Conner, A. Shaffer, G. Tamkin, and S. J. Weber, *"Sesame Street" Revisited: A Case Study in Evaluation Research* (New York: Russell Sage Foundation, 1975), p. 293.

Table 13.2

PRETEST AND GAIN SCORES ON BATTERY OF ACHIEVEMENT TESTS
BY AMOUNT OF "SESAME STREET" VIEWING AND BACKGROUND

| | Quartile (least to most) | | | |
	Q_1	Q_2	Q_3	Q_4
Background				
Total				
Pretest	76	86	94	101
Gain	19	31	39	48
Disadvantaged				
Pretest	76	84	87	97
Gain	19	29	37	47
Advantaged				
Pretest	95	102	113	110
Gain	27	38	40	45

From N. Katzman, "The Impact of Communication Technology: Promises and Prospects," *Journal of Communication* 24, no. 4 (1974): 55. Reprinted by permission.

Refinement of the Hypothesis

In a later study, Donohue, Tichenor, and Olien (1975) began to explore some of the conditions under which a knowledge gap might be reduced or eliminated. Based on analysis of surveys dealing with the relationships between knowledge and other variables from 15 Minnesota communities, the researchers suggested the following modifications of the hypothesis:

1. When there is perceived conflict over a local issue, the knowledge gap is likely to decline.
2. Widening knowledge gaps are more likely to occur in pluralistic communities, with numerous sources of information, than in homogeneous communities, with informal but common communication channels.
3. When an issue has immediate and strong local impact, the knowledge gap is likely to decline.

In general, this study suggested that an important variable is the extent to which an issue arouses basic social concerns. When it does, the knowledge gap is likely to be reduced or eliminated.

Additional evidence for the narrowing of a knowledge gap comes from the data on "Sesame Street" analyzed by Katzman that we have already noted. It is worth taking another look at these data in another form. Figure 13.7 shows a graph of the posttest scores (pretest scores plus gains) for disadvantaged and advantaged children at four levels of viewing. The closing of the gap for heavy viewers becomes readily apparent. In fact, the heavy viewers in the disadvantaged group have reached achievement scores higher than the two lightest viewing groups for the advantaged.

What these results—and the results of some other studies—suggest is that the knowledge gap is widened under certain circumstances and closed under other circumstances. But what are the circumstances? Put another way, what variables determine whether a knowledge gap widens or closes?

Ettema and Kline (1977) cite two explanations for the existence of a knowledge gap. Some researchers have suggested that the knowledge gap is due to basic communication skills and other factors associated with socioeconomic status. This line of thinking explains the knowledge gap in terms of "transsituational" factors. Another group of researchers has suggested that the gap is due to differences in motivation and that individuals of lower socioeconomic status might acquire information just as rapidly as those of higher socioeconomic status when they are motivated to do so. This line of thinking explains the knowledge gap in terms of "situation-specific" factors.

A study pitting these two explanations against one another was conducted by Lovrich and Pierce (1984). These authors used a survey to measure knowledge in the area of water resource management policy, an area of considerable importance in Idaho, where they carried out the study. They compared a set of transsituational variables (education, income, and occupational status) with a set of situation-specific variables (five measures of motivation to acquire information concerning water policy) to see which were most effective in predicting knowledge levels. Their results indicated that both types of variables contributed to knowledge levels, but that the situation-specific variables were the more important ones. In other words, a widening of the knowledge gap might not occur if people of lower socioeconomic status have a particular need or desire to acquire the information.

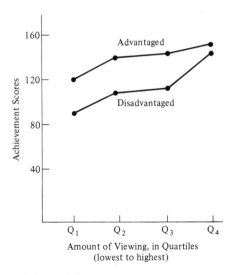

FIGURE 13.7 • POSTTEST ACHIEVEMENT SCORES FOR ADVANTAGED AND DISADVANTAGED CHILDREN AT FOUR LEVELS OF VIEWING "SESAME STREET"

Adapted from N. Katzman, "The Impact of Communication Technology: Promises and Prospects," *Journal of Communication* 24, no. 4 (1974): 55.

Further light is shed on the closing of knowledge gaps in a study by Ettema, Brown, and Luepker (1983). They investigated the effects of a campaign to increase knowledge about cardiovascular disease and health. The study compared a town that received the extensive information campaign (two 20-week exposures) and a control town that did not. Part of the results is shown in Table 13.3. In the treatment community, the one that received the health information campaign, the pretest shows a gap in knowledge level between those with some college and those with no college. The posttest, taken after the campaign, shows a closing of this gap, however, with the means for the two education levels much closer together. The researchers also compared education as a predictor of knowledge acquisition with two measures of motivation to seek information about cardiovascular disease to see which did better. The two measures of motivation were age, based on the assumption that older people would be more worried about heart disease, and a self-rated measure of "threat of heart attack." The two motivational measures were related to knowledge acquisition, while education was not. This study agrees with the Lovrich and Pierce study in suggesting that motivation to acquire information may be the important variable in determining whether a knowledge gap widens or closes.

Television may have a special power to close knowledge gaps, or, if not to close them, at least to keep them from widening. One of the new applications of cable television in a number of communities has been to give live coverage of city council meetings and other government activities, in keeping with the idea that the activities of government should be public and open. It has also been suggested that such television coverage provides a new avenue for the viewer for participating as a citizen. A study of viewers of televised city council meetings in Wichita, Kansas, attempted to see just who the viewers were—and whether a knowledge gap might be occurring (Sharp, 1984). The author found that less-educated, lower-income, and minority individuals were just as likely to watch as their better-off counterparts—in other words, that a widening of the knowledge gap did not occur. Sharp found that viewers of the telecast tended to be persons who "had a stake in the community" and that those people were just as likely to be found in the lower SES levels as the higher. Having a stake in the community was indicated by things like living in the

Table 13.3

MEAN LEVELS OF KNOWLEDGE IN TREATMENT AND
COMPARISON COMMUNITIES SEGMENTED BY EDUCATION

	Treatment Community		Comparison Community	
	Pretest	Posttest	Pretest	Posttest
More educated (some college)	6.09	6.64	5.68	6.31
Less educated (no college)	5.14	6.36	5.46	5.55
Gap between more and less educated	.95*	.28	.22	.76*

*Differences between mean knowledge scores of more and less educated segments are significant ($p < .035$). From J. S. Ettema, J. W. Brown, and R. V. Luepker, "Knowledge Gap Effects in a Health Information Campaign," *Public Opinion Quarterly* 47 (1983): 522. Copyright 1983 by the Trustees of Columbia University. Reprinted by permission of the University of Chicago Press.

the community a long time, belonging to a community organization, and being able to name a community problem.

The Sharp study, then, agrees with those by Lovrich and Pierce and by Ettema, Brown, and Luepker in suggesting that individual motivation is an important factor in information seeking, and that knowledge gaps might narrow rather than widen when motivation to seek information is strong.

The Generality of the Hypothesis

Since the initial formulation of the knowledge-gap hypothesis, several researchers have suggested that it needs to be restated more generally.

Rogers (1976) stated that the gap should apply to attitudinal and overt behavioral effects and not just to effects on knowledge. He stated further that the hypothesis should not be limited to mass media efforts alone, but should include also the effects of interpersonal communication and the combination of mass and interpersonal communication. Finally, he suggested that the gap need not occur between only *two* groups of receivers (those of high and low socioeconomic status, for instance) and that socioeconomic status and its related variables were not the only receiver variables that could be related to a knowledge gap.

A study by McLeod, Bybee, and Durall (1981) also contributed to broadening the knowledge-gap hypothesis. These researchers studied knowledge gain and several other variables in a research project dealing with the effects of the 1976 presidential debates. They investigated a new variable they called *equivalence of informed political participation*. This variable measures five functions that are important in political participation: (1) Stimulation of involvement, (2) Increasing knowledge, (3) Facilitating decision making by clarifying issues, and so forth, (4) Stimulating participation in the form of campaigning, and so forth, (5) Strengthening attachment to the more abstract political system. The equivalence variable measures the extent to which diverse groups are equivalent in knowledge (and some other concerns), and thus is measuring a phenomenon that is basically the opposite of the knowledge gap. The researchers were expanding the gap hypothesis to several other kinds of effects in addition to knowledge. The researchers also looked for gaps between other groups besides just those of high and low education. They investigated possible gaps between young and old and between those of high and low interest in politics. Finally, the researchers looked at nonequivalence of *exposure,* as well as nonequivalence of *predictive strength,* where the latter measured effect on the five functions involved in political participation.

The results showed clear nonequivalence of exposure, with the more interested, older, and better-educated people more likely to have watched the debates. In contrast, the results pertaining to predictive strength showed equivalence for the five functions involved in political participation. That is, the less interested, the young, the less educated were just as likely to have been stimulated by the debates to participate in the political process as the more interested, the old, and the more educated. When nonequivalence of effects did occur with regard to these variables, the effects were often stronger for age and political interest than they were for education. This points out the importance of looking for gaps caused by receiver variables other than education.

Genova and Greenberg (1981) also found evidence that knowledge gaps are more strongly related to audience interest than to socioeconomic status or education. They focused on two kinds of interest—self-interest, or perceived usefulness of news information for one's self; and social interest, or the perceived usefulness of the information to the individual's social milieu or interpersonal networks. They conducted a panel study to examine knowledge of two news events, an ongoing National Football League strike and the Nixon impeachment proceedings.

The findings indicated a combined measure of the two types of interest was a stronger predictor of knowledge levels in respondents than education. Furthermore, of the two types of interest, social interest bore the strongest relationship to knowledge acquisition.

The authors conclude that "this is a more optimistic proposition than the original knowledge gap hypothesis; it offers an alternative route by which public knowledge could be expanded" (p. 504).

An Influence Gap?

In a study of political knowledge in Sweden, Brantgarde (1983) expanded the possible gap to include more than knowledge. Instead of looking just at knowledge, Brantgarde examined effects on information consumption and exposure, on information retention, and on information dissemination and political activity. He found that those low in education were higher in exposure to information than those high in education, that the two groups were about the same in information retention, and that those higher in education were higher in information dissemination and political activity than those low in education. This led him to conclude that the information gap is not a homogeneous phenomenon. Brantgarde also noted that his results are disturbing in that they suggest that the highly educated are more able to disseminate information, and thus might be able to influence decision makers by making opinions known to them. Brantgarde gives as an example of this kind of activity attempts to stop construction projects that might endanger the environment. He calls this possibility an "influence gap," and suggests that it might be more of a real problem than the information gap.

The Knowledge Gap and the New Technology

Communication technology is changing so rapidly that many people speak of a "communication revolution" or an "information explosion." Some of the new technologies in the process of being developed or presently existing are videotape recorders, videocassettes, cable television, home delivery of newspapers, access of computer information services by home computers, and communication between home computers by means of modems. Many of these technologies have the dramatic effect of giving the user much more control over the communication process and the information received.

Theoretically, these new technologies can be used to the benefit of people throughout society. As Parker and Dunn (1972) have noted:

> The greatest single potential of an information utility might be the opportunity to reduce the unit cost of education to the point where our society could afford to provide open and equal access to learning opportunities for all members throughout their lives. (p. 1392)

In actual practice, however, it is not yet clear what the effects of these new technologies will be on levels of information held by the public, particularly by different segments of the public. Many of these new technologies are expensive. Because of the cost, these technologies may be more available to the well-to-do than to the less well-off. For this and other reasons, an unfortunate effect of the technological revolution in communication could be a further widening of the knowledge gap (Lepper, 1985). As Parker and Dunn noted further:

> If access to these information services is not universally available throughout the society, then those already "information-rich" may reap the benefits while the "information-poor" get relatively poorer. A widening of this "information gap" may lead to increased social tension. (p. 1396)

Data on the ownership of home computers provides some preliminary evidence on who will have access to the new technology and who will not. Figure 13.8 shows ownership of home computers looked at by education levels for a sample of Texas residents. The figure shows the likelihood of owning a home computer increasing regularly with increases in education level. Figure 13.9 shows a similar relationship between family income and home computer ownership. The greater the income, the more likely it is that the family will own a home computer.

Ownership of videocassette recorders shows a similar relationship to income and education (Scherer, 1989). Only 9 percent of those with an income of less than $10,000 own a VCR, while 79 percent of those with an income greater than $40,000 own the device. Similarly, 37 percent of those who have not graduated from high school own VCRs, while 73 percent of college graduates possess the technology. Scherer (1989, p. 102) concludes that the VCR is "one in a growing arsenal of media resources that benefit the information-rich more than the information-poor."

The same survey that produced the data on computer ownership also looked at people's attitudes concerning the new communication technology (Reese, Shoemaker, & Danielson, 1984). One of the attitude statements was "Only a small percentage of people will be able to afford these new communication devices." Respondents were asked the extent to which they agreed or disagreed. A majority (57 percent) of the sample answered either "agree" or "strongly agree" for that statement. These results show considerable public awareness that the benefits of the technological revolution might not be available to everyone.

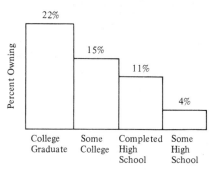

FIGURE 13.8 • HOUSEHOLDS OWNING HOME COMPUTERS, BY EDUCATION OF HEAD OF HOUSE-HOLD

From unpublished data gathered by Wayne A. Danielson, Stephen D. Reese, and Pamela J. Shoemaker.

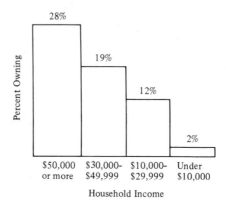

FIGURE 13.9 • HOUSEHOLDS OWNING HOME COMPUTERS, BY INCOME

From unpublished data gathered by Wayne A. Danielson, Stephen D. Reese, and Pamela J. Shoemaker.

Furthermore, the authors found a relationship between belief in the restricted availability of the new communication technology and socioeconomic status. The more well-off individuals tended to believe the new technologies will be available to everyone, while the less-educated and lower-paid were more likely to see the new technologies as widening existing gaps.

Theoretically, the new technology can be used to facilitate grassroots democracy by giving the power of these new devices to political groups and organizations outside the mainstream. In contrast to this hopeful prediction, however, Rubinyi (1989) found evidence that differences between the well-off and the not-so-well-off in their abilities to take advantage of new technology extended even to organized groups. He studied 72 small nonprofit organizations and found that resource-poor groups that adopt computer technology do not benefit in the same way from that technology as more affluent groups.

On the other side of the coin, however, Downing (1989) points out some ways that the new technology can be used to make grassroots democracy work better. As examples, he cites PeaceNet II, an international computer network devoted to peace, and EcoNet, an environmentalist computer network. A different example is Public Data Access, a group devoted to making government data accessible to those sectors of the public most in need of it. One of the products of Public Data Access was *Toxic Wastes and Race in the United States*, a report that showed a correlation between the location of toxic waste dump sites and the location of minority neighborhoods.

Criticism of the Hypothesis

Dervin (1980) has criticized the knowledge-gap hypothesis for being based on the traditional source-sending-messages-to-receiver paradigm of communication. She argued that this paradigm has been pervasive in U.S. communication research, but that it hides certain assumptions. Basically, this view emphasizes attaining source goals and trying to manipulate receivers to those ends. Dervin said this approach leads to a "blaming-the-victim" syndrome. She recommended that communication campaigns (and communication research) be more user based. She issued a call for user-constructed information and user-defined information. This approach emphasizes the user's need for sense making and attempts to determine the questions people are seeking answers to when they are in certain situations, such as seeing a doctor about a health problem.

Conclusions

The original knowledge-gap hypothesis suggested that as the infusion of mass media information into a social system increases, segments of the population with higher socioeconomic status tend to acquire this information at a faster rate than lower-status segments.

The knowledge-gap hypothesis has been refined and broadened in several ways since its original formulation. First of all, it has become clear that information sometimes causes knowledge gaps to widen and sometimes causes them to narrow. One of the crucial variables in this process identified by several studies is interest or motivation. If there is sufficient interest, and particularly if it is evenly distributed throughout a community, then information can help to close a knowledge gap. Second, the gaps that can occur because of communication are not limited to knowledge. They can also involve attitudes and behavior. For this reason, one researcher (Rogers) has suggested that the phenomenon be reconceptualized as a communication effects gap rather than a knowledge gap. Finally, the gaps do not have to be limited to those between people of high and low socioeconomic status (usually measured by education). Significant gaps also occur between people of high and low interest in politics and between the old and the young.

Of course, just because the media can work to narrow a knowledge gap in certain situations does not mean that we should not be concerned about other cases in which the media widen knowledge gaps. The several studies that have found knowledge gaps to narrow have generally shown that motivation to seek knowledge is the key variable leading to a narrowing. But it is not enough to have motivation to seek information—one must also have access to the information. Television may help to serve as a knowledge leveler because it is so universally available. Thus we found a narrowing of the achievement gap for the heaviest viewers of "Sesame Street." In these viewers, we find the combination that is needed—access to the information *plus* motivation to acquire the information.

If access is a key variable, then there is still plenty of reason to be concerned about knowledge gaps. Some media are much more accessible than others. A full selection of the cable television services available in many cities can cost hundreds of dollars a year. The computer equipment needed to access computer information utilities is not cheap, and neither are the access fees for the utilities themselves. Society as a whole may need to take steps to assure that access to information is available to all, or we may indeed expect to see ever-increasing knowledge gaps.

Furthermore, knowledge-gap research indicates that on complex issues like energy, the well-to-do get their information from one medium (newspapers) while the less well-to-do get their information from another medium (television advertisements). These findings suggest that planners of information campaigns need to conduct audience research, and that they will often benefit from choosing different media to reach different segments of the audience. Finally, as Dervin reminds us, information campaigns should probably begin with the needs of the potential user of the information.

References

Ball, S., and G. A. Bogatz (1970). *The First Year of "Sesame Street": An Evaluation.* Princeton, N.J.: Educational Testing Service.

Bishop, G. F., R. W. Oldendick, and A. J. Tuchfarber (1978). Debate watching and the acquisition of political knowledge. *Journal of Communication* 28, no. 4: 99–113.

Brantgarde, L. (1983). The information gap and municipal politics in Sweden. *Communication Research* 10: 367–373.

Childers, T., and J. Post (1975). *The Information-Poor in America.* Metuchen, N.J.: Scarecrow Press.

Cook, T. D., H. Appleton, R. F. Conner, A. Shaffer, G. Tamkin, and S. J. Weber (1975). *"Sesame Street" Revisited: A Case Study in Evaluation Research.* New York: Russell Sage Foundation.

Dervin, B. (1980). Communication gaps and inequities: Moving toward a reconceptualization. In B. Dervin and M. J. Voight (eds.), *Progress in Communication Sciences,* vol. 2, pp. 73–112. Norwood, N.J.: Ablex.

Donohue, G. A., P. J. Tichenor, and C. N. Olien (1975). Mass media and the knowledge gap: A hypothesis reconsidered. *Communication Research* 2: 3–23.

Downing, J. D. H. (1989). Computers for political change: PeaceNet and Public Data Access. *Journal of Communication* 39, no. 3: 154–162.

Ettema, J. S., J. W. Brown, and R. V. Luepker (1983). Knowledge gap effects in a health information campaign. *Public Opinion Quarterly* 47: 516–527.

Ettema, J. S., and F. G. Kline (1977). Deficits, differences and ceilings: Contingent conditions for understanding the knowledge gap. *Communication Research* 4: 179–202.

Genova, B. K. L., and B. S. Greenberg (1981). Interests in news and the knowledge gap. In G. C. Wilhoit and H. de Bock (eds.), *Mass Communication Review Yearbook,* vol. 2, pp. 494–506. Beverly Hills, Cal.: Sage.

Griffin, R. J. (1987). *Energy, education, and media use: A panel study of the knowledge gap.* Paper presented at the annual meeting of the Communication Theory and Methodology Division, Association for Education in Journalism and Mass Communication, San Antonio, Texas, August.

Katzman, N. (1974). The impact of communication technology: Promises and prospects. *Journal of Communication* 24, no. 4: 47–58.

Lazarsfeld, P. F. (1940). *Radio and the Printed Page.* New York: Duell, Sloan, and Pearce.

Lepper, M. R. (1985). Microcomputers in education: Motivational and social issues. *American Psychologist* 40, no. 1: 1–18.

Lesser, G. S. (1974). *Children and Television.* New York: Random House (Vintage Books).

Lovrich, N. P., and J. C. Pierce (1984). "Knowledge gap" phenomena: Effects of situation-specific and transsituational factors. *Communication Research* 11: 415–434.

McLeod, J. M., C. R. Bybee, and J. A. Durall (1981). Equivalence of informed political participation: The 1976 debates as a source of influence. In G. C. Wilhoit and H. de Bock (eds.), *Mass Communication Review Yearbook,* vol. 2, pp. 469–493. Beverly Hills, Cal.: Sage.

Parker, E. B., and D. A. Dunn (1972). Information technology: Its social potential. *Science* 176: 1392–1398.

Reese, S. D., P. J. Shoemaker, and W. A. Danielson (1984). *Social correlates of public attitudes toward the new communication technologies.* Paper presented to the Midwest Association for Public Opinion Research, Chicago.

Rogers, E. M. (1976). Communication and development: The passing of the dominant paradigm. *Communication Research* 3: 213–240.

Rubinyi, R. M. (1989). Computers and community: The organizational impact. *Communication Research* 39, no. 3: 110–123.

Scherer, C. W. (1989). The videocassette recorder and information inequity. *Journal of Communication* 39, no. 3: 94–109.

Sharp, E. B. (1984). Consequences of local government under the klieg lights. *Communication Research* 11: 497–517.

Tichenor, P., G. Donohue, and C. Olien (1970). Mass media flow and differential growth in knowledge. *Public Opinion Quarterly* 34: 159–170.

14 Effects of Mass Communication

What are the general effects of mass communication on people's attitudes, perceptions of the world, and behavior? Are they large or small? These have probably been the major questions communication theorists have grappled with over the past 40 years. Some people might be tempted to say that communication research has not made much progress in answering them. For instance, one author has written, "After four decades of exploration, we are left with one answer to the question of media effects—'it depends'" (Meadow, 1985, p. 158). In contrast with this pessimistic-sounding conclusion, however, we will attempt to show that progress has been made.

This chapter summarizes the current major areas of theory dealing with the effects of mass communication. (Two areas of research—agenda setting and the knowledge gap—are so important that they have been dealt with in chapters of their own [Chapters 12 and 13].) The present chapter also discusses a topic area where there has been extensive research on effects—the area of television violence.

The Bullet Theory

The "bullet theory" is the name given by later researchers to one of the first conceptions of the effects of mass communication. Also referred to as the "hypodermic-needle theory" or the "transmission belt theory" (DeFleur & Ball-Rokeach, 1982), this essentially naive and simplistic view predicts strong and more or less universal effects of mass communication messages on all audience members who happen to be exposed to them. The name "bullet theory" was apparently not used by any of the early thinkers about mass communication effects (Chaffee & Hochheimer, 1985). Nevertheless, the phrase is a good description of a view that apparently was widely held. This view was influenced by the power that propaganda appeared to have in World War I, as we have described in Chapter 6. It was a popular view in the years prior to World War II, when many people shared a fear that a Hitler-style demagogue could rise to power in the United States through the force of mass communication. The Institute for Propaganda Analysis was created in response to this fear, and it began a massive campaign of educating the American people on the techniques of propaganda.

Although the bullet theory has largely been discarded by mass communication researchers, it is apparently something that many people still believe. For instance, Pope John Paul II cautioned in 1980 against what he called the growing "manipulation" of the human mind by radio and television (*Austin American-Statesman*, July 6, 1980). The pope said the mass media bred "passivity and emotionalism, . . . manipulation and consequently evasion and hedonism."

A similar statement was made by Colin Blakemore (1977), a noted researcher on the human brain, in arguing that brain control through implanted electrodes is not likely:

> Are our brains not already more totally disciplined, our opinions more firmly moulded, and our minds more sharply directed by the political and social environment, than by any electrode that could be put in our heads? The stentorian voices of the mass media are more universally powerful than the indiscriminate persuasions of any mind-altering drug. (p. 169)

James Combs, a professor of political science and film studies, sounds an even more ominous warning of mass media potency: "Students of political communication should learn from Orwell that in the future, communication can be used to stamp out human minds—forever" (1985, p. 279).

Still another author, dolphin expert John Lilly, has written, "We have all been educated on the fantastic power of the media in changing public opinion" (Lilly & Lilly, 1976, p. 208).

The Limited-Effects Model

Research on the effects of mass communication, almost from the beginning, did not provide much support for the bullet theory. Rather the evidence supported what came to be called the limited-effects model. Some of the key research leading to this view of mass communication as having small effects included Hovland's Army studies showing that orientation films were effective in transmitting information but not in changing attitudes; Cooper and Jahoda's research on the Mr. Biggott cartoons, indicating that selective perception could reduce the effectiveness of a message; and the election studies of Lazarsfeld and his associates, which showed that few people were influenced by mass communication in election campaigns.

The limited-effects model has been well stated in Joseph Klapper's book *The Effects of Mass Communication* (1960). Klapper presented five generalizations about the effects of mass communication; the first two were the following:

1. Mass communication *ordinarily* does not serve as a necessary and sufficient cause of audience effects, but rather functions among and through a nexus of mediating factors and influences.

2. These mediating factors are such that they typically render mass communication a contributory agent, but not the sole cause, in a process of reinforcing the existing conditions. . . . (p. 8)

The mediating factors that Klapper was referring to include the selective processes (selective perception, selective exposure, and selective retention), group processes and group norms, and opinion leadership.

This position, that the effects of mass communication are limited, is also sometimes referred to as "the law of minimal consequences." This phrase does not appear in

Klapper's book, but was coined by his wife, Hope Lunin Klapper, a faculty member at New York University (Lang & Lang, 1968, p. 273).

Cultivation Theory

Researcher George Gerbner and his colleagues at the Annenberg School of Communication at the University of Pennsylvania developed the cultivation theory using what was probably the longest-running and most extensive program of research on the effects of television. Gerbner argues that television has become the central cultural arm of American society. "The television set has become a key member of the family, the one who tells most of the stories most of the time," Gerbner and his associates have written (Gerbner, Gross, Morgan, & Signorielli, 1980, p. 14). Gerbner points out that the average viewer watches television four hours a day. The heavy viewer watches even more. For heavy viewers, television virtually monopolizes and subsumes other sources of information, ideas, and consciousness, Gerbner says. The effect of all this exposure to the same messages produces what Gerbner calls *cultivation,* or the teaching of a common worldview, common roles, and common values. Gerbner presents research supporting cultivation theory that is based on comparisons of heavy and light television viewers. Gerbner analyzed answers to questions posed in surveys and found that heavy and light television viewers typically give different answers. Furthermore, the heavy television viewers often give answers that are closer to the way the world is portrayed on television.

For instance, surveys have asked what percentage of the world's population lives in the United States (Gerbner & Gross, 1976b). The correct answer is 6 percent. Heavy television viewers tend to overestimate this figure much more than light television viewers. Of course, the leading characters in television entertainment programs are almost always Americans.

Other surveys have asked what percentage of Americans who have jobs work in law enforcement. The correct answer is 1 percent. Heavy television viewers give much higher figures, and they are more likely to do this than light television viewers. On television, about 20 percent of the characters are involved in law enforcement.

Still another question asked of heavy and light television viewers is this: "During any given week, what are your chances of being involved in some type of violence?" The correct or real-world answer is 1 percent or less. The answer presented by television is about 10 percent. Heavy television viewers are more likely than light television viewers to give a larger percentage.

In response to a question like "Can people be trusted?" the heavy television viewers are more likely than the light viewers to check a response such as "Can't be too careful."

The responses to such questions suggest that heavy television viewers are getting a heightened sense of risk and insecurity from television. Television may be leading heavy viewers to perceive a "mean world." Gerbner suggests that this may be one of the primary, and widely shared, cultivation effects due to television.

Gerbner has shown that the differences between heavy and light television viewers show up even across a number of other important variables, including age, education, news reading, and gender (Gerbner & Gross, 1976a). That is, Gerbner realized that the relationship between television viewing and different views of the world could be actually caused by other variables, and he attempted to control for those variables.

Gerbner's procedures have not satisfied all other researchers, however. Gerbner's research has been criticized by Paul Hirsch for not doing an adequate job of controlling for other variables. Hirsch's (1980) further analysis indicated that if one controls for a number of different variables all at the same time, the effect that is left that can be attributed to television becomes very small.

In response to Hirsch's criticisms, Gerbner has revised cultivation theory (Gerbner et al., 1980). He has added two additional concepts—*mainstreaming* and *resonance.* These concepts take account of the fact that heavy television viewing has different outcomes for different social groups. Gerbner says mainstreaming occurs when heavy viewing leads to a convergence of outlooks across groups. For instance, heavy viewers in both low-income and high-income categories share the view that fear of crime is a very serious personal problem. Light viewers in the two categories, however, do not share the same view. The light viewers who are low in income tend to agree with the heavy viewers in both categories that fear of crime is a problem, while the light viewers who are high in income tend not to agree that fear of crime is a problem.

Resonance occurs when the cultivation effect is boosted for a certain group of the population. For instance, heavy viewers among both males and females are more likely than light viewers to agree that fear of crime is a serious problem. But the group that agrees the most strongly is females who are heavy viewers, because their particular vulnerability to crime is said to "resonate" with the portrait of a high-crime world presented on television.

The addition of mainstreaming and resonance to cultivation theory is a substantial modification of the theory. The theory no longer claims uniform, across-the-board effects of television on all heavy viewers. It now claims that television interacts with other variables in ways such that television viewing will have strong effects on some subgroups of persons and not on others. Gerbner is also admitting that Hirsch was right on one important point—when one controls for other variables simultaneously, the remaining effect attributable to television is rather small. Nevertheless, in light of the cumulative effects over time of the substantial exposure to television that most people (in the United States, at least) are receiving, the effects might not be negligible.

Rubin, Perse, and Taylor (1988) cast further doubt on cultivation as a general, across-the-board effect due to heavy, ritualistic television viewing. In their survey of viewers, they found effects of television viewing on perceptions of social reality, but the effects were program specific. That is, viewers of daytime serials tended to score lower in perception of altruism and trust in others, viewers of evening dramas (which often deal with control of others by powerful characters) tended to have lower feelings of political efficacy, and viewers of action and adventure shows showed more feelings of concern about their own safety. They also found that age, gender, socioeconomic status, viewing intention (planning to watch television), and perceived realism (of television content) were better predictors of faith in others than television exposure. These results provide some evidence that viewers actively and differentially evaluate television content, or, to put it another way, that the television audience is an active one.

McLuhan's Media Determinism

Marshall McLuhan startled the entire world in 1964 with his statement that "the medium is the message" (1965, p. 7). McLuhan's writings and speeches were filled with puns and aphorisms to the point of being cryptic, but his classic *Understanding Media* is really fairly clear about what he meant by "the medium is the message." He wrote: "The effects of technology do not occur at the level of opinions or concepts, but alter *sense ratios* or patterns of perception steadily and without resistance" (p. 18). McLuhan is saying that the most important effect of communication media is that they affect our habits of perception and thinking. The concept of "sense ratios" refers to the balance of our senses. Primitive people emphasized all five senses—smell, touch, hearing, sight, taste—but technology, and especially the communication media, have caused people to emphasize one sense over others. Print, McLuhan says, emphasized vision. In turn, it influenced our thinking, making it linear, sequential, regular, repeated, and logical. It allowed human beings to separate thought from feeling. It led to specialization, and technology, but it also led to a sense of alienation and individualism. On the societal level, print led to the possibility of nations and the rise of nationalism.

Television, in contrast to print, emphasized more of the senses. McLuhan described television as a visual, aural, and *tactile* medium. It is more involving and participatory than print. McLuhan proposed that television would restore the balance of the sense ratios that print destroyed. On a grander scale, McLuhan said, television is going to retribalize us. We will move away from individual nation states and become a "global village."

One of the things that bothered many communication theorists and people working in mass communication is that McLuhan was saying that the content of mass communication doesn't matter. McLuhan put it this way: "The 'content' of the medium is like the juicy piece of meat carried by the burglar to distract the watchdog of the mind" (1965, p. 18). That is, the important effects of the medium come from its form, not its content.

McLuhan said that the television generation is the first postliterate generation. He suggested that parents today are watching their children becoming "Third World," and that due to television and other new media, children do not think the same way their parents did. "If Homer was wiped out by literacy, literacy can be wiped out by rock," McLuhan said on a public television program dealing with his life and work.

Researchers have attempted to test some of McLuhan's ideas, but one of the problems is that his notions involve such far-reaching and pervasive effects that it is difficult to test them. Some of the studies were flawed in that they dealt with extremely short-term effects, when McLuhan was obviously talking about effects that would take a long time to show up.

Some of McLuhan's ideas are being taken more seriously now than they were when they were first proposed. For instance, the National Assessment of Educational Progress, attempting to explain why the writing skills of young Americans were deteriorating, cited the role of television watching by young people and stated that "the culture is increasingly less print-oriented" (NAEP, 1975, p. 44). One researcher has argued that relying on television for political information causes a decline in the ability to perform sophisticated intellectual operations on such information and thus is threatening to our democracy (Manheim, 1976).

McLuhan's notion of two different styles of thinking also seems to have anticipated the discussion of the different roles of the right and left hemispheres of the brain, much of which has occurred since the publication of *Understanding Media* in 1964. This work suggests that the two sides of the brain are specialized, the left side being logical, rational, and language oriented while the right side is intuitive, irrational, and picture oriented. McLuhan later related his own work directly to the work on the hemispheres of the brain (1978).

Joshua Meyrowitz (1985) has picked up the baton of McLuhanesque thinking and carried it a bit further. Meyrowitz shares with McLuhan a concern with the social consequences of new electronic media, particularly television. But Meyrowitz felt that the McLuhan notion of sense ratios and sensory balance did not provide a sufficient explanation of how television was affecting people. Meyrowitz attempted to combine the thinking of McLuhan with that of sociologist Erving Goffman. Goffman wrote about how the "definition of the situation" affects behavior, but he focused on face-to-face interaction and ignored the media. Meyrowitz's main argument is that by bringing many different types of people to the same "place," electronic media have brought about the blurring of many formerly distinct roles. Some of the results have been the merging of masculinity and femininity, the blurring of childhood and adulthood, and the lowering of the political leader to the level of everyone else.

The Effects of Synthetic Experience

Funkhouser and Shaw (1990) have argued that motion pictures, television, and computers shape audience perceptions of reality by manipulating and rearranging not only the content but the processes of communicated experience. Some of these techniques for creating synthetic experience include altered speeds of movement (either fast or slow), reenactments of the same action (instant replay), instantaneous cutting from one scene to another, excerpting fragments of events, juxtaposing events widely separated by time or space, and merging and altering visual images (through computer graphics techniques and multiple-exposure processing).

Heavy exposure to this kind of synthetic experience might have a number of effects on viewers. Funkhouser and Shaw list the following five as some of the possible effects:

1. Low tolerance for boredom or inactivity.
2. Heightened expectations of perfection and of high-level performance.
3. Expectations of quick, effective, neat resolutions of problems.
4. Misperceptions of certain classes of physical and social events. For instance, seeing slow-motion violence that doesn't hurt on television programs or in movies might cause people to be less sensitive.
5. Limited contact with, and a superficial view of, one's own inhabited environment.

The authors suggest that electronic media presenting this kind of synthetic experience may be coloring, distorting, and even degrading people's entire cultural worldviews, and that further research should look into these possible effects.

The Spiral of Silence

A theory that gives the mass media more power than many other theories is the "spiral of silence," developed by Elisabeth Noelle-Neumann (1973, 1980). Noelle-Neumann argues that the mass media do have powerful effects on public opinion but that these effects have been underestimated or undetected in the past because of the limitations of research. Noelle-Neumann argues that three characteristics of mass communication—its cumulation, ubiquity, and consonance—combine to produce powerful effects on public opinion. Consonance refers to the unified picture of an event or issue that can develop and is often shared by different newspapers, magazines, television networks, and other media. The effect of consonance is to overcome selective exposure, since people cannot select any other message, and to present the impression that most people look at the issue in the way that the mass media are presenting it.

Another factor that comes into play is the "spiral of silence" (see Figure 14.1). On a controversial issue, people form impressions about the distribution of public opinion. They try to determine whether they are in the majority, and then they try to determine whether public opinion is changing to agree with them. If they feel they are in the minority, they tend to remain silent on the issue. If they think public opinion is changing away from them, they tend to remain silent on the issue. The more they remain silent, the more other people feel that the particular point of view is not represented, and the more they remain silent.

The mass media play an important part because they are the source to which people look to find the distribution of public opinion. The mass media can affect the spiral of silence in three ways: (1) They shape impressions about which opinions are dominant, (2) They shape impressions about which opinions are on the increase, (3) They shape impressions about which opinions one can utter in public without becoming isolated (Noelle-Neumann, 1973, p. 108).

Noelle-Neumann argues that willingness to speak out on issues is influenced largely by perception of the climate of opinion—if the climate of opinion goes against a person, that person will remain silent. The motivating force for this silence is said to be fear of isolation. Lasorsa (1991) questioned whether the fear of a hostile climate of opinion is really that strong, and undertook a study to investigate the question. Lasorsa conducted a survey in which he tested whether political outspokenness is affected not only by one's perception of the climate of opinion, as suggested by Noelle-Neumann, but also by other variables such as age, education, income, interest in politics, level of self-efficacy, the personal rele-

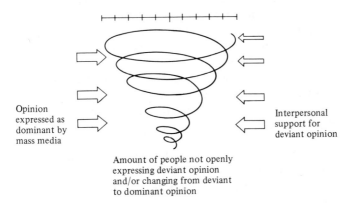

Opinion
expressed as
dominant by
mass media

Interpersonal
support for
deviant opinion

Amount of people not openly
expressing deviant opinion
and/or changing from deviant
to dominant opinion

FIGURE 14.1 • THE SPIRAL OF SILENCE. The mass media's expressing a dominant opinion, combined with an increasing lack of interpersonal support for deviant views, brings about a spiral of silence, with an increasing number of individuals either expressing the dominant opinion or failing to express deviant ones.

From D. McQuail and S. Windahl, *Communication Models for the Study of Mass Communication* (London: Longman, 1981), p. 68.

vance of the issue, one's news media use, and one's certitude in the correctness of one's position. The results of a regression analysis showed outspokenness being affected by the block of demographic variables (age, education, and income), level of self-efficacy, attention to political information in the news media, and certitude in one's position, but not by personal relevance of the issue or news media use in general. Lasorsa says his results show that people are not quite as helpless in the face of public opinion as Noelle-Neumann's theory suggests and that there are conditions under which it is possible to fight the spiral of silence.

The operation of the spiral of silence has also been questioned in the setting of the Philippines during the reign of Ferdinand Marcos (González, 1988). González points out that the mainstream media in the Philippines had all the conditions specified by Noelle-Neumann for powerful media effects to occur—cumulativeness, consonance, and ubiquity. But still the mainstream opinion did not prevail as Marcos went down in a revolution. González gives a major role in overcoming the spiral of silence to the alternative media—including weekly newspapers and a Catholic church radio station—in the Philippines, which presented more diverse reporting than the official media.

Media Hegemony

Another view that attributes wide (if not powerful) influence to the mass media is the concept of media hegemony. Media hegemony is rooted in the ideas of Marxist economics. The concept of hegemony states that the ideas of the ruling class in society become the ruling ideas. The mass media are seen as controlled by the dominant class in society and as aiding in exerting the control of that class over the rest of society (Sallach, 1974). Media hegemony argues that news and other media content in the United States is shaped to the requirements of capitalist, or corporate, ideology.

The idea of media hegemony is a difficult one to test with research. Although suggesting a powerful influence, it is somewhat vague in its actual implications. If it is true, it is describing such a pervasive phenomenon that it becomes difficult to study because it is nearly impossible to set up a control group that is not subject to the effect being researched.

Nevertheless, an attempt to evaluate the idea of media hegemony—at least with regard to news coverage—has been made by one researcher (Altheide, 1984). Altheide says that if you look at the writings on media hegemony, they seem to involve at least three assumptions that could be tested with evidence:

1. The socialization of journalists involves guidelines, work routines, and orientations replete with the dominant ideology.

2. Journalists tend to cover topics and present news reports that are conservative and supportive of the status quo.

3. Journalists tend to present pro-American and negative coverage of foreign countries, especially Third World nations.

Altheide argues that evidence can be found to cast doubt on each of these propositions. In connection with proposition 1, Altheide cites studies showing that foreign affairs reporters take very different approaches to covering détente, depending on their individual backgrounds. In addition, other studies of journalists' backgrounds and attitudes show considerable diversity rather than homogeneity.

In connection with proposition 2, Altheide cites numerous examples, including but not limited to Watergate, in which the reporting done by journalists did not support the status quo. A study of press coverage of the 1971 Indian-Pakistani War (Becker, 1977) provides another example. When the U.S. government shifted its policy to support for West Pakistan, the news coverage by the *New York Times* actually shifted the other way.

And in connection with proposition 3, Altheide cites surveys of journalists that indicate they tend to agree with the Third World position on many issues. Furthermore, research on television coverage of Nicaragua during the Sandinista revolt showed that television presented the rebel case repeatedly and in some detail—not exactly the kind of content that supports the status quo.

Two researchers who attempted to find studies testing the media hegemony idea found only three (Shoemaker & Mayfield, 1984). Two supported the media hegemony idea, while one did not.

Finally, if the mass media are in general giving support to the status quo and corporate values, someone should inform Senator Jesse Helms, and his Fairness in Media group, of this fact. Senator Helms has been involved in efforts to buy the CBS television network because he thinks CBS News is too liberal.

The existence of Fairness in Media may be one of the best arguments that the mass media are ideologically neutral, since they are criticized by the left for presenting a conservative point of view and by the right for presenting a liberal point of view.

Effects of Television Violence

One particular area of possible media effects has been subjected to an extensive amount of research: television violence. Content analysis shows that a massive diet of violent content is served up on television. One set of figures indicates that by the age of 12, the average child will have watched 101,000 violent episodes on television, including 13,400 deaths (Steinfeld, 1973).

A number of different hypotheses have been suggested concerning the possible effects of television violence on human behavior. One is the catharsis hypothesis, which suggests that viewing television violence causes a reduction of aggressive drive through a vicarious expression of aggression. Several stimulation hypotheses predict that watching television violence leads to an increase in actual aggressive behavior. One of these is the imitation hypothesis, which suggests that people learn aggressive behaviors from television and then go out and reproduce them. A slightly different hypothesis is the disinhibition hypothesis, which suggests that television lowers people's inhibitions about behaving aggressively toward other people. If this hypothesis is correct, television violence might be teaching a general norm that violence is an acceptable way to relate to other people.

In all the hundreds of studies investigating the effects of television violence, only a handful support the catharsis hypothesis. Many more studies support the two stimulation hypotheses—imitation and disinhibition. One of the clearest of these studies is the Walters and Llewellyn-Thomas (1963) experiment (see Figure 14.2), which indicated that subjects who saw a violent film segment (a knife fight scene) were more likely to increase the levels of shock they would give another person than subjects who saw a nonviolent film segment (adolescents involved in crafts). This finding supports the disinhibition hypothesis, since the type of aggression engaged in was not the same as that portrayed in the film. A study conducted for the special committee appointed by the surgeon general to look into the effects of television violence reported a similar result. This was the Liebert and Baron (1972) study, which dealt with young children and a violent sequence from the television program *The Untouchables*.

It is possible to criticize these experiments for dealing only with short-term effects of televised violence and for being somewhat artificial in that they take place in laboratory settings. It could be, for instance, that people are more willing to behave aggressively in the laboratory because they do not have to worry about reprisals, which they would almost always have to do in real life.

Some research dealing with long-term effects of televised violence was also reported by the surgeon general's committee. This was a panel study conducted over a 10-year period. Lefkowitz, Eron, Walder, and Huesmann (1972) had started a study of aggression in young people in 1959 and 1960. When the surgeon general's study came along in 1969, Lefkowitz and his colleagues were able to take advantage of their earlier research to do a follow-up study. Their cross-lagged correlation data for boys showed in real life the same relationship that most of the experiments had shown in the laboratory: that watching television violence leads to an increase in aggressive behavior (see Figure 14.3). In fact, the study's best predictor of aggressive behavior at age 19 was violent television watching while in the third grade. The home environment is often thought to have an effect on whether a person becomes violent. The study by Lefkowitz and his associates looked at several aspects of the home environment that might have been related to later aggression:

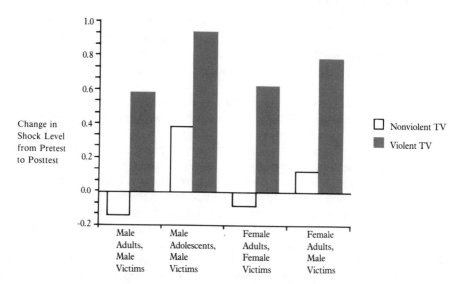

FIGURE 14.2 • CHANGES IN SHOCK LEVEL ADMINISTERED AFTER WATCHING VIOLENT OR NONVIOLENT TELEVISION

Adapted from R. H. Walters and E. Llewellyn-Thomas, "Enhancement of Punitiveness by Visual and Audiovisual Displays," *Canadian Journal of Psychology* 17 (1963): 244–255.

the amount of disharmony between the parents, the tendency of the parents to punish the children, and the regularity of church attendance of the parents. None of these measures taken while boys were in the third grade predicted aggressive behavior at age 19 as well as did viewing television violence in the third grade.

These two types of studies—the experiments in the laboratories and the correlation studies from surveys outside the laboratories—agreed in their general finding, that viewing television violence leads to an increase in aggressive behavior. And that was the conclusion of the report of the surgeon general's advisory committee in 1972, although the committee stated it in a rather qualified manner:

> The two sets of findings converge in three respects: a preliminary and tentative indication of a causal relation between viewing violence on television and aggressive behavior; an indication that any such causal relation operates only on some children (who are predisposed to be aggressive); and an indication that it operates only in some environmental contexts. (Surgeon General's Scientific Advisory Committee on Television and Social Behavior, 1972, p. 11)

Some critics have said this is a watered-down conclusion, heavily influenced by the network members of the committee, and that the research done for the committee really justifies a stronger conclusion. Some researchers have objected particularly to the statement that the causal relationship applies only to those children already predisposed to be aggressive. In the overview to one of the five volumes summarizing the research done for the committee, researcher Robert Liebert concludes that television violence may be contributing to the aggressive behavior "of many normal children" (Liebert, 1972, p. 30).

In 1982, the National Institute of Mental Health issued a report updating the 1972 surgeon general's study. The report offered this conclusion:

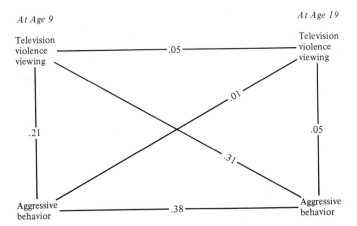

FIGURE 14.3 • CROSS-LAGGED CORRELATIONS OVER A 10-YEAR PERIOD FOR TELEVISION VIEWING AND AGGRESSION SCORES OF 211 MALES

From M. M. Lefkowitz, L. D. Eron, L. O. Walder, and L. R. Huesmann, "Television Violence and Child Aggression: A Followup Study," in G. A. Comstock and E. A. Rubinstein (eds.), *Television and Social Behavior*, vol. 3 (Washington, D.C.: U.S. Government Printing Office, 1972), p. 49.

What is the effect of all this violence? After 10 or more years of research, the consensus among most of the research community is that violence on television does lead to aggressive behavior by children and teenagers who watch the programs. This conclusion is based on laboratory experiments and field studies. Not all children become aggressive, of course, but the correlations between violence and aggression are positive. In magnitude, television violence is as strongly correlated with aggressive behavior as any other behavioral variable that has been measured. The research question has moved from asking whether or not there is an effect to seeking explanations for the effect. (1983, p. 28)

Most researchers seem convinced that watching television violence causes some aggressive behavior, although some might still argue that the effect is small. What seems to be needed now is a different kind of research that would identify the "leverage points" for bringing about positive changes in television (Cook, Kendzierski, & Thomas, 1985). This research would involve an institutional analysis of the broadcasting industry, including the networks, program production companies, local stations, and advertising agencies. It would also examine the institutions that have important relations with the industry, including the FCC, Congress, activist groups, the public, and legal firms representing various players in the scenario. The research would be multidisciplinary, and it would not be easy.

The Powerful-Effects Model

The powerful-effects model was first presented by Elisabeth Noelle-Neumann in her article "Return to the Concept of Powerful Mass Media" (1973). Her spiral of silence theory would fit under the powerful-effects model. Three other studies that also indicate a powerful effect due to the mass media have been conducted by Mendelsohn (1973), Maccoby and Farquhar (1975), and Ball-Rokeach, Rokeach, and Grube (1984a, 1984b).

Mendelsohn describes his own participation in three projects. The first, the CBS "National Drivers Test," resulted in 35,000 viewers enrolling in driver training courses. A second project involved a six-minute film called "A Snort History" that dealt with drinking and driving. The film was entertaining enough to be shown in a first-run motion picture theater along with the Clint Eastwood film *Dirty Harry*. The result of showing the film was that 3 out of 10 viewers said they would consider changing some of their previously held ideas regarding safe driving. A third project, an informational soap opera series aimed at Mexican-Americans in Los Angeles, led to 6 percent of the viewers (13,400 persons) reporting they had joined a community organization, one of the prime objectives of the series.

Mendelsohn says the three campaigns were successful because they were based on certain steps: (1) Spell out clearly the objectives of the campaign. (2) Pinpoint the target audience. (3) Work to overcome indifference of the audience toward the particular issue. (4) Find relevant themes to stress in messages.

Maccoby and Farquhar undertook an ambitious program attempting to use mass communication to reduce heart disease. The study was conducted in three towns, with one (Gilroy) receiving an eight-month mass media campaign, one (Watsonville) receiving the same mass media campaign plus intensive group instruction for a sample of high-risk adults, and the third (Tracy) serving as a control and receiving neither type of communication. Pretests in all three towns before the campaign included measures of information, attitudes, and reported behaviors as well as a physical examination. Both the mass media campaign and the intensive instruction were aimed at producing behavior changes that would reduce the risk of coronary disease. These behaviors included reducing or stopping smoking, improving diets (particularly by eliminating foods high in cholesterol), and increasing amounts of exercise. Results showed that both types of communication campaigns were effective in reducing the amounts of egg consumed and the number of cigarettes smoked and in lowering the cholesterol level as well as an overall measure of heart disease risk, the Cornfield risk score. The greatest effects were in Watsonville, the town with the mass media campaign and the intensive instruction for a selected group, but there were also significant effects in Gilroy, the town with mass media only.

Another example of what might be considered a powerful effect achieved through mass communication comes from *The Great American Values Test* of Ball-Rokeach, Rokeach, and Grube (1984a, 1984b). These researchers developed a model for changing people's values—not an easy task, since our values are usually deeply held and a basic part of our personality. Their model states that people change their values and attitudes—and even their behavior—when they are forced to face inconsistencies in their basic values. This is a theory with some relationship to the consistency theories (see Chapter 8). The researchers argue that people who are forced to recognize inconsistencies in their belief systems experience a sense of dissatisfaction with themselves and that this can lead to reassessment and change.

These researchers designed an extensive experiment to test their theory for changing values. They produced a half-hour television program called "The Great American Values Test." They obtained the cooperation of Ed Asner, former star of "The Mary Tyler Moore Show" and "The Lou Grant Show," and Sandy Hill, the former anchor of "Good Morning America," who agreed to be the hosts for the program. The program begins by discussing results of some public opinion polls that assessed the values of the American people. Then Asner and Hill begin to challenge the audience by pointing out some inconsistencies in the rankings of values. For instance, they point out that the public ranks "freedom" 3rd as a value, but "equality" is ranked 12th. Asner asks what this means, and suggests the possibility that people are interested in freedom for themselves but not for other people. The hosts go on to a similar discussion of the value "a world of beauty," ranked 17th by the public. They contrast that with "a comfortable life," which is ranked much higher. They suggest that the low ranking for "a world of beauty" might explain why so many people are willing to live with pollution and ugliness.

The television program was shown on all three network stations in the Tri-Cities area of eastern Washington at the same time one evening. The program was heavily promoted beforehand, both on the television stations and in publications like *TV Guide*. The program was blacked out in Yakima, a city 80 miles away, so that it could serve as a control.

The researchers studied the impact of the programming by comparing samples from the Tri-Cities area and Yakima. A random sample of residents of each city was selected from the phone book. The 1,699 respondents in the Tri-Cities area were called immediately after the broadcast of the program to see whether they had watched it and whether or not they were interrupted while watching it. Respondents in both cities received a questionnaire in which they were asked to rank 18 basic values, as well as to indicate their attitudes on racism, sexism, and environmental conservatism. They also answered some questions measuring their dependency on television. Then, to measure the effects of the program on behavior, respondents received three solicitations to send money to actual organizations. These came 8, 10, and 13 weeks after the program was broadcast. The solicitations came from a group aimed at providing opportunities for black children, the women's athletic program at Washington State University, and an environmental group attempting to promote antipollution measures.

Because the researchers were able to eliminate competing programs by scheduling the program on all three network stations, the program received an impressive Nielsen rating of 65 percent, meaning that 65 percent of the viewers watching television at that time were watching the values program. Results showed that the program had an effect on donating money to organizations—the Tri-Cities respondents gave significantly more money than the Yakima respondents. Furthermore, viewers who watched without interruption gave more money than viewers who were interrupted.

Viewers of the program also changed their value rankings. They significantly increased their ranking of two of the target values, freedom and equality. They also increased, but less dramatically, their ranking of a third value, a world of beauty. The attitudes related to these values were also affected. Viewers became more antiracist and proenvironment in their attitudes.

The authors also found that the viewers' dependency on television was an important factor in producing effects. Those persons who scored higher in dependency on television were more likely to watch the program, and when they did watch, they were more likely to change their values, change their attitudes, and contribute money to causes related to values discussed on the program.

The *Great American Values Test* experiment had a striking result: a single half-hour television program was able to change viewers' attitudes, their rankings of basic values, and their willingness to engage in behavior of a political nature. And all of this was done in a real-world setting, eliminating any question of whether these results apply outside of the laboratory.

Size of Effects

The numerous theories or research approaches that have been presented during the half-century or so of mass communication research have provided a number of different answers to the question of the size of mass communication effects. These theories can be presented in a time-line diagram that shows the time for each theory and the size of effect that it attributed to the media (see Figure 14.4). The bullet theory, one of the earliest and most simplistic notions about mass communication, attributed quite strong effects to mass communication. After some time had passed, however, this conception was replaced by the limited-effects model. Eventually, though, research began to suggest that the limited-effects model might have swung the pendulum too far in the other direction. Research on a number of topics, including the knowledge gap, agenda setting, and the effects of television violence, indicated that mass communication was having more than limited effects. This position might be called the moderate-effects model. And finally, as we have discussed, a number of recent studies, including those by Noelle-Neumann, Mendelsohn, Maccoby and Farquhar, and Ball-Rokeach, Rokeach, and Grube, have shown mass communication to have powerful effects. It appears, however, that the powerful-effects model will be much more subject to qualifications than the bullet theory. "Powerful effects" do not occur universally or easily, but only when the right communication techniques are used under the right circumstances.

Focusing on the empirical results of studies rather on theories, McGuire (1986) has categorized the notion of sizable effects as a general result of mass communication as a "myth."

McGuire examined research regarding the following dozen types of media effects. The first six are *intended effects:* the effects of commercial advertising on television, the effects of mass media political campaigning on voting, the role of public service announcements

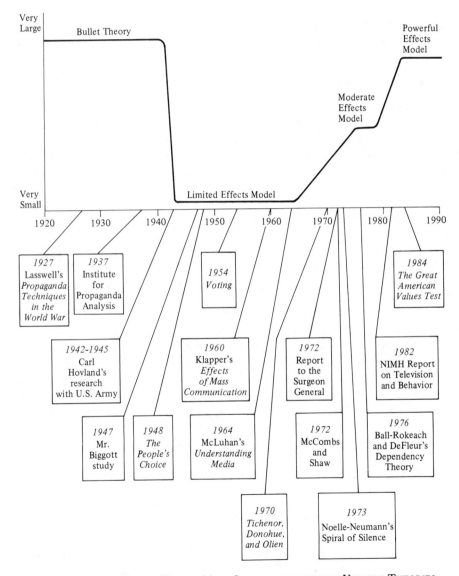

FIGURE 14.4 • SIZE OF EFFECT DUE TO MASS COMMUNICATION, FOR VARIOUS THEORIES

in promoting betterment, the efficacy of prolonged multimedia campaigns in changing life-styles, and the massive monolithic indoctrination effects on ideology. The second six are *unintended effects:* the effects of viewing violent television on aggressive behavior, the effects of underrepresentation of various groups or causes, the effects of misrepresentation on viewer stereotypes, the effects of erotica on sexual thoughts and behaviors, the effect of media differences on cognitive processing, and the impact of new media on thought processes.

In all of these areas, McGuire concluded that the impacts are surprisingly weak, with statistically significant effects found only occasionally and even in those cases, with sizes of effects that were slight.

McGuire's position is not that the data show that the mass media *do not* have a sizable impact, but that the data do not show that the media *do* have a large impact.

Toward a Synthesis

The various theoretical positions presented in this chapter attach a variety of magnitudes to the effects of mass communication, ranging from the relatively weak media of the limited-effects model to the powerful media described by Noelle-Neumann and others. One obvious question is whether there is any way to reconcile these different conceptions of media potency. One approach to reconciling these different theories is presented by Elihu Katz, a researcher who has participated in much of the history of mass communication research. Katz (1980) suggests that the two overridingly important factors in mass communication are selectivity and interpersonal relations. By selectivity, he means the processes that operate to make perception selective—selective exposure, selective perception, and selective retention. By interpersonal relations, he means group membership and the other processes by which groups influence people. The power of the media tends to be limited whenever these two factors intervene in the flow of influence—as the limited-effects model more or less correctly states. The power of the media tends to be greater when the media are able to operate directly, without the intervention of the two factors. For instance, in the spiral of silence, which predicts powerful effects of mass communication, selectivity is prevented by the consonance of the media message, and interpersonal communication is reduced as people stop making their own opinion statements.

Another approach to reconciling the limited-effects and powerful-effects models might come from a theory developed by Ball-Rokeach and DeFleur (1976) called "dependency theory." This theory suggests that people have various dependencies on the media, and that these dependencies vary from person to person, from group to group, and from culture to culture. They argue that, particularly in a modern urban-industrial society, audiences have a high level of dependence on mass media information. In a modern developed society, more and more of the operations of daily life and commerce require reliable, up-to-date information.

This theory stresses the tripartite relationship of media, audience, and society. The relationships between these three and media effects are presented in Figure 14.5.

Within each of the three units—society, media, and audience—factors operate to increase or decrease the amount of media dependency. Within the society, an important element is the amount of disorder, conflict, and change. When there is a great deal of change in society, there is also a great deal of uncertainty in the public. At these times, people's

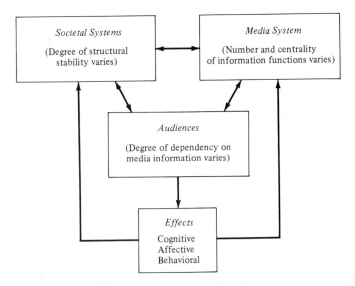

FIGURE 14.5 • THE TRIPARTITE RELATIONSHIP AMONG MEDIA, AUDIENCE, AND SOCIETY

From S. J. Ball-Rokeach and M. L. DeFleur, "A Dependency Model of Mass-Media Effects," *Communication Research* 3 (1976): 8. Copyright 1976 by Sage Publications, Inc. Reprinted by permission of Sage Publications, Inc.

dependency on media information is high. Media systems themselves differ in the number and centrality of information functions they serve. In a modern urban-industrial society, for instance, the media serve a number of functions, including providing information about government and politics to the public so that democratic elections can take place, serving as a watchdog or fourth branch of government, sounding a widespread and general alarm in cases of emergencies, providing information needed to keep the economic system operating, and supplying great quantities of entertainment content to help people relax and fill leisure time. The more of these functions the media serve in a society, the greater the dependency on the media in that society. Similarly, the more important or central some of these functions are to the smooth working of the society, the greater the dependency on the media in that society. Ball-Rokeach and DeFleur suggest that as societies grow more complex, and as media technology grows more complex, the media take on more and more unique functions.

Finally, within the audience, the degree of dependency on media information varies. Some people have a great interest in sports, while others have more interest in the stock market. Some people are highly integrated into the community, and need the media to keep up with what is going on. Others are on the fringes of the community and make little use of the media. Some people are concerned about being good citizens, voting intelligently in elections, and so forth, while others either never become interested in public issues or become alienated from the political system. The factors that affect individuals' dependencies on the media have been described further by Ball-Rokeach (1985).

Dependency theory differs from the uses and gratifications approach by stressing the tripartite relationship of society, media, and audience as the determinant of media dependencies. The uses and gratifications approach focuses more narrowly on the psychological needs of the individual.

The concept of dependency suggested in dependency theory is also similar to the *need for orientation* proposed as an important variable in agenda setting by McCombs and Weaver, although dependency is a broader and more encompassing concept.

Ball-Rokeach and DeFleur argue that the greater the media dependency in connection with a particular message, the greater the likelihood that the message will alter audience cognitions, feelings, and behaviors.

One of people's major needs is to reduce ambiguity. Ball-Rokeach and DeFleur point out that in a complex modern society, there are many matters that the audience can be uncertain about, and new ones are coming up all the time. This ambiguity is stressful, and consequently people may turn to the mass media to reduce it. This may give the mass media a great deal of power in defining and structuring reality.

This tendency for people to turn to the mass media in a time of uncertainty was illustrated at the time of the U.S. attack on Libya in April 1986. Cable News Network's prime-time television coverage received the highest ratings it had received to that time the night after the attack. CNN had an audience of 2.1 million households, compared with an average the month before of 402,000 per night (Donlon & Roush, 1986).

Applying dependency theory may help us to reconcile some of the studies showing large effects of the mass media and studies showing small effects of the mass media. For instance, the powerful effect achieved in *The Great American Values Test* may have come about because audience members felt considerable ambiguity or uncertainty about conflicts between their basic values, such as freedom and equality. Of course, in this case the ambiguity was actually introduced by the television program, and that is an additional way that mass media messages can have increased effectiveness.

In contrast to *The Great American Values Test,* perhaps some of the political campaigns that were studied and that led to the limited effects model did not succeed in creating uncertainty or ambiguity in audience members. Perhaps people did not see much difference between the candidates, so they did not feel much uncertainty. Perhaps they also saw their own vote as not counting for much, and so did not attach much importance to the election.

The dependency theory model might also help us to understand the operation of cultivation, as described by Gerbner. When people are feeling a great deal of ambiguity about some aspect of the world, such as the danger from crime, their dependency on the media may be high, and they may accept a definition of the situation that is presented through television. That is, they may accept a view of the world as a "mean" place. Other people may not feel this uncertainty, however, and may not accept the picture of the world presented by television.

Similarly, the dependency theory model can help us understand agenda setting. Perhaps agenda-setting effects show up most strongly on those issues where there is widespread shared concern, such as inflation or the cost of living. But agenda-setting effects might not show up as uniformly on other issues for which some people feel a great deal of uncertainty but others do not, such as defense spending.

Dependency theory can also be applied to the research on the knowledge gap. Knowledge-gap effects probably occur most strongly when there is a clear difference in media dependency between the well-off and the not-so-well-off in our society. For instance, when it comes to watching "Sesame Street," children from higher-income families come from homes where education is valued, and they are encouraged to watch. Children from lower-income families come from homes where educational values may not be held as strongly, and they may not be encouraged to watch. In this case, a kind of media dependency is essentially passed on in the home from one generation to the next. In contrast to this example, however, there may be certain issues that arouse public interest and concern regardless of educational level or income. This was apparently the case in the study of knowledge of water policy issues conducted by Lovrich and Pierce. In this case, media dependency becomes high across different socioeconomic levels and the knowledge gap disappears.

Several researchers have drawn upon dependency theory to conduct additional research on mass communication. Becker and Whitney (1980) showed that individuals can become dependent on a particular medium for their information, and that people dependent on different media tend to have different pictures of the world. Miller and Reese (1982) found that the more an individual is dependent upon a particular medium, the more likely it is that a message in that medium will have its intended effects. Nigg (1982) used a dependency theory framework to describe the seeking of earthquake-forecasting information from the mass media.

Conclusions

Communication researchers have not yet come up with a unified theory that will explain the effects of mass communication. Instead we have a number of theories, each attempting to explain some particular aspect of mass communication. As communication research advances, perhaps we shall see several of these minitheories combined into one overall theory of mass communication effects. Or, perhaps some of these theories will not survive the test of empirical research and will be winnowed out, while others survive.

The most recent theorizing about mass media effects seems to be suggesting that most mass media effects do not occur "across the board," but are contingent on other variables (Chaffee, 1977). Perry (1988) argues that the truth of a hypothesis differs in different circumstances, and puts in a plea for placing research findings in their context.

Deutsch (1986), discussing the social sciences in general, has commented:

> Probably the structure of society and most social outcomes are the result of a plurality or multiplicity of relatively weak forces and processes. The search for single causes and single models, which has been pursued for a long time, turns out to be less fruitful than once was thought. Outcomes of a particular kind seem to occur most often when "all systems are 'go'"—that is, when all the weak factors, or at least a critical number of them, point in the same direction. Step by step, more of these weak factors are being identified. (pp. 11–12)

Thus, the statement that "it depends" is an accurate description of the answer to many questions about media effects. The answer "it depends" should not be met with despair and a throwing up of the hands, however. The answer "it depends" does not mean that we do not know what is going on. In contrast to what we knew 40 or 50 years ago, we now have some more definite ideas of what "it" depends on. As Katz has noted, the factors of selective perception and interpersonal relations are two important variables that the effects of mass communication depend on. Ball-Rokeach and DeFleur's dependency theory is also helpful. This theory not only gives support in general to the idea that media effects depend on certain other things, but it also gives a complex but useful description of what those things are.

References

Altheide, D. L. (1984). Media hegemony: A failure of perspective. *Public Opinion Quarterly* 48: 476–490.

Ball-Rokeach, S. J. (1985). The origins of individual media-system dependency: A sociological framework. *Communication Research* 12: 485–510.

Ball-Rokeach, S. J., and M. L. DeFleur (1976). A dependency model of mass-media effects. *Communication Research* 3: 3–21.

Ball-Rokeach, S. J., M. Rokeach, and J. W. Grube (1984a). The Great American Values Test. *Psychology Today*, November, pp. 34–41.

Ball-Rokeach, S. J., M. Rokeach, and J. W. Grube (1984b). *The Great American Values Test: Influencing Behavior and Belief through Television.* New York: Free Press.

Becker, L. B. (1977). Foreign policy and press performance. *Journalism Quarterly* 54: 364–368.

Becker, L., and D. C. Whitney (1980). Effects of media dependencies: Audience assessment of government. *Communication Research* 7: 95–120.

Blakemore, C. (1977). *Mechanics of the Mind.* Cambridge: Cambridge University Press.

Chaffee, S. H. (1977). Mass media effects: New research perspectives. In D. Lerner and L. M. Nelson (eds.), *Communication Research—a Half-Century Appraisal,* pp. 210–241. Honolulu: University Press of Hawaii.

Chaffee, S. H., and J. L. Hochheimer (1985). The beginnings of political communication research in the United States: Origins of the 'limited effects model.' In M. Gurevitch and M. R. Levy (eds.), *Mass Communication Review Yearbook,* vol. 5, pp. 75–104. Beverly Hills, Cal.: Sage.

Combs, J. (1985). George Orwell and the demonics of political communication. In K. R. Sanders, L. L. Kaid, and D. Nimmo (eds.), *Political Communication Yearbook 1984,* pp. 262–279. Carbondale: Southern Illinois University Press.

Cook, T. D., D. A. Kendzierski, and S. V. Thomas (1985). The implicit assumptions of television research: An analysis of the 1982 NIMH report on television and behavior. In M. Gurevitch and M. R. Levy (eds.), *Mass Communication Review Yearbook,* vol. 5, pp. 143–183. Beverly Hills, Cal.: Sage.

DeFleur, M. L. and S. Ball-Rokeach (1982). *Theories of Mass Communication.* 4th ed. New York: McKay.

Deutsch, K. W. (1986). What do we mean by advances in the social sciences? In K. W. Deutsch, A. S. Markovits, and J. Platt (eds.), *Advances in the Social Sciences, 1900–1980: What, Who, Where, How?* pp. 1–12. Cambridge, Mass.: Abt Books.

Donlon, B., and M. Roush (1986). News of Libya draws viewers to their TVs. *USA Today,* April 17, p. 1D.

Funkhouser, G. R., and E. F. Shaw (1990). How synthetic experience shapes social reality. *Journal of Communication* 40, no. 2: 75–87.

Gerbner, G., and L. P. Gross (1976a). Living with television: The violence profile. *Journal of Communication* 26, no. 2: 172–199.

——— (1976b). The scary world of TV's heavy viewer. *Psychology Today,* Apr., pp. 41–45, 89.

Gerbner, G., L. Gross, M. Morgan, and N. Signorielli (1980). The "mainstreaming" of America: Violence profile no. 11. *Journal of Communication* 30, no. 3: 10–29.

González, Hernando (1988). Mass media and the spiral of silence: The Philippines from Marcos to Aquino. *Journal of Communication* 38, no. 4: 33–48.

Hirsch, P. (1980). The "scary world" of the nonviewer and other anomalies: A reanalysis of Gerbner et al.'s findings on cultivation analysis. *Communication Research* 7: 403–456.

Katz, E. (1980). On conceptualizing media effects. In T. McCormack (ed.), *Studies in Communications*, vol. 1, pp. 119–141. Greenwich, Conn.: JAI Press.

Klapper, J. T. (1960). *The Effects of Mass Communication*. New York: Free Press.

Lang, K., and G. E. Lang (1968). *Politics and Television*. Chicago: Quadrangle.

Lasorsa, D. L. (1991). Political outspokenness: Factors working against the spiral of silence. *Journalism Quarterly*, in press.

Lefkowitz, M. M., L. D. Eron, L. O. Walder, and L. R. Huesmann (1972). Television violence and child aggression: A followup study. In G. A. Comstock and E. A. Rubinstein (eds.), *Television and Social Behavior*, vol. 3, pp. 35–135. Washington, D.C.: U.S. Government Printing Office.

Liebert, R. M. (1972). Television and social learning: Some relationships between viewing violence and behaving aggressively (overview). In J. P. Murray, E. A. Rubinstein, and G. A. Comstock (eds.), *Television and Social Behavior*, vol. 2, pp. 1–42. Washington, D.C.: U.S. Government Printing Office.

Liebert, R. M., and R. A. Baron (1972). Short-term effects of televised aggression on children's aggressive behavior. In J. P. Murray, E. A. Rubinstein, and G. A. Comstock (eds.), *Television and Social Behavior*, vol. 2, pp. 181–201. Washington, D.C.: U.S. Government Printing Office.

Lilly, J., and A. Lilly (1976). *The Dyadic Cyclone: The Autobiography of a Couple*. New York: Simon & Schuster.

Maccoby, N., and J. W. Farquhar (1975). Communication for health: Unselling heart disease. *Journal of Communication* 25, no. 3: 114–126.

Manheim, J. B. (1976). Can democracy survive television? *Journal of Communication* 26, no. 2: 84–90.

McGuire, W. J. (1986). The myth of massive media impact: Savagings and salvagings. In G. Comstock (ed.), *Public Communication and Behavior*, vol. 1, pp. 173–257. Orlando: Academic Press.

McLuhan, M. (1964). *Understanding Media: The Extensions of Man*. New York: McGraw-Hill.

——— (1978). The brain and the media: The "western" hemisphere. *Journal of Communication* 28, no. 4: 54–60.

Meadow, R. G. (1985). Political communication research in the 1980s. *Journal of Communication* 35, no. 1: 157–173.

Mendelsohn, H. (1973). Some reasons why information campaigns can succeed. *Public Opinion Quarterly* 37: 50–61.

Meyrowitz, J. (1985). *No Sense of Place*. New York: Oxford.

Miller, M. M., and S. D. Reese (1982). Media dependency as interaction: Effects of exposure and reliance on political activity and efficacy. *Communication Research* 9: 227–248.

National Assessment of Educational Progress (1975). *Writing Mechanics, 1969–75: A Capsule Description of Changes in Writing Mechanics*. Washington, D.C.: U.S. Government Printing Office.

National Institute of Mental Health (1983). Television and behavior: Ten years of scientific progress and implications for the eighties. In E. Wartella and D. C. Whitney (eds.), *Mass Communication Review Yearbook*, vol. 4, pp. 23–35. Beverly Hills, Cal.: Sage.

Nigg, J. M. (1982). Communication under conditions of uncertainty: Understanding earthquake forecasting. *Journal of Communication* 32, no. 1: 27–36.

Noelle-Neumann, E. (1973). Return to the concept of powerful mass media. In H. Eguchi and K. Sata (eds.), *Studies of Broadcasting: An International Annual of Broadcasting Science*, pp. 67–112. Tokyo: Nippon Hoso Kyokai.

——— (1980). Mass media and social change in developed societies. In G. C. Wilhoit and H. de Bock (eds.), *Mass Communication Review Yearbook*, vol. 1, pp. 657–678. Beverly Hills, Cal.: Sage.

Perry, D. K. (1988). Implications of a contextualist approach to media-effects research. *Communication Research* 15: 246–264.

Rubin, A. M., E. M. Perse, and D. S. Taylor (1988). A methodological examination of cultivation. *Communication Research* 15: 107–134.

Sallach, D. L. (1974). Class domination and ideological hegemony. *Sociological Quarterly* 15, no. 1: 38–50.

Shoemaker, P. J., and E. K. Mayfield (1984). *Mass media content as a dependent variable: Five media sociology theories*. Paper presented at the annual meeting of the Communication Theory and Methodology Division of the Association for Education in Journalism and Mass Communication, Gainesville, Fla., August.

Steinfeld, J. L. (1973). TV violence is harmful. *Reader's Digest,* Apr., pp. 7–38, 40, 43, 45.

Surgeon General's Scientific Advisory Committee on Television and Social Behavior (1972). *Television and Growing Up: The Impact of Televised Violence.* Washington, D.C.: U.S. Government Printing Office.

Walters, R. H., and E. Llewellyn-Thomas (1963). Enhancement of punitiveness by visual and audio-visual displays. *Canadian Journal of Psychology* 17: 244–255.

15
Uses of the Mass Media

Previous chapters have dealt, for the most part, with what the media do to their audiences. Indeed, many of us, both in the media and out of the media, tend to think of the media "acting" upon their viewers, listeners, and readers. Subconsciously we often continue to accept the model of the media as a hypodermic needle or a bullet directed to a passive target. But audiences are not always passive; indeed, one classic study, titled "The Obstinate Audience," pointed out that the audience is often quite active (Bauer, 1964). Other researchers echo the statement: "The notion of 'the active communicator' is rapidly achieving preeminent status in the communication discipline" (Bryant & Street, 1988, p. 162). In this chapter we shall examine some research on what the audience does with the media, as we take up an area of research often referred to as "the uses and gratifications approach."

In at least one respect the uses and gratifications approach to the media fits well with the Libertarian theory and John Stuart Mill's notions of human rationality. Both stress the potential of the individual for self-realization. As one researcher aptly put it three decades ago:

> The communicator's audience is not a passive recipient—it cannot be regarded as a lump of clay to be molded by the master propagandist. Rather, the audience is made up of individuals who demand something from the communications to which they are exposed, and who select those that are likely to be useful to them. In other words, they must get something from the manipulator if he is to get something from them. A bargain is involved. Sometimes, it is true, the manipulator is able to lead his audience into a bad bargain by emphasizing one need at the expense of another or by representing a change in the significant environment as greater than it actually has been. But audiences, too, can drive a hard bargain. Many communicators who have been widely disregarded or misunderstood know that at their cost. (Davison, 1959, p. 360)

The uses and gratifications approach involves a shift of focus from the purposes of the communicator to the purposes of the receiver. It attempts to determine what functions mass communication is serving for audience members.

Beginnings of the Uses and Gratifications Approach

The uses and gratifications approach was first described in an article by Elihu Katz (1959) in which he was reacting to a claim by Bernard Berelson (1959) that the field of communication research appeared to be dead. Katz argued that the field that was dying was the study of mass communication as persuasion. He pointed out that most communication research up to that time had been aimed at investigating the effects of persuasive campaigns on audiences. Katz said this research was aimed at answering the question "What do media do to people?" Most of this research had shown that mass communication had little effect in persuading people, and so researchers had turned away to variables that did have more of an effect, such as group influences.

Katz suggested that the field might save itself by turning to the question "What do people do with the media?" He cited a few studies of this type already done. One of them was, curiously enough, by Berelson. It was his "What Missing the Newspaper Means," a 1949 study conducted by interviewing people during a newspaper strike about what they missed in their newspapers (Berelson, 1965).

During this two-week strike of deliverymen, most readers were forced to find other sources of news, which is what they overwhelmingly said they missed the most. Many read because they felt it was the socially acceptable thing to do, and some felt that the newspaper was indispensable in finding out about world affairs. Many, however, sought escape, relaxation, entertainment, and social prestige. These people recognized that awareness of public affairs was of value in conversations. Some wanted help in their daily lives by reading material about fashion, recipes, weather forecasts, and other useful information.

Another example cited by Katz was Riley and Riley's study (1951) showing that children well integrated into groups of peers "use" adventure stories in the media for group games while children not well integrated use the same communications for fantasizing and daydreaming. This example illustrates a basic aspect of the uses and gratifications approach—different people can use the same mass communication message for very different purposes.

Another study examined the functions radio soap operas fulfilled for regular listeners. Some listeners found emotional release from their own problems. For others, listening provided escape, while a third group sought solutions to their own problems (Herzog, 1944).

Other early studies that considered the gratifications that the mass media provide their audiences included a series by Lazarsfeld and Stanton (1942, 1944, 1949) that dealt primarily with the functions of radio, one by Suchman (1942) dealing with classical music on radio, and one by Wolfe and Fiske (1949) on the development of children's interests in comics.

Uses and Gratifications in an Election Campaign

Blumler and McQuail (1969) used the uses and gratifications approach as the overall research strategy in a study of the 1964 general election in Britain. The central aim of their study was "to find out why people watch or avoid party broadcasts; what uses they wish to make of them; and what their preferences are between alternative ways of presenting politicians on television" (pp. 10–11). Part of their aim was to answer the challenging question posed by earlier election studies that indicated mass media election campaigns had little effect on voters: if voters are not influenced by mass media election programming, why do they follow it at all? Also, the researchers expected that classifying viewers according to their motives for viewing might disclose some previously undetected relationships between attitude change and campaign exposure, and thus might tell us something about effects after all. The uses and gratifications approach of Blumler and McQuail is reflected in some of their chapter titles—for example, "Why Do People Watch Political Programmes?" and "What Kind of Political Television Do Viewers Want?"

Blumler and McQuail began the task of determining people's motives for watching political broadcasts by interviewing a small sample with open-ended questions. On the basis of the responses to these questions, they drew up a list of eight reasons for watching political broadcasts. This list was used in subsequent interviewing with a large sample survey. On the basis of this interviewing, the researchers determined the frequency with which each reason was cited, as shown in Table 15.1.

The three most frequently mentioned reasons reflect a desire for what Blumler and McQuail call "surveillance of the political environment." These reasons, each cited by more than half the respondents, indicate that people used the political broadcasts as a source of information about political affairs. Other data from the survey indicated that one of the specific purposes of this surveillance was to find out about campaign promises and pledges. Only about a third of the respondents chose "To remind me of my party's strong points," a reason that would indicate the political broadcasts were being used for reinforcement of existing attitudes. This casts some doubt on the indication from some earlier research that people turn to the mass media primarily for reinforcement.

Blumler and McQuail also found some support for their notion that classifying viewers according to motives for viewing might disclose some relationships between attitude change and campaign exposure. The most useful variable they found for this purpose was an index of the strength of a viewer's motivation for following an election campaign on television. They divided viewers into two groups: those "strongly motivated" to follow the campaign and those with "medium and weak" motivation. For those with medium and weak motivation, there was a strong and regular relationship between exposure to Liberal party broadcasts and shift in favor of the Liberal party. This relationship was not found for

Table 15.1

REASONS FOR WATCHING PARTY BROADCASTS IN THE BRITISH
GENERAL ELECTION OF 1964, AS ENDORSED BY TV OWNERS

	Percent
To see what some party will do if it gets into power	55
To keep up with the main issues of the day	52
To judge what political leaders are like	51
To remind me of my party's strong points	36
To judge who is likely to win the election	31
To help make up my mind how to vote	26
To enjoy the excitement of the election race	24
To use as ammunition in arguments with others	10

Note: Respondents could endorse more than one reason.
From Jay G. Blumler and Denis McQuail, *Television in Politics: Its Uses and Influence.* Chicago: University of Chicago Press, 1969. Copyright by Jay G. Blumler and Denis McQuail. Reprinted by permission of Faber and Faber Ltd. and the University of Chicago Press.

those who were strongly motivated to follow the campaign. This finding indicates that a uses and gratifications approach can actually increase our knowledge about *effects* of mass communication. Effects may be dependent upon or related to audience members' needs and motives.

Classifying Individual Needs and Media Uses

A few years later, in a paper summarizing work in the field to that time, Katz, Blumler, and Gurevitch (1974) pointed out that the studies are concerned with:

> (1) the social and psychological origins of (2) needs, which generate (3) expectations of (4) the mass media or other sources, which lead to (5) differential patterns of media exposure (or engagement in other activities), resulting in (6) need gratifications and (7) other consequences, perhaps mostly unintended ones. (p. 20)

They cite two Swedish researchers who in 1968 proposed a "uses and gratifications model" that included the following elements:

> (1) The audience is conceived of as active, that is, an important part of mass media use is assumed to be goal directed.
>
> (2) In the mass communication process much initiative in linking need gratification and media choice lies with the audience member.
>
> (3) The media compete with other sources of need satisfaction. (pp. 22–23)

The uses and gratifications literature has provided several ways of classifying audience needs and gratifications. Some have spoken of "immediate" and "deferred" gratifications (Schramm, Lyle, & Parker, 1961); others have called them "informational-educational" and "fantasist-escapist" (entertainment) (Weiss, 1971).

McQuail, Blumler, and Brown (1972), working in England, suggested the following categories:

1. Diversion (escape from routine and problems; emotional release).

2. Personal relationships (social utility of information in conversations; substitute of the media for companionship).

3. Personal identity or individual psychology (value reinforcement or reassurance; self-understanding; reality exploration, etc.).

4. Surveillance (information about things which might affect one or will help one do or accomplish something).

In 1975, Mark R. Levy (1978b) examined the cross-national applicability of the McQuail, Blumler, and Brown typology with a sample of 240 adults living in Albany County, New York. He was not able to duplicate their classification of television news uses and gratifications but found that their four groupings or clusters of items in England were reduced to three substantially overlapping dimensions. All three clusters contained surveillance items, and the other two clusters were equally mixed. Levy speculated that the differences may be caused by several factors, including the greater availability of television news in the United States, the fact that Americans may rely on it for a greater variety of needs, and the differences in style and presentation of television news.

In a more complete report of the same research Levy (1978a) concluded that besides informing viewers, television news also tests their perceptions and attitudes on "fresh" events and personalities. However, the participation is at a distance with reality "sanitized" and made safe by the celebrity newsreader. Many viewers, he says, "actively" choose between competing newscasts, "arrange their schedules to be near a television set at news time, and pay close, albeit selective, attention to the program" (p. 25). The reasons reported for selection of news programs are shown in Table 15.2.

Katz, Gurevitch, and Haas (1973) see the mass media as a means used by individuals to connect themselves with others (or disconnect). They listed 35 needs taken "from the (largely speculative) literature on the social and psychological functions of the mass media" and put them into five categories:

1. Cognitive needs (acquiring information, knowledge, and understanding)
2. Affective needs (emotional, pleasurable, or aesthetic experience)
3. Personal integrative needs (strengthening credibility, confidence, stability, and status)
4. Social integrative needs (strengthening contacts with family, friends, etc.)
5. Tension release needs (escape and diversion) (pp. 166–167)

The researchers interviewed 1,500 respondents in Israel "on the assumption that people are aware of their needs and able to identify their sources of satisfaction" (p. 179) and reached the following conclusions, among others:

> 1. For all needs examined, the nonmedia sources (combined) were deemed more gratifying than the mass media. Friends, holidays, lectures, and work were nonmedia sources of gratification.

Table 15.2

PERCENT OF RESPONDENTS CITING SPECIFIC CRITERIA FOR NEWS PROGRAM CHOICE

	Newscast		
Reasons for Watching	*6 P.M.*	*11 P.M.*	*Network*
"Active"			
News Quality	12.0	12.4	7.9
Program format	18.1	6.0	1.8
Newscasters	21.3	29.1	41.8
Subtotal	51.4	47.5	51.5
"Passive"			
"Habit"	8.8	4.8	2.2
Channel	24.3	31.2	27.9
Don't Know	5.1	5.8	7.2
Subtotal	38.2	41.8	37.3
Miscellaneous	10.4	10.7	11.2
	(N = 189)	(N = 140)	(N = 125)

From Mark R. Levy, "The Audience Experience with Television News," *Journalism Monographs* 55, April 1978, p. 7. Reprinted by permission.

2. The greater the "distance" from a referent—social, physical, or psychological—the more important the role of the media. Yet, interpersonal communication—formal and informal—competes even in areas relating to political leadership and negative reference groups.

3. Certain comparative processes—such as striving for a higher standard of living, or satisfying oneself that one's time is well spent or that one's country is a good place to live in—seem well served by the media. So are "escapist needs." On the whole, however, friends are more important than the mass media for needs having to do with self-integration, even the need "to be entertained."

4. For individuals who say that matters of state and society are important to them, the rank order of media usefulness in serving these needs is entirely consistent, regardless of the respondent's educational level. Newspapers are the most important medium, followed by radio, then television. Books and films fall far behind. Altogether, the centrality of the newspaper for knowledge and integration in the sociopolitical arena cannot be overstated.

5. Needs having to do with self are associated with different kinds of media, depending on the specific functions involved. Knowing oneself is best served by books; enjoying oneself is associated with films, television, and books; while the newspaper contributes to self-regulation and self-confidence. (p. 180)

Their other five principal findings dealt with the needs the different media fulfill for different types of people. For example, for the better educated, needs associated with the self are better filled by books, while television fills that need for the less educated.

Katz, Gurevitch, and Haas ended with this observation: "Finally, it should be noted that media-related needs are not, by and large, generated by the media. Most predate the emergence of the media and, properly ought to be viewed within the wider range of human needs. . . . " (p. 180).

Katz (1979) has pointed out that in earlier studies, which found avoidance of dissonance and seeking out of consonance, the audience selectivity was based on defensiveness, while in the gratifications studies the audience selectivity is based on interest. In the latter the audience member wants to use the media to serve individual needs and values.

In the late 1970s, researchers turned to the question of gratifications sought and gratifications obtained from the media (Palmgreen, Wenner, & Rayburn, 1981, pp. 451–452). In a telephone survey of 327 male and female heads of households in Lexington, Kentucky, in November 1978, the researchers asked a series of questions regarding the gratifications sought and obtained in watching the three network's evening news. They found that the decision to view a particular news program is a function of viewing choices between one's favorite program and competing programs. In certain cases perceptions of anchorpersons, program format, and news quality are important, but viewing behavior is at least as strongly related as any of the preceding. The researchers close by saying, "Much work remains to be done in illuminating the nature of the relationship between gratifications sought and obtained, the antecedents of such gratifications, and the ways in which such gratifications are related to media behavior" (p. 476).

Criticisms of the Uses and Gratifications Theory

The uses and gratifications approach has come under some criticism, particularly for being nontheoretical, for being vague in defining key concepts (for example, "needs"), and for being basically nothing more than a data-collecting strategy (see Elliott, 1974; Swanson,

1977, 1979; Lometti, Reeves, & Bybee, 1977). Very little has been done to explore the antecedents of gratifications sought (Palmgreen & Rayburn, 1982). Often needs people seek to fulfill through media use are inferred from questions about why they use the media, leading to the suspicion that the need was created by the media, or is a rationalization for media use.

In light of the research since Freud indicating the complexity and obscurity of human motivation, there is also something a little simplistic or naive about using self-reports to determine motives.

One extensive discussion of uses and gratifications theory (McLeod & Baker, 1981) concludes by specifying some additional needs of the uses and gratifications approach. They include:

1. More consistent use of the concepts of motivation and media use.
2. A closer tie between differing patterns of gratifications sought and the meanings and interpretations given specific media messages.
3. No longer equating effects research with the hypodermic all-powerful media model (and an attempt to investigate the consequences of various patterns of media use and motivation).
4. More systematic attempts to develop broader and more complex models of the role of uses and gratifications.
5. Go beyond its present largely individual focus to consider its relevance to social systems.

A 1983 critique of uses and gratification studies and an attempt to link them to psychological value expectancy theory criticizes the confounding of operational definitions and the analytical model, questions internal consistency, cites the lack of theoretical justification for a model offered, and says "the discussion ranges far from the results, which do not support their theoretical underpinnings" (Stanford, 1983, pp. 247–250).

Some respondents are not able to specify the gratifications they get from media use when they are asked open-ended questions, but readily identify a need when it is presented in a list of alternatives (Becker, 1979). However, independent researchers, often using different techniques, have identified very similar needs, which adds confidence in the technique of asking people why they choose certain information.

McQuail (1985), a prominent contributor to uses and gratifications research, has criticized scholars in the area for trying to do too much. He says uses and gratifications research is now attempting to study *culture* (its origin, production, meaning, and use), *people* in audiences (their identity, attributes, and reasons for being there), individual *behavior* (kind, frequency, causes, consequences, and interconnections), and *society* (and the working of media within it). He recommends that the area emphasize one of these four areas, culture, but that it do so with a cultural-empirical approach. Under this approach, attention would be concentrated on the making of choices and the meaningful encounter with cultural products. He argues that this would be a return to the bridge-building between the social sciences and the humanities recommended by Katz in his original call for research on the uses of the media, which was never really achieved.

One criticism of the uses and gratifications approach is that it is focused too narrowly on the individual (Elliott, 1974). It relies on psychological concepts such as need, and it neglects the social structure and the place of the media in that structure. One answer to that criticism has come from Rubin and Windahl (1986), who have proposed a synthesis of the uses and gratifications approach and dependency theory (Ball-Rokeach & DeFleur, 1976). Their "uses and dependency model" places individuals within societal systems, which help shape their needs.

Finally, the finding that exposure to mass communication may not always be highly deliberate or purposeful (discussed in Chapter 4) challenges some of the basic notions of the uses and gratifications approach. People often seem to be making their way through the mass communication environment while on a kind of "automatic pilot" (Donohew, Nair, & Finn, 1984). This view suggests that much use of mass communication might involve a low level of attention, and, in fact, might be appropriately labeled as *ritualistic* or *habitual*. Many people much of the time might not be interested in surveillance or personal guidance as much as they are just interested in some mildly pleasant stimulation.

In a similar point, a massive study of television viewing (Kubey & Csikszentmihalyi, 1990) has suggested recently that the concept of an active audience is misleading when applied to television watching. This study of television viewing by different demographic groups and with respondents ranging in ages from 10 to 82 found that people consistently report their experiences with television as being passive, relaxing, and involving relatively little concentration. They also argue that television and films, in comparison with print, are likely to produce much more uniform cognitive and affective responses in an audience due to the pictorial nature of the media. Uniform effects are not the kind of thing a uses and gratifications approach would predict.

Empirical Tests of the Uses and Gratifications Theory

Bryant and Zillmann (1984) conducted an experimental study of whether an individual's mood influences the selection of television programs. These researchers investigated the selection of exciting and relaxing television programming by students who, prior to an opportunity to choose their viewing, had been purposely either stressed or bored (see Table 15.3):

> Stressed subjects watched nearly six times as much relaxing television as did bored subjects, [while] bored subjects watched nearly twice as much exciting fare as did stressed subjects. . . . Looked at another way, whereas subjects under stress selected approximately the same amount of exciting and relaxing television, bored subjects exposed themselves to exciting programming about 10 times longer than to relaxing fare. (pp. 12–13)

The researchers concluded that "the findings lend strong support to the utility of the selective exposure propositions" and that "subjects make intelligent program choices . . . when using television exposure as a means for alleviating boredom and stress" (p. 20).

The Bryant and Zillmann research, although not called a uses and gratification study, clearly falls into this area. It was a controlled experiment and provides data that do not rely on self-report, one of the criticisms of much of the earlier work in uses and gratifications. In general, it provides some support for uses and gratifications theory.

Several other studies provide less support for basic tenets of the uses and gratifications approach.

Stanford and Riccomini (1984) conducted an experimental investigation of one of the main postulates of the uses and gratifications approach—if the gratifications sought by an

Table 15.3

SELECTIVE EXPOSURE TO RELAXING AND EXCITING
PROGRAMS AS A FUNCTION OF BOREDOM AND STRESS

| Program Type | Experimental Condition | |
	Boredom	Stress
Exciting	793	441
Relaxing	74	427
Combined	867	868

Note: Exposure time is in seconds. Maximally possible time was 900 seconds, or 15 minutes.
From Jennings Bryant and Dolf Zillmann, "Using Television to Alleviate Boredom and Stress: Selective Exposure as a Function of Induced Excitational States," *Journal of Broadcasting* 28 (Winter 1984): 13. Reprinted
with permission.

audience are similar to the gratifications provided by a medium, the audience should show
greater liking for that medium and more willingness to be exposed to it again. The researchers manipulated subjects' orientation (the gratifications sought) by telling them they
were receiving materials for a government instructional course teaching TV literacy. Subjects in one of the three experimental conditions were told government researchers had
discovered that viewing TV for entertainment would increase enjoyment. Students in the
other two conditions were given the same basic instructions, except that the word "entertainment" was replaced by either "information" or "personal guidance." Students in all
three orientations then viewed one of three TV programs. The programs were selected
from the current season to provide the three types of gratification being sought: information ("Washington Week in Review"), entertainment ("Mork and Mindy"), and personal
guidance ("Edge of Night"). Two measures of program enjoyment were obtained by having subjects rate the quality of the program watched and state the likelihood of their viewing another episode, with each variable measured on a scale from 1 to 4.

The results provided no support for the idea that greater enjoyment of TV programs
would result when orientations and program types were matched. In general, the experiment indicated that providing programs that match audience orientations does not help
much in predicting audience reactions to the programs. The authors suggest that orientations operate to encourage selection of appropriate gratifications from *within* program
types rather than operating at the level of programs.

Elliott and Rosenberg (1987), following the example of the pioneering newspaper strike
study of Berelson 40 years earlier, were able to study media use during a newspaper strike
in Philadelphia in September 1985. The researchers took advantage of the strike to look at
the relationship between newspaper gratifications sought and media use during the strike.
Basically, they were investigating whether readers of the Philadelphia newspapers would
turn to other media during the strike to fulfill the functions of surveillance and social contact, killing time, entertainment, and advertising. The results showed mild tendencies for
readers seeking surveillance and social contact to turn to other newspapers, to newsmagazines, and to local and national TV news, but the correlations were not large. The seeking
of the gratifications of killing time, entertainment, and advertising were not associated

with increases of use of other media. The researchers interpret these results as indicating that "media gratifications are primarily the result of the social situation and background factors and may depend more on habit than on internalized need states" (p. 687).

Further evidence that at least some media use may be a matter of habit comes from a study by Stone and Stone (1990). They carried out a telephone survey in which people indicated their reasons for watching evening television soap operas by expressing their extent of agreement with eight statements. One of the statements was "It's an enjoyable habit I like doing." The results showed the respondents rated the habit statement as the reason closest to why they watched continuing evening television dramas.

New Technology and the Active Audience

Researchers have only begun to study the ways that cable television and other new media offering expanded user choices relate to the user's pursuit of uses and gratifications. A few studies done so far provide clues concerning the impact of new technology on how people use the mass media.

Cable television provides new and diverse opportunities for the audience to become active. With cable, the number of channels can increase from the 10 or fewer available with broadcast television to as many as 108. Cable viewers adopt various strategies to cope with this increased number of choices. One strategy is to narrow one's regular watching to a subset of the available channels that correspond to one's interests. This subset has been called an individual's "channel repertoire" (Heeter & Greenberg, 1985).

Viewers differ in their awareness of available cable options. To some extent, viewers appear to be overwhelmed by the number of programs and channels now available. One survey of users of a 35-channel cable system found viewers were able to correctly identify an average of only nine channels by their number or location on the channel selector (Heeter & Greenberg, 1985).

About half the time, cable viewers have a program in mind when they turn on the television set. The other half of the time, programs are chosen at the time of viewing. Viewers use a variety of scanning strategies to decide which programs to watch. These strategies differ in whether they are *automatic* (going from channel to channel in the order that they appear) or *controlled* (going from one selected channel to another on the basis of some desired goal), *elaborated* (involving all or most channels) or *restricted* (involving a limited number of channels), and *exhaustive* (searching all channels before returning to the best choice) or *terminating* (stopping when the first acceptable option is located). The most active viewers of cable television tend to use controlled, elaborated, and exhaustive searching strategies. They tend to be young adults (Heeter & Greenberg, 1985).

The videocassette recorder also gives the television viewer opportunities to be a more active viewer. It offers the user greater flexibility in terms of times for viewing and it increases the choices of available content. Levy (1980) argues that using a VCR to time-shift programs is a demanding task and that the viewers who take the trouble to do it must be among the most active members of the television audience.

Further evidence that VCR users are essentially an active audience comes from additional research by Levy (1987). In a study conducted in Israel, he gave VCR owners questionnaires that measured nine different types of activity. The measuring instrument was the Levy-Windahl typology of audience activity that had been tested previously with television news viewers. The typology measures these nine kinds of activity: selectivity before exposure, during exposure, and after exposure; involvement before exposure, during exposure, and after exposure; and utility before exposure, during exposure, and after exposure. The VCR owners showed higher degrees of activity for most of the items than the television news viewers had shown in earlier research.

A study by Rubin and Bantz (1989) took an explicit uses and gratifications approach to the use of videocassette recorders. These researchers administered a questionnaire soliciting information concerning 11 types of VCR use and 95 statements of motivation for the 11 types of use. Statistical analysis narrowed the list down to 8 motives for using VCRs: (1) library storage of movies and shows, (2) watching music videos, (3) using exercise tapes, (4) renting movies, (5) letting children view, (6) time-shifting, (7) socializing by viewing with others, and (8) critical viewing, including rewatching and studying tapes. Most of these motives involve instrumental use of VCRs for specific purposes rather than just viewing out of habit or to fill time. These results indicate VCR users are deliberately choosing to use their recorders for a number of diverse but specific purposes—a result that follows logically from the uses and gratifications approach.

Conclusions

The uses and gratifications approach reminds us of one very important point—people use the media for many different purposes. To a large extent, the user of mass communication is in control. The uses and gratifications approach can serve as a healthy antidote to the emphasis on passive audiences and persuasion that has dominated much earlier research.

Empirical research testing basic tenets of uses and gratifications theory has so far come up with mixed results. Bryant and Zillmann found evidence that stressed subjects would choose relaxing content while bored subjects would choose exciting content, supporting the idea that viewers choose media content to provide gratifications they are seeking. But the Stanford and Riccomini experiment that introduced subjects to surveillance, entertainment, and personal guidance orientations and then exposed them to various types of television content did not find greater satisfaction when the program content matched the viewer's orientation. Also, Elliott and Rosenberg, in their replication of Berelson's classic newspaper strike study, did not find that readers deprived of their newspapers did a great deal of shifting to other media to fulfill the functions they may have been missing. Elliott and Rosenberg concluded that much of mass media use might be merely a matter of habit. The study by Stone and Stone also suggests the importance of habit in explaining media use.

Despite these mixed results, the uses and gratifications approach may have a chance to come into its own as we move into the information age and media users are confronted with more and more choices. It is obvious that the media user dealing with cable television with as many as 108 channels or with a videocassette recorder that allows time-shifting, archiving, and repeated viewing of television content is a much more active audience member than the traditional media consumer of a few years ago. The uses and gratifications approach should eventually have some things to say about the users of these new media. After all, it is the single area of theory that has attempted most directly to deal with the active audience.

At the very least, the uses and gratifications approach should direct our attention to the audience of mass communication. Brenda Dervin (1980) has recommended that the development of information campaigns should begin with study of the potential information user and the questions that person is attempting to answer in order to make sense of the world. The same lesson probably applies to the producers of much of the content of the mass media. Media planners in many areas should be conducting more research on their potential audiences, and the gratifications those audiences are trying to obtain.

References

Ball-Rokeach, S. J., and M. L. DeFleur (1976). A dependency model of mass-media effects. *Communication Research* 3: 3–21.

Bauer, R. A. (1964). The obstinate audience: The influence process from the point of view of social communication. *American Psychologist* 19: 319–328.

Becker, L. B. (1979). Measurement of gratifications. *Communication Research* 6: 54–73.

Berelson, B. (1959). The state of communication research. *Public Opinion Quarterly* 23: 1–6.

———— (1965). What "missing the newspaper" means. In W. Schramm (ed.), *The Process and Effects of Mass Communication*, pp. 36–47. Urbana: University of Illinois.

Blumler, J. G., and D. McQuail (1969). *Television in Politics: Its Uses and Influence*. Chicago: University of Chicago Press.

Bryant, J., and R. L. Street, Jr. (1988). From reactivity to activity and action: An evolving concept and Weltanschauung in mass and interpersonal communication. In R. P. Hawkins, J. M. Wiemann, and S. Pingree (eds.), *Advancing Communication Science: Merging Mass and Interpersonal Processes*, pp. 162–190.

Bryant, J., and D. Zillmann (1984). Using television to alleviate boredom and stress: Selective exposure as a function of induced excitational states. *Journal of Broadcasting* 28: 1–20.

Davison, W. P. (1959). On the effects of communication. *Public Opinion Quarterly* 23: 343–360.

Dervin, B. (1980). Communication gaps and inequities: Moving toward a reconceptualization. In B. Dervin and M. J. Voight (eds.), *Progress in Communication Sciences*, vol. 2, pp. 73–112. Norwood, N.J.: Ablex.

Donohew, R. L., M. Nair, and S. Finn (1984). Automacity, arousal, and information exposure. In R. N. Bostrom (ed.), *Communication Yearbook 8*, pp. 267–284. Beverly Hills, Cal.: Sage.

Elliott, P. (1974). Uses and gratifications research: A critique and a sociological alternative. In J. G. Blumler and E. Katz (eds.), *The Uses of Mass Communications: Current Perspectives on Gratifications Research*, pp. 249–268. Beverly Hills, Cal.: Sage.

Elliott, W. R., and W. L. Rosenberg (1987). The 1985 Philadelphia newspaper strike: A uses and gratifications study. *Journalism Quarterly* 64: 679–687.

Heeter, C., and B. Greenberg (1985). Cable and program choice. In D. Zillmann and J. Bryant (eds.), *Selective Exposure to Communication*, pp. 203–224. Hillsdale, N.J.: Lawrence Erlbaum.

Herzog, H. (1944). Motivations and gratifications of daily serial listeners. In W. Schramm (ed.), *The Process and Effects of Mass Communication*, pp. 50–55. Urbana: University of Illinois Press.

Katz, E. (1959). Mass communication research and the study of popular culture: An editorial note on a possible future for this journal. *Studies in Public Communication* 2: 1–6.

———— (1979). The uses of Becker, Blumler, and Swanson. *Communication Research* 6: 75–83.

Katz, E., J. G. Blumler, and M. Gurevitch (1974). Utilization of mass communication by the individual. In J. G. Blumler and E. Katz (eds.), *The Uses of Mass Communications: Current Perspectives on Gratifications Research*, pp. 19–32. Beverly Hills, Cal.: Sage.

Katz, E., M. Gurevitch, and H. Haas (1973). On the use of the mass media for important things. *American Sociological Review* 38: 164–181.

Kubey, R., and M. Csikszentmihalyi (1990). *Television and the Quality of Life: How Viewing Shapes Everyday Experience*. Hillsdale, N.J.: Lawrence Erlbaum.

Lazarsfeld, P. F., and F. N. Stanton (eds.) (1942). *Radio Research, 1941*. New York: Duell, Sloan & Pearce.

———— (1944). *Radio Research, 1942-1943*. New York: Duell, Sloan & Pearce.

———— (1949). *Communications Research, 1948-1949.* New York: Harper.

Levy, M. R. (1978a). The audience experience with television news. *Journalism Monographs* no. 55, April.

———— (1978b). Television news uses: A cross-national comparison. *Journalism Quarterly* 55: 334–337.

———— (1980). Home video recorders: A user survey. *Journal of Communication* 30, no. 4: 23–25.

———— (1987). VCR use and the concept of audience activity. *Communication Quarterly* 35: 267–275.

Lometti, G. E., B. Reeves, and C. R. Bybee (1977). Investigating the assumptions of uses and gratifications research. *Communication Research* 4: 321–338.

McLeod, J. M., and L. B. Becker (1981). The uses and gratifications approach. In D. Nimmo and K. Sanders (eds.), *Handbook of Political Communication,* pp. 67–99. Beverly Hills, Cal.: Sage.

McQuail, D. (1985). With the benefit of hindsight: Reflections on uses and gratifications research. In M. Gurevitch and M. R. Levy (eds.), *Mass Communication Review Yearbook,* vol. 5, pp. 125–141.

McQuail, D., J. G. Blumler, and J. R. Brown (1972). The television audience: a revised perspective. In D. McQuail (ed.), *Sociology of Mass Communications,* pp. 135–165. Harmondsworth: Penguin.

Palmgreen, P., and J. D. Rayburn II (1982). Gratifications sought and media exposure: An expectancy value model. *Communications Research* 9: 561–580.

Palmgreen, P., L. A. Wenner, and J. D. Rayburn II (1981). Gratification discrepancies and news program choice. *Communication Research* 8: 451–478.

Riley, M. W., and J. W. Riley, Jr. (1951). A sociological approach to communications research. *Public Opinion Quarterly* 15: 445–460.

Rubin, A. M., and C. R. Bantz (1989). Uses and gratifications of videocassette recorders. In J. L. Salvaggio and J. Bryant (eds.), *Media Use in the Information Age: Emerging Patterns of Adoption and Consumer Use,* pp. 181–195. Hillsdale, N.J.: Lawrence Erlbaum.

Rubin, A. M., and S. Windahl (1986). The uses and dependency model of mass communication. *Critical Studies in Mass Communication* 3: 184–199.

Schramm, W., J. Lyle, and E. B. Parker (1961). *Television in the Lives of Our Children.* Stanford: Stanford University Press.

Stanford, S. W. (1983). Comments on Palmgreen and Rayburn, "Gratifications sought and media exposure." *Communication Research* 10: 247–258.

Stanford, S., and B. Riccomini (1984). Linking TV program orientations and gratifications: An experimental approach. *Journalism Quarterly* 61: 76–82.

Stone, G., and D. B. Stone (1990). Lurking in the literature: Another look at media use habits. *Mass Comm Review* 17, nos. 1 and 2: 25–33, 46.

Suchman, E. (1942). Invitation to music. In P. F. Lazarsfeld and F. N. Stanton (eds.), *Radio Research, 1941,* pp. 140–188. New York: Duell, Sloan & Pearce.

Swanson, D. L. (1977). The uses and misuses of uses and gratifications. *Human Communication Research* 3: 214–221.

———— (1979). Political communication research and the uses and gratifications model: A critique. *Communication Research* 6: 37–53.

Weiss, W. (1971). Mass communication. *Annual Review of Psychology* 22: 309–336.

Wolfe, K. M., and M. Fiske (1949). The children talk about comics. In P. F. Lazarsfeld and F. N. Stanton (eds.), *Communication Research, 1948-1949,* pp. 3–50. New York: Harper & Brothers.

P A R T
VI

The Media as Institutions

Mass communication products are now typically produced by organizations that are complex businesses employing large numbers of people. It is no longer sufficient, if it ever was, to attempt to theorize about mass communication at the level of the individual receiver as an information processor, at the level of the audience as made up of members of groups, or even at the level of individuals linked through interpersonal communication. Certain aspects of mass communication begin to become apparent only when we shift our focus from the individual as a unit of analysis to the society as a whole. Once we do this, we can begin to think about the roles that mass communication plays in society, and the functions that mass communication serves for a society as a whole. Chapter 16 takes this more macro perspective and looks at the relationships between the mass media and society. Chapter 17 deals with an important aspect of the mass media viewed as institutions—the patterns of ownership of the media and the possible consequences of those patterns.

16 Mass Media in Modern Society

Modern society is nearly unimaginable without the mass media: newspapers, magazines, paperbacks, radio, television, and film. The mass media are many things to many people and serve a variety of functions, depending on the type of political and economic system in which the media function, the stage of development of the society, and the interests and needs of specific individuals. In this chapter we will examine several views of what the media should be and do in several types of societies and some observations of how the media actually function.

Some understanding of the role of mass communication in society is necessary for a complete theory of mass communication. One of the goals of communication theory is to make possible accurate predictions of the effects of the mass media. Political, social, and economic forces directly affect media content. Media ownership and control affect media content, which in turn determines media effects.

Four Theories of the Press

One well-known classification of the press systems of the world is presented in the book *Four Theories of the Press*, (Siebert, Peterson, & Schramm, 1956). Its authors divided the world's press into four categories: authoritarian, libertarian, social responsibility, and Soviet-totalitarian (see Table 16.1). These are "normative theories" derived from observation, not from hypothesis testing and replication using social science methods as described in Chapter 2.

Authoritarian Theory

In the West, the invention of the printing press and movable type came at a time when the world was under authoritarian rule by monarchs with absolute power. It is no surprise that the first rationale or theory of the press was that of a press supporting and advancing the policies of the government in power and serving the state. A printer was required to get permission and, in some cases, a patent from the monarch or the government in order to publish. Through the use of patents, licensing, direct censorship, and often self-regulation through printers' guilds, individuals were prevented from criticizing the government in power. In authoritarian systems the press may be either publicly or privately owned; nevertheless it is regarded as an instrument for furthering government policy.

Table 16.1

FOUR RATIONALES FOR THE MASS MEDIA

	Authoritarian	Libertarian	Social Responsibility	Soviet-Totalitarian
Developed	in 16th- and 17th-century England; widely adopted and still practiced in many places	adopted by England after 1688, and in U.S.; influential elsewhere	in U.S. in the 20th century	in Soviet Union, although some of the same things were done by Nazis and Italians
Out of	philosophy of absolute power of monarch, his government, or both	writings of Milton, Locke, Mill, and general philosophy of rationalism and natural rights	writing of W. E. Hocking, Commission on Freedom of Press, and practitioners; media codes	Marxist-Leninist-Stalinist thought, with mixture of Hegel and 19th-century Russian thinking
Chief purpose	to support and advance the policies of the government in power; and to service the state	to inform, entertain, sell—but chiefly to help discover truth, and to check on government	to inform, entertain, sell—but chiefly to raise conflict to the plane of discussion	to contribute to the success and continuance of the Soviet socialist system, and especially to the dictatorship of the party
Who has right to use media?	whoever gets a royal patent or similar permission	anyone with economic means to do so	everyone who has something to say	loyal and orthodox party members

How are media controlled?	government patents, guilds, licensing, sometimes censorship	by "self-righting process of truth" in "free market place of ideas," and by courts	community opinion, consumer action, professional ethics	surveillance and economic or political action of government
What forbidden?	criticism of political machinery and officials in power	defamation, obscenity, indecency, wartime sedition	serious invasion of recognized private rights and vital social interests	criticism of party objectives as distinguished from tactics
Ownership	private or public	chiefly private	private unless government has to take over to insure public service	public
Essential differences from others	instrument for effecting government policy, though not necessarily government-owned	instrument for checking on government and meeting other needs of society	media must assume obligation of social responsibility; and if they do not, someone must see that they do	state-owned and closely controlled media existing solely as arm of state

From F. S. Siebert, T. B. Peterson, and W. Schramm, *Four Theories of the Press* (Urbana: University of Illinois Press, 1956), p. 7. Reprinted by permission.

Libertarian Theory

Out of the Enlightenment and the general theories of rationalism and of natural rights developed a libertarian theory of the press to counter the authoritarian view. From the writings of Milton, Locke, and Mill came the notion that the press was to serve the function of helping discover truth and checking on government as well as informing, entertaining, and selling. Under the libertarian theory the press is chiefly private, and anyone who can afford to do so can publish. The media are controlled in two ways. With a multiplicity of voices, the "self-righting process of truth" in the "free market place of ideas" would enable individuals to differentiate between truth and falsehood. Also, the legal system makes provision for the prosecution of defamation, obscenity, indecency, and wartime sedition. Under the libertarian theory the press is chiefly private and the media are instruments for checking on government as well as meeting the other needs of the society.

The libertarian theory of the press developed in England during the 18th century but was not permitted in the British colonies in North America until the break with the mother country. After 1776 it was implemented in areas not under control of colonial governors and was formally adopted with the First Amendment to the new Bill of Rights appended to the Constitution.

Mill's On Liberty   One of the best concise articulations of the arguments favoring a "free press" was set forth in the mid-19th century by John Stuart Mill in Chapter 2 of *On Liberty*. Mill argues that to silence an opinion we may silence the truth. It is here that we find this oft-quoted passage:

> If all mankind minus one were of one opinion, mankind would be no more justified in silencing that one person than he, if he had the power, would be justified in silencing mankind. . . . If the opinion is right, they [mankind] are deprived of the opportunity of exchanging error for truth; if wrong, they lose, what is almost as great a benefit, the clearer perception and the livelier impression of the truth produced by its collision with error. (1859/1956, p. 21)

Mill argues that since no person is infallible, the question of truth or falsehood of an opinion should be left to every person to judge. He adds that when one lacks trust in one's own opinion, an individual usually relies on the prevailing or majority opinion for support or guidance. (Chapter 10 in this book discusses the findings of modern social psychology on the effects of group judgments on individual judgments.)

Mill quickly points out that the opinions of "the world" in general are no more infallible than those held by an individual because of the limited experiences of groups and entire societies as well as individuals (p. 22). Mill adds:

> Ages are no more infallible than individuals, and every age having held many opinions which subsequent ages have deemed not only false but absurd; and it is as certain that many opinions, now general, will be rejected by future ages, as it is that many, once general, are rejected by the present. (p. 23)

Mill argues that assuming an opinion to be true because every opportunity to disprove it has failed is far different from assuming it to be true and not permitting its refutation. The only justification we have for assuming an opinion to be true is that it has withstood every opportunity to prove it false and this is the only way in which a human being has any rational assurance of being right.

The libertarian theory holds that human beings are capable of correcting their errors, but only when there is the possibility of discussion and argument to bring forth fact and truth eventually. Mill argues that the only way a human being can approach knowing the whole of any subject is by hearing what persons of all varieties of opinions and character of mind may have to say about it (p. 25). (A discussion of abstraction is found in Chapter 5.)

Later Mill argues not only that opinions must be tested and defended to be held on rational grounds but also that opinions not challenged lose their vitality and effect. He says that however true an opinion may be, it will become dead dogma rather than living truth "if it is not fully, frequently and fearlessly discussed." He adds that it is seldom possible to shut out discussion entirely and that once it begins, beliefs not grounded on conviction give way before the slightest argument (p. 43). (McGuire's immunization to counter persuasion in Chapter 9 relates directly to this point.)

The libertarian theory, with its notion of truth eventually winning out in the marketplace of ideas, was useful and viable before the industrial revolution made itself felt in publishing and later in broadcasting. As technology made possible ever-faster and ever-wider distribution of newspapers, the economies of mass production became more and more important. Larger newspapers began buying out or merging with smaller newspapers until today very few cities have competing newspapers. This caused thoughtful individuals, both inside and outside the media, to question the usefulness of the libertarian theory in a democratic society. It was argued that with fewer and fewer media voices, it was becoming more and more difficult for significant and sometimes unpopular views to gain a hearing.

In addition, 20th-century psychology has demonstrated that human beings do not always deal with information in seemingly rational ways. Rationalization is itself an attempt to provide a rational explanation for an irrational act. These findings undercut the "rational man" philosophies upon which the libertarian theory is based.

Social Responsibility Theory

In the 20th century in the United States the notion developed that the media, the only industry singled out for protection in the Bill of Rights, must meet a social responsibility. This social responsibility theory, evolving from media practitioners, media codes, and the work of the Commission on Freedom of the Press (Hutchins Commission), holds that while the media inform, entertain, and sell (as in the libertarian theory) they must also raise conflict to the plane of discussion.

The social responsibility theory holds that everyone who has something of significance to say should be allowed a forum and that if the media do not assume their obligation, somebody must see to it that they do. Under this theory, the media are controlled by community opinion, consumer action, professional ethics, and, in the case of broadcasting, governmental regulatory agencies because of technical limits on the number of channels or frequencies available (Siebert et al., 1956). (In the United States, as of this writing, there has been a trend for many years to "deregulate" broadcasting. The argument put forth is that with the new technologies such as cable television and low-power broadcasting, enough channels are now available in each community to make regulation unnecessary.)

The social responsibility theory has generated considerable discussion over who should see to it that the media act in a socially responsible manner and how decisions should be made as to what is or is not a significant opinion worthy of media space or time.

Soviet-Totalitarian Theory

In the meantime, the authoritarian theory of the press has, in many parts of the world, evolved into the Soviet-totalitarian theory of the press. The Soviets view the chief purpose of the media to be that of contributing to the success and continuance of the Soviet system. The media are controlled by the economic and political actions of the government as well as by surveillance, and only loyal and orthodox party members can use the media regularly. The tactics of the party may be criticized, but the objectives or goals may not. The media in the Soviet system are state owned and controlled and exist solely as an arm of the state to further the state.

Since *Four Theories of the Press* was written there have been many changes in the socialist countries. In the People's Republic of China private ownership of newspapers was allowed on a limited scale during the 1980s. More criticism has been tolerated, especially if it is criticism of individuals or local policies that undermine the goals of the nation's "four modernizations" program. Today more changes of political direction are again taking place in the People's Republic of China.

Pravda, the Communist party daily, began publishing criticisms of the special privileges enjoyed by the political elite in the Soviet Union (Kimelman, 1986). By 1989 the Soviet Union was in a state of political, social, and economic flux. A Soviet magazine published a scathing attack on the Communist party, including the Soviet leader Mikhail S. Gorbachev (Keller, 1989a), and the government newspaper *Izvestia,* in the first disclosure of crime statistics in 56 years, reported a 17.6 percent increase over the previous year, with especially sharp increases in violent crimes (Fein, 1989). Later in 1989 three committees of the Soviet legislature proposed a law to permit any citizen or group to publish without prior censorship, described by Soviet journalists as "the most important broadening of press freedom in Soviet history" (Keller, 1989b).

During 1989 press restrictions were also lifted in the East European satellite nations. Hungarians learned from television and the press of the existence of widespread poverty after four decades of claims by the Communist party that it had been eradicated (Kamm, 1989). The year ended with Rumanians throughout the country learning of widespread discontent from their television network. President Nicolae Ceausescu had called an orchestrated morning rally to denounce anti-Communist forces. Students began booing, but before technicians could "voice over" a sound track of canned applause viewers were aware that their all-powerful leader was vulnerable. An afternoon of demonstrations was soon followed by the violent overthrow of the regime (Bohlen & Haberman, 1989).

The News Media as Agents of Power

J. Herbert Altschull, in his book *Agents of Power* (1984), argues that the categories in *Four Theories of the Press,* which were formulated during the cold war, are no longer relevant. He maintains that the analysis is an "us-versus-them" approach that reflects the hostility of the period. Altschull says, "One of the most critical of all difficulties we face in efforts to avoid the perils of global confrontation lies in labeling and in the language of conflict" (p. 108). He maintains that an independent press cannot exist and that the mass media are the agents of those who hold the economic, political, and social power in any system.

After a sweeping review of the history and functioning of the world's press systems, much of it based on personal experience, Altschull concludes that today there are three models of the press. These are: the market (or capitalist) model; the Marxist (or socialist) model; and the advancing (or, less accurately, developing countries) model. Altschull's comparisons of purposes, articles of faith, and views on press freedom of the three models appear in Tables 16.2, 16.3, and 16.4.

Altschull reaches the following conclusions:

1. In all press systems, the news media are agents of the people who exercise political and economic power. Newspapers, magazines, and broadcasting outlets thus are not independent actors, although they have the potential to exercise independent power.

2. The content of the news media always reflects the interests of those who finance the press.

3. All press systems are based on a belief in free expression, although free expression is defined in different ways.

4. All press systems endorse the doctrine of social responsibility, proclaim that they serve the needs and interests of the people, and state their willingness to provide access to the people.

5. In each of the three press models, the press of the other models is perceived to be deviant.

6. Schools of journalism transmit ideologies and value systems of the society in which they exist and inevitably assist people in power in maintaining their control of the news media.

7. Press practices always differ from theory.

Table 16.2
PURPOSES OF JOURNALISM

Market	Marxist	Advancing
To seek truth	To search for truth	To serve truth
To be socially responsible	To educate the people and enlist allies (in a political way)	To be socially responsible
To inform (or educate) in a non-political way	To serve the people by demanding support for socialist doctrine	To educate (in a political way)
To serve the people impartially; to support capitalist doctrine	To mold views and change behavior	To serve the people, by seeking, in partnership with government, change for beneficial purposes
To serve as a watchdog on government		To serve as an instrument of peace

From J. H. Altschull, *Agents of Power: The Role of the News Media in Human Affairs* (White Plains, N.Y.: Longman, 1984), p. 284. Reprinted with permission.

Table 16.3

ARTICLES OF FAITH

Market	Marxist	Advancing
The press is free of outside interference	The press transforms false consciousness and educates workers into class consciousness	The press is a unifying and not a divisive force
The press serves the public's right to know	The press provides for the objective needs of the people	The press is a device for beneficial social change
The press seeks to learn and present the truth	The press facilitates effective change	The press is an instrument of social justice
The press reports fairly and objectively	The press reports objectively about the realities of experience	The press is meant to be used for two-way exchanges between journalists and readers

From J. H. Altschull, *Agents of Power: The Role of the News Media in Human Affairs* (White Plains, N.Y.: Longman, 1984), p. 287. Reprinted with permission.

Table 16.4

VIEWS ON PRESS FREEDOM

Market	Marxist	Advancing
A free press means that journalists are free of all outside controls	A free press means that the opinions of all people are published, not only those of the rich	A free press means freedom of conscience for journalists
A free press is one in which the press is not servile to power and is not manipulated by power	A free press is required to counter oppression	Press freedom is less important than the viability of the nation
No national press policy is needed to insure a free press	A national press policy is required to guarantee that a free press takes the correct form	A national press policy is needed to provide legal safeguards for freedom

From J. H. Altschull, *Agents of Power: The Role of the News Media in Human Affairs* (White Plains, N.Y.: Longman, 1984), p. 294. Reprinted with permission.

Altschull sums up:

> The history of the press demonstrates that newspapers and the more modern variations of the press have tended to serve the selfish interests of the paymasters, while at the same time perpetuating the image of a press operating in the service of the consumers of the news. To expect that the news media will make a dramatic U-turn and scoff at the wishes of the paymasters is to engage in the wildest kind of utopian fantasies. (1984, p. 299)

Functions of the Media

Harold Lasswell and Charles Wright are among the many scholars who have seriously considered the functions and role of the mass media in society. Wright (1959) defines mass communication in terms of the nature of the audience, the nature of the communication experience, and the nature of the communicator.

Lasswell (1948/1960), scholar of communication and professor of law at Yale, noted three functions of the mass media: surveillance of the environment, the correlation of the parts of society in responding to the environment, and the transmission of the social heritage from one generation to the next. To these three functions Wright (1959, p. 16) adds a fourth, entertainment. In addition to functions, the media may also have dysfunctions, consequences that are undesirable for the society or its members. A single act may be both functional and dysfunctional.

Surveillance, the first function, informs and provides news. In performing this function the media often warn us of expected dangers such as extreme or dangerous weather conditions or a threatening military situation. The surveillance function also includes the news the media provide that is essential to the economy, the public, and society, such as stock market reports, traffic reports, weather conditions, and so on.

The surveillance function can also cause several dysfunctions. Panic may result through the overemphasis of dangers or threats to the society. Lazarsfeld and Merton (1948/1960) have noted a "narcotizing" dysfunction when individuals fall into a state of apathy or passivity as a result of too much information to assimilate. Besides that, too much exposure to "news" (the unusual, abnormal, extraordinary) may leave many audience members with little perspective of what is the usual, normal, or ordinary in a society.

A good example of media surveillance is a story published at the time of the major Soviet nuclear accident at Chernobyl in 1986. The article described five U.S. reactors used to produce nuclear weapons that lack containment domes to trap escaping radiation. The article also described other major structural problems that, it was charged, could lead to a similar accident (Associated Press, May 1, 1986).

However, when Hurricane Gilbert threatened the Gulf Coast, "media coverage and other constant reminders gripped Houston not with panic, but with deep anxiety." Gayle Beck, a psychologist who runs a panic-disorder center at the University of Houston said,

> There's a range of ways people demonstrate that they're not merely scared, but scared to the bone—profoundly frightened. We were informed this is the largest storm in the history of civilization, or some such thing. That kind of thing makes people feel as if their usual methods of coping are insufficient. (Petzinger, 1988)

Correlation, the second function, is the selection and interpretation of information about the environment. The media often include criticism and prescribe how one should react to events. Correlation is thus the editorial and propaganda content of the media. The correlation function serves to enforce social norms and maintain consensus by exposing deviants, confers status by highlighting selected individuals, and can operate as a check on government. In carrying out the correlation function the media can often impede threats to social stability and may often monitor or manage public opinion.

The correlation function can become dysfunctional when the media perpetuate stereotypes and enhance conformity, impede social change and innovation, minimize criticism, enforce majority views at the expense of minority opinions that are not aired, and preserve and extend power that may need to be checked.

One of the frequently cited major dysfunctions of media correlation is the creation of what Daniel Boorstin has termed "pseudoevents" or the manufacture of "images" or "personalities"—much of the stock in trade of the public relations industry. Products and corporations are given "images," and individuals have public "personalities" manufactured for them through the creation of "events" contrived to gain media exposure. Aspiring politicians and entertainers seek exposure for public recognition and acceptance, and corporations seek a respected image and sought-after products and services.

John Wayne, known to the world as the stereotypical macho man and all-around tough guy, was filmed in dozens of western shoot-outs and military battles, yet he never served a day in the armed forces. Bing Crosby was a cool, reserved man whose image as a bright, friendly, cheerful movie star was projected and defended by Hollywood publicists (Scott, 1986).

In late October 1990, less than two days after the conclusion of the bruising congressional debates over the federal deficit reduction tax bill and only eight days before the 1990 congressional elections, U.S. representative J. J. Pickle of Austin, Texas, wearing a veterans' organization hat, spoke at the dedication of a new Veterans Administration outpatient medical clinic in Austin. However, the clinic was not scheduled to open until January 1991, more than two months later. This was clearly a pseudoevent, arranged for media coverage, which emphasized to voters that their congressman "delivers the goods." The dedication of the clinic, with Congressman Pickle speaking, was carried by local television stations, on the 5 P.M., 6 P.M., and 10 P.M. news. His television campaign commercials, on those same stations at the time, stressed his "effectiveness." An article in the *Austin American-Statesman* (October 29, 1990, p. B3), which carried a three-column headline, pointed out that Representative Pickle and Senator Phil Gramm, both scheduled to speak at the dedication and both campaigning for reelection, had joined efforts to bring the clinic to Austin despite federal budget cutbacks.

As *transmitters of culture,* the media function to communicate information, values, and norms from one generation to another or from the members of a society to newcomers. In this way they serve to increase social cohesion by widening the base of common experience. They aid the integration of individuals into a society by continuing socialization after formal education has ended as well as by beginning it during the preschool years. It has been noted that the media can reduce an individual's sense of estrangement (anomie) or feeling of rootlessness by providing a society to identify with.

However, because of the impersonal nature of the mass media, it has been charged that the media contribute to the depersonalization of society (a dysfunction). Mass media are interposed between individuals and remove personal contact in communication.

It has also been charged that the media serve to reduce the variety of subcultures and help augment mass society. This is the notion that because of the mass media, we tend more and more to speak the same way, dress the same way, think the same way, and act and react the same way. It is based on the idea that thousands of hours of media exposure cause millions of people to accept role models presented by the media. Along with this tendency for standardization goes the charge that the mass media impede cultural growth.

Probably most media content is intended as *entertainment*, even in newspapers, if one considers the many columns, features, and fillers. Media entertainment serves to provide respite from everyday problems and fills leisure time. The media expose millions to a mass culture of art and music, and some people contend that they raise public taste and preference in the arts. However, there are others who argue that the media encourage escapism, corrupt fine art, lower public taste, and prevent the growth of an appreciation for the arts. The various functions and dysfunctions of the media are summarized in Table 16.5.

Values and Ideology in Support of the Society

Harold Lasswell (1948/1960) pointed out that in every society, values that are shaped and distributed constitute an ideology in support of the network as a whole (1960, p. 123). He notes that in the ideological conflict of world politics, "the ruling elites view one another as potential enemies . . . [and] the ideology of the other may appeal to disaffected elements at home and weaken the internal power position of each ruling class" (1960, p. 124).

Lasswell adds that "one ruling element is especially alert to the other, and relies upon communication as a means of preserving power" (1960, p. 124). Discussing barriers to efficient communication in a society, Lasswell notes:

> Some of the most serious threats to efficient communication for the community as a whole relate to the values of power, wealth, and respect. Perhaps the most striking examples of power distortion occur when the content of communication is deliberately adjusted to fit an ideology or counterideology. Distortions related to wealth not only arise from attempts to influence the market, for instance, but from rigid conceptions of economic interest. A typical instance of inefficiencies connected with respect (social class) occurs when an upper class person mixes only with persons of his own stratum and forgets to correct his perspective by being exposed to members of other classes. (1960, pp. 126–127)

Ever larger segments of the U.S. mass media now strive for more "upscale" audiences (those with higher educations and incomes and more prestigious occupations) in order to attract the advertisers of "high-ticket" consumer products. In the process these media tailor their content to meet the interests of the upscale audiences they seek and, it is charged, fail to acknowledge the concerns, views, and perspective of other classes that Lasswell refers to. Often cited as a major cause of the urban riots that swept U.S. cities in the mid and late 1960s were the frustrations of minority members over their inability to communicate their grievances to the general population.

In the early 1980s, the editor of the *Detroit News* told his staff to aim stories at people aged 28 to 40 who earn more than $18,000 per year. The stories "won't have a damn thing to do with Detroit and its internal problems" (Holuska, 1982).

Nearly a decade later the president of the American Society of Newspaper Editors, Loren Ghiglione, at their annual convention, scolded editors for "looking at the world increasingly through the eyes of the comfortable." He said, "We often think of ourselves

Table 16.5

FUNCTIONAL ANALYSIS OF MASS COMMUNICATION BASED ON LASSWELL AND WRIGHT

Function	Dysfunction
1. Surveillance: informs, provides news	
Warning—natural dangers	Possibility of panic, overemphasis
Instrumental—news essential to economy, public, society	Narcotization—apathy, passivity, too much to assimilate
Exposure to norms—personalities, events	Overexposure, little perspective
2. Correlation: selects, interprets, criticizes	
Enforces social norms—consensus, exposes deviants	Enhances conformity, perpetuates stereotypes
Status conferral—opinion leaders	Creates pseudoevents, images, "personalities"
Impedes threats to social stability, panic	Impedes social change, innovation
Monitors, manages public opinion	Minimizes criticism, tyranny of majority
Checks on government, safeguards	Preserves, extends power
3. Transmission of culture: teaches	
Increases social cohesion—widens base of common experience	Reduces variety of subcultures, augments mass society
Reduces anomie—sense of estrangement	Depersonalizes, lack of personal contact
Continues socialization—before/after education, aids integration	Tendency for standardization, impedes cultural growth
4. Entertainment	
Private respite, escapism, fills leisure time	Encourages escapism, preoccupation with leisure
Creates mass culture—art, music—mass exposure	Corrupts fine art
Raises taste, preference	Lowers taste, impedes growth

Adapted from C. R. Wright, "Functional Analysis in Mass Communication, *Public Opinion Quarterly* 24 (1960): 605–620 (Winter). Also see: C. R. Wright, *Mass Communication: A Sociological Perspective*, pp. 4–6. 3rd ed. (New York: Random House, 1986); and H. D. Lasswell, "The Structure and Function of Communication in Society," in W. Schramm, *Mass Communication* (Urbana: University of Illinois Press, 1960), pp. 117–130.

as Davids, fighting the establishment, but the public sees us more as status-quo, establishment Goliaths" (Jones, 1990).

As the media use more "upscale" content, reporters, editors, camera operators, and news anchors are also more frequently drawn from the upper middle class, or aspire to it, and identify with the officials they cover. It is often charged that this identification and these aspirations bias their perspective on the society they report, often unconsciously. Media people usually vehemently deny this charge, but too often their reporting and editing betray them. One early-career local newspaper reporter, in a story about the crash of a jet from a nearby military base, wrote that it "was similar to Phantom rides given to journalists, civic leaders, and other important visitors" (Gamino, 1986). Presumably the copy and makeup editors agreed, at least subconsciously, since the quoted phrase appeared at the top center of page one, a position that normally comes under close editorial scrutiny.

Another example occurred during the Monday morning "debut" of a much-heralded co-anchor on the morning news of a national television network. That weekend had seen considerable violence by California growers during attempts by United Farm Workers representatives to organize field workers. After televising a sequence showing children harvesting crops under the hot August sun, the new co-anchor commented that she had always thought that "child labor" meant being sent to her room to tidy it up. This is not surprising since it came from someone who had only recently been a society reporter on a major metropolitan daily and whose father had been a career military officer and a general. However, to many her response indicated a lack of sensitivity to a serious social problem. It was made all the more poignant because that same news organization had, 13 years earlier, produced *the* classic documentary on migrant farm labor, "Harvest of Shame," narrated by Edward R. Murrow, the generally acknowledged "father of broadcast journalism."

In a documentary dealing with press coverage of a presidential primary, a national television network followed a candidate and the working press. The following comments by working reporters at a soup kitchen for the destitute, where a presidential candidate was to appear, were broadcast:

> "I'm just wondering whether they had to go out this morning and round up some winos to get in line."
>
> "What wine are they serving for lunch?"
>
> "That's what this guy said, this big guy. He gets our producer aside and he says, 'This is a shame, you people coming in here, the press, invading these people's privacy, these poor people, and so forth.'" ("Frontline," February 27, 1984).

In 1980 the owners of *Book Digest* magazine selectively cut the magazine's circulation from 1 million to 400,000 to concentrate on reaching only the higher-income readers. The selected audience has more appeal to advertisers and is less costly to serve. Donald A. Macdonald, vice chairman of Dow Jones, which was one of the magazine's owners, said, "It's a positive move because it will give us control over the magazine's demographics, which we haven't been particularly pleased with" (*Wall Street Journal,* June 4, 1980, p. 16).

In the past, television network officials strongly denied that the sponsors had any voice in the programs that were aired or their content. Either procedures have changed, or the industry has become much more candid in discussing its operations. The lead of a syndicated column about the season's forthcoming entertainment on one network read: "The nation's television critics are months away from reviewing the new fall shows, but CBS has been given an enthusiastic nod from the group whose criticism counts most: the sponsors" (Gendel, 1986).

The former network morning news, once produced by their news divisions, is now a group of shows under the jurisdiction of the entertainment divisions. These "infotainment" programs have very little of what has traditionally been regarded as news; instead they feature entertainment designed to attract the "upscale" audience that advertisers demand. The difference between hard realities and the content of the new infotainment "shows" is sometimes glaring.

This difference was especially apparent to correspondents covering the Philippine election campaign in early 1986. During that campaign hundreds of opposition workers were beaten by Ferdinand Marcos's forces and many were murdered. Veteran correspondents, both Philippine and foreign, risked their personal safety by traveling in the backcountry to report the story. Some correspondents traveled to remote islands to report on serious social problems, including the frequent death of babies in a hospital ward crowded with malnourished children on Negros Island.

In Manila correspondents' frustration mounted as it became apparent that many of the stories they were risking their lives for were not used in the U.S. media, while air time and space was filled with what many considered fluff and trivia.

Speaking of the flow of information within a society, Lasswell says:

> When the ruling classes fear the masses, the rulers do not share their picture of reality with the rank and file. When the reality picture of kings, presidents, and cabinets is not permitted to circulate through the state as a whole, the degree of discrepancy shows the extent to which the ruling groups assume that their power depends upon distortion.
>
> Or to express the matter another way: If the "truth" is not shared, the ruling elements expect internal conflict, rather than harmonious adjustment to the external environment of the state. Hence the channels of communication are controlled in the hope of organizing the attention of the community at large in such a way that only responses will be forthcoming which are deemed favorable to the power position of the ruling classes. (1960, p. 129)

The revelations contained in the "Pentagon Papers" of truths about the Vietnam War not shared with the American public are a good example of the point Lasswell makes. Another example is the continuing struggle for economic and political control of the Corporation for Public Broadcasting. In violation of the basic principles established in the 1967 act that created the corporation, Congress, presidents Nixon and Reagan, and a number of economic and political groups have used a wide variety of methods to influence content and eliminate views different from their own. These have included attempts to eliminate all government funding for public broadcasting (Wicklein, 1986).

Under present funding and administration, corporate sponsors select many of PBS's programs. "Great Performances" programs are picked by Exxon programmers; miniseries for "Masterpiece Theater" are selected by Mobil programmers. AT&T chose to sponsor the "MacNeil/Lehrer NewsHour" (considered a "safe" public affairs program) because they want to be identified as the electronic information source for the nation. Station managers were unable to see the need for "the nation's first hour-long news program" but quickly changed their minds when AT&T offered them $10 million (Wicklein, 1986, pp. 32–33).

Our Mental Picture of the World

The distinguished political columnist Walter Lippmann, writing in his classic *Public Opinion* (1922), discussed the discrepancy between the world and the "realities" we perceive and act upon. He pointed out that most of what we know of the environment we live in comes to us indirectly, but "whatever we believe to be a true picture, we treat as if it were the environment itself" (p. 4). Lippmann pointed out that although we find it hard to apply this notion to the beliefs upon which we are now acting, it becomes easy to apply it to other people and other ages and to the ludicrous pictures of the world about which they were in dead earnest.

Fictions and symbols, aside from their value to the existing social order, are important to human communication. Nearly every individual deals with events that are out of sight and hard to grasp. Lippmann observes, "The only feeling that anyone can have about an event he does not experience is the feeling aroused by his mental image of that event." He adds that at certain times we respond as powerfully to fictions as to realities, and often we help create those fictions. In every case there has been inserted between us and the environment a pseudoenvironment, and it is to this pseudoenvironment that we respond. If these responses are acts, they are in the real environment, not the pseudoenvironment that stimulated them. For this reason, Lippmann says, "what is called the adjustment of man to his environment takes place through the medium of fictions" (pp. 13, 15).

Lippmann does not mean that these fictions are lies but rather that we react to a representation of an environment that we manufacture ourselves. We do this because the real environment is too big, too complex, and too fleeting for direct experience. (See Chapter 5 on abstraction.) To act on the environment we must reconstruct it as a simpler model before we are able to deal with it.

Lippmann then discusses "the world-wide spectacle of men acting upon their environment, moved by stimuli from their pseudo-environments" (p. 20). These actions can result in commands " . . . which set armies in motion or make peace, conscript life, tax, exile, imprison, protect property or confiscate it, encourage one kind of enterprise and discourage another, facilitate immigration or obstruct it, improve communication or censor it, establish schools, build navies, proclaim "policies," and "destiny," raise economic barriers, make property or unmake it, bring one people under the rule of another, or favor one class against another" (pp. 20, 21).

What we do, then, is not based on certain and direct knowledge but on our pictures of the world, usually provided by someone else. The way we imagine the world determines what we do, our efforts, feelings, and hopes, but not our achievements or results. Propaganda, Lippmann points out, is an effort to alter the pictures to which we respond.

A good example of Lippmann's "men acting upon their environment moved by stimuli from their pseudo-environments" is when American grain and livestock futures speculators bid up prices by the maximum amount allowed daily on U.S. commodity markets immediately upon hearing only the most fragmentary news of a Soviet nuclear accident in the Ukraine, the "breadbasket" of the USSR. They were speculating that the accident would force the Soviet Union to make large foreign purchases of agricultural products.

In *Public Opinion*, Lippmann deals with the reasons why pictures inside our heads often mislead us in our dealings with the outside world. Among the factors that limit our access to the facts he lists the following: censorship, limitations of social contact, meager time available each day for paying attention to public affairs, distortions as a result of compressing events into short messages (abstraction), the use of a small vocabulary to describe a complex world (Chapter 5), and the fear of facing facts that threaten our lives (Chapter 8).

Popular Taste and Social Action

In an article titled "Mass Communication, Popular Taste, and Organized Social Action" (1948/1960), two well-known and respected communication researchers and sociologists, Paul F. Lazarsfeld and Robert K. Merton, raise several important questions about the use of the media in our society. One of the major concerns they express is use of the mass media by powerful interest groups to exercise social control. They point out that organized business, which "occupies the most spectacular place" among the chief power groups, has replaced the more direct means of control of mass publics through the use of propaganda called "public relations." The authors say:

> Economic power seems to have reduced direct exploitation, achieved largely by disseminating propaganda through the mass media of communication. . . . The radio program and the institutional advertisement serve in place of intimidation and coercion . . . media have taken on the job of rendering mass publics conformative to the social and economic status quo. (1948, pp. 96–97; 1960, pp. 493–494)

A good example of this occurred in late 1990 when the Exxon Corporation gave the Alaska Visitors Association $7 million to win back potential tourists still scared away by the 1989 oil spill. Had Exxon run commercials claiming that Prince William Sound is "nearly recovered" and "nearly restored" it would have invited skepticism. Instead, Exxon gave tax-deductible dollars, written off as a business expense, to the Alaska Visitors Association, an innocuous-sounding group with greater credibility (Creed, 1990).

Lazarsfeld and Merton then go on to discuss several of the functions of the media: status conferral; enforcement of social norms; and the narcotizing dysfunction.

Status conferral, or recognition by the mass media, indicates that one is important enough to single out from the mass and that one's behavior and opinions are significant enough to demand media attention. By legitimating the status of individuals and groups the media confer status and prestige.

The mass media may enforce social norms as a result of their "exposure" of conditions that deviate from professed public morality. Publicity forces members of a group to acknowledge that these deviations have occurred and requires that individuals take a stand. A person is forced to choose between repudiating the norm and being identified as outside the moral framework or supporting the norms, whatever his or her private beliefs. Lazarsfeld and Merton say, "Publicity closes the gap between 'private attitudes' and 'public morality'" (1948, p. 103). By preventing continued evasion of an issue, publicity brings about pressure for a single rather than a dual morality. The mass media reaffirm social norms by publicly exposing deviations from them.

The authors observe that another consequence of the mass media is a "narcotizing" of the average reader or listener as a result of the flood of media stimuli. They call this the "narcotizing dysfunction" on the assumption that it is not in society's best interest to have a large portion of the population apathetic and inert. The authors suggest that the result of a flood of communications may be a superficial concern with problems and that this superficiality may cloak mass apathy. The interested and informed individual may know about the problems of the society without recognizing that he or she has failed to make decisions and do something about them. In this way, the authors say, mass media are among the most respectable and efficient of social narcotics, and increasing dosages may be transforming our energies from active participation to passive knowledge (pp. 105–106).

Social Conformism

In much of Western society the media are supported by the corporate business world as a result of the social and economic system. The media, in turn, support that system. Lazarsfeld and Merton note that this support comes not only in the form of advertising but also in the content of the media, which usually confirms and approves the present structure of society. In their words, "this continuing reaffirmation underscores the duty to accept" (1948, p. 107).

The authors charge that this comes about not only through what is said but, more important, from what is not said, for the media "fail to raise essential questions about the structure of society." The authors say that the commercially sponsored media provide little basis for the critical appraisal of society and "restrain the cogent development of a genuinely critical outlook" (p. 107). They note that there are occasional critical articles or programs but that they are so few that they are overwhelmed by the tide of conformist materials.

They note that social objectives are abandoned by commercial media when those objectives interfere with profits and that this economic pressure results in conformity by omitting sensitive issues (p. 108).

George F. Kennan, former United States ambassador to the Soviet Union, charged that the media caused a prolongation of the cold war through their lack of critical analysis because they have become bland as a result of the influence of advertising ("MacNeil/Lehrer NewsHour," Dec. 23, 1988).

Conditions of Media Effectiveness

Lazarsfeld and Merton say three conditions are required for media effectiveness: monopolization; canalization rather than change of basic values; and supplementary face-to-face contact.

Monopolization occurs in the absence of mass media counterpropaganda. It exists not only in authoritarian societies but also in any society in which there is an absence of countering views on any issue, value, policy, or public image. Sometimes this near or complete absence is illustrated by the fact that when a "sacred" institution is questioned by the media, the article or program becomes the center of a storm of controversy and is remembered years later as an outstanding exception to the norm. An example is the CBS documentary "The Selling of the Pentagon," which raised the question of what were termed "improper military information activities."

Many critics of the documentary generalized their criticism and said the program was an attack on the entire military when in fact it dealt only with military public relations programs.

Other memorable exceptions to the prevailing norm that raised storms of protest were the CBS documentaries "Harvest of Shame," dealing with migrant farm labor, and "Hunger in America," as well as the PBS documentaries "Who Invited US?" which questioned U.S. foreign policy, and "Banks and the Poor" (Brown, 1971, pp. 328–332).

Critics observe that the commercial television networks have, in their quest for higher ratings and upscale audiences, largely abandoned the controversial hard-hitting documentaries of the past.

Bill Moyers, known nationally for his television documentaries, said:

> Our center of gravity shifted from the standards and practices of the news business to show business. . . . It is no coincidence that in an era when the president says, "America's back," CBS News's promotional campaign is "We keep America on top of the world." That's what happens when you decide not to examine your culture but to flatter it. (*Newsweek*, Sept. 15, 1986, p. 53)

The spread of cable and videocassettes has caused a decline in network audience shares and a loss of revenue. As a result the networks have cut expenditures, including those for documentaries. An article about network cost cutting observes:

> Back when the networks were fat and happy . . . [there] was a strong commitment to news and public affairs programming. CBS used to maintain two-dozen full-time documentary makers; they now have one. In the place of thoughtful, sometimes ponderous and usually low-rated documentaries have come magazine shows . . . and snappy instant documentaries . . . specifically designed to perform in the ratings. (Boyer, 1986, pp. 1, 28)

Many other underlying assumptions, issues, policies, and values are dealt with only peripherally, if at all. The television documentary "The Business of Religion" questioned some aspects of some religions, but the larger question of the overall value of religion in society is seldom, if ever, discussed in the major media. During recent years the media have increasingly questioned business methods without ever questioning the underlying assumptions—for example, the private ownership of natural resources. Whatever the intent of the framers of the First Amendment, whatever the arguments of the Enlightenment that truth will win out in the marketplace of ideas, whatever the logic of Mill in his arguments for the liberty of thought and discussion, including the idea that beliefs not vigorously defended lose their vitality, many basic assumptions that underlie society are never questioned or challenged in any meaningful way.

Lazarsfeld and Merton point out that advertising usually attempts to "canalize" existing patterns of behavior or attitudes. It often attempts to get the consumer to switch brands of a product he or she is already habituated to use, be it toothpaste or automobiles. Once a pattern of behavior or an attitude has been established, it can be canalized in one direction or another. Propaganda, in contrast, usually deals with more complex matters. Its objectives may be at odds with deep-seated attitudes that must be reshaped, rather than the simple canalizing of existing value systems. The authors conclude that although the mass media have been effective in canalizing basic attitudes, there is little evidence of their bringing about attitude change by themselves.

Lazarsfeld and Merton cite a third condition: supplementation through face-to-face contacts. Here mass media that are neither monopolistic nor canalizing may, nevertheless, prove effective. The authors cite Father Coughlin, who combined propagandistic radio talks with local organizations. Members listened to him and then followed his radio talks with group discussions of the views he had expressed. The combination of radio talks, the distribution of newspapers and pamphlets, and the coordinated locally organized small discussion groups, all reinforcing one another, proved especially successful. ("Media forums" were discussed in Chapter 11.)

Such combinations of the mass media and reinforcing discussion groups are expensive and are usually found only in cases of planned change in the service of the status quo or in the case of the diffusion of innovation in developing countries. Often such combinations of mass media and discussion groups are used in political systems where central authorities have almost total control. These systems are then used to implement policies and directives from the central leadership. As Lazarsfeld and Merton point out, such media and discussion group collaboration has seldom been achieved by groups trying to bring about social change in modern industrial society. They say, "The forward looking groups at the edges of the power structure do not ordinarily have the large financial means of the contented groups at the center" (1948, p. 117).

The authors add, "Organized business does approach a virtual 'psychological monopoly' of the mass media. Radio commercials and newspaper advertisements are, of course, premised on a system which has been termed free enterprise." They close by saying, "Face-to-face contacts with those who have been socialized in our culture serve primarily to reinforce the prevailing culture patterns." (Indeed, when those contacts do not do so, we often suffer the psychological discomfort of dissonance discussed in Chapter 8.) "Thus," the authors conclude, "the very conditions which make for the maximum effectiveness of the mass media of communication operate toward the maintenance of the ongoing social and cultural structure rather than toward its change" (p. 118).

One has only to look critically at the myriad of "special sections" that bloat most metropolitan dailies or fill local newscasts to see that the media are designed for merchants, not consumers. The only exceptions seem to be those that critique books, films, the performing arts, and restaurants. The largest single purchase for most people is a house. The real estate or housing section of most Sunday newspapers is filled not only with ads but with "editorial" content that is, more often than not, puffery for local developers, builders, and real estate agents. One finds here articles that are, in fact, public relations handouts extolling the virtues of various housing developments or the benefits of using agents in home purchases and sales. Rare indeed is the housing section that *critiques* designs, floor plans, quality of construction, subdivision planning, cost compared to value offered, financing available, or other relevant matters. The same can be said for the automotive, food, fashion, and travel sections. One is hard pressed to find a travel article in which the waiters were not unfailingly prompt, the natives uniformly cheerful, the service completely efficient, the accommodations totally comfortable, the costs entirely reasonable, and the skies ever sunny and blue.

The business community complains that in recent years the media have become increasingly biased against business. One group of academic business researchers investigated the attitudes of newspaper business editors toward capitalism (Peterson, Albaum, Kozmetsky, & Cunningham, 1984). Based on 454 usable questionnaires returned by newspaper business and financial editors, the researchers concluded:

> The newspaper business editors surveyed are not only positively disposed toward capitalism in an absolute sense; as a group they are more favorably disposed toward capitalism than is the general public. . . . the editors report their attitude toward business has become more positive in recent years and their overwhelming belief that capitalism is compatible with freedom of the press. . . . the more experience a survey participant possesses as an

editor, the more positive that individual's attitude toward capitalism. . . . editors not favorably disposed toward capitalism may serve in that occupational capacity for only a relatively short period of time. (p. 65)

Enduring Values in the News

Sociologist Herbert J. Gans argues that "the news does not limit itself to reality judgments; it also contains values, or preference statements" (Gans, 1979, p. 40). He says that underlying the news in the United States is a picture of the nation and society as the media think it ought to be. These values are rarely explicit and must be inferred because journalists do not, in most instances, insert these values into the news.

Gans calls these *enduring values* and says they can be found in many different kinds of news stories over a long period of time. Often, he says, they help define news and affect what activities become news.

From a continual scrutiny of the news he identified eight enduring values (see Table 16.6). They emerged from the way events were described, the tone used in stories, and the connotations of verbs, nouns, and adjectives commonly used by journalists.

The first of Gans's enduring values is *ethnocentrism* (the attitude that one's own race, nation, or culture is superior to all others), as, he observes, is the case for other countries. This, he says, is most explicit in foreign news, which evaluates others by the extent to

Table 16.6
GANS'S ENDURING VALUES IN THE NEWS

Ethnocentrism	to value one's own nation above all others (most explicit in foreign news)
Altruistic Democracy	news implies that politics should be based on the public interest and service
Responsible Capitalism	news implies that business people will refrain from unreasonable profits and gross exploitation of workers or customers
Small-Town Pastoralism	favoring of small towns over other types of settlements (including the desirability of nature and smallness per se)
Individualism	preservation of the freedom of the individual against the encroachments of nation and society
Moderatism	discouragement of excess or extremism (violations of the law, the dominant mores, or enduring values)
Order	respect for authority and relevant enduring values; concern for social cohesion
Leadership	moral and otherwise competent leadership; honest and candid, with vision, physical stamina, and courage

Adapted from H. J. Gans, "The Messages Behind the News," *Columbia Journalism Review,* Jan.-Feb. 1979, pp. 40–45.

which they follow American values and practices. He adds that the news carries many stories critical of domestic conditions, but only as deviations from American ideals.

The clearest expression of ethnocentrism in all countries, says Gans, is war news. For example, atrocities committed by one's own forces do not often get into the news. For nearly two years the American mass media did not use the pictures of the Mylai massacre in which American soldiers were later found guilty of having murdered at least 109 un-armed civilian prisoners. Only after a former GI, Ron Ridenhour, began a letter-writing campaign to members of Congress and an investigation into the massacre was opened were the pictures finally given national exposure, 20 months after the actual event (*Life*, Dec. 5, 1969). Seymour M. Hersh, the reporter who finally broke the story, detailed the refusals he got at *Life* and *Look* as well as Ron Ridenhour's earlier refusal by *Life* before the story was finally made public, even though photographs were available (Hersh, 1969). Finally, the story and photos of the Mylai massacre were first published on Nov. 20, 1969, in a daily newspaper, the *Cleveland Plain Dealer*.

Domestic news stresses *altruistic democracy*, according to Gans. Domestic news indicates how American democracy should perform by frequently citing deviations from un-stated ideals. This can be seen in stories of corruption, conflict, protest, and bureaucratic malfunctioning. However, Gans says, the news is selective when it keeps track of violations of official norms. While the media have been concerned with freedom of the press and related civil liberties, it has not been as concerned with the violations of the civil liberties of radicals, of due process, of habeas corpus, and of other constitutional protections, particularly for criminals.

In one city a television reporter interviewed several former mayors for a series titled "Water Woes," dealing with the lack of pumping, filtration, and distribution facilities. She allowed them to blame the shortages on the voters who had, over the previous decade, rejected several bond issues. At no time in the series did the reporter allude to the fact that for more than a decade in that city there had been strong opposition to rapid population growth. At no time did she ask why the city had continued, for more than a decade, to issue building permits after the voters had rejected utility bonds. The long-time control of the city council by developers and builders was never mentioned (KTBC-TV, Oct. 2-3, 1985).

Although the media are consistent in reporting political and legal failures in achieving altruistic and official democracy, the press concerns itself much less with the economic barriers that prevent its realization, according to Gans. The media, he says, pay little attention to the relationship between poverty and powerlessness or to the difficulty that middle-class Americans have in gaining political access. There is an assumption, according to Gans, that the polity and the economy are separate and independent of each other. Private industry's intervention in the government is, typically, not viewed as seriously as government intervention in the economy. As a result, the news rarely notes the extent of public subsidy to private interests.

The enduring news value of *responsible capitalism* is, according to Gans, "an optimistic faith that, in the good society, businessmen and women will compete with each other . . . but that they will refrain from unreasonable profits and gross exploitation of workers or customers" (1979, p. 41). He says that there is little explicit or implicit criticism of the oligopolistic nature of much of today's economy.

One daily newspaper in Texas ran a wire service story that reported on "oil firms that cheat the government by underestimating their oil production on federal land. The cheating is estimated to cost the United States as much as a half-billion dollars annually in lost royalties." However, the newspaper headline on the story was "Oil Firms That *Skimp* on Federal Royalties" (*Austin American-Statesman,* Jan. 22, 1982, p. 1) (emphasis added). *Cheat* on or *steal* would have easily fit the headline space and would have been far more accurate.

Gans points out that "'welfare cheaters' are a continuing menace and are more newsworthy than people, other than the very rich, who cheat on their taxes" (1979, p. 42). A recent exception to this are the scandals in the financial industries in 1990, although some critics claim the media reported them only after they were exposed by government agencies.

Buried in one newspaper was the report that only 16.3 percent of the state's half-million jobless were receiving any unemployment benefits, the lowest among the 11 most populous states. The last paragraph said that only 1.5 percent of the state's work force was covered by unemployment insurance (*Daily Texan,* Nov. 6, 1985, p. 14).

In reporting on the Internal Revenue Service's desire to close tax loopholes, Jane Bryant Quinn said the IRS estimated that at that time only 3 percent of wages were unreported, while 30 percent of self-employment income, 50 percent of rents, and 22 percent of capital gains went unreported for tax purposes (CBS, Mar. 4, 1983). Seldom do the media mention that "the richest one-half percent of American families own over 40 percent of all corporate stock and virtually control corporate America" (*ISR Newsletter,* 1986–87). Frequent citation of such data in the media would imply criticism of the "upscale" segments of the population, although some media discussion of this occurred during the debates on tax revision in late 1990. These are the very segments the media want as readers and viewers, those with the large discretionary incomes that the media's advertisers want to reach.

Other enduring values that Gans cites are *small town pastoralism,* or a favoring of small towns over other types of settlements; *individualism,* the preservation of the freedom of the rugged individualist against the encroachments of society and the nation; *moderatism,* the discouragement of excess or extremism; *order,* both moral and social, including disapproval of any rejection of prevailing ethics or rules; and *leadership,* the method of maintaining moral and social order.

Gans contends that the news contains not only values but also ideology, even if it consists of ideas that are only partly thought out. He calls "this aggregate of values and the *reality judgments* associated with it paraideology, partly to distinguish it from the deliberate, integrated, and more doctrinaire set of values usually defined as ideology; it is ideology nevertheless" (1979, p. 45) (emphasis added). He says that the beliefs that are reflected in the news are neither liberal nor conservative but actually professional values, especially the reformist value or the belief "in honest, fair, and competent public and private institutions and leaders." Reports of violations of this value anger those in power, whether they be liberal or conservative (Gans, 1985, p. 32).

Making News: The Social Construction of Reality

Sociologist Gaye Tuchman, in her book *Making News* (1978), contends that news is the social construction of reality. The book is based on a series of participant observations in media newsrooms and interviews of newspeople over a period of 10 years. The act of making news, Tuchman says, is the act of constructing reality itself rather than a picture of reality (p. 12). She asserts that the news is an ally of legitimated institutions and that it also legitimates the status quo. Tuchman links news professionalism and news organizations to the emergence of corporate capitalism. She argues that news is a social resource whose construction limits an analytic understanding of contemporary life (p. 215). She contends that "through its routine practices and the claims of news professionals to arbitrate knowledge and to present factual accounts, news legitimates the status quo" (p. 14).

Jim Fox, former city editor of the *St. Louis Post-Dispatch*, is quoted as saying: "On any given day of publication, there are only about six stories that have to be printed. The rest are chosen by editorial whim. Life could go on if most stories were not printed" (Fox, 1982).

According to writer Mark Dowie, ABC News "spiked" three hard-hitting exposés before the 1984 presidential elections. "The selection and editing process is designed to produce, along with news and entertainment, an aura of objectivity." All three stories were about powerful Republicans: the U.S. Information Agency director, the secretary of labor, and a powerful Republican senator. "ABC had spent tens of thousands of dollars and hundreds of work hours on each of them. Reporters and crews were flown around the country on investigations that lasted for months" (Dowie, 1985, p. 34). He argues that all three stories had merit, importance, and news value, yet none of the three stories was aired.

A review of Dowie's article in one journalism review concluded:

> He ascribes the three instances of self-censorship . . . to some impersonal yet perceptible corporate "tone" that filtered on down to everyone in the company, including those at ABC News. The tone, Dowie asserts, was dictated by the company's vital economic interest in keeping Laxalt (who as chairman of the Senate appropriations subcommittee had the power to influence legislation affecting the FCC) in Congress, and in keeping the FCC in Republican hands. (As things turned out, of course, the FCC did make a much-lobbied-for revision in the ownership rule, a revision so crucial to ABC's attractiveness to a potential buyer that a clause in its merger agreement with Capital Cities Communications stated that if the new rule did not actually go into effect, the deal was off.)
>
> Although his story this time deals with ABC, similar pressures, Dowie depressingly observes, can be felt in any newsroom owned by a company with bottom-line interests in government decisions, and especially in broadcast deregulation. Undeniably, money talks, and sometimes the message is to just shut up. ("Discretionary Journalism," 1986)

Controlling the News Staff and Maintaining the Status Quo

Why and how media maintain news and editorial policy was explored in two articles by Warren Breed, former newspaper reporter, Columbia Ph.D., and long-time faculty member at Tulane University. In "Social Control in the Newsroom" (1955), Breed explored the areas in which news and editorial policy is usually maintained and where it is bypassed. Breed observed that the newspaper publisher, as owner or a representative of ownership, has the right to set and enforce the newspaper's policy. However, conformity is not automatic.

By *policy* Breed means the orientation shown by a newspaper in its editorials, news columns, and headlines regarding certain issues and events. "Slanting" almost never means prevarication, Breed points out, but rather it is the "omission, differential selection, and preferential placement, such as 'featuring' a pro-policy item, 'burying' an anti-policy story, etc." (1955, p. 327). Breed contends that every newspaper, whether it admits it or not, has a policy. Politics, business, and labor are the major areas of policy, much of which results from considerations of class. Breed points out that policy is usually covert because it is often against the ethical norms of journalism and media executives want to avoid being embarrassed by accusations that they have ordered the slanting of a news story.

An example of burying a story negative about business is one that told about "America's richest and most sophisticated real-estate investors" worried "that too many of the country's savings and loan associations and commercial banks have abused their federal insurance charters to finance office buildings, hotels, and housing projects that will go belly up before the end of the decade." It was run on page 4 of section E on a Saturday (Harney, 1985). Within three years the newspaper that buried this item found itself in the midst of the biggest savings and loan crisis in the history of the United States.

Martin Feldstein, president of the National Bureau of Economic Research, observed on the "Nightly Business Report" that local newspapers were not reporting on the riskiness of local savings and loans (March 20, 1989). He added that if there were no 100 percent depositor's insurance (i.e., coinsurance) in an institution's failure, individuals would have some of their own money at risk and would be more interested in the management of local savings and loan companies.

Because of the covert nature of policy a new reporter cannot be told what the policy is but must learn to anticipate what is expected in order to win rewards and avoid punishments. Since policy is never made explicit, a new reporter learns policy in a number of indirect ways. First, the staffer reads the newspaper every day and learns to diagnose its characteristics. Usually his or her own output is patterned after that of newsroom colleagues. The newcomer's stories tend to reflect what is defined as standard procedure. The editing of a newcomer's copy is another guide to what is or is not acceptable. Occasionally a staffer may, in an oblique way, be reprimanded. The implication is that punishment will follow if policy is not adhered to.

Through gossip among staffers and by other means the new reporter learns of the interests, affiliations, and characteristics of the executives. Conferences at which the staffer outlines findings and executives discuss how to shape a story offer insight through what the executives say and do not say. Again, policy is not stated explicitly. Other sources of information for staffers about executives are house organs, observation of executives in meetings with various leaders, and opinions executives voice in unguarded moments.

In 1990, the publisher of the *Austin American-Statesman,* Roger Kintzel, was also the chairman of the Greater Austin Chamber of Commerce. Observers commented on the seeming lack of objective reporting about the drive to woo the computer chip-making consortium U.S. Memories to Austin with large tax concessions and other inducements (Forrest, 1989).

Apparently stung by criticism, the newspaper ran a long article defending this seeming conflict of interest (Ladendorf, 1990). Among other things, the article said:

> Even before he officially took over as 1990 chairman of the Greater Austin Chamber of Commerce, his appointment was being criticized as an unholy alliance between the *Austin American-Statesman* and the business establishment. . . .
>
> In this case, the concern was whether Kintzel's responsibilities at the chamber of commerce would influence the paper's coverage of business-related issues.

A conflict would not occur, Kintzel maintained, because he would not allow one to exist. . . .
"It's very easy for me to keep those things separate," he said. "I'm surprised that people should think that I would feel the need to manage the news because of a one-year volunteer job at the chamber."
There is no compromising the integrity of the newspaper."
End of subject. (p. H1)

Two years earlier, a veteran high-tech reporter, Kathleen Sullivan, who was a skeptic, not a booster, at that same Austin daily, lost her job. When Sullivan reported about worker safety and health problems at a big Austin semiconductor chip manufacturer after an unreported fire and a chemical leak, she angered a local power broker. When she reported the public and private incentives used to lure Sematech, a federally funded consortium to improve the manufacture of computer chips, the power broker reportedly complained to the publisher, Kintzel, who had been deputy vice chairman of the chamber of commerce's economic development council that the power broker chaired. As she was finishing a story critical of another Austin high-tech company, Sullivan was forced to resign for reasons the paper won't explain and "was offered $8,000 if she would promise not to criticize the paper, sue it, use the notes she had gathered at the *Statesman* for future stories" (Curtis, 1988). Three weeks after she left the *Statesman,* Sullivan was hired for the high-tech beat for the *San Francisco Examiner* (Shahin, 1988). One of Sullivan's early stories for the *Examiner,* that the Austin Dell Computer Company's top-selling computer did not comply with Federal Communications Commission standards for radio frequency emissions, is one she claims was squelched by the *Statesman* (Shahin & Forest, 1988).

Breed lists a number of reasons a staffer conforms to policy. The publisher's power to fire or demote is one. However, editors have many opportunities to prevent a situation from reaching this point. Editors can ignore stories that allow for deviation from policy, or, if the story cannot be ignored, it can be assigned to a "safe" reporter. Should a story reach an editor in an unacceptable form, it can be edited, and reasons other than policy—such as pressures of time and space—can be given.

New reporters may feel obligation and esteem toward the people who hired them, helped show them the ropes, or did them other favors. Breed says that these "obligations and warm personal sentiments toward superiors play a strategic role in the pull to conformity" (1955, p. 330). This factor seems to determine not only conformity to policy but morale and good news policy as well.

The desires that most young staffers have for status achievement are another reason for conforming to policy. Many reporters noted that a good path for advancement is to get big page one stories, and this means stories that do not oppose policy. Many staffers view newspapering as a stepping stone to more lucrative positions, and a reputation as a "troublemaker" is a serious hurdle.

Among the other reasons for conformity to policy that Breed notes are the absence of conflicting group allegiance, the pleasant nature of the activity (e.g., the in-groupness in the newsroom, the interesting nature of the work, nonfinancial perquisites), and the fact that news becomes a value and is a continuous challenge.

Through these many factors the new staffer identifies with veteran staffers and executives. Because of shared norms, the newcomer's performance soon emulates theirs. The new staffer usually learns rapidly to put aside personal beliefs or ethical ideals brought to the job and to conform to policy norms.

Possibilities for Policy Deviation

There are situations that permit deviations from policy. Because policy is covert, its norms are not always entirely clear. If policy were spelled out explicitly, motivations, reasons, alternatives, and other complicating material would have to be provided. Because policies are not spelled out, a reporter often has an undefined zone that allows a certain amount of freedom.

Staffers who gather the news can use their superior knowledge of a story to subvert policy because executives may be ignorant of particular facts. Staffers are in a position to make decisions at many points. If a staffer cannot get "play" for a story because it violates policy, the story can be "planted" through a friendly staffer with a competitor. The reporter can then argue that the story has become too big to ignore.

Staffers covering "beats" (police, fire, city hall, courts, etc.) have greater leeway in deciding which stories to cover and which to ignore than those working on individual assignments from the editor. Beat reporters can sometimes ignore stories that would support policies they dislike or feel run counter to professional codes. Of course, this is possible only if potential competitors cooperate. And as one might expect, reporters who are considered "stars" can more often violate policy than others.

Breed contends that to the extent that policy is maintained, the existing system of power relationships is maintained. He says, "Policy usually protects property and class interests, and thus the strata and groups holding these interests are better able to retain them" (1955, p. 334). Although much news is printed objectively so that the community can form opinions openly, important information is often denied the citizenry when policy news is buried or slanted.

Breed concludes that because the newsperson's source of rewards is from colleagues and superiors rather than from readers, the staffer abandons societal and professional ideals in favor of the more pragmatic level of newsroom values. The staffer thereby gains both status rewards and group acceptance. Breed says:

> Thus the cultural patterns of the newsroom produce results insufficient for wider democratic needs. Any important change toward a more "free and responsible press" must stem from various possible pressures on the publisher, who epitomizes the policy making and coordinating role. (1955, p. 335)

One of the often-stated reasons for the urban riots by minorities in the 1960s was the feeling that their grievances were not being communicated to the general public. They recognized correctly, of course, that before one can hope for change the problem must be recognized. Since that time this has come to be called "consciousness raising."

Thirteen years after the publication of Breed's article, the *Report of the National Advisory Commission on Civil Disorders* (the Kerner Report) said this about media coverage of urban minority grievances:

> Our second and fundamental criticism is that the news media have failed to analyze and report adequately on racial problems in the United States and, as a related matter, to meet the Negro's legitimate expectations in journalism. By and large, news organizations have failed to communicate to both their black and white audiences a sense of the problems America faces and the sources of potential solutions. The media report and write from the standpoint of the white man's world. The ills of the ghetto, the difficulties of life there, the Negro's burning sense of grievance, are seldom conveyed. Slights and indignities are part

of the Negro's daily life, and many of them come from what he now calls "the white press"—a press that repeatedly, if unconsciously, reflects the biases, the paternalism, the indifference of white America. This may be understandable, but it is not excusable in an institution that has the mission to inform and educate the whole of our society. (NACCD, 1968, p. 366)

Mass Communication and Sociocultural Integration

In a second article, Warren Breed (1958) looked at the ways in which the media function to maintain the status quo. He points out that in a conflict of values the mass media sometimes sacrifice accurate reporting of significant events for the virtues of respect for convention, public decency, and orderliness. Breed observes that newspapers generally speak well of the hometown and its leaders. Most of his examples are concerned with protecting the dominant values and interests of American society.

Breed begins by observing that a major problem for any society is the maintenance of order and social cohesion, including consensus over a value system. He quotes E. C. Devereau: "Such head-on conflicts are prevented also by various barriers to communication embedded in the social structure; taboo'd areas simply are not to be discussed, and hence the conflict need not be 'faced'" (1958, p. 109).

A good example is illustrated by a conversation one of the authors of this book had with a middle-aged black parking attendant while writing this chapter. The author, summoned to jury duty, observed the number of spaces reserved for the media in the county court's parking garage. The attendant, without prompting, observed, "The court gives them parking space so they will keep certain things out of the papers." Correct or incorrect, this was that man's perception of reality. The predominantly white, middle-class media make a mistake if they believe that the poor and uneducated do not make such observations.

A rather dramatic example of "taboo'd areas" can be seen in the paucity of media discussion about the inequities of the draft during the Vietnam War, even after the war ended. In most cases the sons of the middle class went to college while the sons of the poor went to Asia. In a rare and unusually candid article one writer, James Fallows (1976), described how in his senior year at an Ivy League university the draft lottery had been instituted and his number indicated that he would probably be called for military service. He and his fellow students devised ways to escape service while the less sophisticated lads from across town were being drafted wholesale. Fallows concluded:

> Our heritage from Vietnam is rich with potential for class hatred. World War II forced different classes of people to live together; Vietnam kept them rigidly apart, a process in which people like me were only too glad to cooperate. . . . Among those who went to war, there is a residual resentment, the natural result of a cool look at who ended up paying what price. On the part of those who were spared, there is a residual guilt often so deeply buried that it surfaces only in unnaturally vehement denials that there is anything to feel guilty about. (p. 14)

The Reverend Theodore M. Hesburgh, president of the University of Notre Dame, in the foreword to a book dealing with this topic, wrote:

> The great bulk of all those Americans deeply scarred by Vietnam were those already economically, socially, and educationally disadvantaged. They not only carried the burden of the fighting and dying, they now bear the lion's share of the penalties occasioned by the

war and its aftermath. One often hears shocked people excoriating the President for pardoning deserters, but do these self-righteous critics ever advert to the fact that 15 million men of draft age completely avoided even one day of military service without penalty . . . ? (Baskir & Strauss, 1978, pp. xi–xii)

An article titled "America's Foreign Legion" (Stern, 1966), published in *Ramparts,* a magazine of relatively small circulation at that time, pointed out that while blacks were then being drafted at a rate of 11 percent, 22 percent of the total Vietnam casualties were black. Meanwhile, back home the rate of unemployment among blacks was twice as high as among whites.

The article went on to say:

> During recent hearings before the House Armed Services Committee, Representative Alvin E. O'Konski told General Hershey, "The system is undemocratic and unAmerican. It nauseates me. How can I defend it to my people? They say that the poor are always with us, but if the draft goes on this way the poor won't be around much longer." O'Konski cited the shocking statistic that of 100 men drafted from his district in the previous six months, not one had come from a family with an annual income of more than $5,000. Speaking was not a left wing populist but a relatively conservative Republican. (p. 6)

The article added:

> [President Johnson's] son-in-law, Pat Nugent, managed a convenient six month reserve stint in the Air Force that put him in Washington. Actor George Hamilton, a sometimes rumored-to-be future son-in-law of the President, managed to avoid even that inconvenience. He is the sole supporter (a $200,000 home, a $30,000 Rolls Royce and a $100,000 income) of his four times married mother. That, according to Selective Service regulations, is a hardship case. . . . A total of 146 senators and congressmen have one or more sons between the ages of 18 and 26—there are a total of 191 such sons in all. RAMPARTS was able to track down the whereabouts of all but 13 of them. Of the 178 thus accounted for, only 16 were serving in the Armed Services, and only one was in Vietnam. (p. 8)

The one man serving in Vietnam was a 22-year-old paratrooper with Special Forces (both volunteer military specialties) who obviously wanted to be there. The other 15 were mostly commissioned officers or had enlisted in the Navy or the Air Force. None, apparently, had been drafted, and none was serving in Vietnam (Stern, 1966).

A generation later, when the United States was deploying the largest army abroad since the Vietnam War, the issue was raised again when President Bush announced that an additional 100,000 troops would be sent to the Middle East to augment the 225,000 already there. *Washington Post* columnist Mark Shields, speaking on the MacNeil/Lehrer NewsHour (Nov. 2, 1990), expressed his "anger and disappointment" that the people in Washington making decisions on the Persian Gulf were out of contact with the American people. He said:

> The reality is that at any Washington dinner party whether it's a Democrat or Republican, or conservative or liberal, there is nobody there who knows anybody of the 1.8 million American enlisted personnel. Because they come from a different America. They don't come from the journalistic establishment. There are no sons of senators, there are no sons of CEO's, there are no sons of anchormen or syndicated columnists there. There's something desperately wrong when people talk about policy abstractions, about sending people there to the very likelihood of death. . . . If the U.S. national interest is really involved

here, then the President of the United States and the leaders of this country have the responsibility to say that it's everybody's fight.

Shields observed that nobody mentions the draft and he called for exposing everybody to the risk of war in the Middle East.

Five days later (Nov. 7, 1990), John Kenneth Galbraith, in an article on the op-ed page of the *New York Times,* expanded on this criticism. After pointing out that the young men and women deployed in Saudi Arabia and facing possible extinction are drawn from the poorer families of America, he suggested, facetiously:

> Instead, let us establish a special volunteer service corps for the duration of the Middle Eastern troubles. These battalions, recruited at the universities and in the better suburbs, and from among the numerous young men and women now or recently at work in Wall Street, would provide opportunity for military service for those now so undemocratically exempted by their wealth or comparative affluence. . . . A large response . . . would show that we are not risking the lives only of the poor for the gasoline the economically more fortunate consume and, in the words of President Bush, for the "way of life" which those with higher incomes especially enjoy.
>
> A limited response, which is not entirely to be ruled out, would drive home the fact that we are, indeed, asking the poor to protect the rich. (p. A21)

While other writers have said that the media maintain consensus through the dramatization of proper behavior, Breed set out to demonstrate that they also do this by omission. He says that the media "omit or bury items which might jeopardize the sociocultural structure and man's faith in it" (1958, p. 111). An example of Breed's charge can be seen in the treatment of two articles on the same day in a daily newspaper in a state capital. The first article, from the Washington Post Service, was played full-page width across the top of page 1, headlined, "Up to 100,000 Soviets Believed Exposed to Radiation Harms." The other, on page 5, from the New York Times Service, carried a two-column headline reading, "Nuclear Experts List Similarity of Plants in Chernobyl, U.S." (*Austin American-Statesman,* May 19, 1986).

When falling crude oil prices caused a fiscal crisis for one state, the daily newspaper in the state capital, where the major state university is located, ran a story headlined "State Woes Spark Fear of Scholar Exodus." The article, which expressed the fear that top faculty might leave the state, was buried on a page with the daily listing of deaths and funerals and a quarter-page advertisement for a chain of chiropractic centers (*Austin American-Statesman,* May 12, 1986, p. B5).

It took biographer Robert Caro (1990) to reconstruct the wartime service of Lyndon Johnson, which consisted of "a total of 13 minutes" of action while a passenger in a B-26 on a bombing mission over New Guinea that drew fire from Japanese Zeros. Caro says Johnson had promised Texas voters in 1941 that if the United States entered the war he would "be in the front line, in the trenches, in the mud and blood." Caro adds, Johnson spent "the first five months of the war trying to further his political future while ensconcing himself in precisely the type of bureaucratic 'safe, warm naval berth' he had promised to avoid." Only an upcoming election compelled Johnson to fly to a Pacific combat zone, not to fight but as an observer. After his one combat mission Johnson "left the combat zone on the next plane out," Caro wrote. Neither the pilot nor the corporal who shot down a Zero was decorated for the mission, but Johnson was awarded the Silver Star, the Army's third-highest combat award. In later years, Johnson often wore the miniature of the award in the buttonhole of his lapel. A Texas newspaperman, Horace Busby, who occasionally worked for Johnson from 1948 to 1968, said, "for about 40 years I have been wondering when this story would be told. It's just been there waiting for somebody to find it" (Trueheart, 1989).

Breed found that items in the political and economic areas were most frequently omitted. Typically they involved "an elite individual or group obtaining privilege through non-democratic means." He notes that the most striking fact is that the word *class* is seldom mentioned in the media: "class, being social inequality, is the very antithesis of the American creed," Breed observes (1958, p. 114). Other sacrosanct areas that Breed identifies are religion, the family, patriotism, the community, medicine, and law and justice.

Of religion Breed says, "It should be noted that religion is of double significance to social integration: It is not only a value in itself but it justifies and rationalizes other sentiments which bring order to a society" (1958, p. 112). Clergymen are rarely sentenced to prison. More rare, however, is prominent display of this uncommon event, even considering the major role religion and the clergy play in our society. One such story told of a clergyman who had been sentenced to 20 years in prison. He had admitted to sexually abusing more than three dozen children. In plea bargaining, prosecutors dropped an aggravated rape charge in return for guilty pleas on 11 counts each of child pornography, crime against nature, and contributing to the delinquency of a minor (Associated Press, 1985).

Breed contends that the media portray the family as an institution without which society would perish. It may be true that in recent years the media have devoted some time and space to alternate life-styles, but in general it seems difficult to dispute Breed's contention.

Patriotism

Breed observes that patriotism is another value protected by the media. He says, "When an individual is accused of disloyalty, favorable discussion of him by the media is sharply checked. He cannot be dramatized as an individual or a leader, only as a 'controversial' person under suspicion" (1958, p. 113).

When Muhammad Ali (then known as Cassius Clay), the world heavyweight champion, reacted to the possibility of being drafted with "I've got nothing against them Viet Congs," boxing commissioners, promoters, and veterans' groups found the remark "unpatriotic" and "disgusting." A title bout was called off, six other cities turned down the fight, and, finally, it was rescheduled for Toronto. Then sponsors of the radio broadcast and most of the theaters planning to show the fight on closed-circuit TV canceled their contracts. Ali was even denounced on the floor of the House of Representatives. Ali's heavyweight title was taken away from him and when he chose the Black Muslim name Muhammad Ali, the media scoffed and refused to use it for many months (Stone, 1966).

Of the press and its policy regarding patriotism and national ethnocentrism, Breed says:

> American soldiers overseas may violate norms involving persons and property for which they would be publicly punished in the country, but the press here minimizes overseas derelictions. In other countries, they are "representatives" of our nationality and thus in a quasi-sacred position. (1958, p. 113)

Community Coverage

Of the media's coverage of their communities Breed says, "The progress, growth, and achievements of a city are praised, the failures buried" (1958, p. 113). Breed notes the "chamber of commerce" attitude on the part of the media; another author, journalism professor Gene Burd, has dubbed this the "civic superlative."

Burd wrote:

> As gatekeeper of the civic symbols and custodian of the civic relics, the press is the city's civic salesman and press agent who points with pride or cries with shame and alarm. It reminds the public of the central business district as the city with civic superlatives, the centerpiece, the showcase, the crown jewels, the face and facade, the newest, the biggest, the tallest, the longest, the largest, the cleanest, the safest, the greatest. (1969, p. 307)

Later Burd wrote, "Such boosterism is most evident in news on sports and new urban developments, in news of national recognition of local natives" (1972, p. 3).

Violations of Burd's "civic superlative" often meet with a strong reaction. When NBC correspondent Linda Ellerbee traveled to San Antonio to do a story as part of the Texas Sesquicentennial, she did one report from the Alamo (Feb. 24, 1986). In her report she stated that not all of those at the Alamo were Texans, that not all present chose to "fight and die" at the Alamo (at least one went over the wall before the battle started), that at that time Texas was a part of Mexico, and that the southerners who immigrated into Texas wanted to keep slaves, which were not allowed under Mexican law. This report created considerable dissonance and the Daughters of the Texas Revolution threatened to boycott the local network affiliate.

The civic boosterism in sports referred to by Burd can reach into even the smallest communities and down to the junior high school level, as an "ABC Evening News" report by Bob Brown on November 23, 1978, illustrated. He reported, "Football isn't everything in Thomaston, but it is an important source of prestige." Brown cited cases of students at the junior high school who repeated years, although their grades were fine, in order to improve their prowess at football before their limited high school eligibility of eight semesters began. The local coach said that parental permission must be received in advance, that "two or three" players were probably repeating the eighth grade at the time, that half the repeaters took exactly the same courses that they had passed the year before, and that the situation was probably the same in other towns in Georgia. At that time there were nine such cases of repeaters in the Thomaston schools, and the extra years in junior high school for these nine players alone cost about $10,000. Brown closed his report with, "As in many other communities, football here is viewed as a measure of a town's image, reflected in its youth."

A decade later the *Wall Street Journal* reported:

> In the big cities, sport is part of a larger culture. In the big corporations, its jargon and images are now common, part of that culture too. But in countless small towns all across the country, sport is much more than that. It practically *is* the culture, the social cement that holds these towns together. . . . "High school teams offer small communities a sense of identity that's hard to find anywhere else," says Steven Padgitt, a rural sociologist at Iowa State University. . . . Rich town, poor town, it makes no difference. When Highland Park, a chi-chi Dallas suburb, made the state finals . . . residents chartered nine Boeing 727s to shuttle them 300 miles to the game. (Duke, 1988)

When a nationally ranked college baseball team lost its first home double-header in four years, which was also its first loss to that team in 70 years, the story was headlined, "Top-ranked Longhorns Drop Double-Header to Wesleyan" (Frisbie, 1983). *Lose* would have been the more accurate verb, but, of course, it's hard to admit that "our team" lost.

Sometimes the "civic superlative" takes a more subtle turn, accomplishing its aim through mild "card stacking" by the omission of information. A story on the departure of a young cellist for the prestigious Tchaikovsky Competition in Moscow identified her as a University of Texas honors student and a native of the People's Republic of China (Garcia, 1986). Nowhere did the story mention that at the time she went to Moscow she had been in the United States for less than 18 months and that her prior musical education had taken place at the Shanghai Academy of Music and the Shanghai Conservatory.

A relatively rare example of a news item that included facts disturbing to Vidich and Bensman's (1960) "accepted system of illusions" concerned a graduation ceremony. The son of a former governor and, at that time, a presidential hopeful had just graduated from the Air Force officer training school at the height of the Vietnam War. The father of the graduate, speaking at the ceremony, was quoted, "In the times we live in there are so many who have doubts about their country that it's critical that our young men recognize their responsibility to serve their nation. I'm particularly proud that my son has chosen to meet his responsibility."

The last paragraph of the story, surprisingly uncut, read, "Lt. Connally will serve with headquarters, Texas Air National Guard in Austin, where he will attend law school" (Associated Press, June 30, 1969).

Medicine

"Physicians are almost never shown in a bad light by the press, and the treatment of doctors in other media such as daytime serials is often worshipful," says Breed (1958, p. 113). Even three decades later, it is rare indeed to see coverage like the five-part in-depth series by the *New York Times* discussing the number of unfit physicians, incompetent surgeries, bad prescriptions, and medical cover-ups (Jan. 26–30, 1976), the six-part series by the *Milwaukee Journal* titled "The Ailing Blues" examining medical and surgical insurance in depth (May 30–June 4, 1976), or a long article in the *Wall Street Journal* (Feb. 27, 1989) about the widespread practice of hospital kickbacks to physicians who refer patients (sometimes specifically excluding Medicare and Medicaid patients) (Bogdanich & Waldholz, 1989).

Even rarer are stories showing "doctors acting in selfish rather than professional fashion" (Breed, 1958, p. 114). One of these rare stories told of a white Alabama doctor who removed the freshly sewn stitches from the arm of a 13-year-old black youngster when the youth's father couldn't pay the $25 fee (Associated Press, 1976).

Law and Justice

Justice is another media policy area noted by Breed. On the subject of differential attention to crime, a former attorney general of the United States has said:

> The crimes to which we pay least attention are those committed by people of advantage who have an easier, less offensive, less visible way of doing wrong. White-collar crime is usually the act of respected and successful people. Illicit gains from white-collar crime far exceed those of all other crimes combined. . . . One corporate price-fixing conspiracy criminally converted more money each year it continued than all of the hundreds of thousands of burglaries, larcenies or thefts in the entire nation during those same years. . . . White-collar crime is the most corrosive of all crimes. The trusted prove untrustworthy; the advantaged dishonest. It shows the capability of people with better opportunities for creating a decent life for themselves to take property belonging to others. As no other crime, it questions our moral fiber. (Clark, 1970, p. 38)

When Michael K. Deaver, once one of the most powerful officials in the White House, was given a suspended three-year prison sentence for lying about his lobbying activities after leaving the White House, Representative John D. Dingell said:

> An ordinary citizen who steals a Social Security check, goes for a joy ride or is caught with a few grams of marijuana goes to jail, but someone of wealth and influence who lies to a grand jury and Congress has little to fear. The message is: The powerful can get away with things most people can't. (Shenon, 1988)

Two researchers examined crime reporting during one month by the two daily newspapers in one of America's largest cities. They found that although nearly 36 percent (2,814 of the 7,901 crimes reported) were larcenies, neither newspaper carried a story about any of them during that month (Antunes & Hurley, 1977).

However, as a result of publicity about John Zaccaro, Jr., having served a four-month term for cocaine trafficking in a $1,500-a-month luxury apartment, the governor of Vermont ruled that future drug offenders would be excluded from Vermont's program of house arrest. The case got special media attention because Zaccaro is the son of Geraldine A. Ferraro, the Democratic vice presidential candidate in 1984 (Associated Press, 1988).

Breed contends that the media function to protect "power" and "class." He observes that "critics have for centuries noted the disproportionate power of elites and the winking by the media at their actions" (1958, p. 111).

Breed says that when television dramas portray a businessman as a villain, for example, they focus on the individual, not on the institution. When newspapers report investigations detailing the structural faults of campaign financing, lobbying, concentrations of economic power, or the like, Breed contends that they are usually not featured. He says that the media "do not challenge basic institutions by exploring the flaws in the working of institutions" (p. 116).

Conclusions

The world has changed considerably since the end of World War II. Many media systems no longer fit the old classifications of *Four Theories of the Press,* especially in the developing countries. Moreover, the late 1980s have seen radical and continuing changes in media functions and control in the socialist countries.

It is apparent that in the West the ideal functions of the mass media as defined by the libertarian and social responsibility theories of the press and the rationale so logically developed by John Stuart Mill are at considerable variance with actual practice. Wright, Lasswell, Lippmann, Lazarsfeld, Merton, Breed, Altschull, Gans, and Tuchman are but a few of the many who have made such observations. Although it is true that the media omissions cited by Warren Breed four decades ago are still present, they are probably much less prevalent today than they were at the time he wrote. However, the gap between the ideal and the reality remains a major problem for a democratic society.

References

Altschull, J. H. (1984). *Agents of Power: The Role of the News Media in Human Affairs.* New York: Longman.

Antunes, G., and P. Hurley (1977). The representation of criminal events in Houston's two daily newspapers. *Journalism Quarterly* 54: 756–760.

Associated Press (1969). Connally pins AF bars on son. June 30.
———— (1976). Patient can't pay, so doc pulls stitches. Apr. 16.
———— (1985). Ex-Louisiana priest draws 20 years in child sex case. Oct. 15.
———— (1988). Vermont to exclude all drug offenders from house arrests. Sept. 3.
Baskir, L., and W. Strauss (1978). *Chance and Circumstance: The Draft, the War, and the Vietnam Generation.* New York: Alfred A. Knopf.
Bogdanich, W., and M. Waldholz (1989). Hospitals that need patients pay bounties for doctor's referrals. *Wall Street Journal,* Feb. 27, pp. A1, A4.
Bohlen, C., and C. Haberman (1990). How the Ceausescus fell: harnessing popular rage. *New York Times,* Jan. 7, pp. 1, 11.
Boyer, P. J. (1986). Trauma times on network TV. *New York Times,* Nov. 2, Sect. 3, pp. 1, 28.
Breed, W. (1955). Social control in the newsroom. *Social Forces,* May, pp. 326–335. Also in W. Schramm (ed.), *Mass Communication,* 2nd. ed. Urbana: University of Illinois Press, 1960.
———— *(1958). Mass communication and sociocultural integration. Social Forces,* pp. 109–116. Reprinted in L. Dexter and D. White (eds.) (1964), *People, Society and Mass Communications.* New York: Free Press.
Brown, L. (1971). *Televi$ion: The Business Behind the Box.* New York: Harcourt Brace Jovanovich.
Burd, G. (1969). The mass media in urban society. In H. Schmandt and W. Bloomberg, Jr. (eds.), *The Quality of Urban Life.* Beverly Hills, Cal.: Sage.
———— *(1972). The civic superlative: We're no. 1. The press as civic cheer-leader. Twin Cities Journalism Review* 1 (April-May). Minneapolis, Minn.
Caro, R. (1990). *Means of Ascent* New York: Knopf.
Clark, R. (1970). *Crime in America.* New York: Simon & Schuster.
Creed, J. (1990). Exxon's slick trick. *New York Times,* Nov. 4, Sect. 4, p. 19.
Curtis, T. (1988). Altered statesman. *Texas Monthly,* April, p. 176.
Discretionary journalism: How ABC spikes the news (1986). *Columbia Journalism Review,* March/April, p. 65.
Dowie, M. (1985). How ABC spikes the news. *Mother Jones,* Nov.-Dec., pp. 33–40.
Duke, P. (1988). Teams make towns winners. *Wall Street Journal,* Feb. 26, p. 4D.
Fallows, J. (1976). Vietnam—the class war. *National Observer,* Feb. 21, p. 14.
Fein, E. (1989). Ending long silence, Soviets report big increase in crime. *New York Times,* Feb. 15, p. 46.
Forrest, H. (1989) Media clips. *Austin Chronicle,* Nov. 17, p. 4.
Fox, J. (1982). Interview. St. Louis, Mo., Nov. 29. Quoted in University of Missouri Freedom of Information Center Report 471, p. 3.
Frisbie, B. (1983). Top-ranked Longhorns drop double-header to Wesleyan. *Daily Texan,* Mar. 22, p. 11.
"Frontline" (1984). The campaign for page one. Boston: WGBH transcripts, Feb. 27, p. 19.
Gamino, D. (1986). Work reward carries Bergstrom airman on flight to death. *Austin American-Statesman,* May 25, p. 1.
Gans, H. J. (1979). *Deciding What's News.* New York: Random House.
———— (1979). The messages behind the news. *Columbia Journalism Review,* Jan.-Feb., pp. 40–45.
———— (1985). Are U.S. journalists dangerously liberal? *Columbia Journalism Review,* Nov.-Dec., pp. 29–33.
Garcia, G. (1986). Students previewed to cellist's Moscow competition. *Austin American-Statesman,* June 14, p. B1.
Gendel, M. (1986). CBS's new lineup pleases sponsors. *Austin American-Statesman,* May 18, Show World (insert), p. 15.
Harney, K. (1985). Economic trouble brewing. *Austin American-Statesman,* Oct. 19, p. E4.
Hersh, S. M. (1969). Notes on the art: The story everyone ignored. *Columbia Journalism Review,* Winter, pp. 55–58.
———— (1970). How I broke the Mylai 4 story. *Saturday Review,* July 11, pp. 46–49.
———— (1972). The story everyone ignored. In M. Emery and T. Smythe (eds.), *Readings in Mass Communications,* 1st ed. Dubuque, Iowa: Wm. C. Brown.

Holuska, J. (1982). Rival papers in Detroit bar no holds. *New York Times,* June 6, p. 49.

ISR Newsletter (1986–87). Wealth in America. Winter, p. 3. Ann Arbor: Institute for Social Research, University of Michigan.

Jones, A. S. (1990). At U.S. newspaper editors' talks, criticism and 1960's headliners. *New York Times,* April 6, p. A12.

Kamm, H. (1989). Hungarians shocked by news of vast poverty in their midst. *New York Times,* Feb. 6, p. 3.

Keller, B. (1989a). Another Soviet taboo is broken: paper attacks Communist party. *New York Times,* Feb. 9, 1989, p. 1.

———— (1989b). A proposed Soviet law limits press censorship. *New York Times,* Sept. 27, p. 8.

Kimelman, D. (1986). Soviet newspaper prints criticism of privileges. *Austin American-Statesman,* Feb. 16, p. C5.

Ladendorf, K. (1990). Controversy greets chamber tenure of publisher Kintzel. *Austin American-Statesman,* Mar. 4, pp. H1, H5.

Lasswell, H. (1948, 1960). The structure and function of communication in society. In L. Bryson (ed.), *The Communication of Ideas* (1948). New York: Institute for Religious and Social Studies. Reprinted in W. Schramm (ed.), *Mass Communications* (1960). Urbana: University of Illinois Press.

Lazarsfeld, P., and R. Merton (1948). Mass communication, popular taste and organized social action. In L. Bryson (ed.), *The Communication of Ideas* (1948). New York: Institute for Religious and Social Studies. Reprinted in W. Schramm (ed.), *Mass Communications* (1960). Urbana: University of Illinois Press.

Lippmann, W. (1922). *Public Opinion.* New York: Macmillan. Ch. 1 reprinted in W. Schramm (ed.), *Mass Communications* (1960). Urbana: University of Illinois Press.

Mill, J. (1859, reprinted 1956). *On Liberty.* Indianapolis: Bobbs-Merrill.

National Advisory Commission on Civil Disorders (1968). *Report of the National Advisory Commission on Civil Disorders* (The Kerner Report). New York: Bantam Books.

Peterson, R., G. Albaum, G. Kozmetsky, and I. Cunningham (1984). Attitudes of newspaper business editors and general public toward capitalism. *Journalism Quarterly* 61: 56–65.

Petzinger, T. (1988). Houstonians find there is no escape from storm of hype. *Wall Street Journal,* Sept. 16, p. 4.

Scott, W. (1986). Personality Parade. *Parade.* Apr. 27.

Shahin, J. (1988). Austin redux: The Kathleen Sullivan mystery. *Columbia Journalism Review,* July-Aug., p. 14.

————, and H. Forest (1988). *Austin Chronicle,* July 1, p. 4.

Shenon, P. (1988). Deaver gets fine of $100,000 and a suspended sentence. *New York Times,* Sept. 24, p. 1.

Siebert, F. S., T. B. Peterson, and W. Schramm (1956). *Four Theories of the Press.* Urbana: University of Illinois Press.

Stern, S. (1966). America's foreign legion. *Ramparts,* Nov., pp. 6–8.

Stone, I. F. (1966). No free speech for Cassius Clay. *I. F. Stone's Weekly,* Mar. 28, p. 2.

Trueheart, C. (1989). LBJ embroidered scanty record in war, his biographer says. *San Francisco Chronicle,* Nov. 2, p. A22.

Tuchman, G. (1978). *Making News: A Study in the Construction of Reality.* New York: Free Press.

Vidich, A., and J. Bensman (1960). *Small Town in Mass Society.* New York: Doubleday.

Wicklein, J. (1986). The assault on public television. *Columbia Journalism Review,* Jan.-Feb., pp. 27–34.

Wright, C. (1959). *Mass Communication.* New York: Random

17

Media Chains and Conglomerates

The Gerbner verbal model (see Chapter 3) recognizes that communication takes place "through some means, to make available materials. . . . " For these two aspects of the communication process—means and availability—Gerbner lists as areas of study "investigation of channels, media, controls over facilities" and "administration; distribution; freedom of access to materials."

As mentioned in Chapter 16, Warren Breed (1955) points out that the media "omit or bury items which might jeopardize the sociocultural structure" and that "policy usually protects property and class interests" (p. 334). Closely related to this and also cited in Chapter 16 are Lazarsfeld and Merton's discussion of "social conformism," Gans's "responsible capitalism," Tuchman's comments concerning "the social construction of reality," and Altschull's observations that the news media are agents of the people who exercise political and economic power and that the content of the news media always reflects the interests of those who finance the press. If these observations are correct, some knowledge of mass media ownership is necessary to understand fully the workings of mass communication.

Newspaper Chains

Twelve large conglomerates, many of which are also involved in broadcasting, cable, magazine and book publishing, and other media, control nearly half of the nation's daily newspaper circulation (Table 17.1).

The number of daily newspapers in the United States has declined steadily since 1920, while the population has more than doubled. Of greater concern is the fact that the number of cities with competing dailies has dropped from 552 in 1920 to 28 in 1986 (Table 17.2). As John C. Busterna points out, between 1960 and 1986 the number of cities with competing dailies declined from 4.2 percent to 1.9 percent. In 1960 those cities with competing dailies constituted 42 percent of total daily circulation, but by 1986 the 28 cities that still had competition accounted for only 21 percent of total daily circulation (1988, p. 833).

Busterna says:

> The decline in head-to-head daily newspaper competition can be explained in terms of a few economic factors. There is little product differentiation among daily newspapers. The content of typical competing dailies is very similar giving readers no reason to purchase more than one. This similarity is a product of a decline of the partisan press and the establishment of objectivity in presenting news and balance in selecting editorial page features.

Table 17.1
PROPORTION OF TOTAL DAILY CIRCULATION CONTROLLED BY LARGEST CHAINS

	Chain	Number of Dailies	Circulation	Percent of Total Circulation	Cumulative Percent
1.	Gannett	90	5,887,787	9.43%	9.43%
2.	Knight-Ridder	33	3,848,495	6.16	15.59
3.	Newhouse	27	3,034,836	4.86	20.45
4.	Times Mirror	9	2,714,165	4.35	24.80
5.	Tribune	9	2,685,124	4.30	29.10
6.	Dow Jones	23	2,519,287	4.03	33.13
7.	New York Times	26	1,768,209	2.83	35.96
8.	Scripps Howard	20	1,531,200	2.45	38.41
9.	Thomson	96	1,481,047	2.37	40.78
10.	Hearst	15	1,456,093	2.33	43.11
11.	Cox	20	1,287,363	2.06	45.17
12.	News America	3	1,256,941	2.01	47.18

From 1987 *Editor & Publisher International Yearbook,* as cited in J. C. Busterna, "Trends in Daily Newspaper Ownership," *Journalism Quarterly* 65 (1988): 836. Reprinted with permission.

> The lack of different content typically creates homogeneous audiences for advertisers. As a result, advertisers flock disproportionately to the larger circulation daily. With no special content to attract readers and a smaller audience for advertisers, competition is often doomed. (pp. 833–834)

Busterna adds that other media complement daily newspapers rather than provide substantial competition for news, opinion, and advertising. He concludes that other media don't appear to be good substitutes for the loss of competing daily newspapers (p. 835).

The number of chain-owned newspapers has doubled from 1960 to 1986, reducing the proportion of independently owned dailies during the same period from 68 percent to 30 percent. Busterna points out that the number of chains peaked in 1978 with 169, and since then there has been a sharp decline in their number, suggesting that chains are merging with other chains (p. 835). Indeed, the average number of dailies per chain almost doubled from 1960 to 1986, at a time when the total number of dailies declined by 106 (Table 17.2). Busterna points out that this has "caused a large jump in the proportion of absentee-owned chain dailies. . . . the foreseeable future should find the continuing consolidation of daily newspapers into the hands of a small number of distant firms" (p. 838).

Earlier, James N. Rosse (1980) attributed the dramatic decline in newspaper competition to several factors, including these:

1. Loss of effective newspaper market segmentation, or an inability to find an audience for which a newspaper could differentiate itself from competitors and for which advertisers were willing to pay enough to make publication profitable

Table 17.2
TRENDS IN OWNERSHIP OF DAILY NEWSPAPERS: 1920–1986

	1920	1940	1960	1986
Circulation (000)	27,791	41,132	58,881	62,453
Total Dailies	2,042	1,878	1,763	1,657
Total Daily Cities	1,295	1,426	1,461	1,513
One-Daily Cities	716	1,092	1,222	1,389
% of Total	55.3	76.6	83.6	91.8
Joint Monopoly Cities	27	149	160	75
Joint Operating Cities	0	4	18	21
Total Non-Competitive	743	1,245	1,400	1,485
% of Total	57.4	87.3	95.8	98.1
Competing Daily Cities	552	181	61	28
Newspaper Chains	31	60	109	127
Chain Newspapers	153	319	560	1,158
Average Dailies per Chain	4.9	5.3	5.1	9.1
Independent Newspapers	1,889	1,559	1,203	499
% of Total	92.5	83.0	68.2	30.1
Newspaper Owners	1,920	1,619	1,312	626

From 1987 *Editor & Publisher International Yearbook* for 1986 figures. All earlier figures from Raymond B. Nixon and Jean Ward, "Trends in Newspaper Ownership and Inter-Media Competition," *Journalism Quarterly* 38:3–14 (Winter 1961), p. 5. As cited in J. C. Busterna, "Trends in Daily Newspaper Ownership," *Journalism Quarterly* 65 (1988): 833. Reprinted with permission.

2. Competition for advertising revenue from the broadcast media
3. Decline in readership of newspapers per household
4. Population shifts from inner cities with great population diversity to more homogeneous suburbs with individual suburban newspapers that serve the more homogeneous population more efficiently.

With each passing year there are fewer and fewer independent newspapers, or even small chains of newspapers, as the giants in the field continue to buy them up. Katharine Graham, publisher of the *Washington Post* and chairman of the Washington Post Company (*Washington Post, Newsweek,* four television stations, and a one-third interest in the *International Herald Tribune*), was quoted as saying in a rare series of articles in a newspaper about the newspaper industry, "You have an irreversible trend going, and nothing can stop it short of government intervention and then, at that point, we all choke" (Jones & Anderson, 1977, p. 25).

The editor and publisher of the then family-owned *Louisville Courier-Journal,* Barry Bingham, Jr., said, "The idea of a family-owned newspaper in the future is not probable" ("The Big Money," 1977, p. 58). His prophecy became reality in less than a decade when it was announced that the prestigious *Courier-Journal* and its sister paper, the *Louisville Times* (winners of eight Pulitzer Prizes), a CBS-affiliated TV station, two radio stations, and Standard Gravure (printers of Sunday magazine sections and advertising inserts) were sold to Gannett for a reported $445 million. Other bids for the highly coveted properties were made by the Washington Post Company, the New York Times Company, and the Tribune Company of Chicago (Associated Press, May 19, 1986).

Many reasons exist for the growth of media conglomerates. This phenomenon is, of course, part of the larger economic trend in our society that favors concentration in general with the advantages of large-scale operation. Another factor is the inheritance tax laws, which make it difficult for a family-owned newspaper to be passed on to heirs when large sums are needed to pay taxes. There is also the inability to challenge chain ownership under current antitrust laws. Senator Edward Kennedy, chair of the subcommittee on antitrust and monopoly, has expressed concern about this, as have many others.

Another factor is the tremendous real or potential profitability of many of the media. Profit figures in the newspaper industry are hard to come by since only a minority of the nearly 1,657 dailies sell public stock and issue public business reports. Even in recession years and in the face of long strikes, newspapers have shown growth in profits exceeding that in most other industries.

The largest newspaper chain is Gannett, which publishes *USA Today,* transmitted by satellite daily to printing plants throughout the United States, and 89 other daily newspapers with a total daily circulation of nearly 6 million in 34 states plus Guam and the Virgin Islands. Gannett also owns 7 AM, 9 FM, and 10 television stations in some of the nation's largest cities (*Broadcasting and Cablecasting Yearbook,* 1989, pp. A43, A58). (For details on Gannett, see Bagdikian, 1990, Chapter 4; Winski, 1981; and Tate, 1981.)

Knight-Ridder, which has a reputation for excellence, is second in size after Gannett, with 33 daily newspapers and 3.8 million circulation in 15 states. The chain also owns nine TV stations (*Broadcasting and Cablecasting Yearbook,* 1989, pp. A46).

Newhouse, the largest privately owned U.S. newspaper chain, with 27 dailies and 3 million circulation, ranks third. Newhouse Newspapers owns the Booth Newspapers chain of Michigan, which it bought in 1976 for $305 million. (For a look at how journalism is practiced at one of the Newhouse-owned Booth newspapers, see Michael Moore's "How to Keep 'em Happy in Flint," 1985. This detailed examination of what many would call systematic bias over a period of more than a half-century illustrates many of the points made in Chapter 17.)

Newhouse also owns radio stations, major cable systems, widely read Conde Nast magazines, Random House book publishers, a Sunday magazine supplement, and printing plants. In 1985 one newspaper analyst estimated the value of the privately owned chain at $3 billion and estimated that its 1984 revenues were around $2 billion, and its after-tax profits $180 million (Hoyt & Schoonmaker, 1985, p. 38).

The Times-Mirror Company is the publisher of six dailies, including the *Los Angeles Times;* eight magazines; several book publishing houses; four television stations; and cable properties (*Broadcasting and Cablecasting Yearbook,* 1989, pp. A61). It also owns newsprint mills and timberland.

Otis Chandler of the Times-Mirror Company stresses local media competition as one of the biggest considerations in any prospective acquisition. The choicest property is one that has a market almost to itself. Chandler was quoted as saying, "In these markets [large metropolitan areas] you worry about cost per thousand, or the other media buys that an advertiser could make. All that doesn't mean a thing in smaller media markets because the advertiser has no competitive buys." He added that if a newspaper is noncompetitive, "it gives you a franchise to do what you want with profitability. You can engineer your profits. You can control expenses and generate revenue almost arbitrarily." Times-Mirror Company bought *Newsday* in 1970 and increased profits by 72 percent in the first year, in part by doubling the price of the paper ("The Big Money," 1977, pp. 58–59).

An article about the buying up of independent newspapers by chains referred to papers "that either earn or have the potential to earn pretax profit margins of 25% to 30% or higher. The Speidel chain [of 13 newspapers] acquired by Gannett [for $178 million], had pretax margins of 34%" ("The Big Money," 1977, p. 57). Such rates in the banking industry would be usurious in most states. Chains have the expectation that their local managers will produce high profits. Usually these profits are not put back into the community to improve local media but are returned to the corporate headquarters to enable the conglomerate to purchase additional media elsewhere, called by some a form of economic colonialism.

Harte-Hanks Communications, Inc., a San Antonio–based nationwide communications company that went public from family ownership, owns 10 daily newspapers and other media outlets (50 nondaily publications, a television station, and the world's largest direct-mail shopper organization) (*Editor and Publisher International Yearbook 1989*, pp. 1–374). Harte-Hanks's president and chief executive officer, Robert Marbut, a 1963 Harvard M.B.A., said, "There are about 7,500 weeklies all over the country, and 1,762 dailies. Out of those dailies, only 39 cities have competing newspapers. We don't try to get a paper in those 39 cities" (Cook, 1977, p. 36).

Former secretary of the treasury John Connally called the media conglomerates "massive business empires built by entrepreneurs under the shelter of our free enterprise system" (Phillips, 1977, pp. 23–24). At the other end of the political spectrum, Senator Edward Kennedy called for the antitrust laws to be ready and able to promote a "diverse and competitive press." Representative Morris Udall of Arizona and others have introduced legislation in Congress for studies of concentration in newspapers as well as in other industries. Udall told an audience at the National Press Club that he feared "chain-store news is upon us" as, he said, are chain-store drugs and chain-store gasoline. Udall saw disturbing social implications in this trend (Jones & Anderson, 1977, p. 25).

Concern about "chain-store news," the maintenance of a "diverse and competitive press," and the effects of "massive business empires" on our media have been voiced for at least 50 years. A nationally known and highly regarded media critic pointed out that residents of most American cities have access to competing automobile dealerships, even though we have only four manufacturers of automobiles in the United States. Not so with newspapers—most U.S. cities have no competition in newspapers (Bagdikian, 1978, p. 31).

Defenders of newspaper chains and monopoly newspaper cities reply that other sources of news, including newsmagazines, radio, and television, are available. The fact is that most of the news in all the media comes from two wire services, the Associated Press and United Press International, who in turn rely very heavily on their local members and clients. The wire service clients most apt to gather news are the daily newspapers, which are, increasingly, in one-owner cities.

National newsmagazines are of little help to the individual who wants and needs information about his or her own community—the actions of the city council and county commissioners on tax increases and zoning ordinances, school board policies, fire and police protection, maintenance and construction of roads, water and sewage treatment facilities, and the myriad of other local issues that affect a person's everyday life.

Although local television evening news programs now often run one hour, in reality that hour is usually split into two highly redundant half-hour segments, preceding and following the national evening news. After making allowances for commercials, weather, sports, "fillers," network feeds of items not used on the national news, PR handouts, and "happy talk," most local evening news programs, with few exceptions, probably contain less than five minutes of local news.

Significant local news coverage on radio is so unusual that when it does occur the rare exception merits special recognition. Despite all of the arguments that there is now greater diversity in local communities because of increasing numbers of local media outlets, many stations in a locality even duplicate one another. One local radio station, in a television promo, says, "If you like KOKE-FM, you should know there's another station in town just like it, KOKE-AM." Today some radio stations in a community are not only similar but identical.

Broadcasting Chains

Ownership of broadcasting is equally concentrated. In 1989 nearly four of every five television stations in the 100 largest markets in the United States were group owned (Table 17.3). The total number of regular commercial TV stations (exclusive of low-power stations) in the 100 largest markets increased from 420 in 1982 to 677 in 1989. Of these 677 TV stations in the 100 largest population centers, 529 or 78.1 percent were licensed to groups. On the basis of the Federal Communications Commission's market reach formula, only three groups (the network owned-and-operated stations of ABC, CBS, and NBC) reach more than 20 percent of the nation's TV households. However these three networks are also able to reach more than 95 percent of the nation's households when their affiliated stations are included.

Howard (1989) observes that the number of television stations under group ownership (two or more stations under single ownership) has increased since 1982, and the number of groups has increased from 158 in 1982 to 205 in 1989 (p. 791). However, 5 groups reached the limit of 12 TV stations each, and 24 groups now own more than the former limit of 7 stations each (p. 791). In 1989 the overwhelming number of group-owned stations, 189 or 92 percent, could reach fewer than 5 percent of the nation's television homes (p. 789).

Media Cross Ownership

From the standpoint of the individual citizen, probably one of the greatest threats to diversity of news and opinion about local issues is media cross ownership or joint ownership (a newspaper and a television station under single ownership in one community). In 1975 the Federal Communications Commission proposed a ban on single-community broadcast-newspaper links in the future. It did, however, "grandfather" or make immune from divestiture all existing combinations except those amounting to outright monopolies. The exemption for existing cross ownerships was challenged in D.C. Circuit Court by the Justice Department. Although the court ruled against exempting existing cross ownerships, the U.S. Supreme Court ruled in a unanimous (8-0) decision in 1978 that the FCC had reasonably exercised the power delegated to it by Congress.

The Newhouse Broadcasting Corporation announced in December 1978 the sale of five

Table 17.3

MULTIPLE OWNERSHIP OF TV STATIONS BY MARKET RANK, JANUARY 1, 1989

Market Ranking	No. of Stations			No. of Stations Group-Owned			Percentage of Stations Group-Owned		
	VHF	UHF	All TV	VHF	UHF	All TV	VHF	UHF	All TV
1–10	43	80	123	42	47	89	97.7	58.8	72.4
11–25	58	66	124	53	50	103	91.4	75.8	83.1
26–50	70	87	157	64	62	126	91.4	71.3	80.3
51–75	73	80	153	64	56	120	87.7	70.0	78.4
76–100	60	60	120	51	40	91	85.0	66.7	75.8
Total (1–100)	304	373	677	274	255	529	90.1	68.4	78.1

From H. H. Howard, "Group and Cross-Media Ownership of TV Stations: A 1989 Update," *Journalism Quarterly* 66 (1989): 788. Reprinted by permission.

television stations to the Times-Mirror Company for $82 million. The reason given for the sale was the growing opposition by federal regulatory agencies to cross ownership of newspapers and television stations in the same communities. The Newhouse group published newspapers in each of the cities in which the five television stations they sold were located. Newhouse retained its radio, cable television, and microwave facilities as well as its newspaper properties.

In a large-scale study of joint ownership of a newspaper and a television station in the same city, one researcher concluded that it often means less diversity in coverage (Gormley, 1977). The author noted that more than 60 million Americans live in cities where at least one newspaper and one television station have the same owner. In 1975 there were 66 newspaper-television cross ownerships.

The investigator sent questionnaires to 349 news directors and managing editors of both cross owned and separately owned media. As a result of the 214 responses received he visited 10 cross ownership cities, where he interviewed 44 news executives and reporters. Then he analyzed 9,335 news stories for a comparison of overlap of coverage between cross owned and separately owned pairs of newspaper and television stations.

He reported:

> What I found was that jointly owned newspaper and television news staffs were engaged in cooperative practices that might not be described as "abuses" but which nevertheless belied assurances by owners of newspaper-television combinations that their news staffs functioned separately and independently. (Gormley, 1977, p. 39)

He added that cross ownership increases the likelihood of three situations:

1. A newspaper and a television station will share carbons (copies).
2. A television station will hire a reporter or editor who has worked for the newspaper that owns the television station.
3. A newspaper and a television station will be located within the same complex of buildings. Gormley pointed out that "sharing the same roof, the same parking lot, or the same cafeteria reminds newspaper and television reporters that they are members of the same corporate family—which encourages cooperation." (1977, pp. 42–43)

Besides undermining diversity in the flow of news, Gormley indicated that while one-fourth of the stations not owned by a newspaper never editorialized, more than half of those that are newspaper owned never editorialized. A newspaper-owned television station that editorializes in accordance with a newspaper's views faces charges of collusion, yet if it editorializes against those views, it tends to offset the view of a corporate partner. If it chooses not to editorialize, it avoids the dilemma, which is what most choose to do. By not editorializing, television stations increase dependence on local newspapers for views on local issues. Gormley found that the "homogenizing effects of newspaper-television cross-ownership are strongest in cities with populations under 125,000" (1977, p. 43). It is precisely these cities that can least afford reduced diversity, since they usually have so few media voices.

If one accepts the notions of the libertarian and social responsibility theories of the press, the arguments put forth by Mill regarding the liberty of thought and discussion, and the position of Judge Learned Hand, who wrote in U.S. v. Associated Press that "right conclusions are more likely to be gathered out of a multitude of tongues," one must agree that when cross ownership reduces diversity in news and opinions, it also threatens truth and understanding.

As of early 1989 nearly one-fourth of the television stations in the nation's 100 largest population centers were affiliated with newspaper publishers (Table 17.4). Of the 677 TV stations in the 100 most populous cities, 167 were newspaper related, an increase of 27 stations between 1982 and 1989. However, because of the large increase in the number of new stations in the 100 largest markets (especially UHF) the actual percentage of newspaper affiliated TV stations *declined* from 33.3 percent in 1982 to 24.7 percent in 1989 (Howard, 1989, p. 790)

Howard also reports a *steady decline* in both percent and number of local newspaper-television cross ownerships in the top 100 markets. They have dropped from 16.1 percent (60 stations) at the beginning of 1973, to 8.3 percent (35 stations) in 1982, to 3.7 percent (25 stations) at the beginning of 1989 (1989, p. 790).

Howard says:

> Three reasons seem to account for the increase in the number of newspaper-affiliated television stations:
>
> 1. Although the FCC has sought to eliminate local cross-media ownerships of newspaper and TV properties, it has not objected to newspaper ownership of broadcast stations in markets where a publisher does not engage in the newspaper business.
>
> 2. Media companies with holdings in both the publishing and broadcast fields (and often cable as well) have experienced rapid growth during recent years.
>
> 3. Finally, existing media companies have added new television stations to their broadcast holdings. (1989, pp. 790–791)

Howard points out that newspaper chains such as Gannett, Times-Mirror, and Murdoch's News America (through Fox Television) have become big players in broadcasting, while radio-TV companies like ABC/Capital Cities and Park Communications have entered the publishing business. At the same time corporations like Cox Enterprises, Hearst, Scripps-Howard, and Tribune Company have added television stations to their holdings. The Tribune Company, through its super stations in Chicago and New York, currently leads all other groups in weekly audience reach (1989, pp. 790–791).

He concludes:

> Media companies which operate both TV stations and newspapers, but in separate market areas, have become highly visible components of the communications industry structure. The list of the 25 largest television group owners includes such prominent publishers as Tribune Company, Gannett, Cox, Scripps-Howard, Hearst, Belo, Post-Newsweek, Knight-Ridder, Times-Mirror, and Pulitzer. (p. 792)

Media Conglomerates

One of the most rapidly expanding areas of media ownership is that of media conglomerates. A parent corporation may own newspapers, magazines, book publishing houses, news services, public opinion polling organizations, radio and television stations, cable TV, broadcasting networks, and companies that produce records and tapes and the associated "clubs" that promote, sell, and distribute those records and tapes.

Often a conglomerate derives only a fraction of its annual revenue from media activities,

Table 17.4
NEWSPAPER-AFFILIATED TELEVISION STATIONS, JANUARY 1, 1989

Market Rank	VHF		UHF		Both VHF and UHF	
	No.	%	No.	%	No.	%
1–10	25	58.1	8	10.0	33	26.8
11–25	19	32.8	5	7.5	24	19.4
26–50	31	44.3	9	10.3	40	25.5
51–75	30	41.1	7	8.8	37	24.2
76–100	26	43.3	7	11.7	33	27.5
TOTAL (1–100)	131	43.1	36	9.6	167	24.7

From H. H. Howard, "Group and Cross-Media Ownership of TV Stations: A 1989 Update," *Journalism Quarterly* 66 (1989): 791. Reprinted by permission.

the bulk of its operations being in manufacturing and sales. These include such diverse activities as international telecommunications, the manufacture of electronic systems for defense and space, musical instruments, frozen foods, investment corporations, paper and wood products, timberlands, furniture manufacturing, vehicle rental agencies, cement, sugar, citrus, livestock, cigars, and candy. If these seem like a varied mixture indeed, that is, after all, the definition of conglomerate. A number of these conglomerates involved in the mass media rank well up among the *Fortune* 500 listings of the largest corporations in the United States.

The dean of Columbia's graduate school of journalism, Osborn Elliott, speaking at the presentation of the Alfred I. du Pont–Columbia University broadcast journalism awards in 1986, said:

> News divisions, which once may have enjoyed some kind of special standing within their companies, may now be perceived as just another chicken in the corporate henhouse, to be stuffed or starved as may serve the corporate purpose. (Boyer, 1986)

The General Electric Company, the tenth largest U.S. corporation, bought Radio Corporation of America in 1985 for $6.28 billion. RCA, in turn, owns NBC and seven television stations in the nation's largest cities (*Broadcasting and Cablecasting Yearbook 1989*, p. A49). However, only a fraction of RCA's total revenues are derived from broadcasting; twice as much has traditionally come from electronic products and services, much of it from defense and space contracts. The rest of RCA's revenues have come from its publishing houses and such diverse operations as frozen foods and vehicle rental.

One writer has pointed out that RCA is a major defense contractor supplying radar, electronic warfare and laser systems, guidance systems for missiles and bombs, intelligence processing hardware, and other items. Through RCA Global Communications it controls telecommunications among 200 nations, and it was also a major supplier for the Alaska pipeline. RCA produced the guidance systems for the *Apollo* and *Skylab* spacecraft, and the writer wonders what RCA might have lost in multimillion-dollar space contracts if its broadcasting network, NBC, had produced a powerful documentary against the vast expenditures on space exploration (Bagdikian, 1977, p. 20).

With the sale of RCA to General Electric, one cannot help but speculate on the kind of news coverage RCA's subsidiary NBC would provide should GE become involved in another conspiracy and price-fixing scandal. Between 1911 and 1967 GE was the defendant in 65 antitrust actions. One resulted in jail sentences for three GE officials and fines and settlements reaching more than $58 million (Moskowitz, Katz, & Levering, 1980, p. 178.)

Perhaps even more disturbing is the fact that General Electric is the nation's largest manufacturer of nuclear power plants (28 in operation in the United States and dozens more overseas). Following the Chernobyl nuclear disaster, experts in this country asserted that there are construction similarities between the Soviet plant and those in the United States (Diamond, 1986). The Union of Concerned Scientists and others have repeatedly raised questions about the safety of GE nuclear power plants (as in their full-page advertisement in the *New York Times* on May 19, 1986, p. 9). This raises obvious questions about how GE-owned NBC News will cover such vital issues.

The New York Times Company owns, besides the *New York Times,* dailies and weeklies in 10 states, two radio and five television stations in several states, a one-third interest in the *International Herald-Tribune,* book publishers, and a half-dozen magazines (*Broadcasting and Cablecasting Yearbook 1989,* pp. A49, A60). In 1976 it sold eight professional magazines to publisher and then theme park operator Harcourt Brace and Jovanovich.

Among the magazines the New York Times Company sold was *Modern Medicine,* one of seven specialized journals in the health field that it had bought from another media conglomerate, Cowles Communications, Inc. (former publisher of *Look* magazine, among other ventures). After the *New York Times* ran a series of articles (cited in Chapter 16) dealing with medical incompetence, it lost 260 pages of advertising from medical-related industries, not in the *New York Times* but in its magazine *Modern Medicine.* Respected media critic Ben Bagdikian writes:

> One wonders whether Harcourt Brace Jovanovich will now think twice before publishing an otherwise acceptable manuscript if it contains material displeasing to the advertisers who are now a source of the concern's revenue. One wonders, moreover, if other newspaper conglomerates would have been as willing as the Times Company to get rid of such a property: it would strike many as simpler not to assign reporters to stories that might offend someone doing business with a subsidiary. (Bagdikian, 1977, p. 20)

In 1989 Time Inc. and Warner Communications merged to become the largest media corporation in the world. Time Inc. had published not only *Time, Life, Fortune, Sports Illustrated, Money,* and *People* magazines but also Time-Life Books; Little, Brown books; and weekly newspapers. It was heavily into films, broadcasting, cable television, investment corporations, and forest products (pulp, paperboard, packaging, building materials, interior wall products, bedroom furniture, timberland, etc.). Today the new Time Inc.–Warner Communications is the largest magazine publisher in the United States and has a total worldwide readership of more than 120 million. As the world's largest video company, second largest cable company, and one of the largest book publishers it conducts operations on five continents (Bagdikian, 1990, p. 240).

Paramount Communications Inc. (before mid-1989 called Gulf + Western), near the top of the *Fortune* 500, deals in insurance, manufacturing, zinc, cement, apparel, paper, building products, auto replacement parts (both in the United States and overseas), rocket engineering, jet engines and missile parts, nuclear power plants, sugar, citrus and frozen juices, mining (on four continents), livestock, cigars, candy, and a host of other industries. It also produces prime-time television shows, and owns Paramount Pictures and Simon & Schuster book publishers (Bagdikian, 1990, pp. 28–30). It took a full-page ad in the *New York Times* to list its many entertainment and publishing activities (June 5, 1989, p. 29). It operates in all 50 states and 50 other countries.

Ben Bagdikian, dean emeritus of journalism at Berkeley and formerly the first ombudsman at the *Washington Post,* relates in his book *The Media Monopoly* the fate of a book manuscript critical of big corporations that was submitted to Simon & Schuster, a subsidiary of Gulf + Western (now Paramount Communications Inc.). Although one of Simon' & Schuster's editors and her staff were unanimous in supporting publication of the book, the corporation president opposed publication, even though it never mentioned Gulf + Western, because he felt it made all corporations look bad (Bagdikian, 1990, pp. 27–30). The book in question, *Corporate Murders,* wasn't published. Bagdikian cites other similar examples.

When the first edition (1983) of Bagdikian's book *The Media Monopoly* was about to be published, Simon & Schuster asked Beacon Press to delete criticism of it from the book and asked to see the manuscript. When Beacon Press refused, Simon & Schuster threatened the publisher with a libel suit. Beacon Press stood firm, and the incident has been related in Bagdikian's book through three editions (1990, pp. 27–30). (Beacon Press, the Boston-based publishing arm of the Unitarian Church, published the *Pentagon Papers* in 1971 over the objections of the Nixon administration. They described the origins of U.S. intervention in Vietnam [*Wall Street Journal*, April 7, 1983, p. 10; McDowell, 1983].)

Before Bagdikian sent the manuscript of *The Media Monopoly* to Beacon Press the manuscript had been turned down by 12 major commercial publishing houses, including the publisher of most of his earlier books. None of the publishers were ones he had written about, and none provided reasons for their rejections of the manuscript (Rips, 1988, p. 16).

In March 1985, ABC, third largest U.S. television network, was bought by Capital Cities Communications for $3.5 billion. At that time ABC owned television stations in New York, Chicago, Detroit, Los Angeles, and San Francisco, as well as 12 radio stations in major markets, a publishing business, and a film company. ABC reported revenues in 1984 of $3.7 billion and profits of $195 million. Capital Cities, which reported 1984 profits of $135.2 million on revenues of $939.7 million, owned 7 television stations (including stations in Philadelphia and Houston), 12 radio stations, 8 daily newspapers, 9 weeklies, and several cable television systems.

Capital Cities/ABC Inc. owned in 1989, in addition to the ABC television network, 11 AM, 10 FM, and 8 TV stations, a newspaper chain of 8 dailies, 28 community weeklies and 12 shopping guides, cable companies, ESPN and Lifetime cable channels, Hollywood studios, and a score of consumer, medical, professional, trade, and agricultural magazines (*Broadcasting and Cablecasting Yearbook 1989*, pp. A40, A57; Bagdikian, 1990, pp. 241–242.

In January 1979 the American Express Company attempted to take over one of the nation's largest publishers, McGraw-Hill, Inc. In addition to book publishing the company also, at that time, published 60 magazines, including *Business Week*, and owned Standard and Poor's investment advisory service. The offer of $830 million (later increased to $976 million) or $34 per share (later $40) in cash or securities to stockholders, made it one of the biggest takeover attempts on record to that time. The day after the announcement, McGraw-Hill stock jumped $4^7/_8$ on the New York Stock Exchange. The reaction of Chairman Harold W. McGraw, Jr., to the attempted takeover was "negative" (*New York Times*, Jan. 10, 1979, sec. 4, p. 16).

In February the Federal Trade Commission expressed four "serious concerns" about the takeover effort, now "bitterly opposed" by McGraw-Hill directors:

1. Possible unfair advantage to American Express from advance notice of business information to be published in McGraw-Hill publications and possible influence by American Express on the selection of material published by McGraw-Hill

2. Potential conflict of interest if McGraw-Hill, a leading bond rating firm, is taken over by American Express, a leading underwriter of bonds

3. The possibility of a reduction in competition between the two companies in services related to bond sales

4. Possible unfair business advantage to American Express through reduced advertising rates in McGraw-Hill publications

McGraw-Hill was almost taken over by American Express because two individuals with inside knowledge of the publishing firm's finances switched sides in the attempted "hostile" takeover. One was McGraw-Hill's banker, the other was from the American Express Company. Both were members of McGraw-Hill's board of directors.

Ben Bagdikian has called for a series of changes (1977, p. 22; 1978, p. 34)—for the professional staffs of newspapers and broadcasting stations to choose their own top editors, to have representatives on the board of directors, and to have a voice in determining the annual news budget. He points out that this is done on a number of quality European papers including *Le Monde,* often cited as one of the best newspapers in the world. Bagdikian gets to the heart of the matter when he says:

> Broadcast and newspaper news is too important an ingredient in the collective American brain to be constantly exposed to journalistically irrelevant corporate policy. . . . Staff autonomy in the newsroom has not been the ordinary way of running business, even the news business. But there is no reason to expect that a person skilled at building a corporate empire is a good judge of what the generality of citizens in a community need and want to know. Today, news is increasingly a monopoly medium in its locality, its entrepreneurs are increasingly absent ones who know little about and have no commitment to the social and political knowledge of a community's citizens. More and more, the news in America is a by-product of some other business, controlled by a small group of distant corporate chieftains. If the integrity of news and the full information of communities are to be protected, more can be expected from autonomous news staffs than from empire builders mainly concerned with other businesses in other places. (1977, p. 22)

More recently, Bagdikian (1990) has explored at book length the accelerating concentration of media ownership, now in the hands of 23 corporations who control the majority of United States media (p. 4); interlocking directorates and the corporate desire for only positive information; the trend to mass advertising directed at "upscale" audiences and its impact on media content, especially as it affects minorities and the poor; media monopoly and the myth of media competition; the use of media power to obtain, through political means, special economic considerations; the reduction of local media coverage in favor of cheaper syndicated material and its impact on citizen knowledge of local affairs; the result of maintaining the status quo when news is not put into its social, economic, and political context; and a series of other media issues.

Among the remedies Bagdikian suggests are:

> 1. A limit on the number of broadcasting stations, newspapers, magazines, and book publishers under a single ownership (During the 1980s the FCC nearly doubled the limit on broadcasting stations allowed under single ownership, and seems to be moving toward eliminating limits on ownership altogether. Of course, there has never been a limit in the print media.)
> 2. Limits on the cross ownership of media
> 3. Free broadcasting time for political candidates to help prevent their having to become beholden to large financial contributors
> 4. A progressive tax on advertising

5. The selection of top editors by professional newspaper staffs

6. Mandated free prime-time for the representatives of all political parties in political campaigns. (pp. 223–237)

Other suggestions that have been made include divestiture of cross owned media in single communities, divestiture of network-owned and operated stations, reductions in the amount of programming originated by the network, and more autonomy for news staffs, including employee ownership.

Employee Ownership

Milwaukee Journal

One major daily newspaper, the *Milwaukee Journal,* found a way in 1937 to prevent the "irreversible trend" of chain ownership (Conrad, Wilson, & Wilson, 1964, pp. 175–181). Today nearly all the stock in the *Journal* is in employee hands. The Employees' Stock Trust Agreement of 1937 ensures that it will probably remain so (Severin, 1979). The agreement was set up to prevent ownership of the actual stock from passing into the hands of persons not directly involved with the company. A former editor and president of the company, John Donald Ferguson, said, "The allotment of stock has been such that no single group, and no possible combinations of two or three groups, including the executive group, could control the company" (Conrad, Wilson, & Wilson, p. 179).

In 1947, on the 10th anniversary of the employee ownership plan, employees presented former owners with scrolls that stated:

> Employee ownership knits our lives together. We don't work *for* the *Journal.* We *are* the *Journal.* . . . Above all we are grateful for the security which sharing ownership has brought into our lives. . . . We stand on guard to preserve and perpetuate this institution in our time, and beyond. (Conrad, Wilson, & Wilson, p. 181)

Over one 10-year period the price per share increased nearly 154 percent with an average annual return of 23.7 percent, including dividends paid and increases in value (Severin, 1979).

Irwin Maier, chairman of the board of directors of the Journal Company from 1968 to 1977, said:

> What this stock plan has done has been not only to keep secure a newspaper's future, but it has helped finance college educations for children, helped buy homes and secure loans for home remodeling, supported parents in nursing homes, and paid for parents' medical expenses. (Severin, 1979, p. 786)

Employees can use their shares in the company as collateral for loans at Milwaukee banks and get favorable interest rates.

The annual balance sheet shows that the employee ownership plan has paid off financially. But, many hold that there is another balance sheet to be considered in the only industry named in and protected by the Constitution: the fulfillment of a social responsibility to a community.

Nearly any national poll of the best daily newspapers in the United States includes the *Milwaukee Journal,* often ranked near the top. Over the years the newspaper has been awarded five Pulitzer Prizes. Its 1968 Pulitzer, for distinguished public service, was for a color Sunday magazine supplement dealing with water pollution. Shortly thereafter, Wisconsin passed a law to regulate the pollution of public waters that became a model for other states.

Irwin Maier says, "The employees take pride in ownership, they want it to succeed." Of his own role in the company, which spanned more than half a century, Maier says:

> You feel that anything you do affects them, so you give it extra thought. You are working as an owner, but you are also working for all the other owners, who are your friends and associates. You don't go to New York to report to security analysts. The people you report to are right here—they are us. I wouldn't want it any other way. (Severin, 1979, p. 787)

The then editorial page editor of the *Journal*, Sig Gissler, said:

> We have preserved many of the features of a family-owned newspaper but have avoided the eccentricities of family ownership. Whoever is chairman of the board here cannot say, "This is my newspaper" and do whatever he wants. It is amazing that we can still preserve a family feeling with 2,000 employees and our many subdivisions.

He adds, "I think primarily the difference between the *Journal* and other newspapers is the depth and diligence of its local, regional and state coverage. We plow an awful lot of our resources into coverage" (Severin, 1979, p. 787).

The Employees' Stock Trust Agreement is now more than a half-century old, and there is no indication that the *Journal* will ever become part of a chain or conglomerate. In October 1986 the Journal Company rejected an offer by Affiliated Publications of Boston to buy the company for $626 million. The offer was worth $87 a share, more than double the share value under the employee trust. "The company is not for sale," said Jack Knake, Journal Company vice president (*Wall Street Journal*, Oct. 31, 1986, p. 12). When an earlier attempt was made to buy the company, Chairman of the Board Donald B. Abert said, "We are employee-owned and we intend to remain so" (*Wall Street Journal*, June 4, 1980, p. 18).

The Journal Company started experiments with radio in 1924 and a year later station WTMJ was established. Its regular broadcasts have been heard since 1927. In 1929 the company began TV experimentation and WTMJ-TV went on the air in 1947 as the nation's first TV station west of the Alleghenies (*History*).

The Journal Company bought the morning *Milwaukee Sentinel* from the Hearst Corporation in 1962 after the *Sentinel* had stopped publishing because of a lengthy strike. The paper, known for its investigative reporting, is the state's largest morning newspaper.

Journal Communications, as it is now known, also owns five radio and three television stations, nine weekly newspapers, six commercial printing plants, and other communication properties. It employs nearly 4,000 full-time people and has operations in 15 states.

By January 1989, the value of the units owned by employees and retirees had risen to $338,522,000. As of the end of that year 2,610 people were part of the employee ownership plan.

The Unitholders Council has been expanded into three, the Journal-Sentinel Council, the Telecom Council, and the Printing Council. The 35 representatives on the three councils elect seven of their members to the board of directors of Journal Communications. During its first 40 years, more than 500 employee-owners have served on the council and more than 250 have been elected to the board of directors (*Partners*, p. 18).

Peoria Journal Star

In 1983 the *Peoria* (Illinois) *Journal Star* established a similar ownership plan, using employee stock ownership plans (ESOPs) and retirement plans such as 401(k) plans on a voluntary basis. In 1984, reflecting the company's profitability, high prices paid by chains for other independently owned newspapers, and the rising value of publicly owned newspaper stocks, the *Journal Star*'s value went up nearly 25 percent to $49 million. Earnings for 1984 were $1.3 million on revenues of $49.7 million, an increase of 8.5 percent from the previous year, a strong indication that the incentive of employee ownership has had a positive effect on company performance. At the end of the second year of the plan's operation, the average employee had more than $25,000 worth of *Journal Star* stock. The initial stock was acquired in 1984 at $39 per share and by 1990 the appraised value had grown to $125 per share (Koch, 1990). By December 1985 *Journal Star* employees owned 25 percent of their newspaper and were scheduled to own the company outright by 1994 (*Profile*, Dec. 1985, p. 1). However, by early 1990 the ESOP owned 82 percent of the shares through subsequent purchases and has the right to acquire the remaining 18 percent (Koch, 1990).

The newspaper has been in the Slane family since its founding in 1889. Henry Slane, principal owner and current president, began to search for a means to keep the paper independent and locally owned when he decided to sell. Slane says that he had no intention to allow the company "to fall into the hands of any of the large chains who would be forced to bleed it instead of expanding it" (*Profile*, Dec. 1985, pp. 3–4). His two principal objectives were to ensure local, community ownership of the paper; and to provide employees with a stake in the business and therefore with a powerful incentive to be productive and efficient.

This was *not* the sale of a faltering business to a group of employees who had to save their jobs. In addition to the sale of the newspaper (with a circulation of more than 100,000, making it the largest Illinois daily outside of Chicago), the company also owned five national-circulation magazines and six radio stations. In 1983 the company's appraised value was $39 million.

One of two corporate pension plans was terminated and proceeds were rolled over into the ESOP. The transaction required no wage or benefit reductions from the *Journal Star*'s employees. Nearly all of the company's employees are participants in the ESOP, including union members.

In addition, a 401(k) salary deferral plan is also incorporated into the ESOP whereby the company matches, dollar for dollar, employee contributions to the plan up to 5 percent of compensation. An employee can invest 5 percent of pretax income, have it matched with 5 percent from the company, and receive an additional 12.5 percent in corporate contributions for a total contribution of 22.5 percent of his or her earnings each year.

The company provides employees with annual corporate reports, quarterly reports with full financial disclosure, and a company newsletter called *In Business for Ourselves*.

Departing employees are given an option of receiving their plan distributions in a lump-sum payment, in stock, or in installments. The company retains the right of first refusal on repurchase of all distributed stock to ensure that 100 percent ownership will continue to reside in employee hands.

The following statement, issued at the time the ESOP was established in 1984 by Henry Slane, the third-generation owner-publisher and chairman, greets the visitor inside the front door of the *Journal Star:*

I feel strongly that this newspaper and its affiliated companies should ultimately belong to those who have worked as a team to make this group what it is today. Far too many organizations, such as ours, have ended in the hands of large communication conglomerates. I have no intention of seeing such a fate befall our group.

In 1989 the *Journal Star*'s ESOP participated, along with the Thomson Newspaper Group of Canada, in bidding for the purchase of the *Register-Mail,* a 19,000 circulation daily in nearby Galesburg, Illinois. The *Journal Star* was the successful bidder, in part because of the benefits available under the ESOP. The employees in Galesburg will join the ESOP and the newspaper will remain locally owned (S. Koch, personal communication, Feb. 2, 1990).

The Peoria *Journal Star* ESOP could be the way to maintain local ownership in the future.

Conclusions

Several media scholars have pointed out that media ownership determines media control, which, in turn, determines media content, which is probably the major cause of media effects. Media ownership is an important concern of communication theorists dealing with media effects.

A number of reasons have been advanced opposing the increasing concentration of ownership in the U.S. media. Nearly all are concerned with the effects of ownership on media content and its ultimate effects on society. This chapter has discussed some of the many possible remedies that have been suggested.

References

Associated Press (1986). Gannett chain purchases Louisville newspaper firm. May 19.
Bagdikian, B. (1977). Newspaper mergers: The final phase. *Columbia Journalism Review,* Mar.-Apr., pp. 17–22.
——— (1978). The media monopolies. *Progressive,* June, pp. 31–37.
——— (1990). *The Media Monopoly.* Boston: Beacon Press.
Boyer, P. (1986). *Nightline* wins journalism prize. *Austin American-Statesman,* Feb. 9, p. 46.
Breed, W. (1955). Social control in the newsroom. *Social Forces,* May, pp. 326–335.
Broadcasting and Cablecasting Yearbook (1989). Washington, D.C.: Broadcasting Publications, Inc.
Business Week (1977). The big money hunts for independent newspapers. Feb. 21, pp. 56–60; 62.
Busterna, J. C. (1988). Trends in daily newspaper ownership. *Journalism Quarterly* 65: 831–838.
Conrad, W., K. Wilson, and D. Wilson (1964). *The Milwaukee Journal: The First Eighty Years.* Madison: University of Wisconsin Press.
Cook, A. (1977). Extra! extra! read all about it! *Texas Parade,* October, pp. 35–36.
Diamond, S. (1986). Chernobyl design found to include new safety plans. *New York Times,* May 19, pp. 1, 6.
Gormley, W. (1977) How cross-ownership affects news-gathering. *Columbia Journalism Review,* May-June, pp. 38–46.
History. Milwaukee, Wisc.: Journal Communications, no date. (Company internal publication.)
Howard, H. H. (1989). Group and cross-media ownership of TV stations: A 1989 update. *Journalism Quarterly* 66: 785–792.
Hoyt, M., and M. Schoonmaker (1985). Onward—and upward?—with the Newhouse boys. *Columbia Journalism Review,* July-Aug., pp. 37–44.
Jones, W., and L. Anderson (1977). The newspaper business. Madison, Wis., *Capital Times,* Aug. 15, p. 25.

Koch, S. (1990). Personal correspondence from vice-president and treasurer of *Peoria Journal Star,* Inc. to W. J. Severin, Feb. 2.

McDowell, E. (1983). Censorship raised in book dispute. *New York Times,* April 9, p. 19.

Moore, M. (1985). How to keep 'em happy in Flint. *Columbia Journalism Review,* Sept.-Oct., pp. 40–43.

Moskowitz, M., M. Katz, & R. Levering (eds.) (1980). *Everybody's Business.* New York: Harper & Row.

Partners. Milwaukee, Wisc.: Journal Communications, no date. (Company internal publication.)

Phillips, K. (1977). Busting the media trusts. *Harper's,* July, pp. 23–34.

Rips, G. (1988). All the news that's fit to print. *Texas Observer,* Feb. 12, pp. 12–16.

Rosse, J. (1980). The decline of direct newspaper competition. *Journal of Communication* 30: 65–71.

Severin, W. (1979). The *Milwaukee Journal:* Employee-owned prizewinner. *Journalism Quarterly* 56: 783–787.

Tate, C. (1981). Gannett in Salem: Protecting the franchise. *Columbia Journalism Review,* July-Aug., pp. 51–56.

Winski, J. (1981). Case study: How Gannett took Oregon. *Advertising Age* 52, July 6, p. 1. Reprinted in M. Emery and T. Smythe, *Readings in Mass Communication: Concepts and Issues in the Mass Media.* Dubuque, Iowa: Wm. C. Brown. 6th ed. (1986), pp. 50–61. 5th ed. (1983), pp. 69–79.

PART

VII

Bringing It All Together

Throughout this book we have approached the process of mass communication from several different perspectives, including that of the individual receiver, the individual as a member of a group, the individual as a recipient of mass media effects, the individual as a user of the mass media, and the mass media as institutions in society. In covering these perspectives, we have summarized a large number of theories and a great deal of research dealing with mass communication.

There is probably no framework or model that would successfully bring all these diverse perspectives, theories, and research findings together. In the final chapter of the book, Chapter 18, we attempt to bring together as much as we can of this material through the use of one particular communication model—the Westley-MacLean model.

The search for a more unified theory of mass communication goes on, but in the meantime, communication research and theory have produced a rich body of findings that can help us to communicate better and perhaps even to live better lives.

18
The Overall Picture

Early in this book we discussed the need for research and theory in communication and their application to the fields of journalism, advertising, radio, television, film, and public relations. After discussing the scientific method, a number of models of the communication process were presented and discussed. We now attempt to bring most of the material discussed in earlier chapters together by relating it to an overall model, the Westley-MacLean model.

The Westley-MacLean model (Figure 3.4[d] in Chapter 3, reprinted here as Figure 18.1) expanded the Newcomb model of interpersonal symmetry (Chapters 3 and 8) to include a communicator role (C) and to accommodate a number of "objects of orientation" (X). When they presented their model in 1957, Westley and MacLean said:

> Communications research and theory have blossomed from a variety of disciplinary sources in recent years. People probing the communications area have here focused on theoretical issues and there on "practical" concerns. Thus, one finds today a jungle of unrelated concepts and systems of concepts on the one hand and a mass of undigested, often sterile empirical data on the other. (p. 31)

They added:

> In this paper, we are trying to develop a single communication model which may help to order existing findings. It also may provide a system of concepts which will evoke new and interrelated research directions, compose old theoretical and disciplinary differences, and in general bring some order out of a chaotic situation. . . . Can a simple, parsimonious model be built capable of drawing together many of the existing approaches to mass communications without serious loss in utility? (p. 31)

The Model and Communication Research

In the Westley-MacLean model, the As (advocacy roles) or communicators select and transmit messages purposively. Information theory, explored in Chapter 3, deals with sources that select messages out of all those possible and produce suitable signals for transmission over whatever channel is used. Chapter 3 also discussed the role of gatekeepers and coupling. Chapter 5 dealt with the effects of language on perception, including assumptions built into languages about the nature of reality, and abstraction and the misuses of language, including overgeneralization, two-valued thinking, and unconscious projection.

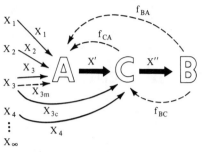

The messages C transmits to B (X″) represent his selections from both messages to him from As (X′) and C's selections and abstractions from Xs in his own sensory field (X_{3c}, X_4), which may or may not be Xs in A's field. Feedback not only moves from B to A (f_{BA}) and from B to C (f_{BC}) but also from C to A (f_{CA}). Clearly, in the mass communication situation, a large number of Cs receive from a very large number of As and transmit to a vastly larger number of Bs, who simultaneously receive from other Cs.

FIGURE 18.1 • WESTLEY-MACLEAN MODEL

From B. H. Westley and M. MacLean, "A Conceptual Model for Communication Research," *Journalism Quarterly* 34 (1957): 35. Reprinted with permission.

Consistency theories have equal meaning for both communicators and receivers. To a greater or lesser extent, depending on the issue, we all practice selective attention and perception. Persuasion research (Chapter 9) indicates the active role of the receiver and that single messages are unlikely to change strongly held attitudes. Research about the communication of innovation indicates that such attitudes are probably best changed with a combination of interpersonal and media messages used as "media forums" (Chapters 9 and 11). The studies dealing with the credibility of the source (Chapter 9) or communicator are, of course, of direct application here. As pointed out earlier, the concept of agenda setting raises important questions for the journalist. Whether the public pays attention to the issues connected with an event can be influenced by the labels a journalist applies to that event, and, as research has demonstrated, whether the report of an event is accompanied by photographs and their size. Newsmakers have long sought to place items on the media agenda, and we now have evidence of intermedia agenda setting, whereby certain media systematically influence other media.

The Cs (channel roles) provide the Bs (behavioral system roles) with a more extended environment by selecting and transmitting the information Bs require, especially information that is beyond B's immediate reach. Cs make abstractions from objects (X) appropriate to satisfying B's needs or solving B's problem. We have already mentioned information theory, semantics, and selective attention as they relate to abstraction in connection with A roles. In a like manner they apply to C roles.

In the Westley-MacLean model, Cs select and transmit nonpurposively the information Bs require. Nonpurposively means without intent to influence. However, as gatekeepers, Cs often engage in transmitting messages designed to engender attitude change, as in the case of advertising and public relations campaigns and in more general ways (compare

Lasswell and Breed). Cs also serve different roles in various types of societies and may have several functions as well as dysfunctions. Lasswell has pointed to distortions of media content as a method of achieving or maintaining social control. Breed discusses news policy and slanting, areas omitted or seldom dealt with by communicators, and the distortions brought about by civic boosterism. Media chains, conglomerates, and cross ownership in single communities can all result in distortions and omissions of news and a reduction in the diversity of news as a threat to truth and understanding. Some researchers suggest that the communicator is often in a position to exercise great influence as to what readers and viewers will think about (the agenda-setting function), even if not the conclusions they will reach about an issue. Agenda-setting research suggests that the media shape people's views about the major problems facing society. However, the problems emphasized by the media may not be those that are in reality the most pressing. The mass media can also work to close the knowledge gaps that exist in society, particularly when lower-status segments need a particular type of information. This is especially true in pluralistic communities with numerous sources of information. Some researchers have concluded that because the more highly educated are more able to disseminate information there may be an information gap, which may be a bigger problem than a knowledge gap. Unfortunately, as indicated in Chapter 17, there is some evidence that many of the media are not interested in reaching the lower-status segments of society because these are unwanted by advertisers.

The Bs in the Westley-MacLean model are the behavioral system roles or the "receivers." They can be an individual (a personality system), a primary group, or a social system. A B needs "transmissible messages as a means of orienting itself in its environment and as a means of securing problem solutions and need satisfactions." Bs can select from a number of Cs, as diffusion studies have shown, which is why C remains an agent of B only so long as C fulfills B's needs. Bs are the destination in information theory terms and must decode the messages. Bs bring their backgrounds to the messages to provide connotative meanings. As pointed out in Chapter 4, "meaning is something invented, assigned, given, rather than something received." Bs exercise selective perception and often make information fit an existing schema as a result of their past experiences, cultural expectations, needs, moods, and attitudes. They also use selective exposure, attention, and retention when dealing with messages. As Chapter 10 (Groups and Communication) points out, how we interpret and act on message content is often the result of the groups we are members of, identify with, or aspire to. There is also evidence (Chapter 4) that much use of mass communication may be ritualistic or habitual and involve a low level of attention.

Consistency theories predict that when messages that cause psychological discomfort are directed to Bs (receivers), they will use selective attention, perception, and retention or fall back on rationalization, incredulity, or attacks on source credibility to avoid or reduce the psychological discomfort. However, if the messages offer rewards (utility, novelty, etc.) great enough to offset the discomfort, Bs may not avoid them. Communicators who wish to change attitudes held by receivers must first understand the functions of those attitudes for receivers if any measure of success is to be achieved. Inoculation theory provides the other side of the coin, making attitudes resistant to persuasion.

If receivers are to be reached through opinion leaders, two-step flow and communication of innovation research indicate that media appropriate to the particular sphere of influence must be carefully selected.

Uses and gratifications research helps to explain to communicators some selective behavior in media use by receivers and the reasons for it. The findings should help communicators better tailor their messages for their audiences.

The media serve several functions for receivers, but as we have seen, they can also have a number of dysfunctions. Walter Lippmann, more than a half-century ago, discussed the gap between reality and the pictures of reality we carry around in our heads. For the receiver the media supply information, gratify needs, and have other uses. These areas need further research along with the effects of the media on political behavior and the effects of viewing violence on television.

In the model "messages" about Xs (objects or events "out there" that have characteristics capable of being transmitted in some abstracted form) are transmitted through channels from As and/or Cs to Bs. These messages can inform, persuade, and educate. Information theory introduces the concepts of channel capacity, the notion that in one sense information is not meaning, the important use of redundancy to offset noise, and the use of entropy as a measure of the difficulty of a message. General semantics sheds light on the problems we encounter in using language to communicate abstractions about reality, and readability measures provide a way of judging the difficulty of textual materials. As was noted, more research is needed on the effects of organization of material, directness of approach, and the conceptual difficulty of textual materials, and probably on the "listenability" of spoken messages.

Messages often contain the techniques identified in studies of propaganda, an area that provided the roots for attitude-change research and the general studies of the effects of mass communication. An understanding of these techniques for designing messages is of considerable value to the receiver as well as the communicator. Message content is under increasing scrutiny, especially for sex and violence during prime-time television.

Mass Media Research

Communication research is the application of social science research methods to the problems communicators deal with. It is an attempt to replace as much guesswork as possible with verified theories. Theories and research methods in the social sciences are not as accurate or refined as those used in the physical sciences. Understanding and predicting human behavior is extremely difficult; nevertheless, the imperfect statements that can be made about human behavior as a result of research are better than the guesswork upon which much of communication has been based.

Research provides the information to help plan communication and evaluate its results. To sum up what we have learned about the uses of research in mass communication, we offer the following survey:

1. *Audience studies* are usually survey-type research designed to measure the amount of interest in various mass media content and the reasons for it. With print media, audience studies are usually in the form of "one-time" surveys, whereas television ratings most often use an adaptation of the "panel" method where samples of the audience are repeatedly measured over a period of years. Studies of media use and media credibility, reader interest surveys, and broadcast "ratings" are examples of this type of research.

2. *Message content and design* immediately brings to mind the content analysis of messages, but content analysis can often be used in conjunction with other research methods

to great advantage. Experimental designs in a laboratory setting are often used to determine the most effective version of a message to achieve a desired objective with a specific population. Research on the advantages of presenting one side of an issue or two sides of an issue, the use of fear appeals, the optimum levels of repetition (both in Chapter 9), the uses of language, and the various methods of counterpersuasion are examples of message content and design studies. So are field studies done by advertising agencies and public relations firms to determine the most effective form or versions for their commercials and advertisements.

3. *Effect studies* involve the planning and evaluation of the effects of media campaigns as well as the choice of media used. Studies involving the diffusion of innovations, the functions and dysfunctions of the media, the agenda-setting function of the media, and the effects of viewing television violence are obvious examples. In the commercial world, advertisers are interested in the most effective means of increasing sales, public relations practitioners seek the best ways to improve a corporate image, campaign managers need the means to get a candidate elected, and statesmen want the best ways to win acceptance for a policy or a program. Effect studies can use many research methods: experimental designs, survey research, content analysis, and case studies, as well as combinations of these.

4. *Communicator analysis* has traditionally been linked with "gatekeeper" studies (case studies). Studies dealing with the effects of language on perception and abstraction can also be classified as communicator analysis. The effects of source credibility on the acceptance of a message are also directly related to communicator studies. Research into the effects of media chains, conglomerates, and cross ownership on the content of the media are all examples of communicator analysis.

As can be seen, any listing of research in mass communication contains a great deal of overlap. One cannot separate media effects from message content, or communicator analysis from message content. Communicators, messages, audiences, and effects are all interrelated—that interrelation is necessary for communication. Research methods are tools to aid communicators in understanding the communication process and predicting the effects of their efforts.

In Conclusion

As we pointed out in our preface, this book is intended as an introduction to the development of mass communication theory. It provides the reader with a grounding in the beginnings of an ongoing field of research.

By now you are aware that communications theory and research stands at the crossroads of many other fields. The student seeking related courses and the practitioner seeking related reading might wish to consider some of the following, which is by no means an exhaustive list.

Psychology: social psychology, perception, psychology of language, sensory psychology, information processing, human learning

Sociology: public opinion, collective behavior, formal organizations, social change, communication

Government: public opinion, theory construction, empirical theory and modeling, research design

Philosophy: philosophy of science, science and the modern world, communication and culture

Linguistics: study of language, language and society

Computer sciences: computer application courses

Also, research methods (survey research, experimental design, content analysis, case studies, etc.) and statistics in a number of fields, especially psychology, educational psychology, sociology, government, and communications.

The student or practitioner who wishes to keep abreast of the most recent developments in this field can find them in a number of publications. Found in academic and other libraries, these journals regularly publish articles about the most recent advances in communication theory and research, and the function, effects, and role of the mass media. Among the best of them are (in alphabetical order): *Columbia Journalism Review; ETC.: A Review of General Semantics; Journal of Broadcasting and Electronic Media; Journal of Communication; Journalism Quarterly;* and *Public Opinion Quarterly.*

We wish our readers well in their ongoing quest to understand the functions, effects, and role of the mass media in modern society.

Reference

Westley, B., and M. MacLean (1957). A conceptual model for communication research. *Journalism Quarterly* 34: 31–38.

Index

Abelson, R. P., 143
Absolute sleeper effect, 157. *See also* Sleeper effect
Abstraction
  language as, 74–77
  levels of, 77–78, 88
Abstraction ladder, 75
Advertising
  canalizing attempt of, 302
  cloze procedure applied to, 125
  price, 30
  as propaganda, 91
  readability of, 120
  repetition in, 175
  subliminal, 67
  use of band wagon device in, 103
  use of sex in, 173–175
  use of testimonial in, 99–100
  use of transfer in, 99
  use of virtue words in, 96–97
Affiliated Publications of Boston, 335
Agenda building, 221–222
Agenda setting
  agenda building and, 221–222
  bias and, 220
  Chapel Hill study of, 208–212
  Charlotte study of, 211–213, 219, 221
  conceptualization of, 225
  effect of television program on, 217–219
  evolution of thinking in, 209–210
  experimental evidence in, 213–215
  explanation of, 207–208
  intermedia, 224
  media, 223–225
  obtrusiveness of issues, 219–220
  orientation needs and, 222–223, 264

presidential, 216–217
priming and, 215–216
process of, 225–227
reality and, 210–211
in television, 213–219, 222, 223
time lag and, 220–221
Aggressive behavior, 256–257
Agnew, Spiro, 86–87
AIDS, fear appeals in communication regarding, 161
AIETA model
  applied to print media, 171
  explanation of, 5–6
Alaska Visitors Association, 300
Alcoholics Anonymous, 188
Ali, Muhammad, 314
Allen, Irvin L., 201
"All in the Family" program, 63–65, 70
Allport, Gordon W., 64, 148, 201
Altheide, D. L., 254–255
Altruistic democracy, 304, 305
Altschull, J. Herbert, 290–293, 320
American Broadcasting Company (ABC), 217, 307, 328, 332
American Express Company, 332, 333
American Jewish Committee, 63
Ames, Adelbert, Jr., 58
Anderson, N. H., 156
Anderson, Norman, 176
Annual report readability, 120–121
Apple, R. W., 62n, 224
Appleton, H., 236n, 237n
Arafat, Fathi, 102
Army, U.S., 148–149
Asch, Solomon, 181, 183–184
Asner, Ed, 259

Associated Press, 118, 324
Assumptions
  hidden, 77
  meaning of, 3
  perception and, 58
Atkinson, J. W., 59, 60n
Attitude change, 6, 90
  appeals to humor to accomplish, 172–173
  appeals to sex to accomplish, 173–175
  cognitive change and, 141
  consistency theory approach to, 165. *See also*
    Consistency theories
  directions in theory of, 176, 209
  effects of repetition on, 175
  fear appeals and, 157–161
  following forced compliance, 141–142
  functional approach to, 165–167
  incongruity and, 137
  inconsistency of, 133
  inoculation theory of, 162–164
  learning theory approach to, 148, 165
  low involvement theory of, 171–172
  resistance to counterpropaganda and, 162,
    163
  source credibility and, 153–157
  symmetry theory and, 134–135
Attitude change research
  Hovland's, 147–150
  overview of, 176–177
  Yale Communication Research Program,
    152–153
Attitudes
  behavior and, 166, 168–170
  classical conditioning of, 170–171
  concept of, 148
  functions of, 165–167
  perception and, 61
  psychological needs and, 165
Attractiveness
  of models, 174
  source credibility and, 156
Audience
  activity level of, 269, 276
  impact of technology on, 278–279
  relationship between, media, society, and,
    262–263
  socioeconomic status of, 295–297
  studies of, 344
Austin American-Statesman, 308–309
Authoritarian theory of press, 285–287

Authority, 19
Autokinetic light effect, 182
Automatic exposure, 69
Awareness threshold, 67

Bagby, J. W., 58–59
Bagdikian, Ben, 331–334
Balance theory (Heider), 133, 134
Ballachey, E. L., 148
Ball-Rokeach, S. J., 188, 258, 259, 262–264,
  266
Band wagon appeals, 103–105
Bantz, C. R., 279
Barnlund, Dean C., 70
Barnum, P. T., 69
Baron, R. A., 256
Baskir, L., 311–312
Battle of Britain, The, film, 149, 150
Bavelas, Alex, 184
Beacon Press, 332
Beatty, S. E., 67
Beck, Gayle, 293
Becker, Hal, 68
Becker, L. B., 175, 265
Behavior, attitudes and, 166, 168–170
Behaviorism, 210
Bell, Daniel, 97
Bensman, J., 316
Bentsen, Lloyd, 234–235
Berelson, Bernard R., 68, 185, 186n, 269, 270
Berkowitz, D., 31
Bernays, Edward L., 95–96
Bias
  by agenda, 220
  in news coverage, 84–86
  safeguards against, 22–23
  use of negative, 84–85
Bingham, Barry, Jr., 322
Binocular rivalry, 58, 59
Black, Hugo, 234, 235
Black Americans
  literacy rates of, 122
  in Vietnam War, 312
Blair, E., 125
Blakemore, Colin, 248
Blumler, Jay G., 270–272
Bonjean, Charles M., 201
Book Digest magazine, 297
Boorstin, Daniel, 294
Booth Newspapers, 323

Bormuth, J. R., 124
Brain hemispheres, 251
Brantgarde, L., 242
Breed, Warren, 307–311, 313–317, 320, 343
Brigham, J. C., 64
Broad, W. J., 23
Broadcast news, 120. *See also* News; News coverage
Broadcast ownership, 325–328
Bronowski, J., 76
Brooker, G. W., 175, 176n
Brown, Bob, 315
Brown, H. Jackson, Jr., 81–82
Brown, J. R., 272
Brown, J. W., 240
Brown, Roger, 91, 105, 152
Bryan, Sam Dunn, 115, 119
Bryan, William Jennings, 147
Bryant, J., 143, 276, 277n
Bryson, Lyman, 112
Buddha, 73
Bullet theory, 105–106, 247–248, 260. *See also* Hypodermic-needle theory
Burd, Gene, 315
Busby, Horace, 314
Bush, George, 93, 224, 234–235, 312
Business
  glittering generalities in, 97
  media bias against, 303–304
Busterna, John C., 320–321
Bybee, C. R., 241

Cable News Network (CNN), 264
Cable television. *See also* Television
  impact of, 8, 12–13
  opportunities for active audience in, 278
  role in closing knowledge gap, 240
Cacioppo, J. T., 175
Campaigns. *See* Political campaigning; Presidential campaigns
Cantril, Hadley, 61–62, 92
Capital Cities Communications, 332
Capitalism, responsible, 304–306
Capra, Frank, 149
Card stacking. *See also* Slanting
  effectiveness of, 104, 150
  as propaganda device, 101–103
Caro, Robert, 313
Carter, Jimmy, 62, 207, 215, 216
Cartoons, antiprejudice, 63

Case studies, 30–32
Casual groups, 181
Categorical thinking, 78
Categorization, language use for, 76
Catharsis hypothesis, television violence and, 255
Causality, experimental design to deal with, 28, 213
CD-ROM (Compact Disk-Read Only Memory), 9
Ceausescu, Nicolae, 290
Census, 24
Chains. *See also* Conglomerates
  broadcasting, 325
  employee ownership as alternative to, 334–337
  media cross-ownership in, 325–328
  newspaper, 320–325
Chall, J. S., 126
Chandler, Otis, 323–324
Chang, T. K., 28
Change agents
  explanation of, 200
  role of, 200–201
Channel capacity, 40–41
Chapel Hill study, 208–212
Chappaquiddick incident, 209, 215
Charisma, source credibility and, 156
Charlotte study, 211–213, 219, 221
Childers, T., 230
Civil rights issues, 221
Clark, R., 316
Classical conditioning, 170–171
Cleaver, Eldridge, 73
Closure, 22
Cloze procedure, 44, 123–126
Cognitive consistency, 6
Cognitive dissonance, 64
  theory of, 140–144
Cognitive psychology, 210
Cohen, Arthur R., 166
Cohen, Bernard, 209
Cohen, M. R., 22
Colby, William, 80
Colfax, J. David, 201
Collective bargaining agreements, 121–122
Columbia Broadcasting System (CBS), 136, 220, 255
Columbus, Christopher, 139
Combs, James, 248

Commercials, 101. *See also* Advertising
Commission on Freedom of the Press, 289
Communication. *See also* Mass communication
  application of mathematical theory to, 43
  decentralization of, 12
  in information theory terms, 44
  monopoly in, 105
  social nature of, 46
  Westley-MacLean model and research in, 341–344
Communication channels, 200
Communication effects, 4–6
Communication media
  examples of, 8–10
  map of, 10–12
Communication models
  Gerbner's, 50–51
  Lasswell's, 38
  mathematical theory, 38–39, 46. *See also* Information theory
  Newcomb symmetry, 47–50
  Osgood, 45–46
  Schramm, 46–47
  Westley-MacLean, 48–50, 341–344
Communication networks, 44
Communication systems, 43–44
Communication technology
  advances in, 7–8
  consequences of new, 8–10
  impact on audience of, 278–279
  impact on communication theory of, 12–13
  knowledge gap and, 242–244
  origins of digital, 39
Communication theory
  effects of, 6
  explanation of, 4
  goals of, 285
  impact of new technology on, 12–13
  uses of, 6
Communicator analysis, 345
Communicator credibility. *See* Media credibility; Source credibility
Community
  coverage of news in local, 324–325
  role in decision making, 194–196
Competence
  opinion leaders and, 195
  source credibility and, 156

CompuServe, 12
Computers. *See also* Communication technology
  future uses of, 13
  impact of home, 8
  ownership of home, 243, 244
  readability formulas, 115
Conditioning. *See* Classical conditioning
Confidence interval, 24
Conformism, social, 301
Conglomerates. *See also* Chains
  control of newspapers by, 320
  overview of, 328, 330–334
Congruity theory (Osgood), 135–140
Connally, John, 324
Conner, R. F., 236n, 237n
Consequences, 199–200
Consistency, 131–132
Consistency theories
  attitude change and, 165. *See also* Attitude change
  Festinger's theory of cognitive dissonance, 140–144
  Heider's balance theory, 133
  Newcomb's symmetry theory, 133–135
  Osgood's congruity theory, 135–140
Consonance, 252–253
Content analysis
  case study of television news gatekeeping using, 31
  to examine news bias, 85
  explanation and examples of, 26–28
  of State of the Union address, 216
Cook, Thomas D., 157, 236, 237n
Cooper, Eunice, 63, 248
Copernicus, Nicolaus, 20, 21
Corporate reports, 120–121
Correlation function of media, 293–294, 296
Corresponding systems, 43
Cosby, Bill, 99–100
Cosmopolite communication channels, 200
Cotton, J. L., 65, 143
Coughlin, Charles E., 92, 99, 189, 302
Counterpropaganda
  attitude change and resistance to, 162, 163
  monopolization in absense of, 301
Cousins, Norman, 67
Cowles Communications, Inc., 331
Cox Enterprises, 321, 328
Credibility. *See* Source credibility

Cronkite, Walter, 136
Crouse, Timothy, 224
Crutchfield, R. S., 148
Cueing, 66
Culhane, J. W., 124
Cultivation theory, 249–250
Cultural expectations, 58–59
Cultural truisms, 163–164
Culture transmission, 294–296
Cutbirth, C., 222
Cybernetics (Wiener), 38, 41

Dale, Edgar, 92, 126
Daley, Lee, 98
Danielian, L. H., 224
Danielson, Wayne, 115, 118, 119, 201
Davison, W. P., 269
"Day After, The," 217–219
Dead-level abstracting, 77–78. *See also*
    Abstraction
Deaver, Michael K., 317
De Bock, H., 65
Decision making
    dissonance and, 140–141
    role of community in, 194–196
Decoding process, 57
Deduction, 23, 24
De Fleur, Melvin L., 188, 196, 201–202,
    262–264, 266
DeGeorge, W. F., 221
Democracy, altruistic, 304, 305
Dempsey, G. R., 157
Dependency theory, 262–264
Dervin, Brenda, 244–245, 280
Deutsch, K., 36, 37, 265
Devereau, E. C., 311
Diffusion
    definition of, 199
    explanation of, 194
    of innovations, 197–201
    of news, 201–202
Digital communication technology, 39
Dingell, John D., 317
Discussion groups, 302–303
Disinhibition hypothesis, television violence
    and, 255
Dissonance
    avoidance of, 274
    postdecision, 141

theory of, 140, 141. *See also* Cognitive
    dissonance
Distraction theory, 175–176
Documentaries, 302
Document readability, 121–122
Dollard, Charles, 149
Donohew, R. L., 69
Donohue, G., 231–234, 238
Doob, Leonard, 92
Doolittle, J. C., 175
Dow Chemical Company, 96, 98
Dowie, Mark, 307
Downing, J. D. H., 244
Draft, during Vietnam War, 311–312
Drug diffusion study, 194–195, 197
Drug use, 224
Dukakis, Michael, 93, 224, 234–235
Duke, P., 315
Dulles, John Foster, 95
Dunn, D. A., 242, 243
Durall, J. A., 241
Dynamism, 156

E. F. Hutton, 99–100
EcoNet, 244
Edison, Thomas, 74
Education
    acquisition of knowledge and, 233, 241
    effect of one- and two-sided messages on
        people with varying levels of, 151–152
    exposure to information and, 242
    portrayal by prime-time television of, 28
    propaganda, 92–93
    and viewing of "Sesame Street," 236, 237,
        265
Effect studies, 345
Ehrenhaus, P., 139–140
Einstein, Albert, 19
Either-or thinking, 79
Election campaigns. *See* Political campaigning;
        Presidential campaigns
Electronic delivery of news, 9, 10
Eliot, T. S., 73
Ellerbee, Linda, 315
Elliot, W. R., 277
Elliott, Osborn, 330
Ellul, Jacques, 106
El Salvador, 85–86
Embeds, 68
Empirical data acquisition, 24–32

Employee ownership of newspapers, 334–337
Encoding
  characteristics of language and, 72–77
  explanation of, 72
  implications for, 87–88
  misuses of language and, 77–82
  objectivity and, 84–87
Enduring values, 304–306
Energy issue, 235–236
Engel, Gladys, 209
Engel, R., 174
English, A. C., 148
English, H. B., 148
Entertainment
  choices in, 143
  function of media, 295, 296
Entrophy
  balance between redundancy and, 42
  cloze procedure and, 44, 45, 125
  information and, 41, 42
  message composed of, 38
Environment, men acting upon their,
  298–299
Equivalence of informed political participa-
  tion, 241
Eron, L. D., 256, 257n
Ethnocentrism, 304
Ettema, J. S., 239, 240
Evaluation
  multivalued, 80–81
  two-valued, 79–80
Expectations, perception and cultural, 58–59
Experimental designs, 28–30
Experiments
  causality issues and, 28, 213
  explanation of natural, 30
Expertness, source credibility and, 156
Exposure, automatic, 69
External validity, 33
Exxon Corporation, 300
Eyal, C. H., 216, 217, 221

Fairness in Media, 220, 255
Falkland Islands war, 104
Fallows, James, 311
Fantel, H., 39
Farquhar, J. W., 258
Farrell, Barry, 100
Farr-Jenkins-Paterson readability formula,
  121, 126

Fatoullah, E., 156
Fear appeals
  impact on attitude change of,
    157–158
  research on effect of, 158–161
Fearing, Franklin, 70
Fedler, F. M., 85, 86
Feedback, 41
Feldstein, Martin, 308
Ferguson, John Donald, 334
Ferraro, Geraldine A., 317
Feshbach, S., 158–159, 166, 168
Festinger, Leon A., 64, 165, 166, 170
Fiction
  passage of time and readability of, 119
  sentence length in, 118, 119
Filene, Edward A., 92
Films, for training and motivation during
    World War II, 149–150
Finckenauer, J. O., 160
Finn, Seth, 45, 69, 125
Fischman, J. F., 220n
Fishbein, Martin, 168, 169
Fiske, M., 270
Fiske, S. T., 66
Flay, B. R., 157, 189
Flesch, Rudolf, 112–116, 118, 126
Flesch readability formulas, 112–115,
    117–121, 124, 126
Fog index. See Gunning fog index
Food habits, 184–185
Foot, R., 101–102
Ford, Gerald, 62
FORTH, 12
Fowles, Jib, 175
Fox, Jim, 307
Framing, 222
Fraud, safeguards against, 22–23
Freedman, J. L., 143
Freedom of press, Altschull's views of, 291,
    292
Functional approach to attitude change,
    165–166
Fund drives, 188
Funkhouser, G. Ray, 210–211, 216, 223, 252

Galbraith, John Kenneth, 313
Galilei Galilei, 20, 21, 90, 91
Gamble, L. G., 124
Gannett Corporation, 321, 323, 328

Gans, Herbert J., 23, 224, 304–306, 320
Gatekeepers
  as change agents, 200
  purpose of, 43, 44
  role of media, 138–140
  studies of, 30–31
General Electric Company, 330
Generality, glittering, 96–98
Generalizations. *See also* Hypothesis
  definition of, 24
  scientific, 21–23
General semanticists, 72, 88
General semantics, 88
Genova, B. K. L., 241–242
Gerber, C. H., 13
Gerbner, George, 50, 52, 53n, 249–250, 264
Gerbner verbal model, 50, 52, 320
Ghiglione, Loren, 295–296
Giesbrecht, L. W., 64
Gilbert, S., 216, 217
Gillig, P. M., 157
Gissler, Sig, 335
Gitlin, Todd, 224
Glittering generality, 96–98, 171
Global warming, 21
Goebbels, Joseph, 92, 105
Goffman, Erving, 252
González, Hernando, 254
Gorbachev, Mikhail S., 290
Gormley, W., 327
Graber, Doris, 66
Graham, Katharine, 322
Gramm, Phil, 294
Gratifications. *See* Uses and gratifications
  approach
Gray, W. S., 111–112, 117, 118
Great American Values Test, The, 259, 260,
  264
Greenberg, Bradley S., 201, 241–242
Greenwald, A. G., 157
Griffin, R. J., 236
Gross, N., 198
Groups
  as instruments of change, 188–189
  mass communication and, 189–190
  norms of, 181–182
  political attitudes and, 185–187
  pressures exerted by, 183–184
  types of, 181
Grube, J. W., 258, 259

Gulf of Tonkin, 103
Gunning, Robert, 114, 118
Gunning fog index, 114–115, 120, 121
Gurevitch, M., 272–274

Haas, H., 273–274
Hackworth, David H., 132
Hage, Jerald, 14
Hall, J., 86
Hand, Learned, 327
Harcourt Brace Jovanovich, 331
Harte-Hanks Communications, Inc., 324
Hastorf, A. H., 61–62
Hawkins, D. I., 67
Hayakawa, S. I., 75, 82, 83, 86, 87
Hearability of news, 120
Hegemony, 254–255
Heider, Fritz, 133, 134, 165
Helms, Jesse, 220, 255
Helms, Richard, 138
Heraclitus, 73
Herman, E. S., 85–86
Hersh, Seymour M., 305
Hesburgh, Theodore M., 311–312
Heterophily, 199
Hieser, R. A., 65
High definition television (HDTV), 9–10
High-level abstractions, 77–78
Hill, R. P., 161
Hill, Richard J., 201
Hill, Sandy, 259
Hirsch, Paul, 250
Hispanic Americans, literacy rates of, 122
Histories, as case studies, 31–32
Hitchens, Christopher, 93–94
Hite, Shere, 33
Hitler, Adolf, 92, 192
Homeowner's insurance policies, readability
  of, 122
Homophily, 199
Horai, J., 156
Horst, Paul, 155–156
Hovland, Carl I., 29, 147–157, 159n, 162,
  175, 248
Howard, Edward Lee, 142
Howard, H. H., 325, 328
Huesmann, L. R., 256, 257n
Hull, Clark, 148
Human communication systems, as functional
  systems, 43

Human interest formula, 113–115
Human rationality, 269
Humor, persuasion through, 172–173
Huxley, Thomas H., 19
Hybrid seed corn study, 198
Hypercard, 9
Hypermedia, 9
Hypodermic-needle theory, 105–106, 193, 196, 247–248, 269
Hypothesis
  definition of, 24
  explanation of, 21–22
  operationally defining, 33

Ideogram, 77
Imagination, in science, 19–20
Imitation hypothesis, television violence and, 255
Immunity, 163, 164
Incongruity
  existence of, 135, 136
  media and, 136–138
  methods of dealing with, 137–138
Index numbers, 79
Individualism, as enduring value in news, 304, 306
Induction, 23–24
Inferences
  definition of, 82
  labeled, 83
Influence gap, 242
Information
  delivery of useful, 41–43
  diffusion of, 202. See also Diffusion
  distribution of, 230–231
  meaning and, 7, 41
  socioeconomic status and exposure to, 234, 235, 242
Information age, 1
Information anxiety, 7
Information overload, 7
Information theory
  application of, 43–44
  applied to readability, 44–45
  explanation of, 39–41
  origins of, 39
Infotainment programs, 297–298
Innovation
  decision process of, 199–200
  diffusion and, 197–199

opinion leadership and, 195
role of change agents in, 200–201
spread of, 199
Inoculation theory
  explanation of, 162–163
  research on, 163–164
Inquiry. See Scientific inquiry
Institute for Propaganda Analysis, 92, 104–106, 147, 153, 247
Insurance policy readability, 122
Interest types, 242
Intermedia agenda setting, 224
Internal validity, 33
International affairs
  card stacking used in, 101–102
  glittering generalities in, 97–98
International Herald-Tribune, 331
Interpersonal communication
  diffusion of innovations and, 197–202
  role of community in decision making and, 194–196
  two-step flow and, 197
  voting behavior and, 192–194
Interpersonal environment, 196
Interpersonal relations, 262
Intuition, 19
IQuest, 12
Issues
  importance of news, 208–211, 213–215
  obtrusiveness of, 219–220
Iyengar, Shanto, 207, 213–215
Izvestia, 290

Jacobson, J. M., 125
Jahoda, Marie, 63, 248
James, William, 113
Janis, I., 158–159, 162, 163n, 166, 168
Janis, Irving, 149, 152
Japanese people, 138
Johnson, Lyndon B., 103, 138, 313–314
Johnson, Wendell, 72, 74, 77, 80, 81
Jones, E. E., 64, 144
Jong, Erica, 81
Journal Communications, 335
Journalism
  media hegemony theory and, 254–255
  purposes of, 291
Journalists
  intended effect of, 4
Joyce, James, 123, 124

Judgment, definition of, 83
Justice, policy regarding, 316–317

Kamal, Mohamed, 79
Katz, Daniel, 165, 166, 167n, 177
Katz, E., 193
Katz, Elihu, 262, 265–266, 269–270, 272–274
Katzman, N., 238, 239n
Kelley, Earl C., 81
Kelley, H. H., 159n
Kennan, George F., 301
Kennedy, Edward, 208, 215, 324
Kennedy, John F., 98, 201
Key, Wilson Bryan, 68
Kincaid, J. P., 124
Kinder, Donald R., 66, 207, 213, 214n, 215
Kintzel, Roger, 308, 309
Kitson, H. D., 110
Klapp, Orrin E., 7
Klapper, Joseph, 106, 209, 248–249
Klare, G. R., 110, 126
Kline, F. G., 239
Knake, Jack, 335
Knight-Ridder, Inc., 321, 323
Knowledge gap
   dependency theory and, 264–265
   existence of, 234, 239
   influence gap and, 242
   new technology and, 242–244
   in public affairs, 234–236
   "Sesame Street" and, 231, 236–239, 265
Knowledge-gap hypothesis
   criticism of, 244–245
   explanation of, 231–234, 245
   generality of, 241–242
   refinement of, 238–241
Koffka, Kurt, 113
Kohler, R., 64, 144
Korzybski, Alfred, 72, 75, 81
Krech, D., 148
Krugman, Herbert E., 171–172, 175, 177
Ku Klux Klan, 93, 98, 99

Labeled inferences, 83
Lang, Gladys Engel, 221, 222
Lang, Kurt, 209, 221, 222
Language
   to categorize, 76
   characteristics of, 72–77
   learning of emotional meaning of, 170–171

misuses of, 77–82
LaPiere, Richard, 166
Larsen, O., 196
Lasorsa, D. L., 119, 253–254
Lasswell, Harold D., 38, 49, 90–92, 293, 295, 298, 343
Lavidge, R., 4
Law
   definition of, 24
   policy regarding, 316–317
Lazarsfeld, Paul F., 106, 185, 186n, 235n, 270, 300–302, 320
Leadership
   characteristics of, 195
   differentiation of leaders from followers in, 195
   as enduring value in news, 304, 306
   opinion, 194–197, 199
Lear, Norman, 63, 64
Learning theory
   applied to attitude change, 148, 165, 170–171
   humor and, 175
Leary, B. E., 111–112, 117, 118
Lee, Alfred McClung, 92–93
Lee, Elizabeth Briant, 92–93
Lefkowitz, M.M., 256, 257n
Leggett, D., 221
Leuba, C., 60
Leventhal, H., 159
Levine, J. M., 64, 144
Levy, Mark R., 272–273, 278
Levy-Windahl typology of audience activity, 278–279
Lewin, Kurt, 181, 184, 185
Lewis, P., 141
Libertarian theory of press, 286–289, 327–328
Liddy, G. Gordon, 184
Liebert, Robert M., 256, 257
Lilly, John, 248
Limited-effects model, 209–210, 248–249, 260
Lin, N., 197
Lippmann, Walter, 227, 298–299, 344
Literacy, adult, 122
Lively, B. A., 110, 111, 117, 118
Llewellyn-Thomas, E., 255–256
Long, Norton, 209
Lorge, Irving, 112
Louisville Courier Journal, 322–323
Louisville Times, 322–323

Lovrich, N. P., 239, 265
Low involvement theory, 171–172
Low-level abstractions, 78
Lowry, Dennis, 86–87
Lucas, C., 60
Luepker, R. V., 240
Lumsdaine, Arthur A., 149, 151n, 152, 154,
    162, 163n
Lusitania, 102–103
Lysenko, Trofim, 21

Maccoby, Nathan, 149, 258
Macdonald, Donald A., 297
MacLean, M., 49–50, 341
Magazines. *See also* Print media
    coverage of Vietnam War objectors by, 27
    perception of importance of issues in news
        and coverage of news in, 210–211
    perceptions and messages from, 62
Maier, Irwin, 334, 335
Mail questionnaires, 25
Mainstreaming, in television viewing, 250
Manheim, J. B., 226–227
Mann, Leon, 83
Marbut, Robert, 324
Marcos, Ferdinand, 254, 298
Markiewicz, D., 175
Mass communication. *See also* Communica-
        tion
    explanations of, 3, 7
    exposure to, 69
    general effects of, 90
    groups and, 189–190
    limited-effects model of, 248–249, 260
    media hegemony and, 254–255
    and mental picture of world, 298–299
    perception and, 62–64
    powerful effects model and, 258–260
    scientific method as approach through, 1–2
    social action and popular taste and, 300–301
    sociocultural integration and, 311–317
    spiral of silence and, 252–254, 258
    user control of, 13–14
    values and ideology and, 295–298
Mass communication effects
    bullet theory of, 247–248, 260. *See also*
        Hypodermic-needle theory
    cultivation theory of, 249–250
    media determinism and, 250–252
    size of, 260–262

synthesis of, 262–265
synthetic experience and, 252
television violence and, 255–258
Mass media
    communication channels of, 200
    conditions for effectiveness of, 301–304
    credibility of, 25–26, 85
    criticism of, 6–7
    cross-ownership of, 325–328, 343. *See also*
        Chains; Conglomerates
    employee ownership of, 334–337
    functions of, 231–232, 293–295
    as high amplifiers, 44
    incongruity and, 136–138
    press theories of, 285–290
    research in, 344–345
    social conformism and, 301, 320
    voting behavior and, 192–194
Mathematical theory, 38–39
Mathematical Theory of Communication, The
        (Shannon & Weaver), 38–39
Mayerle, J., 28
McCann, Thomas P., 95
McClelland, D. C., 59, 60n
McClintock, Charles, 165
McCombs, Maxwell E., 209, 212n, 216, 217,
        220–222
McGinnies, E., 155
McGraw, Harold W., Jr., 332
McGraw-Hill, Inc., 332–333
McGuire, W. J., 261–262
McGuire, William, 4–5, 162–164, 177
McLeod, J. M., 241
McLuhan, Marshall, 250–252
McPhee, W. N., 185, 186n
McQuail, Denis, 253n, 270–272, 275
Mead, Margaret, 184
Meadowcraft, J. M., 61
Meaning, information and, 7, 41, 42
Meaning lag, 13
Media. *See* Mass media
Media agenda
    dimensions of, 226
    presidential agenda and, 216–217
    public agenda vs., 221
    who sets, 223–225
Media conglomerates, newspaper, 320–325
Media coverage. *See also* News coverage
    of communities, 314–316
    public opinion and, 210

reality and, 210–211, 223
of urban minority issues, 310–311
Media credibility. *See also* Source credibility
explanation of, 85
survey on, 25–26
Media determinism, 250–252
Media effectiveness conditions, 301–304
Media forums, 201
Media hegemony, 254–255
Media Monopoly, The (Bagdikian), 331–332
Media policy
creation of, 27–28
deviation from, 310–311
process of conforming to, 307–309
regarding law and justice, 316–317
regarding medicine, 316
regarding patriotism, 314
Media users
concerns of, 6–7
types of, 25–26
Medical coverage, 316
Meeske, M., 86
Mendelsohn, H., 258
Merrill, John, 84, 86
Merton, Robert K., 20, 106, 300–302, 320
Message design and content, 344–345
Messages
one-sided vs. two-sided, 104, 150–152, 162
processing of print vs. television, 171
source of. *See* Source credibility
Mewborn, C. R., 159–160, 161n
Meyrowitz, Joshua, 252
Mill, John Stuart, 269, 288, 289, 317
Miller, M. Mark, 217, 219, 265
Miller, Thomas Haven, 119, 120
Mills, J., 143
Milwaukee Journal, 334–335
Milwaukee Sentinel, 335
Models. *See also* Communication models
evaluation of, 37
explanation of, 24, 36–37
functions of, 37
Moderate-effects model, 260
Moderatism, 304, 306
Modern Medicine, 331
Monocular distorted room, 58
Mood
perception and, 60–61
television program selection and, 276, 277
Moore, Michael, 323

Motivation
fear appeals and, 161
information seeking and, 241
perception and, 59–60
Moyers, Bill, 302
Muckraking journalism, 207
Mudd, Roger, 208
Multivalued evaluation, 80–81
Murphy, G., 64, 144
Murphy, G.L.B., 148
Murphy, T. M., 148
Murrow, Edward R., 297
Music, transfer through use of, 99

Naccari, N., 156
Nagel, E., 22
Nair, M., 69
Name calling, 93–96, 171
Narcotizing dysfunction, 300
National Broadcasting Company (NBC), 330
National Organization for Women (NOW), 223
Natural experiments, 30
Nazi propaganda, 92, 105
Negative labels, 80
Net effect, 151
Newcomb, Theodore M., 47–49, 133–135, 148, 165
New Deal, 97
Newhouse Broadcasting Corporation, 325, 327
Newhouse Newspapers, 321, 323
Newman, L. S., 169
News. *See also* Broadcast news; Television news
diffusion of, 201–202
electronic delivery of, 9, 10
enduring values in, 304–306
mail questionnaires to check on accuracy of, 25
readability of, 118–120
schemas to process, 66
as social construction of reality, 306–307
News America, 328
News coverage. *See also* Media coverage; Television news
bias in, 84–86
perception of importance of issues and, 208–211, 213–215
policy deviation in, 310–311

News coverage (*continued*)
  socioeconomic status and, 295–297
News magazines. *See* Magazines
News media, 290–293. *See also* Mass media
Newspaper ownership
  chains, 320–325, 343
  cross-ownership issues in, 325–328
  employee, 334–337
Newspapers. *See also* Print media
  agenda setting coverage of news in, 215
  bias in, 85–86
  circulation of, 320, 321
  coverage of political policy by, 27–28
  policy of individual, 307–311
  readability formulas for, 118–119
News releases, readability of, 119–120
News staff
  controlling, 307–309
  media hegemony theory and, 254–255
  policy deviation and, 310–311
Newton, Isaac, 20
New York Times, 85–86, 330
New York Times Company, 321, 330–331
Nicaragua, coverage of 1984 elections in,
  85–86
Nicholas, D., 216
Nigg, J. M., 265
Niles, P., 159
Nixon, Richard M., 81, 184, 217
Noelle-Neumann, Elisabeth, 13, 252–254, 258
Noise, 42
Noncorresponding systems, 43
Noriega, Manuel Antonio, 97, 101
Norms, group, 181–182
Novels. *See* Fiction
Nuclear war, 217–219

Objectivity
  absolute, 83–84
  controversy over, 82
  studies of, 84–87
Obtrusive issues, 219–220
O'Connor, Carroll, 63
O'Connor, D. Vincent, 62
Olien, C. N., 231–234, 238
Olsen, Don, 122
One-sided messages
  counterpropaganda and, 162
  effectiveness of, 104

research in, 150–152
Operationally defining the hypothesis, 33
Opinion leaders
  characteristics of, 194–196
  and similarity to followers, 199
  vs. non-opinion leaders, 197
Orientation, 222–223, 264
Osgood, C. E., 45–46, 135, 165
Overgeneralization, 78, 79

Page, B. I., 157
Paisley, W. J., 44
Papageorgis, Demetrios, 162–164, 177
Paramount Communications, Inc., 331
Park Communications, 328
Parker, E. B., 242, 243
Pastoralism, 304, 306
Patriotism, 314
PeaceNet II, 244
Peer review process, 23
Pelz, Edith Bennett, 185
Pentagon Papers, 139, 298, 332
People's Republic of China, 290
Peoria Journal Star, 336–337
Perception
  assumptions and, 58
  attitude and, 61–62
  automatic exposure and, 69
  cultural expectations and, 58–59
  mass communication and, 62–64
  mood and, 60–61
  motivation and, 59–60
  process of, 57–58
  schemata theory and, 65–66
  selective, 57, 62, 64–65
  subliminal, 66–69
  transactional view of, 58
Perse, E. M., 250
Persian Gulf War, 312–313
Personal references, readability of, 112–113
Persuasion. *See also* Attitude change
  appeals to humor as, 172–173
  appeals to sex as, 173–175
  definition of, 91
  effects of repetition on, 175
  study of mass communication as, 270
  uses of, 147
Persuasion theory, 176. *See also* Attitude
  change

Peters, M. D., 213, 214n
Peterson, T. B., 285, 286n
Petty, R. E., 175
Photograph size, 215
Physical attractiveness
  of models, 174
  source credibility and, 156
Physicians, 316
Pickle, J. J., 294
Pierce, J. C., 239, 265
Plain folks device, 100–101
Policy. *See* Media policy
Policy agenda, 226
Political attitudes, 185–187
Political campaigning
  in Philippines, 298
  as propaganda, 91
  uses and gratifications approach in, 270–272
  use of testimonial in, 99–100
Political participation, 241
Politics
  group pressures and, 184
  propaganda in, 97, 104
Post, J., 230
Postman, Lee, 64, 201
Power
  communication as means of preserving, 295
  news media as agent of, 290–293
Powerful-effects model, 258–261
Pravda, 290
Predictability, 131
Predictions, 37
Prejudice
  effect of group attitude on, 181
  effect of satire on reducing, 63–64
Presidential campaigns
  agenda setting and, 207–209, 212–214, 222, 224
  debates during, 62, 234–235
Presidents, agenda setting for, 216–217, 224
Press
  Altschull's views of, 290–293
  freedom of, 291, 292
  theories of, 285–290
Pressey, S. L., 110, 111, 117, 118
Price, Vincent, 187
Price advertising, 30
Primary group, 188
Primary groups, 181

Priming, 215–216
Principles of Gestalt Psychology (Koffka), 113
Print media. *See also* Magazines; Newspapers
  drug coverage by, 224
  message processing of, 171
Professionalism, 156
Professional journals, 23, 346
Projection, unconscious, 81–82
Propaganda
  counter-, 162, 163, 301
  education in techniques of, 92–93
  meaning of, 90–91
  views of, 90
  wartime, 90–92, 94, 101–105
Propaganda devices
  band wagon as, 103–104
  card stacking as, 101–103
  efffectiveness of, 104–106
  glittering generalities as, 96–98
  name calling as, 93–96
  plain folks method as, 100–101
  testimonial as, 99–100
  transfer as, 98–99
Propaganda education, 92–93
Prose literacy, adult, 122
Protective motivation theory, 159–160
Ptolemy, 20
Public access television channels, 8
Public affairs
  interest in, 1
  knowledge gap in, 234–236
Public agenda
  dimensions of, 226
  media agenda vs., 221
Public Broadcasting System (PBS), 298
Public Data Access, 244
Public opinion
  effect of mass communication on, 157
  social identification model and, 187
  view of importance of issues in news, 208–211, 213–215
Public relations
  control through, 300
  as propaganda, 91, 98

Quarles, Jan P., 217, 219
Quayle, Dan, 98, 234–235

Racial discrimination, 223
Radio Corporation of America (RCA), 330
Rankin, E. F., 124
Rarick, D., 28
Rather, Dan, 136
Rationalization, 131, 132
Raven, Bertram H., 184
Readability
  cloze procedure to measure, 122–126
  history of measurement of, 110–113
  importance of, 109
  information theory applied to, 44–45
Readability formulas
  for advertising copy, 120
  for broadcast news, 120
  for corporate reports, 120–121
  for documents, 121–122
  Farr-Jenkins-Paterson, 121, 126
  Flesch's, 112–115, 117–121, 124, 126
  Gunning fog index, 114–115, 120, 121
  for newspapers and wire services, 118–119
  for news releases, 119–120
  for novels, 119
  sample application of, 115–117
  for textbooks, 113, 117–118
Reading ease formula, 113–115, 119–120, 124
Reagan, Ronald, 27–28, 93, 137, 207, 224
Reality
  dynamic nature of, 72–74
  relationship between media coverage and, 210–211, 223
  scientific generalizations about, 21–23
  social construction of, 306–307
  unlimited nature of, 74
Reality judgments, 306
Reardon, K. K., 161, 190
Redundancy
  balance between entrophy and, 42
  cloze procedure and, 44, 123
  explanation of, 42
  message composed of, 38–39
Reese, S. D., 224, 225, 265
Reference groups, 181
Reliability, 33
Repetition, persuasion through, 175
Reports, 82
Resonance, in television viewing, 250
Responsible capitalism, 304–306
Riccomini, B., 276–277

Ridenhour, Ron, 305
Riis, Jake, 207
Riley, J. W., Jr., 270
Riley, M. W., 270
"Risky-shift," 184
Roberts, D., 45
Robinson, Michael J., 220
Rogers, Everett, 6, 190, 197–200, 202–203, 241
Rogers, R. W., 159–160, 161n
Rokeach, Milton, 63, 64, 258, 259
Roosevelt, Franklin D., 97, 192, 234, 235
Rosenberg, M. J., 148
Rosenberg, W. L., 277
Ross, Raymond S., 161, 176
Rosse, James N., 321
Rovere study, 193–194, 196
Rubin, A. M., 250, 276, 279
Rucker, E., 69
Rumor transmission studies, 64
Ryan, B., 198
Ryan, M., 25

Sample surveys, 24–25
San Francisco Examiner, 309
Sarnoff, Irving, 165
Satellite transmission, 8–9
Satire, 63–64
Schema, 65–66
Schema theory, 65–66
Schramm, W., 43, 44, 46, 285, 286n
Schulte, R., 59
Science
  cumulative nature of, 20–21
  imagination in, 19–20
Scientific inquiry, 23–24
Scientific journals, 23
Scientific method
  approaching mass communication through, 1–2
  explanation of, 19
  and generalizations about reality, 21–23
  and methods of acquiring empirical data, 24–32
  nature of science and, 20–21
  and process of scientific inquiry, 23–24
  and reasoning about empirical data, 32–33
Scott, C., 121–122
Scripps-Howard, 321, 328

Sears, D., 143
Seib, Charles, 118
Selective attention
  dissonance theory and, 142–143
  explanation of, 64
Selective exposure, 14
  dissonance theory and, 142–143
  example of, 65
  explanation of, 64, 262
Selective perception, 14
  examples of, 62, 64
  explanation of, 57, 137
  as variables, 262, 265–266
Selective processes, 64–65
Selective retention
  explanation of, 64, 138, 262
  studies in, 143–144
Self-realization, 269
Sentence length, 110, 112, 118, 122
"Sesame Street," 231, 236–239, 264
Severin, W., 25, 26, 335
Sex, persuasion through, 173–175
Shaffer, A., 236n, 237n
Shakespeare, William, 81
Shamir, Yitzhak, 94
Shannon, Claude, 38, 39, 45, 46, 49, 125
Shapiro, M., 222
Shapiro, R. Y., 157
Sharp, E. B., 241
Shaw, D. L., 209, 212n
Shaw, E. F., 252
Shaw, George Bernard, 73
Sheffield, Fred D., 149, 151n, 152, 154,
  162
Shenon, P., 317
Sherif, Muzafer, 181, 182
Sherman, L. A., 110
Shields, Mark, 312–313
Shoemaker, F., 197, 202–203, 224, 225
Shoemaker, P. J., 221
Shoup, David M., 132
Showalter, S. W., 27, 28
Siebert, F. S., 32, 285, 286n
Signal transmission, 38–41
Simon & Schuster, 331, 332
Slane, Henry, 336–337
Slanting, 83, 84. See also Card stacking
Sleeper effect
  example of, 154

source of, 150
  varying views on, 157
Small-town pastoralism, 304, 306
Smith, G. H., 174
Smith, Mary John, 176
Social action, 300–301
Social conformism, 301, 320
Social identification model, 187
Social location, strategic, 195
Social responsibility theory of press, 286–287,
  289, 327–328
Social sciences, use of communication models
  in, 36, 37, 265
Society
  media's role in support of, 295–298
  relationship between, media, audience, and,
  262–263
Socioeconomic status
  of audience, 295–297
  availability of communication technology
  and, 244
  information and, 231–232
  knowledge gap and, 234, 239
Solzhenitsyn, Alexander, 20
Source credibility. See also Media credibility
  audience and, 138
  experiment in, 29–30
  low vs. high, 104, 154, 155
  research in, 153–157
Soviet-totalitarian theory of press, 286–287,
  290
Speakes, Larry, 224
Spiedel newspaper chain, 324
Spinoza, Baruch, 181
Spiral of silence theory, 252–254, 258
Split-run technique, 30
Staats, A. W., 170, 171, 175
Staats, C. K., 170, 171, 175
Stanford, S. W., 276–277
Stanton, F. N., 270
Statements, 82–84
State of the Union address, 216–217
Static nature of language, 72–73
Statistics, 32
Statue of Liberty, 98–99
Steffens, Lincoln, 207–208
Stein, Gertrude, 123, 124
Steiner, G. A., 4, 68
Stereotyping, 78

Stern, S., 312
Stevens, Leonard Arthur, 120
Stevens, S. S., 113, 117
Stimulus-response theory, 106
Stone, D. B., 278
Stone, Gerald, 113, 117, 220–221, 278
Storey, J. D., 190
Stouffer, Samuel, 149
Strategic social location, 195
Strauss, W., 311–312
Strong, B., 139
Structural differential, 75
Student Nonviolent Coordinating Committee (SNCC), 223
Subliminal perception, 66–69
Suchan, J., 121–122
Suchman, E., 270
Sullivan, Kathleen, 309
Sun Tsu, 91
Surveillance function of media, 293, 296
Survey research, 24–26
Swanson, C., 118
Symbionese Liberation Army, 80, 87
Symmetry theory (Newcomb), 133–135
Synthetic experience, 252
Systems, 43. *See also* Communication systems

Tajfel, Henri, 186–187
Tamkin, G., 236n, 237n
Tankard, J., 25
Tannenbaum, Percy, 136, 165
Taste, popular, 300–301
Taylor, D. S., 250
Taylor, Wilson L., 44, 122–124
Teacher's Word Book (Thorndike), 110–111
Technology. *See* Communication technology
Teletext, 9, 10
Television
  criticism of, 6–7
  high definition, 9–10
  impact of cable, 8, 12–13. *See also* Cable television
  as medium, 251
  prejudice and effect of, 63–64
  processing of messages from, 171
  role in closing knowledge gap, 240
Television commercials, 101. *See also* Advertising
Television networks

cost-cutting by, 302
ownership of, 325–328
Television news. *See also* News coverage
  agenda setting in, 213–219, 222, 223
  coverage of local news in, 325
  effects on presidential elections, 215
  gatekeeping case study of, 31
  gratification and, 272–273
  source credibility and, 157
Television programs
  influence of mood on selection of, 276, 277
  violence in, 255–258
Television viewing
  active vs. passive, 276, 278
  cultivation theory and, 249–250
  negative effects of, 251–252
Television violence, 255–258
Tenacity, 19
Terrorism, 93–95
Testimonials
  effectiveness of, 104
  as propaganda device, 99–100
Textbook readability formulas, 113, 117–118
Theory, 3, 20, 24
Thinking with the excluded middle, 79
Thomas, W. I., 148
Thomas Newspaper Group of Canada, 337
Thorndike, E. L., 110–111
Tichenor, P., 231–234, 238
Time Inc.-Warner Communications, 331
Time lag, 220–221
Time magazine, 62, 83–85
Times-Mirror Company, 321, 323–324, 327, 328
Toch, H. H., 59
Toffler, Alvin, 73, 81, 87–88
Totalitarian theory of press. *See* Soviet-totalitarian theory of press
Transfer, as propaganda device, 98–99
Transmissibility, 20
Transmission belt theory. *See* Hypodermic-needle theory
Transmission rates, 43
Treffert, D. A., 80
Tribune Company, 321, 328
Troldahl, V., 197
Trustworthiness, source credibility and, 156
Tuchman, Gaye, 306–307
Turner, John C., 186–187

Two-sided messages
    counterpropaganda and, 162
    effectiveness of, 104
    research in, 150–152
Two-step flow model, 197–199
Two-valued evaluation, 79–80

Udall, Morris, 324
Uncertainty, 198
Unconscious projection, 81–82
Undue identification, 78–79
United Press International, 324
Unobtrusive issues, 219–220
USA Today, 10, 323
User control, 13–14
Uses and gratifications approach
    audience needs and, 272–274
    criticisms of, 274–276, 279
    in election campaign, 270–272
    origin of, 269–270
    and study of mass communication, 6, 12,
        343–344
    tests of, 276–278
Ustinov, Peter, 100

Validity, 32–33
Values
    in news, 304–306
    personification of, 195
Van Dam, R., 197
VCRs. *See* Videocassette recorders
Vicary, James M., 66–67
Videocassette recorders (VCRs)
    active audience and, 278–279
    impact of, 8, 12–13
    ownership of, 243
Videotex, 9, 10
Vidich, A., 316
Vidmar, Neil, 63, 64
Vietnam War
    chemicals used during, 98
    draft during, 311–312
    exposure to information regarding, 139, 298
    Gulf of Tonkin resolution and, 103
    measurement of positions taken toward ob-
        jectors to, 27
    selective attention and, 142
    support for, 131–132
Violence, effects of television, 255–258

Virtue words, 96
Vocabulary difficulties, 110
Voting behavior
    groups and, 185–187
    mass media and, 192–194

Walder, L. O., 256, 257n
Walters, R. H., 255–256
Wanta, W., 215, 221, 226
Ward, C. D., 155
Warner Communications, 331
Wartime propaganda, 90–92, 94, 101–105. *See
    also* Propaganda
Watergate affair, 139, 221, 222
Weaver, D. H., 222, 226
Weaver, Warren, 38–42, 45, 46
Weber, S. J., 236n, 237n
Weigel, R. H., 169
Weiner, Norbert, 38, 41
Weiss, W., 29, 153–156, 175
Weizman, Ezer, 94
Wesson, D. A., 120
Westheimer, Ruth, 94–95
Westley, Bruce, 25, 26, 49–50, 197, 213, 223,
    341
Westley-MacLean model, 48–50, 341–344
White, D., 30
Whitehead, J. L., 156
Whitney, D. C., 265
Whorf, Benjamin Lee, 77
"Why We Fly" films, 149–150
Wicker, A. W., 168
Wilhoit, G. C., 65
Williams, W., 222
Wilson, M. L., 184
Windahl, S., 253n, 276
Winter, J. P., 221
Wire copy readability, 115, 118–119
Wire editor, as gatekeeper, 30–31
Wolfe, K. M., 270
Words
    abstract, 76, 112
    difficulty with, 110
    number in English language, 74
    syllables per, 113, 114
World War I, 90–92, 102–103
World War II
    research on attitude change during,
        149–151

source credibility and, 153, 154
  use of propaganda during, 90, 103–105
Wright, Charles R., 7, 293, 296n
Wurman, Richard Saul, 7

Yale Communication Research Program,
  152–153

Zaccaro, John, Jr., 317
Zajonc, R. B., 134n, 135n, 136n
Zapping, 12
Zielske, H. A., 175
Zillmann, D., 61, 143, 276, 277n
Zinkhan, G., 125
Znaniecki, F., 148
Zucker, Harold Gene, 219, 220, 223, 226